the FIRST TWELVE CROCHET BOOKS *of* MLLE. RIEGO DE LA BRANCHARDIERE

[1847 - 1852]

LACIS
PUBLICATIONS

The materials in this volume have been reproduced from original printed editions as bound in two volumes, without the original covers. Each volume contained a random edition of six of the Crochet Books, notated in a "Series" format.

Pages of the original small format editions have been combined placing two of the original pages on each page of this edition. The fold-out, tipped in illustrations of the original editions have been reprinted on a full page. Some rearrangement of pages has been made for the sake of consistency, and some of the duplicated pages of advertising have been eliminated.

The original bound volumes remain the property of Maryvonne Wetsch.

Published by

LACIS
PUBLICATIONS
3163 Adeline Street, Berkeley, CA 94703

lacis.com

For

THE LACIS MUSEUM OF LACE AND TEXTILES

LacisMuseum.org

ISBN 978-1-891656-79-8

INTRODUCTION

Much mystery abounds concerning Mlle. Riego, one the foremost and most prolific authorities on needlework of the nineteenth century. We are not sure when or where she was born, if she was married or had a family, and although hundreds of publications have been assigned to her, there is no bibliographic listing. We do know that she died in 1887, shortly after writing her last book, *Lace Tatting* in 1886. Her name is often referenced as Mlle. Riego de la Branchardiere, sometimes Eleonore Riego de la Branchardiere, and more commonly Mlle. Riego. A picture of her in Annie Louise Potter's *A Living Mystery Crochet* is the only one that I am aware of.

We know of at least eighteen Crochet Books, the first twelve of which are included herein, eleven tatting books, numerous knitting books and a periodical called *The Needle* published regularly between 1852 and 1854. Here Mlle. Riego offered further designs, working and material suggestions as well as solicitating readers to approach her should they have any problems or designs which she would convert to specific patterns.

Her memory, however, is forever engraved as the leading influence of 19th c. needlework due to her extraordinary talents in beauty of design and innovative techniques in the areas of lacemaking, tatting, crochet, and knitting, as well as her philanthropic efforts in supporting these arts.

There is a consensus that she was born in England to a father of Franco-Spanish nobility and a mother of Irish heritage, shortly after their exile from France at the height of the French revolution. It was this Irish connection that directed many of her energies throughout her life.

Her dedication to helping the Irish in the trying times of the mid-century famine supported her development of a new concept of a 'free' crochet, soon called Irish Crochet which would become the salvation of the Irish peasantry. Her early devotion to crochet was based on her belief that lace comparable to the precious and valuable needle laces of the 17th and 18th centuries could be made by crochet, with the obvious advantages that it could be made in a quarter of the time, would take less time to learn, and could be made without a pattern thanks to her innovation of clear written instructions. This new concept was a free crochet technique where separate elements of varying complexity could be made by workers of different skill levels, and then joined by a common ground in a viable commercial community pursuit. With her formidable marketing and design skills she did much to establish and popularize Irish Crochet as a world commodity.

A prolific writer and publisher, endowed with the wealth to support these interests, she was able to produce the most authoritative books of the time, enhancing her clear written instructions with beautiful illustrations, many embellished with color, a mid century novelty. Prior to this time, any illustrations were expensive and thus rare, the best pattern books having simply having actual swatches showing the finished design and demanding fluency in technique.

Well educated, Mlle. Riego was familiar with the valuable laces of the past and well aware of their value and popularity in contemporary fashion. She was soon emulating in crochet not only the Spanish and Venetian point laces, but also the geometric patterns of Reticella.

Her first books date from 1846 and were devoted to crochet; the 1848 Leicester Journal described them as "among the most useful and cheapest" to guide and stimulate the needle arts. In 1864, the English magazine *Queen* made the following reference:

> *"...with Mlle. Riego's directions we may always feel safe, and when they are illustrated we may rest secure that the piece of work in hand will not bring disappointment with completion, for, if the rules are only carried out attentively, the result generally surpasses the representation—and this cannot be said of most work patterns."*

Her ability to translate the most complex designs into easy-to-follow instructions brought her an enormous following and multitple editions of the already published books.

She won many awards at the Exhibitions of 1851, 1855, 1862 and 1872, where her exquisite yet simple style was noted as 'true brilliance.'

Astute in fashion and politics she was often in communication with most of the courts of Europe, designing and instructing within these spheres, working primarily in the courts of England and Germany. Her books spread quickly throughout Europe, and in Turkey her dimensional flower crochet designs became the now traditional Oyas. In England she was named by special appointment "Artiste in Needlework" to HRH The Princess of Wales.

Mlle. Riego bequeathed the greater part of her fortune to Irish agencies supporting the peasants of Ireland, and endowments, viz through the Royal Dublin Society (RDS), which still offers monetary prizes in support of needlework under her name.

Jules Kliot, Director

the FIRST TWELVE CROCHET BOOKS *of* Mille Riego de la Branchardiere

TABLE OF CONTENTS

THE

CROCHET BOOK,

FIRST SERIES.

BY

MLLE. RIEGO DE LA BRANCHARDIERE.

Twelfth Edition--60,000.

LONDON:
SIMPKIN, MARSHALL, AND CO.,
ACKERMANN & CO., STRAND; OLIVER AND BOYD, EDINBURGH;
AND ALL THE BERLIN WAREHOUSES.

1853.

Entered at Stationers' Hall.

CONTENTS.

LONDON:
Printed at the Office of E. RIEGO DE LA BRANCHARDIERE, 106, New Bond Street,

PREFACE.

THE flattering success my Work on Knitting, Netting, and Crochet, received, and the numerous testimonials to the correctness of the receipts, forwarded to me by ladies from all parts of the kingdom, combined with the advice of many of my kind patrons, whom I have the honour to instruct, has induced me to publish, in a cheap form, a series of works, suitable to all classes, on the various branches of Ornamental Needle-work. It is necessary to observe, that in this, my first of the series, the patterns are designed from the picturesque costumes of past times; and I have endeavoured, from experience as an instructress, to give clear illustrated elementary instructions, with concise details of the various patterns. And it is humbly hoped that the time, great care, and expense incurred to obtain correctness of the receipts, the originality and elegance of the designs, with the beauty of the illustrations, will secure for this work a place in the drawing-room of every lady, and the cordial approval of all for its general utility.

E. RIEGO DE LA BRANCHARDIERE.

106, New Bond Street,
Jan. 30th, 1847.

Ladies experiencing any difficulty in the following directions, may communicate personally, or by Letter enclosing a directed stamped envelope, *with an* extra stamp *for a reply, addressed to the Authoress,* 106, New Bond Street.

INSTRUCTIONS IN CROCHET,

AND

EXPLANATION OF THE TERMS.

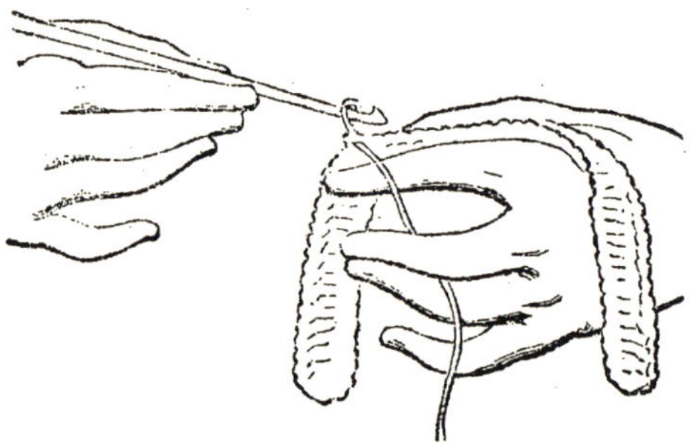

THE Work should be held between the first finger and thumb of the left hand, as in sewing, the thread hanging over the first finger, and falling between the second and third fingers; the needle should be held lightly in the right hand as a pen.

To Make a Chain.

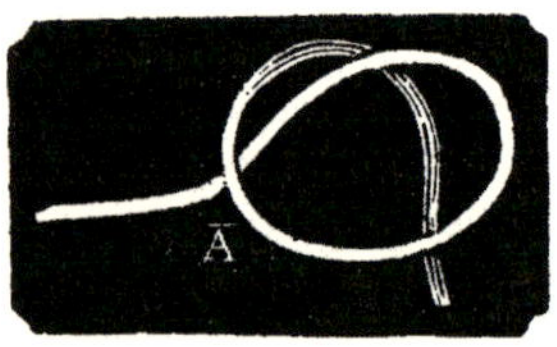

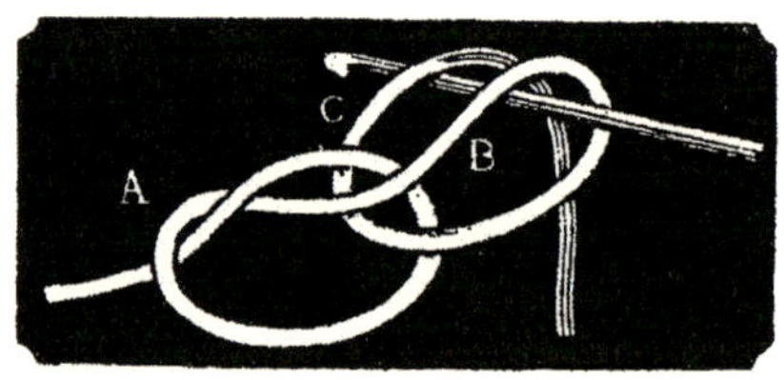

The foundation stitch of all crochet; make a loop with the thread, holding it at A, and put the needle into it then take the thread on the needle and draw it through the loop as B; this forms another chain loop. Repeat as C.

Plain Stitch, called French or Double Crochet.

After making a chain, keep the loop A on the needle; put the needle into the last chain stitch, and draw the thread through. There will now be two loops, A, B, on the needle; take up the thread, C, and draw it through the two. This forms one stitch.

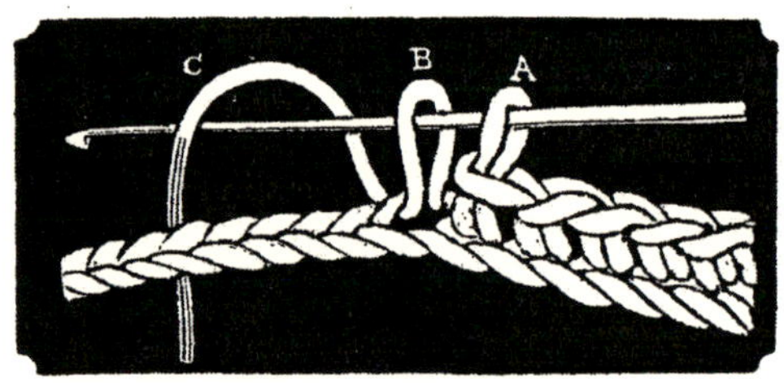

Treble Stitch.

Keep the loop on the needle as A, then take the thread on the needle, B; put the needle in a stitch; draw the thread through: this makes three loops, as A, B, C. Take up the thread, D, and draw it through the two loops, C and B. Take it up again, and draw it through the two loops formed by D and A. This finishes one stitch.

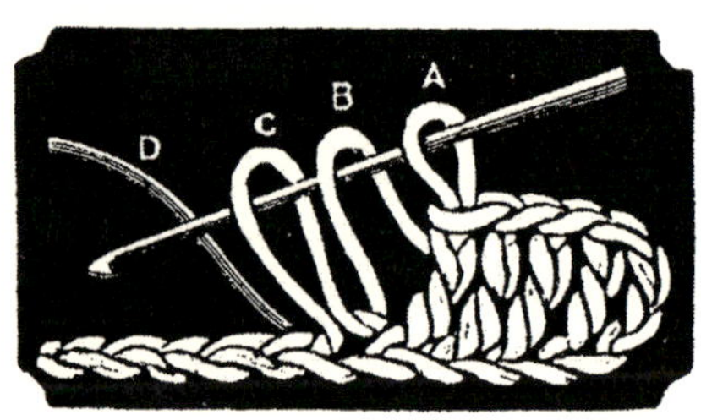

Miss a Stitch.

To pass over a stitch of the preceding row.

To Work in the Chain.

Put the needle in the space formed by the chain stitches of the row before: this renders the working easier, and obviates the necessity of counting stitches that are to be missed.

When this mark * occurs, the stitches before it are not to be repeated. Thus, 1 treble, 1 chain, *, 3 treble, 3 chain, 1 plain. In repeating, work from 3 treble, 3 chain, 1 plain.

The stitches in a parenthesis, thus—(3 treble, 3 chain, miss 1, 3 times), are to be worked 3 treble, 3 chain, miss 1, 3 treble, 3 chain, miss 1, 3 treble, 3 chain, miss 1: also when chain stitches divide treble stitches without missing any, as thus—(5 treble, 3 chain, 5 treble), these 10 treble are all to be worked in the chain of the last row.

The needles to be used are fine steel crochet needles, Nos. 20, 22, and 24, Bell Gauge; and all the collars are to be worked backwards and forwards.

COLLAR—MARY STUART.

Taylor's Crochet Thread, No. 8; Needle, No. 22, Bell Gauge. Chain of 190 stitches.

1st row—1 chain, miss 4, 4 treble in one chain stitch of the foundation. Repeat to the end of the chain, turn back.

2nd and 3rd—1 chain, miss 4, 4 treble in the chain of the last row. Repeat.

4th—1 chain, miss 4, (2 treble, 5 chain, 2 treble: these 4 treble stitches are all to be worked in the 1 chain of the last row).

5th and 6th—3 chain, miss 2 *, (2 treble, 5 chain, 2 treble: these 4 treble stitches are all to be worked in the 5 chain of the last row), 1 chain, miss 5: repeat from * and finish with 2 treble, 5 chain, 2 treble in the 5 chain.

7th—3 chain, miss 2 *, (3 treble, 5 chain, 3 treble in the 5 chain of last row), 3 chain, miss 5. Repeat from *, finish with 3 treble, 5 chain, 3 treble as before.

8th—3 chain, miss 3, (3 treble, 5 chain, 3 treble in the 5 chain of last row), 3 chain, miss 3, 1 plain in the 3 chain of last row. Repeat.

9th—1 chain, miss 1, 1 plain, 3 chain, miss 5, (4 treble, 5 chain, 4 treble in the 5 chain of the last row), 3 chain, miss 5, 1 plain. The plain stitches in this row are to be worked in the 3 chain of the last row; at the end cut off the cotton and fasten off.

10th and 12th—Commence this row at the foundation, and work down the sides, same as 9th row, working the treble stitch between the spaces down the side; at the end of the row, work the other side to correspond.

12th—1 chain, miss 1, 1 plain, 4 chain, miss 5, (5 treble, 5 chain, 5 treble in the 5 chain), 4 chain, miss 5, 1 plain. This finishes the collar; but should it be required deeper, add two or three more rows same as the 12th.

Cuffs to Match.

Make a chain of 100 stitches, and work the same pattern.

POINT DE GUISE.

Taylor's Crochet Thread, No. 6, or Fine Black Netting Silk; Needle, No. 20, Bell Gauge. Chain of 240 stitches.

1st and 2nd rows—1 chain, miss 1, 1 treble at the end of the 2nd row. Cut the cotton off, and leaving 50 stitches of the foundation, commence the 3rd row in the 51st stitch.

3rd.—3 plain, 5 chain, miss 3. Repeat 22 times; then 3 plain, this finishes the 3rd row; turn back to work the 4th row, leaving 50 stitches to correspond with the other side.

4th.—3 chain, miss 5, *, (1 plain, 5 chain, 1 plain; *these 2 plain stitches* are both to be worked in the 5 chain of last row); then 7 chain, miss 7. Repeat from * 22 times. This brings the thread to the 50 stitches left, work 4 plain stitches on them and turn back.

5th—5 chain, miss 5, *, 1 plain in the 7 chain of last row; 5 chain, miss 5, 5 plain in the 5 chain of last row, 5 chain, miss 5. Repeat from * 22 times, then 1 plain, 5 chain, and on the 2nd row, miss 3, 6 plain.

6th—5 chain, miss 9, 1 plain in the 5 chain of last row, 5 chain, miss 5, 1 plain. Repeat 23 times, then 5 chain on 2nd row, miss 3, 1 plain.

7th—7 chain, miss the 5 chain of last row, (1 plain, 5 chain, 1 plain, *these* 2 *plain* are both to be worked in the 5 chain of last row). Repeat 23 times, then 5 chain on 2 row, 4 plain.

8th—7 chain, miss 9, 7 plain in the 5 chain of last row Repeat 23 times; then 7 chain, miss 9, on 2nd row work 1 plain, 5 chain, miss 1, 1 plain.

9th—7 chain, miss 7, (1 plain, 5 chain, 1 plain, 5 chain, 1 plain, these 3 plain stitches to be worked in the 7 chain of last row.) Repeat 24 times, and on the 2nd row, 7 chain, 1 plain, 5 chain, miss 2, 3 plain.

10th—5 chain, miss 5, 1 plain, 7 chain, miss 11, 1 plain, (the plain stitches in this row are to be worked in the 5 chain of last row). Repeat 25 times, work the last stitch on the 2nd row, then 5 chain, miss 1, 7 plain.

11th—9 chain, miss 9, (1 plain, 5 chain, 1 plain; these 2 plain stitches are both to be worked in the 5 chain of last row.) Repeat 26 timet, then 9 chain, and on the 2nd row, miss 4, 1 plain, 5 chain, 1 plain.

12th—5 plain in the 5 chain of the last row, 3 chain, (1 plain, 5 chain, 1 plain; these 2 plain in the 9 chain of the last row), 3 chain. Repeat 27 times, then on the 2nd row, 5 plain, 3 chain, miss 2, 1 plain, 5 chain, miss 2, 3 plain.

13th—5 chain, miss 5, 1 plain in the 5 chain of the last row; 5 chain, miss 4, 1 plain in the 3 chain of the last row, 5 chain, miss 7, 1 plain. Repeat 28 times more, work the last stitch on the 2nd row, (then 5 chain, miss 2, 1 plain, 3 times.)

14th—7 chain, miss the 5 chain of last row, 1 plain in the 5 chain, 5 chain, miss 5, 1 plain. Repeat 29 times; then 7 chain, and on the 2nd row, 1 plain, 5 chain, miss 2, 4 plain.

15th—5 chain, miss 5, *, (1 plain, 5 chain, 1 plain; these 2 plain in the 5 chain of the last row), 9 chain, miss 11. Repeat from * 30 times, and on the 2nd row, 1 plain, 5 chain 7 plain.

16th—9 chain, misss 9, 5 plain in the 5 chain of last row. Repeat 32 times, then 9 chain on the 2nd row, 5 plain, 9 chain, miss 3, 5 plain.

17th—7 chain, miss the 5 plain, (1 plain, 9 chain, 1 plain, 11 chain, 1 plain, 9 chain, 1 plain; these 4 plain stitches are all to be worked in the 9 chain of the last row.) Repeat to the end. This finishes the collar.

POINT A'NGLETERRE.

Taylor's Crochet Thread, No. 10, *or Fine Black Netting Silk; Needle, No.* 22, *Bell Gauge. Chain of* 216 *stitches.*

1st row—Treble in every stitch of the chain.

2nd—3 chain, miss 3, 3 treble. Repeat.

3rd—The same as 2nd, working the 3 treble in the 3 chain.

4th—4 chain, miss 3, 4 treble in the 3 chain, at the end of this row work 10 plain stitches down the side, so as to bring the thread to the foundation chain.

5th—All treble, at the end work 10 treble stitches down the side.

6th—5 chain, miss1, 1 plain. Repeat 5 times, *, 5 chain, miss 4, 1 plain. Repeat from * to to the 10 stitcnes at he end, (then 5 chain, miss 1, 1 plain, 5 times).

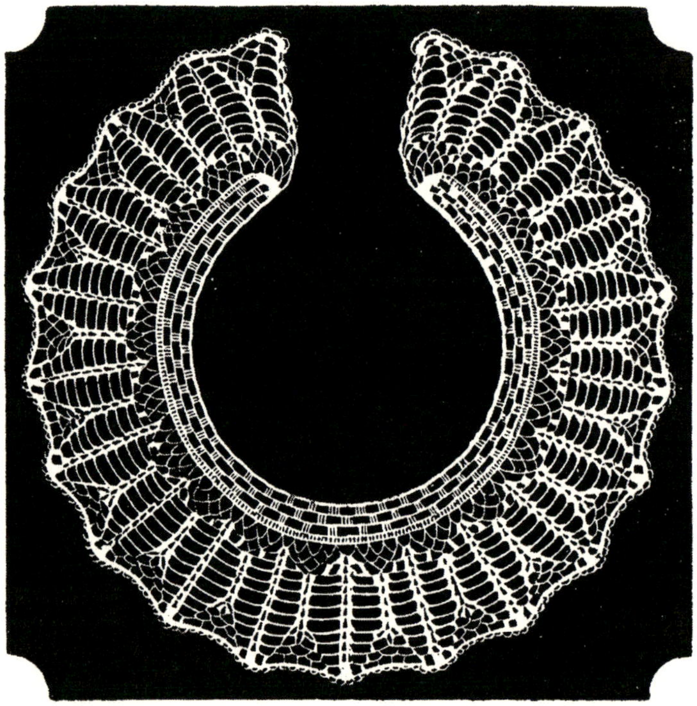

7th—3 chain, miss 4, (3 treble, 3 chain, 3 treble; these 6 treble are all to bworked in the 5 chain of last row); then 3 chain, miss 4, 1 plain, 5 chain, miss 5, 1 plain, 5 chain, miss 5, 1 plain, the plain stitches are to be worked in the 5 chain. Repeat, finish with 3 chain, miss 4, (3 treble; 3 chain, 3 treble in the 5 chain).

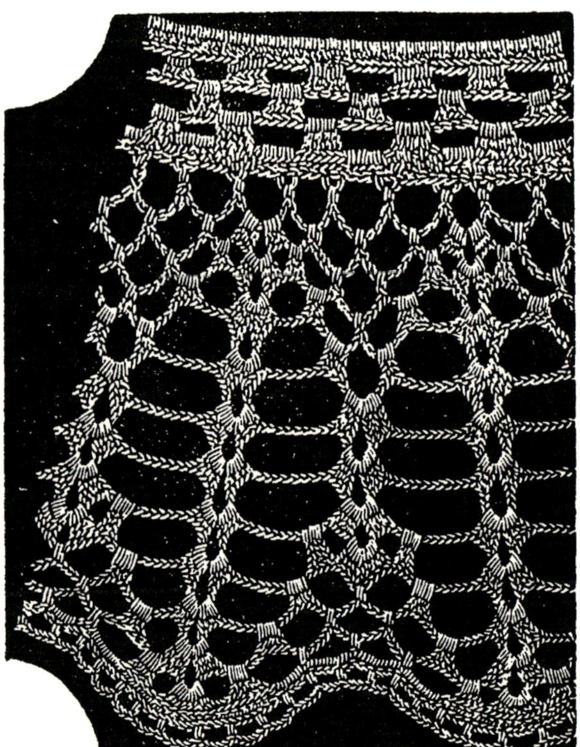

8th—1 chain, miss 3, (3 treble, 3 chain, 3 treble, these 6 treble are to be worked in the 3 chain between the 6th treble of last row), 1 chain, miss 3, 3 treble in the 3 chain of the last row, 3 chain, miss 3, 1 plain, 5 chain, miss 5, 1 plain, the plain stitches are to be worked in the 5 chain of last row, 3 chain, miss 3, 3 treble. Repeat and end with 1 chain, miss 3, (3 treble, 3 chain, 3 treble in the 3 chain).

9th—3 chain, miss 3, *, (3 treble, 3 chain, 3 treble in the 3 chain of last row), 3 chain, miss 7, 3 treble, 3 chain, miss 4, 1 plain in the 5 chain, 3 chain, miss 4, 3 treble, 3 chain, miss 7. Repeat from *. Now end every row with 3 treble, 8 chain, 3 treble.

10th—3 chain, miss 3, *, (3 treble, 3 chain, 3 treble in the 3 chain of last row), 5 chain, miss 9, 3 treble in the 3 chain of last row, 5 chain, miss 1, 3 treble, 5 chain, miss 9. Repeat from *, end as last row.

11th—3 chain, miss 3, *, (3 treble, 3 chain, 3 treble in the 3 chain), 7 chain, miss 11. Repeat from *.

12th—Same as 11th, missing 13 instead of 11.

13th—Same as 12th.

14th—3 chain, miss 3, *, (3 treble, 3 chain, 3 treble in the 3 chain), 9 chain, miss 7, 3 treble in 7 chain of last row 1 chain, miss 3, (3 treble, 3 chain, 3 treble in the 3 chain), 1 chain, miss 3, 3 treble, 9 chain, miss 7. Repeat from *.

15th—3 chain, miss 3, *, (3 treble, 3 chain, 3 treble in the 3 chain), 7 chain,, miss 9, 3 treble in the 9 chain, 5 chain, miss 7, 1 plain in the 3 chain, 5 chain, miss 9, 3 treble, 7 chain, miss 9. Repeat from *.

16th—3 chain, miss 3, *, (3 treble, 3 chain, 3 treble in the 3 chain), 3 chain, miss 7, 3 treble in the 7 chain, 5 chain, miss 5, 1 plain, 5 chain, miss 5, 1 plain; the plain stitches in the 5 chain, 5 chain, miss 5, 4 treble, 3 chain, miss 7. Repeat from *.

17th—3 chain, miss 3, *, (9 treble in the 3 chain), 1 chain, miss 3, 3 treble, 5 chain, miss 5, 1 plain, 5 chain, miss 5, 1 plain, 5 chain, miss 5, 1 plain, 5 chain, miss 5, 3 treble, 1 chain, miss 3. Repeat from *; the plain stitches are to be worked in the 5 chain.

18th—All plain.

19th—4 chain, miss 2, 1 plain. Repeat, and fasten off.

POINT DE MONTPENSIER.

Taylor's Crochet Thread, No. 12, *or Fine Black Netting Silk; Needle, No.* 24, *Bell Gauge. Chain of* 208 *stitches.*

1st and 2nd rows.—Treble in every stitch, turn back.

3rd.—4 chain, miss 1, 7 treble. Repeat.

4th.—6 chain, miss 1, *, 5 treble, 6 chain, miss 6. Rrepeat from *, at the end of the row, 5 treble, 6 chain, miss 1, 1 treble.

5th—4 chain, miss 3, 2 treble, 4 chain, miss 3, 3 treble. Repeat, end with 4 chain, miss 3, 2 treble.

6th—5 chain, 4 treble, *, 3 chain, miss 3, 1 treble, 3 chain, miss 3, 6 treble. Repeat from *, end with 3 treble instead of 6.

7th—4 chain. 1 treble, *, 4 chain, miss 4, 3 treble, 4 chain, miss 4, 2 treble. Repeat from *.

8th—6 chain, miss 4, *, 7 treble, 6 chain, miss 6. Repeat from *, end miss 3 instead of 6, 1 treble

9th—3 chain, 3 treble, *, 3 chain, miss 2, 11 treble. Repeat from *, end with 3 chain, 2 treble.

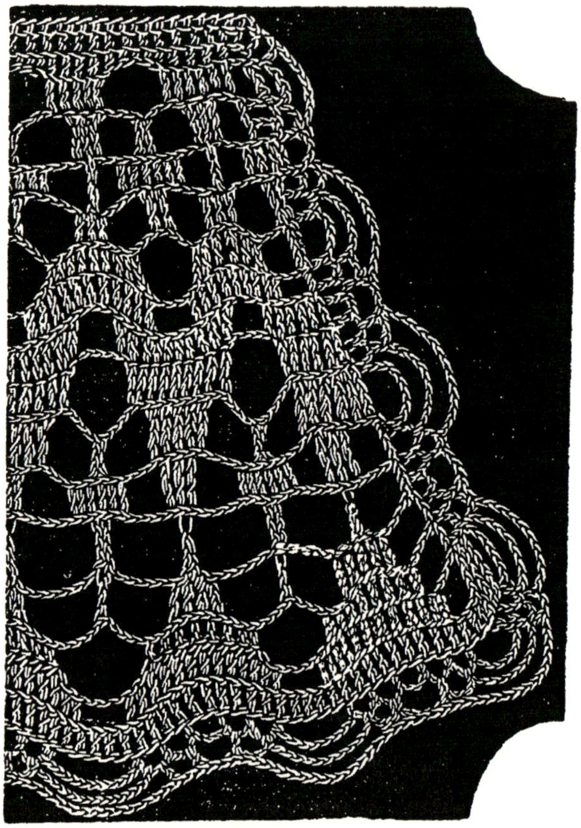

10th—4 chain, 9 treble, *, 4 chain, miss 3, 11 treble. Repeat from *.

11th—4 chain, miss 1, *, 9 treble 6 chain, miss 6. Repeat from *, end with 9 treble.

12th—5 chain, miss 2, *, 5 treble, 5 chain, miss 4, 2 treble, 5 chain, miss 4. Repeat from *, end with miss 1, 2 treble.

13th—4 chain, 4 treble, *, 5 chain, miss 4, 3 treble, 5 chain, miss 4, 6 treble. Repeat from *, end 3 treble instead of 6.

14th—4 chain, 1 treble, *, 7 chain, miss 8, 1 treble, 7 chain, miss 8, 2 treble. Repeat from *.

15th—5 chain, 1 treble, *, 5 chain, miss 6, 5 treble, 5 chain, miss 5, 1 treble. Repeat from *.

16th—7 chain, miss4, *,9 treble, 7 chain, miss 7. Repeat from *, end 3 treble.

17th—3 chain, 5 treble, *, 3 chain, miss 3, 13 treble. Repeat from *.

18th—All treble. This finishes the collar. Then work the écaille pattern edging, commencing at the 4th row, down the sides and round the collar.

COLLAR—POINT D'ESPAGNE.

Taylor's Crochet Thread, No. 12, or Fine Black Netting Silk; Needle, No. 24, Bell Gauge. Chain of 226 stitches.

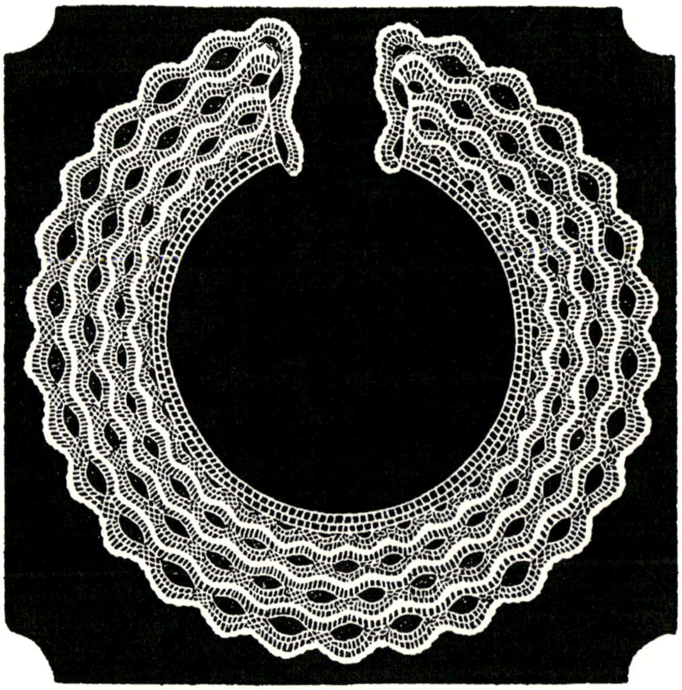

1st row—1 chain, miss 1, 1 treble. Repeat to the end and turn back.

2nd—Same as 1st, working the treble stitch in the chain stitch of the last row.

3rd—5 chain, miss 2, 1 plain, 3 chain, miss 1, 1 plain, 3 chain, miss 1, 1 plain, 3 chain, miss 1, 1 plain. Repeat and finish the row with 5 chain, miss 2, 1 plain.

4th—(1 chain, and 1 treble, 5 times, to be worked in the 5 chain of the last row), then 1 chain, miss 2, 1 plain. The plain stitches in this row, are to be worked in the 3 chain of last row, 3 chain, miss 3, 1 plain, 3 chain, miss 3, 1 plain, miss 2. Repeat. Finish with (1 chain and 1 treble, 6 times.)

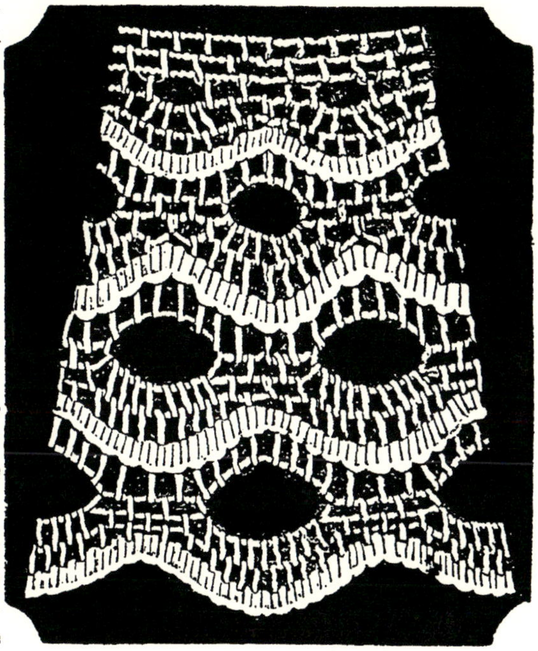

5th—(1 chain, miss 1, 1 treble, 6 times), then 1 chain, miss 2, 1 plain, 3 chain, miss 3, 1 plain, miss 2. Repeat; end with (1 chain, 1 treble, 6 times.)

6th—1 plain, and 3 treble in every chain stitch of last row. Repeat to the end.

7th—1 chain, miss 3, 1 treble. Repeat.

8th—6 chain, miss 1, *, (1 plain, 3 chain, miss 1, 3 times), 1 plain, 6 chain, miss 9. Repeat from *, and finish with 6 chain, miss 1, 1 plain.

9th—(1 chain and 1 treble, 6 times, to be worked in the 6 chain of the last row), 1 chain, miss 2, 1 plain, 3 chain, miss 3, 1 plain, 3 chain, miss 3, 1 plain, miss 2. Repeat, end with (1 chain and 1 treble, 7 times). the plain stitches in this row, are to be worked in the 3 chain of 8th row

10th—(1 chain, miss 1, and 1 treble, 7 times), 1 chain, miss 2, 1 plain 3 chain, miss 3, 1 plain, miss 2. Repeat; end with (1 chain, miss 1 and 1 treble, 7 times).

11th—Same as 6th. 12th—Same as 7th.

13th—8 chain, miss 4, 1 plain, *, (3 chain, miss 1, 1 plain, 3 times), 8 chain, miss 11, 1 plain. Repeat from *.

14th—(1 chain, and 1 treble, 8 times in the 8 chain of last row), 1 chain, miss 2, 1 plain, 3 chain, miss 3, 1 plain, 3 chain, miss 3, 1 plain, miss 2, repeat, finish with (1 chain, and 1 treble, 9 times).

15th—(1 chain, miss 1, and 1 treble, 9 times), 1 chain, miss 2, 1 plain, 3 chain, miss 3, 1 plain, miss 2, (end with 1 chain, miss 1, and 1 treble, 9 times).

16th—Same as 6th; at the end work 40 plain stitches down the side of the collar; this brings it to the foundation.

17th—Same as 7th, continuing the row to the foundation, to correspond with the other side.

18th—9 chain, miss 3, 1 plain, *, (3 chain, miss 3, 1 plain, 3 times), 9 chain, miss 15, 1 plain. Repeat from *, at the sides, miss 7, instead of 15.

19th—(1 chain and 1 treble, 9 times), 1 chain, miss 2, 1 plain, 3 chain, miss 3, 1 plain, 3 chain, miss 2. Repeat, finish with (1 chain, and 1 treble, 10 times).

20th—(1 chain, miss 1, 1 treble, 10 times), 1 chain, miss 2, 1 plain, 3 chain, miss 3, 1 plain miss 2. Repeat.

21st—Same as 6th. This finishes the Collar.

POINT DE VALOIS.

Taylor's Crochet Thread, No. 12, *or Fine Black Netting Silk; Needle, No.* 24, *Bell Gauge. Chain of* 240 *stitches.*

1st row—Treble in every stitch, at the end turn back.

2nd—7 chain, miss 4, 1 plain, 5 chain, miss 4, 1 plain, 7 chain, miss 4, 1 plain. Repeat to the end, and finish with 4 plain.

3rd—7 chain, miss 7, 1 plain, 3 chain, miss 4, (4 treble, 1 chain, 4 treble; these 8 treble stitches are to be worked in the 5 chain of the last row), then 3 chain, miss 4, 1 plain Repeat to the end, the plain stitches are to be worked in the 7 chain of the last row.

4th—3 chain, miss 3, 5 treble in the 3 chain, 3 chain, miss 4, 1 treble in the 1 chain, 3 chain, miss 4, 5 treble in the 3 chain, 3 chain, miss 3, 1 plain in the 7 chain. Repeat.

5th—3 chain, miss 1, 5 treble, 5 chain, miss 5, 2 treble, 1 chain, miss 3, 2 treble, 5 chain, miss 5, 5 treble; the treble stitches are to be worked in the 3 chain of last row. Repeat.

6th—3 chain, miss 5, 5 treble, 4 chain, miss 2, 1 treble, 4 chain, miss 2, 5 treble, 3 chain, miss 5, 1 plain. Repeat; the 5 treble stitches are worked in the 5 chain, and the 1 treble in the 1 chain of last row.

7th—7 chain, miss 3, 1 plain, 5 chain, miss 6, 4 treble, 1 chain, miss 1, 4 treble, 5 chain, miss 5, 1 plain. Repeat, end with 7 chain, miss 1, 1 plain.

8th—7 chain, miss 1, 4 treble, *, 3 chain, miss 4, 1 plain, 7 chain, miss 6, 1 plain, 7 chain, miss 6, 1 plain, 3 chain, miss 4, (4 treble, 1 chain, 4 treble in the 7 chain.) Repeat from *; end with 4 treble instead of 8, then 5 chain, 1 plain.

9th—5 chain, miss 4, 1 treble, 5 chain, miss 4, 5 treble, 3 chain, miss 3, 1 plain, 7 chain, miss 7, 1 plain, 3 chain, miss 3, 5 treble. Repeat; end with 5 chain, miss 4, 1 treble.

10th—1 chain, miss 1, 2 treble, 5 chain, miss 7, 5 treble, 5 chain, miss 4, 1 plain, 5 chain, miss 4, 5 treble, 5 chain, miss 7, 2 treble. Repeat; end with 5 chain, miss 1, 2 treble, 5 chain, treble.

11th—5 chain, miss 5, 5 treble, 5 chain, miss 2, 1 treble, 5 chain, miss 2, 5 treble, 6 chain, miss 7, 1 plain, 1 chain, miss 5, 1plain. Repeat; end with 6 chain, miss 7, 5 treble, 5 chain, miss 2, 1 treble, 5 chain, 5 treble.

12th—5 chain, miss 7, 5 treble, 1 chain, miss 1, 5 treble, 5 chain, miss 7, 1 plain, 7 chain, miss 9, 1 plain. Repeat; end with miss 1, instead of 9.

13th—Same as 8th. 14th—Same as 9th.

15th—Same as 10th. 16th—Same as 11th.

17th—3 chain, miss 5, 9 treble, 1 chain, miss 1, 9 treble, 3 chain, miss 5, 1 plain, 3 chain, miss 6, 1 plain, 3 chain, miss 6, 1 plain. Repeat; commence at the foundation and work up the side.

18th—5 chain, miss 2, 1 plain, repeat, at the end work down the other side to the foundation.

19th—7 chain, miss 11, 1 plain. Repeat; and fasten off.

COIFFURE DE LA VALLIERE; OR, HEAD DRESS.

Taylor's Crochet Thread, No. 10, or Fine Black Silk; Needle, No. 24, Bell Gauge.
Make a chain of 330 stitches. This chain forms the centre of the Coiffure.

See Engraving, at A.

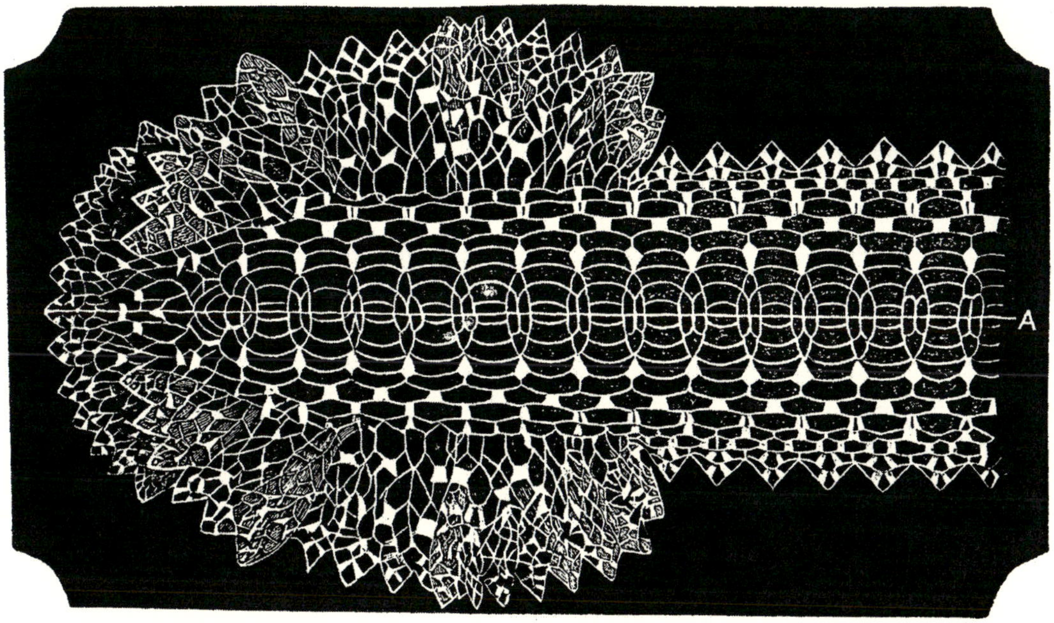

1st round—5 chain, miss 2, 1 plain: repeat to the end of the foundation chain, then turn the work so as to crochet on the other side of the chain; work 5 chain, miss 2, 1 plain as before, working the plain stitch in the same stitch as the one plain on the other side. Repeat to the end.

2nd—5 chain, miss 5, 1 plain, 7 chain, miss 11, 1 plain; the plain stitches are to be worked in the 5 chain of 1st round. Repeat all round.

3rd—9 chain, miss 11, 1 plain, 3 chain, 1 plain; both these plain stitches are to be worked in the 5 chain of 2nd round. Repeat all round.

4th—5 chain, miss 11, 5 treble in the 3 chain of 3rd round. Repeat all round.

5th—(8 chain, miss 5, 1 treble, repeat 8 times), then 8 chain, miss 11, 1 treble in the centre of the 5 treble, repeat 30 times, (then 8 chain, miss 5, 1 treble, 14 times), then 8 chain miss 11, 1 treble as before, 30 times, (8 chain, miss 5, 1 treble, 6 times); this finishes the round..

6th—6 chain, miss 6, 1 plain in the 8 chain, 6 chain, miss 6, 5 treble in the 8 chain. Repeat all round.

7th—5 chain, miss 5, (2 treble, 3 chain, 2 treble, these 4 treble stitches are all to be worked in the 6 chain of 6th round.) Repeat all round.

8th—4 chain, miss 5, 6 treble in the 3 chain, 4 chain, miss 5, 1 plain in the 5 chain. Repeat all round: at the end cut off the thread, and fasten it, count 484 stitches, or 32 patterns, and commence in the 485th stitch, this stitch is the centre of the 6 treble in the 8th round, the 5 following rows are worked backwards and forwards round the corner only, thus:—

9th—9 chain, miss 4, 1 treble. Repeat 65 times, then work 2 plain stitches, and turn back to work the 10th row, 5 chain, miss 7, 5 treble in the 9 chain of 9th row, 6 chain, miss 7, 1 plain in the 9 chain. Repeat 33 times, turn back.

11th—Same as 7th round, repeating the pattern 66 times, then 1 chain, miss 5, 1 plain on the plain stitch in the 8th round, turn back.

12th—Same as 8th round, repeating the pattern 66 times, work 1 plain on the 8th round, and turn back.

13th—3 chain, miss 6, 2 treble in the 4 chain of 8th round. Repeat 132 times, this finishes one corner, then work across the front thus:—3 chain, miss 6, 2 treble in the 4 chain of 8th round. Repeat 43 times, then 3 chain, miss 3, 1 plain. Repeat the 9th, 10th, 11th

12th, and 13th rows, then work across the front thus:—3 chain, miss 6, 2 treble. Repeat 43 times as before. The two following rounds are worked all round the coiffure thus:—

14th—3 chain, miss 3, (2 treble, 3 chain, 2 treble, these 4 treble are all worked in the 3 chain of 13th round), 3 chain, miss 3, 1 plain in the 3 chain. Repeat all round.

15th—1 chain, miss 1, 1 plain, 3 chain, miss 3, (2 treble, 3 chain, 2 treble in the 3 chain), 3 chain, miss 3, 1 plain. Repeat all round. Fasten off.

BERTHE, OR CAPE—POINT D'ITALIE.

Taylor's Crochet Thread, No. 10, *or Fine Black Netting Silk; Needle, No.* 22, *Bell Gauge. Commence at A. with a chain of* 650 *stitches; the plain stitches are always worked in the chain of the row before.*

1st row—All treble.

2nd—5 chain, miss 3, 1 plain. Repeat to the end.

3rd—5 chain, miss 3, 1 plain in the 5 chain, 5 chain, miss 3, (2 treble, 3 chain, 2 treble, these 4 treble are all to be worked in the 5 chain of 2nd row). Repeat to end.

4th—3 chain, miss 3, 1 plain, 3 chain, miss 3, 1 plain, 5 chain, miss 9, 1 plain. Repeat.

5th—5 chain, miss 3, 1 plain, 5 chain, miss 3, (2 treble, 3 chain, 2 treble, these 4 treble in the 3 chain of the 4th row), 3 chain, miss 1, (2 treble, 3 chain, 2 treble, these 4 treble as before). Repeat.

6th—5 chain, miss 7, (2 treble, 3 chain, 2 treble in the 3 chain), 5 chain, miss 7, 1 plain, 1 chain, miss 9, 1 plain. Repeat, end 3 chain, 1 plain.

7th—5 chain, miss 11, 1 plain, 7 chain, miss 9, 1 plain. Repeat.

8th—5 chain, miss 4, 1 plain, 5 chain, miss 4, (2 treble, 3 chain, 2 treble in the 5 chain.) Repeat.

9th—Same as 4th. 10th as 5th. 11th as 6th. 12th as 7th. 13th as 8th row.

14th—5 chain, miss 3, 1 plain, 5 chain, miss 3, 1 plain, 7 chain, miss 9, 1 plain. Repeat.

15th—5 chain, miss 4, 1 plain, 5 chain, miss 4, (2 treble, 3 chain, 2 treble in the 5 chain), 3 chain, miss 1, (2 treble, 3 chain, 2 treble as before.) Repeat.

16th—Same as 6th.

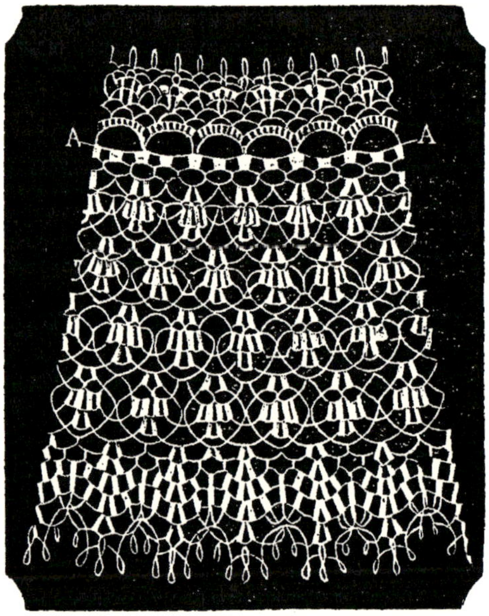

17th—7 chain, miss 11, 1 plain, 9 chain, miss 9, 1 plain. Repeat.

18th—5 chain, miss 5, 1 plain, 5 chain, (3 treble, 3 chain, 3 treble in the 7 chain). Repeat.

19th—5 chain, miss 4, 1 plain, 5 chain, miss 4, 1 plain, 9 chain, miss 9, 1 plain. Repeat.

20th—5 chain, miss 5, 1 plain, 5 chain, miss 5, (3 treble, 3 chain, 3 treble, these 6 treble in the 5 chain), 5 chain, miss 1, (3 treble, 3 chain, 3 treble, as before). Repeat.

21st—5 chain, miss 9, (3 treble, 3 chain, 3 treble in the 5 chain), 5 chain, miss 9, 1 plain, 3 chain, miss 9, 1 plain. Repeat, and end with 3 chain, 1 plain.

22nd—7 chain, miss 11, 1 plain, 9 chain, miss 11, 1 plain. Repeat.

23rd—Same as 18th.

24th—3 chain, miss 3, (3 treble, 3 chain, 3 treble in the 3 chain), 3 chain, miss 3, 1 plain, 7 chain, miss 9, 1 plain. Repeat.

25th—3 chain, miss 3, 1 plain, 3 chain, 1 plain, both these plain stitches in the 7 chain of 24th row, (3 chain, miss 3, 2 treble, 3 chain, 2 treble in the 3 chain. Repeat 3 times), Repeat, end with 3 chain, 1 plain.

26th—(3 chain, miss 7, 2 treble, 3 chain, 2 treble. Repeat 3 times), then 3 chain, miss 7, 1 plain. Repeat to end.

27th—5 chain, miss 6, 1 plain, 5 chain, miss 7, (3 treble, 3 chain, 3 treble in the 3 chain), 5 chain, miss 7, 1 plain, 5 chain, miss 6, 1 plain on the plain stitch in 26th row.

28th—13 chain; put the needle in the 4th chain stitch, and work 1 plain stitch in it, this forms a round loop of 9 stitches, then 3 chain, miss 5, 1 plain. Repeat 3 times, then 13 chain, 1 plain in the 4th stitch as before, 3 chain, 1 plain in the same stitch as the last plain stitch, then 13 chain, 1 plain in the 4th stitch as before, 3 chain, miss 5, 1 plain, 13 chain, 1 plain in the 4th stitch, miss 5, 1 plain. Repeat to the end, and cut off the cotton. Now commence upon the foundation, and work as follows:—

1st row—2 treble, 12 chain, miss 6. Repeat; end with 2 treble.

2nd—8 treble, miss 6; end with 8 treble. This is for the ribbon. Now commence at the 28th row, and work up the side of the berthe, 5 chain, miss 3, 1 plain. Repeat 20 times, and work the same along the treble row, and 20 times down the other side; then work the 3rd, 4th, 5th, and 6th rows as in the first part of the direction, working them along the top and down the sides.

For the Edging—13 chain, 1 plain in the 4th stitch as in the 28th row, 3 chain, miss 5, 1 plain. Repeat once more; then 13 chain, 1 plain in the 4th stitch, 3 chain, 1 plain in the same stitch as the last plain stitch; then 13 chain, 1 plain in the 4th stitch, 3 chain, miss 5, 1 plain. Repeat to the end, and fasten off.

INSERTION—MOSAIC.

Taylor's Crochet Thread, No. 10; Needle, No. 20, Bell Gauge. Chain of 500 stitches per yard.

1st row—Treble in every stitch of the foundation.

2nd—1 treble, 2 chain, miss 2, 3 treble, 2 chain, miss 2. Repeat; finish with 1 treble, 2 chain to turn the corner.

3rd—2 treble, 2 chain, miss 2, 1 treble, 2 chain, miss 2, 1 treble. Repeat; at the end, 1 treble, 2 chain.

4th—Same as 2nd. 5th—Same as 1st.

INSERTION—A-LA-GRECQUE.

Taylor's Crochet Thread, No. 10; Needle, No. 22, Bell Gauge. Chain of 500 stitches, work rather loose.

1st row—1 plain, 2 chain, miss 2, 5 treble in 1 stitch, 2 chain, miss 2. Repeat; end 1 plain.

2nd—6 chain, miss 9, 1 plain, the plain stitch to be worked in the centre of 5 treble of last row.

3rd—1 chain, 1 plain, 6 treble, 1 plain; the plain stitches and the treble are all to be worked in

the 6 chain of last row; miss 1, and repeat; now turn the work so as to work on the foundation chain.

4th—Same as 1st, working the plain stitch and the 5 treble in the same chain stitches as the 1st row. 5th—Same as 2nd. 6th—Same as 3rd.

MANCHETTE, OR UNDER SLEEVE.

Taylor's Crochet Thread, No. 10; *Needle, No.* 22, *Bell Gauge. Chain of* 90 *stitches.*

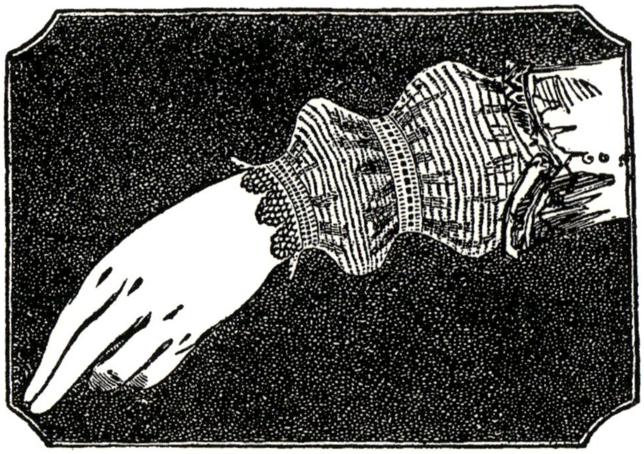

1st and 2nd rows—Treble in every stitch.

3rd—1 chain, miss 1, 1 treble. Repeat.

4th and 5th—Same as 1st and 2nd.

6th—3 chain, 1 plain. Repeat.

7th—3 chain, miss 3, 1 plain in the 3 chain of the last row. Repeat this last row, 15 times more.

23rd—1 plain, miss 3. Repeat; this reduces the Manchette to 90 stitches. Repeat from 1st row once more; then repeat the first 5 rows, and finish with Vandyke Edging.

VANDYKE EDGING.

Taylor's, No. 10, *Needle, No.* 22, *Bell Gauge. Make a chain af* 500 *stitches per yard.*

1st row—4 chain, miss 1, 1 plain. Repeat.

2nd—1 chain, 1 plain, the 1 plain are always worked in the chain in last row; (4 chain, miss 5, 1 plain, twice), turn back so as to work on the 2nd row.

3rd—1 chain, miss 1, 1 plain, (4 chain, miss 5, 1 plain, twice), turn back.

4th—1 chain, miss 1, 1 plain, 4 chain, miss 5, 1 plain; work 6 single down the side of the Vandyke, so as to bring the thread to the 1st row; this forms one Vandyke. Repeat from 2nd row.

MONTPENSIER CUFF.

Taylor's Crochet Thread, No. 12; *Needle, No.* 24, *Bell Gauge. Chain of* 85 *stitches.*

1st row—All treble.

2nd—5 treble, 3 chain, miss 3, 4 treble. Repeat, at the end of every row work 1 treble, 2 chain, beside the pattern.

3rd—4 treble, 2 chain, miss 2, 1 treble, 2 chain, miss 2, 3 treble. Repeat.

4th—3 treble, 2 chain, miss 2, 1 treble, 1 chain, miss 1, 1 treble, 2 chain, miss 2, 2 treble. Repeat.

5th—2 treble, 2 chain, miss 2, 1 treble, (1 chain, miss 1, 1 treble, twice), 2 chain, miss 2, 1 treble. Repeat.

6th—1 treble, 2 chain, miss 2, (1 treble, 1 chain, miss 1, 3 times), 1 treble, 2 chain, miss 2. Repeat.

7th—Same as 5th. 8th—Same as 4th.

9th—Same as 3rd. 10th—Same as 2nd.

11th—Same as 1st. Then work the écaille pattern edging, commencing at the 4th row.

ECAILLE PATTERN EDGING.

Taylor's Crochet Thread, No. 8, *or Fine Black Netting Silk; Needle, No.* 20, *Bell Gauge. Chain of* 500 *stitches for each yard.*

1st row—4 chain, miss 4, 4 treble.

2nd and 3rd—The same as 1st, working the 4 treble in the 4 chain of last row.

4th—2 chain, miss 3, *, 1 plain, 9 chain, miss 5, (1 plain, 3 chain, miss 1, 5 times). Repeat from *, and end with 1 plain.

5th—5 chain, *, 1 plain, 3 chain, miss 3, 1 plain, 7 chain, miss 7, 1 plain, 3 chain, miss 3, 1 plain, 11 chain, miss 11. Repeat from * end with 1 plain: the plain stitches in this row are to be worked in the 3 chain of last row.

6th—13 chain, miss 13, 1 plain, 1 chain, 3 plain in the 7 chain of the last row, 1 chain, 1 plain. Repeat; end with 1 plain.

EDGING—EGYPTIAN.

Taylor's Crochet Thread, No. 8; *Needle, No.* 20, *Bell Gauge.* 500 *stitches per yard, or Thread, No.* 6, *and* 400 *stitches.*

1st row—1 chain, miss 3, 3 treble in 1 chain stitch. Repeat; end with 2 chain.

2nd—Miss 3, 3 treble in the 1 chain of last row, 1 chain. Repeat 5 times; then miss 3, 1 treble, 3 chain; turn back so as to work the next row on the 2nd row.

3rd—Miss 5, *, 3 treble in the 1 chain, 1 chain, miss 3. Repeat from * 4 times, then 1 treble, 3 chain; turn back.

4th—Miss 5, *, 3 treble in the 1 chain, 1 chain, miss 3. Repeat from * 3 times, then 1 treble, 3 chain; turn back.

5th—Miss 5, *, 3 treble in the 1 chain, 1 chain, miss 3. Repeat from * twice, then 1 treble, 3 chain; turn back.

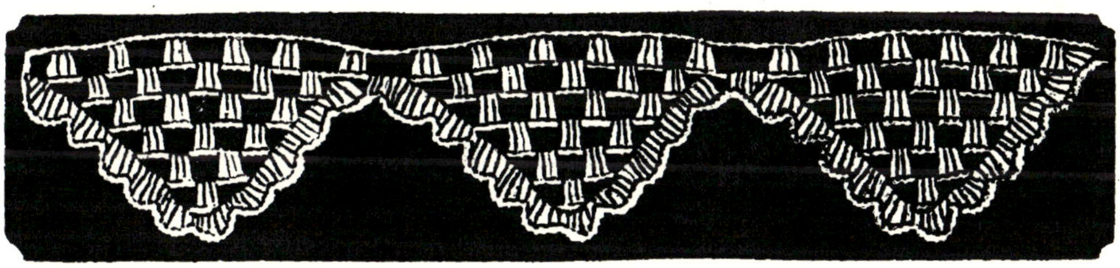

6th—Miss 5, 3 treble in the 1 chain, 3 chain, miss 3, 1 plain; work 8 single stitches down the side of the Vandyke, so as to bring the thread to 1st row; work 2 treble stitches in the same stitch as the 1 treble in the 2nd row, then 1 chain, and repeat the 2nd and following rows until the whole length is worked; then work a row round the Vandyke, thus—1 plain, 5 treble, 1 plain; these 7 stitches are to be worked in every space formed by the turning of the rows.

THE END.

THE

CROCHET BOOK,

SECOND SERIES.

IN WHICH IS GIVEN AN ENTIRELY NEW STYLE IN

FLOWERS AND LEAVES,

BY

MDLLE. RIEGO DE LA BRANCHARDIERE.

Tenth Edition--50,000.

LONDON:
SIMPKIN, MARSHALL, AND CO.;
ACKERMANN & CO., STRAND; OLIVER AND BOYD, EDINBURGH;
AND ALL THE BERLIN WAREHOUSES.
1850.

CONTENTS.

PREVIOUS to presenting the First Series of Instructions in Crochet to the public, I conceived the idea of carrying the art to greater perfection than had been hitherto attained. How far I have succeeded, must be left to the unbiassed judgment of my numerous friends and patronesses. The Illustrated Instructions, and the variety of patterns given in the First Series of THE CROCHET BOOK, are a necessary and preliminary course (combined with the new instructions in *this* Series), to assist the learner, or even the proficient, in acquiring a readier knowledge of the mode of working the improved designs in the present production. Flowers and Leaves in Crochet, were studies which I found comparatively easy in their separate forms; but to combine them with effect in *one* design, with concise and simple directions, was a task of great difficulty, labour, and time. This, and the care that has been bestowed in perfecting the engravings, will fully account for the delay of the work, since its announcement in June last.

Encouraged in my endeavours to forward this delightful accomplishment by the approbation and flattering testimonials my works have received, I beg respectfully to intimate that a Third Series of New Patterns are in course of preparation.

E. R. DE LA BRANCHARDIERE.

106, *New Bond Street*,
Jan. 1*st*, 1848.

CROCHET.

INSTRUCTION, AND EXPLANATION OF TERMS.

SINGLE CROCHET, OR SHEPHERD'S KNITTING.

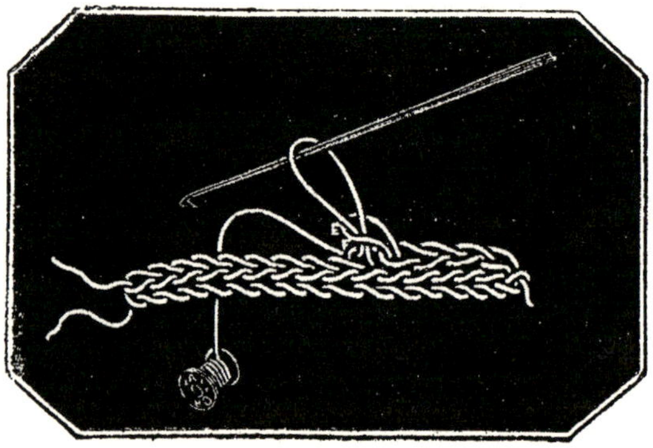

After making a chain, the loop E being on the needle, put the needle in a stitch as F, draw the thread through, forming a loop, and also through the loop on the needle E. This stitch is only used in the following direction at the end of a round, to prevent the stitches from appearing higher than those at the commencement of the round; also in rows, to bring the thread to another part of the work without the stitches being perceived.

TO COMMENCE AND END A ROW IN TREBLE CROCHET.

Work a chain stitch as G, leaving an end of the thread about two inches; turn the thread round the needle, and then putting the needle into the 1st stitch of the work, finish the treble stitch; end the row as in plain crochet.

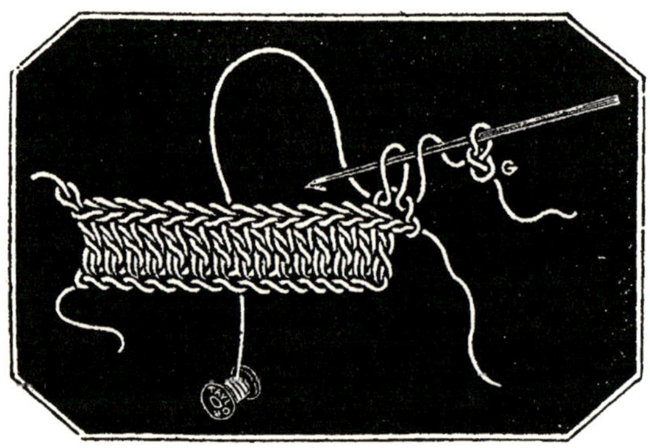

DOUBLE CROCHET,

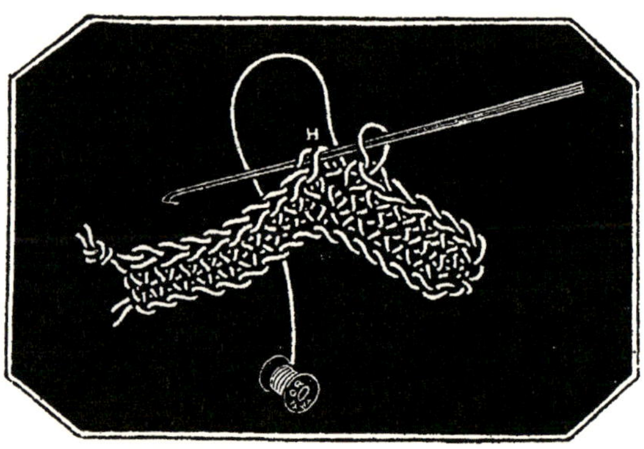

Is a variation of plain crochet; and formed by taking up both sides of the stitch in the previous row on the needle as H, instead of the usual method of putting it in the stitch; this makes the work stronger, and is suited for fine thread.

TO COMMENCE AND END A ROW IN PLAIN CROCHET.

When the thread is cut off, work a chain stitch, leaving an end about 2 inches; put the needle into the 1st stitch of the work and finish the plain stitch. At the end of the row work a chain stitch, cut off the thread, leaving about 2 inches, and draw it through to fasten it; when the work is finished, knot every 2 ends of the thread together and cut them close.

A ROUND LOOP.

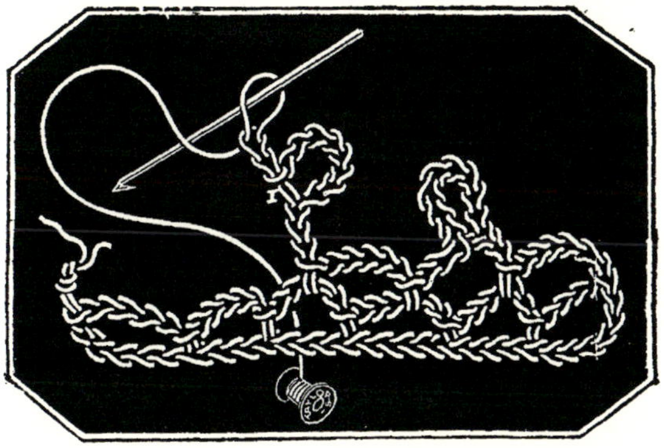

Make a chain of 11 stitches or more according to the direction; put the needle back into the 3d stitch of the 11 chain, and work a plain stitch in it as I, leaving the 1st 2 chain stitches of the 11 chain; then work 2 chain to correspond with the other side. This round loop is varied in the direction, in size and position, according to the pattern.

TO WORK BACKWARDS AND FORWARDS.

After working the required number of foundation stitches, for plain crochet, work 1 chain stitch, and commence the direction in the 2d stitch, leaving the 1 chain stitch to turn the corner. For treble crocnet, work 2 chain stitches, and commence in the 3d stitch. This rule should be observed at the commencement of every row.

TO TURN BACK,

Is to turn the work on the contrary side of the stitches last worked.

TO TURN,

Is to place the work so as to crochet on the opposite side of the stitches or chain last worked, still keeping the work on the right side.

TO JOIN FLOWERS AND LEAVES TOGETHER.

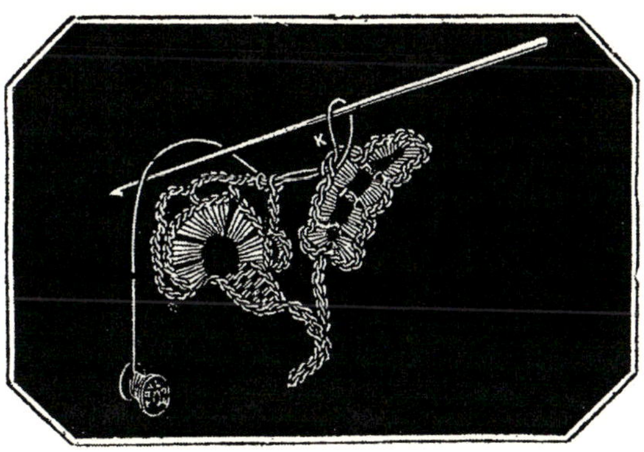

Work 1 chain stitch, take the needle out of the loop, insert the needle in the stitch marked in *italics* in the direction; then put the needle in the loop as K, and draw the loop through the stitch, and work 1 chain as L.

Note.—To make a chain. Plain stitch, treble stitch, miss a stitch. To work in the chain * and a parenthesis ( ) see First Series of the Crochet Book.

COLLAR—LA REINE DES FLEURS.

COLLAR—LA REINE DES FLEURS.

Taylor's Crochet Thread, No. 12, or Fine Black Netting Silk; Needle, No. 24, Bell Gauge

The plain and treble stitches are to be worked in double crochet, except when they are worked in the chain. "To join the Flowers and Leaves together," "Round Loop," "to Turn," and "to Turn Back,"—See Instructions. Commence by working a Leaf, thus:—

1st Leaf—13 chain, turn, miss 3, 1 plain in the 4th chain stitch, 2 chain, miss 2, 1 treble, 2 chain, miss 2, 1 treble, 2 chain, miss 2, 1 plain; turn so as to crochet on the other side and leaving one chain stitch for the stem, work 1 chain to cross the stem, then (miss 1, 5, treble, and 1 plain in the 2 chain 4 times), turn, and work on the other side, (miss 1, 5 treble and 1 plain in the 2 chain 3 times as before); turn back, and on the wrong side work 21 single stitches, which will bring the thread to the point of the Leaf; turn the Leaf on the right side, and work a Flower, thus:—

1st Flower.—22 chain, put the needle into the 12th stitch of these 22 chain, and work a plain stitch in it, to form a round loop; then for the calyx, 5 treble, 2 plain, turn, leaving 5 chain for the stem; then work 1 chain to cross the stem; and in the same stitches as those on the other side, 2 plain and 5 treble, 1 plain; then work in the round loop, (3 plain and 5 chain 5 times), 2 plain and 1 plain on the 1st plain stitch of the calyx, 3 chain, and turning the Flower on the wrong side, join it to the 2nd 5 *treble* of the Leaf; then on the Flower work (1 chain, miss 3, and 5 treble in the 5 chain 5 times), miss 2, 1 plain, and down the calyx work 9 single stitches, and commence the

2nd Flower.—22 chain, put the needle into the 11th stitch, and work 1 plain stitch in it to form a round loop; for the calyx, 5 treble, 2 plain, turn, leaving 3 chain stitches for the stem, and work 1 chain to cross it, 2 plain, 5 treble, 1 plain on the same stitches as those on the other side; then in the round loop (3 plain and 5 chain 7 times) 2 plain, and 1 plain on the 1st plain stitch of the calyx, turn back, (1 chain, miss 3, and 5 treble in the 5 chain 7 times) miss 1, 1 plain, turn back, (7 chain miss 5, and 1 plain in the 1 chain 7 times) turn back, miss 1, 3 plain in the 7 chain, join it to the last 1 *chain* of the 1st flower; then on the 2d flower, 4 plain in the same 7 chain as the 3 plain, then (miss 1, and 7 plain in the 7 chain 6 times), miss 1, and down the calyx, 1 plain, 5 treble, 2 plain as before; then on the stem, 4 plain, and work the

2d Leaf.—15 chain, turn, 1 plain in the 4th chain stitch, 2 chain miss 2, 1 treble, 2 chain, miss 2, 1 treble, 2 chain, miss 2, 1 plain, turn, leaving 2 chain for the stem, work 1 chain to cross it, (miss 1, 5 treble, and 1 plain in the 2 chain twice), join to the 2d flower by working in the centre stitch of *the* 7 *plain*, then miss 1, (5 treble and 1 plain in the 2 chain as before twice), turn so as to work on the other side, (miss 1, 5 treble and 1 plain 3 times in the 2 chain as before), then 2 plain on the stem, and 4 plain on the stem of the 1st flower, 10 chain, turn back, 9 plain on the 10 chain, and leaving them for the stem, work the

3d Flower.—19 chain, 1 plain in the 10th stitch to form a round loop; then for the calyx, 5 treble, 2 plain, turn, leaving 2 stitches for the stem, work 1 chain to cross it, then 2 plain, 5 treble, 1 plain in the same stitches as those on the other side, and in the round loop (3 plain; and 5 chain 5 times), 2 plain, and 1 plain on the calyx, 3 chain, turn back, and join it to 2*d* 5 *treble* of the 2d leaf; then (1 chain miss 3, and 5 treble in the 5 chain, 5 times), then join to the stem by working 1 plain stitch on the 1st stitch of the 9 plain left for the stem, turn back, and work 15 single stitches on the wrong side of the flower, which will bring the thread to the centre of it.

This finishes the 1st pattern, and is not repeated, as a leaf is omitted between the 1st and 2d flowers to shape the side of the collar, and as the next pattern must necessarily join to the 1st pattern, the direction is slightly varied, although the shape and position of the leaves and flowers remain the same.

SECOND PATTERN.

1st Leaf.—Same as the 1st leaf.

1st Flower.—22 chain, and work 1 plain in the 12th stitch, to form a round loop; then for the calyx, 5 treble, 2 plain, turn, leaving 5 chain for the stem, work 1 chain to cross it, and on the other side 2 plain, 5 treble, 1 plain; then in the round loop, (3 plain, and 5 chain 5 times,) 2 plain and 1 plain on the calyx, 3 chain, and turning this flower on the wrong side, join it to the 2*d* 5 *treble* of the 1*st leaf*; then on the flower (1 chain miss 3, and 5 treble in the 5 chain twice), join to the 1st 1 *chain* of the 3d flower, then 1 chain miss 3, 2 treble as before, and join to the 1*st* 5 *treble* in the 2d leaf; then (1 chain miss 3, and 5 treble twice as before), then miss 2, 1 plain, and down the calyx work 7 single stitches commence the large leaf thus:—

Large Leaf.—28 chain, turn, miss 3, 1 plain in the 4th stitch, 2 chain, miss 2, 1 plain (2 chain miss 2, and 1 treble 4 times), 2 chain, miss 2, 1 plain, turn, and leavin

6 chain for the stem, work 1 chain to cross it, and on the other side (miss 1, 5 treble, 1 plain in the 2 chain twice), join to the *last* 1 *chain* of the 1st flower; then miss 1,

[SECTION OF COLLAR.]

5 treble and 1 plain in the 2 chain, join to the *point* of the 2nd leaf, then miss 1, 5 treble and 1 plain in the 2 chain, join to the centre of the 7 *plain* of the 2nd *flower*; then (miss 1, 5 treble, and 1 plain in the 2 chain 3 times): turn, and on the other side (miss 1, 5 treble, and 1 plain in the 2 chain as on the other side 6 times); then on the stem, 5 plain, and work the 2d flower as in 1st pattern, joining it to the *4th* 5 *treble* of the large leaf; then work the 2d small leaf, the stems, and 3d flower the same as in 1st pattern: repeat this pattern 11 times more; then work 5 rows for the Neck along the pattern thus:—

1st row.—(5 chain, miss 4, 1 plain 3 times), on the 15 single stitches of the flower; then 5 chain, 1 plain in the 15th stitch of the 21 single stitches of the leaf; then 5 chain, miss 4, and 1 plain 3 times), on the leaf—repeat to the end, work 2 plain stitches, and turn back.

2d and 3d.—5 chain, miss 5, 1 plain in the 5 chain of last row: repeat, and end with 2 plain.

4th.—3 chain, miss 5, 1 plain in the 5 chain of the last row: repeat to the end.

5th.—Miss 2, and 2 plain in the 3 chain; repeat, and fasten off.

POINT D'EGLANTIER.

Taylor's Crochet Thread, No. 10.—Needle No. 22, Bell Gauge.

This Collar is worked backwards and forwards. For the round loops, see Instructions. Make a chain of 270 stitches.

1st row.—(8 chain, one plain in the 3d stitch, 2 chain, forming a round loop), miss 1 stitch of the foundation, 13 plain, repeat 20 times, end with 5 plain instead of 13 plain.

2d.—Miss 7, (1 plain, 9 chain, 1 plain, 11 chain, 1 plain, 9 chain, 1 plain, these 4 plain in the round loop of the 1st row), 3 chain, miss 7, 1 plain, 5 chain, miss 1, 1 plain, 3 chain, repeat, end with miss 7, 1 plain, 9 chain, 1 plain, 11 chain, 1 plain, 9 chain, 1 plain, as before.

3d.—Miss 1, *, 10 treble, 1 plain, these 11 stitches in the 9 chain of the 2d row, miss 1, 1 plain, 11 treble, 1 plain, these 13 stitches are worked in the 11 chain, miss 1, 1 plain, 10 treble, these 11 stitches in the 9 chain, miss 6, 1 plain, in the 5 chain of the 2d row, (11 chain, 1 plain, in the 3d stitch, 2 chain forming a round loop,) 1 plain in the same 5 chain, miss 6, repeat from *, and end with 10 treble, 1 plain, miss 1, 1 plain, 11 treble, 1 plain, miss 1, 1 plain, 10 treble as before.

4th.—16 plain *, 1 plain, 3 chain, 1 plain, both these plain stitches in the centre stitch of the 11 treble in the last row, 7 chain, miss 11, 1 plain, 3 chain, miss 11, (1 plain, 9 chain, 1 plain, 11 chain, 1 plain, 9 chain, 1 plain; these 4 plain in the round loop of the 3d row), 3 chain, miss 11, 1 plain, 7 chain, miss 11, repeat from *, and end with 1 plain.

5th.—3 chain, miss 5, 1 plain in the 7 chain of last row, miss 7, 10 treble, 1 plain, these 11 stitches in the 9 chain of 4th row, miss 1, 1 plain, 11 treble, 1 plain, these 13 stitches in the

11 chain, miss 1, 1 plain and 10 treble in the 9 chain, miss 7, 1 plain in the 7 chain, 3 chain, miss 5, 1 plain in the chain of the 4th row, 9 chain, 1 plain in the 3rd stitch, 2

[SECTION OF COLLAR.]

chain to form a round loop, 1 plain in the same 3 chain. Repeat, and end with 1 plain in the 3 chain, instead of the 9 chain for the round loop.

6th.—Miss 4, 16 plain, and repeat from * in the 4th row.

7th.—Same as 5th.

8th.—Same as 6th.

9th.—Same as 5th.

10th.—Same as 4th.

11th.—1 chain, miss 5, 1 plain in the 7 chain of last row, miss 7, (10 treble, and 1 plain, in the 9 chain), miss 1, (1 plain, 11 treble, 1 plain, in the 11 chain,) miss 1, (1 plain and 10 treble as before), miss 7, 1 plain, 1 chain, miss 5, (1 plain, 5 chain, 1 plain, 7 chain. 1 plain, 9 chain, 1 plain, 7 chain, 1 plain, 5 chain, 1 plain, these 6 plain are all to be worked in the 3 chain of 10th row,) repeat to the end and fasten off.

COLLAR—POINT DES FLEURS.

Taylor's Crochet Thread, No. 12; Needle, No. 23, Bell Gauge. This Collar is to be worked backwards and forwards. Work the plain and treble stitches in Double Crochet, except when they are worked in the chain.

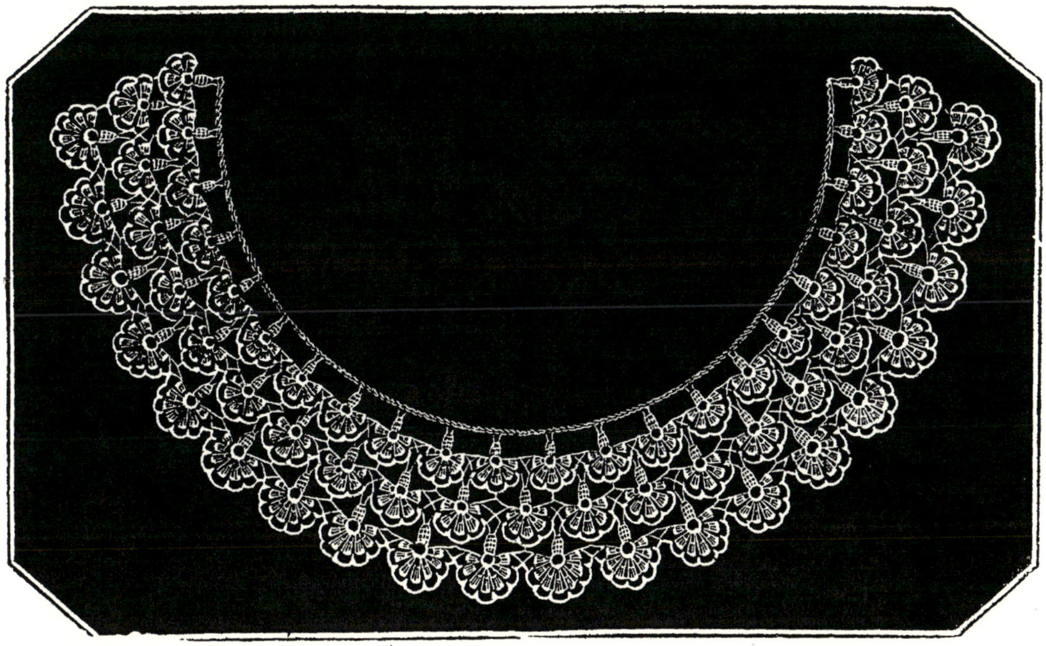

1st row—31 chain, put the needle in the 22d stitch of these 31 to form a round loop, 2 plain, 4 treble, 1 plain, these 7 stitches are worked on 7 stitches of the chain, for the Calyx, turn the work so as to Crochet on the other side, leaving 14 chain stitches for the stem, 1 chain, to cross the stem, 1 plain, 4 treble, 2 plain, in the same stitches as on the other side, *then for the flower*, (3 plain and 5 chain, 5 times in the round loop), 2 plain, and 1 plain on the Calyx, turn back. (1 chain, miss the 3 plain, and 5 treble in the 5 chain, 5 times), 1 chain, miss 3, and on the Calyx, 2 plain, 4 treble, 1 plain, as before; this forms one complete flower; repeat for 22 flowers, and turn back to work the 2nd row, which will join the flowers together.

2d.—7 plain up the calyx of the 22d flower, 1 plain in the 1 chain, (7 chain, miss 5, and 1 plain in the 1 chain of the 1st row 5 times), *, 3 chain, 1 plain in the 1st 1 chain of the 21st flower, 3 chain, join to the 7 chain of the 22d flower, 3 chain, miss 5, 1 plain in the 1 chain of the 21st flower, (7 chain, miss 5, and 1 plain 4 times) in the 1 chain of the 21st flower, repeat from * to the end, and turn back.

3d.—(miss 1, and 7 plain in the 7 chain of the 2d row 4 times), * miss 1, 3 plain in the 3 chain, of the 2d row, then 18 chain, put the needle into the 9th stitch of these 18, to form a round loop, 2 plain, 4 treble, 1 plain, these 7 stitches on 7 stitches of the chain, turn the work to crochet on the other side, finish the calyx and flower as in the 1st row, then miss 1, 3 plain in the 3 chain of the 2d row, (miss 1, and 7 plain, in the 7 chain of the 2d row, 3 times), repeat from * for 21 flowers and end with miss 1, 7 plain.

4th.—18 plain, on 18 plain stitches of the 3d row, 3 chain, 1 plain, in the 1 chain of the 21st flower in the 3d row, (then 7 chain, miss 5, 1 plain in the 1 chain of the 3d row, 5 times,) * 3 chain, miss 13 stitches of the 3d row, 1 plain in the centre of the flower in the 1st row,

3 chain, miss 13, 1 plain in the 1 chain of 20th flower in 3rd row, 3 chain, 1 plain in the

[SECTION OF COLLAR.]

7 chain of the 21st flower, 3 chain, miss 5, 1 plain in the 1 chain of the 20th flower, then (7 chain, miss 5 and 1 plain, 4 times.) Repeat from *, and end with miss 13, 1 plain.

5th.—(Miss 1, and 7 plain in the 7 chain of the 4th row 4 times), * miss 1, 3 plain in the 3 chain, of the 4th row, then work a flower and calyx in the same manner as tnose in the 1st and 3d rows but larger, (thus:—20 chain, put the needle into the 9th stitch of these 20 chain, 2 plain, 4 treble, 1 plain, then on the other side 1 chain, 1 plain, 4 treble, 2 plain,) and in the round loop, work (3 plain, and 5 chain 7 times), 2 plain and 1 plain on the calyx, turn back, (1 chain, miss 5, and 5 treble in the 5 chain 7 times), 1 chain, miss 3, and on the calyx 2 plain, 4 treble, 1 plain, then miss 1, 3 plain in the 3 chain of the 4th row, (miss 1, and 7 plain in the 7 chain of the 4th row 3 times), repeat from * for 20 flowers, and end with miss 1, 7 plain.

6th.—18 plain on 18 plain stitches of the 5th row, 1 plain in the one chain of the 20th flower, in the 5th row, (7 chain, miss 5, and 1 plain 7 times), *, 3 chain, miss 13 stitches of the 5th row, 1 plain in the centre of the flower in the 3d row, 3 chain, miss 13, 1 plain in the one chain of the 19th flower of the 5th row, 3 chain, join to the 7 chain of the 20th flower of the 5th row, 3 chain, miss 5, 1 plain in the 1 chain of the 19th flower, then (7 chain, miss 5, and 1 plain 6 times), repeat from *, and end with miss 13, 1 plain.

7th.—(Miss 1, and 7 plain in the 7 chain of the 6th row 6 times), *, miss 1, 3 plain in the 3 chain of 6th row, miss 1, 3 plain in the 3 chain, then (miss 1, and 7 plain 5 times in the 7 chain of the 6th row,) repeat from * to the end and fasten off, then work a row of plain crochet along the neck.

COLLAR—POINT DE VENISE

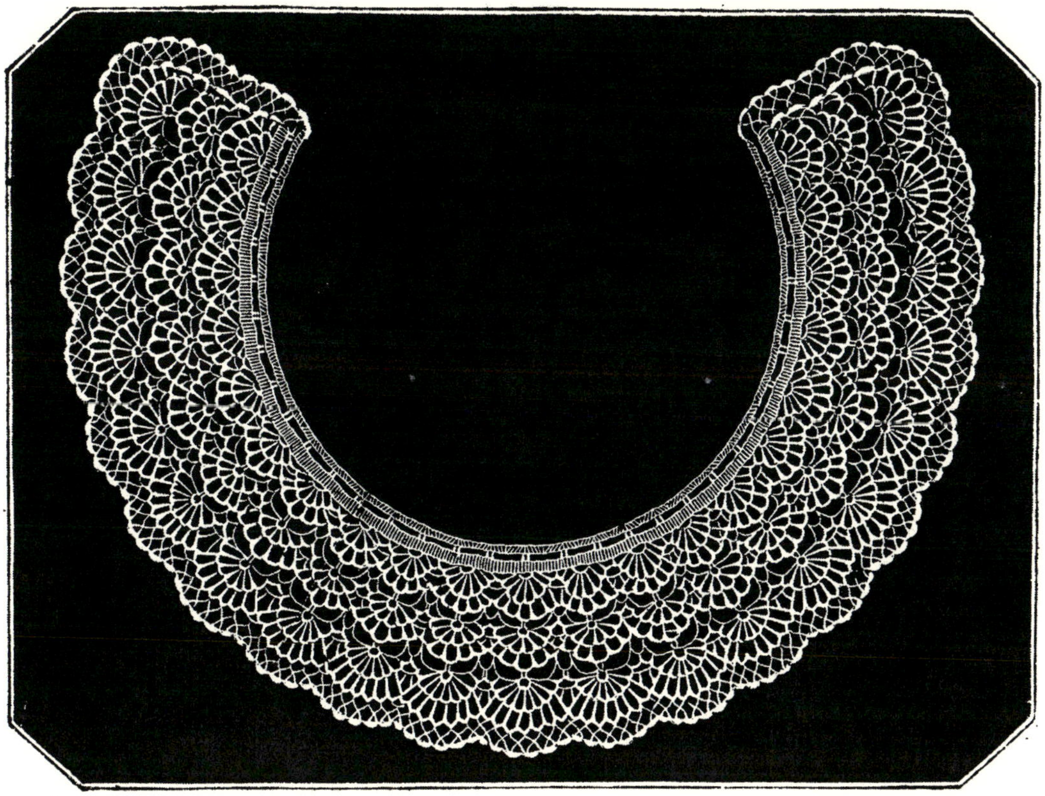

Taylor's Crochet Thread, No. 12, or Fine Black Silk.—Needle, No. 22, Bell Gauge.

Make a chain of 253 stitches.

1st row.—6 plain, *, 5 chain, miss 1, 11 plain, repeat from *, and end with 5 plain, turn back.

2d.—3 chain, miss 2, 1 plain, miss 2, (3 chain, and 1 treble, 5 times in the 5 chain of the 1st row,) 3 chain, miss 2, 1 plain, 3 chain, miss 2, 1 plain, repeat, and at the end turn back.

3d.—Miss 1, and 3 plain in the 3 chain of the last row, repeat, and turn back.

4th.—1 chain, miss 4, 1 plain, *, (5 chain, miss 2, and 1 plain 5 times), 1 chain, miss 8, 1 plain, repeat from *, and end with miss 4 instead of 8, turn back, the plain stitches in this now are worked in the centre of the 3 plain in the last row.

5th.—5 chain, *, (miss 1, and 5 plain in the 5 chain of the 4th row 5 times), miss 2, repeat from *, and end with 5 chain, 1 plain, then cut off the thread and commence at the other end.

6th.—1 plain in the 5 chain of the beginning of the 5th row, *, 5 chain, miss 4, 1 plain, 7 chain, miss 9, (1 plain, 6 chain, 1 plain, both these plain stitches are to be worked in the same stitch), 7 chain, miss 9, 1 plain, repeat from *, end with 5 chain, miss 4, 1 plain, turn back.

7th.—Miss 3, 1 plain, *, 3 chain, miss 5, 1 plain in the 7 chain of 6th row, miss 5, (3 chain and 1 treble, 5 times in the 6th chain of last row), 3 chain, miss 5, 1 plain, 3 chain, miss 5, 1 plain in the 5 chain of the last row, repeat from *, turn back.

8th—Same as 3rd. 9th same as 4th. 10th same as 5th. Cut off the thread and commence at the other end. 11th same as 6th.

[SECTION OF COLLAR.]

12th—Miss 3, 1 plain, *, 3 chain, miss 5, 1 plain, miss 5, (3 chain and 1 treble, 7 times in the 6th chain of the last row), 3 chain, miss 5, 1 plain, 3 chain, miss 5, 1 plain, repeat from* turn back.

13th.—Same as 3d.

14th.—1 chain, miss 4,*, 1 plain, (5 chain, miss 2, and 1 plain 7 times), 1 chain, miss 8, repeat from*, end with miss 4, instead of 8; turn back.

15th.—7 chain,*, (miss 1, and 5 plain in the 5 chain of the 14th row 7 times), miss 2, repeat from* and end with 7 chain, 1 plain. Cut off the thread and commence at the foundation to work the edging.

16th.—9 chain, 1 plain in the 2nd stitch of these 9 chain to form a round loop; then 1 chain, miss 3, 1 plain, repeat 8 times up one side; the last plain stitch should be in 7 chain at the commencement of the 15th row,*, 1 chain, miss 4, 1 plain, (9 chain, and 1 plain in 2nd stitch to form a round loop, 1 chain, miss 4, 1 plain 6 times), repeat from*, along the 15th row, and work down the other side 8 times as before, the plain stitches in this row are worked on the centre stitch of the 5 plain in the 15th row

17th—Miss 5, and 5 plain in the round loop; repeat and fasten off.

BAND FOR RIBBON.

To be worked on the Foundation Chain.

1st. row.—Treble.

2d.—2 treble, 6 chain, miss 4, repeat, and end with 2 treble.

3d.—Miss 2, 6 treble on the 6 chain, repeat and fasten off.

COLLAR—MIGNONNETTE.

Taylor's Crochet Thread, No. 10; Needle, No. 22, Bell Gauge. Make a chain of 265 stitches, and work backwards and forwards.

1st row—5 chain, miss 2, 1 plain. Repeat, and end with 2 plain.

2nd—5 chain, miss 5, 1 plain in the 5 chain of 1st row. Repeat.

3rd—5 chain, miss 3, 1 plain, *, (7chain, 1 plain in the 2nd chain stitch to form a round loop 1 chain, miss 5, 1 plain in the 5 chain of last row, 5 chain, miss 5, 1 plain in the 5 chain of last row: repeat from *, and end with 1 plain.

4th.—5 chain, miss 9, *, (1 plain, and 3 chain 3 times, 1 plain, these four plain stitches are all to be worked in the round loop of the 3rd row;) 7 chain, 1 plain in the 2nd chain stitch, to form a round loop, 1 chain, miss 7, repeat from *, and end with (1 plain, and 3 chain 3 times,) 1 plain in the round loop as before, 2 chain, miss 3, 1 plain in the 5 chain.

5th.—5 chain, miss 17, *, (1 plain, and 3 chain 3 times, 1 plain, these 4 plain are to be worked in the round loop of 4th row,) 11 chain, 1 plain in the 3rd chain stitch, to form a round loop, 2 chain, miss 17, repeat from *, end with 1 plain, and 3 chain 3 times, 1 plain, the plain stitches in the round loop as before, 2 chain, miss 7, 1 plain in the centre loop of the 4th row.

6th.—5 chain, miss 17 *, (1 plain, and 4 chain 4 times, 1 plain, these 5 plain stitches are to be worked in the round loop, of 5th row,) 11 chain, 1 plain in the 3d chain stitch, to form a round loop, 2 chain, miss 17, repeat from *, end with 1 plain, and four chain 4 times, 1 plain, the plain stitches are worked as before, 2 chain, miss 7, 1 plain in loop of the 5th row.

7th and 8th.—The same; missing 25 instead of 17, and, at the end of the 8th row, cut off the thread and fasten it.

9th—Commence at the foundation and work up the side, thus:—11 chain, 1 plain in the 3d stitch, to form a loop as before, 2 chain, 1 plain in the chain at the side, repeat 5 times,

11 chain, 1 plain in the 3rd stitch as before, 2 chain, and repeat from the * in the 6th row missing 25 instead of 17 as before, at the end work 6 round loops down the side as at the commencement of this row.

[SECTION OF COLLAR.]

10th.—3 chain, miss 3, 7 plain in the round loop, of the 9th row,*, 3 chain, miss 5, (1 plain 9 chain, 1 plain, 11 chain, 1 plain, 9 chain, 1 plain; these 4 plain are worked in the next round loop of the 9th row,) 3 chain, miss 5, 7 plain in the next round loop, repeat from * once more, for the side, and work the same along the 9th row, missing 24 instead of 5 stitches.

11th.—(1 plain, and 4 chain, 6 times, 1 plain; these 7 plain stitches are to be worked in the 9 chain of last row) miss 3, (1 plain and 4 chain, 9 times, 1 plain; these 10 plain stitches are worked in the 11 chain of last row) miss 3, (1 plain, and four chain, 6 times, 1 plain; these 7 plain stitches in the 9 chain of last row), 2 chain, miss 6, 1 plain on the centre of the 7 plain in last row, 2 chain, miss 6, repeat, end with 1 plain, and fasten off.

Taylor's Crochet Thread, No. 10; Needle, No. 22, Bell Gauge.—Make a chain of 658 stitches, or 16 stitches for each pattern. Commence and end every row with 1 treble stitch, beside the pattern, to form a perfect edge, and cut off the thread at the end of each row.

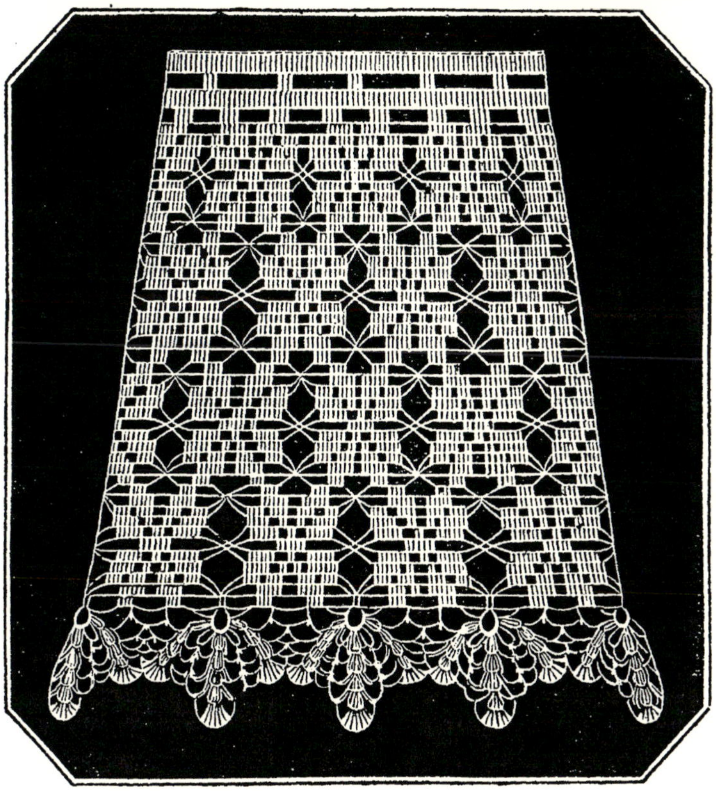

1st row.—4 chain, miss 2, *, 4 treble, 4 chain, miss 4, 4 treble, 6 chain miss 4: repeat from *, and end with 2 chain, instead of 6.

2d.—2 chain, miss 2, 6 treble, 7 chain, miss 4, 6 treble: repeat.

3d.—2 chain, miss 2, 4 treble, 2 chain, miss 1, 4 treble, 3 chain, miss 1, 4 treble, 2 chain, miss 1, 4 treble, repeat.

4th.—2 chain, miss 2, 2 treble, 2 chain, miss 2, 6 treble, 3 chain, miss 3, 6 treble, 2 chain miss 2, 2 treble; repeat.

5th.—2 treble, 2 chain, miss 2, 6 treble, 3 chain, miss 3, 1 plain, 3 chain, miss 3, 6 treble 2 chain, miss 2; repeat.

6th.—4 treble, *, 8 chain, miss 8, 3 plain, 8 chain, miss 8, 6 treble, repeat from *, and end with 4 treble instead of 6.

7th.—Same as 5th.

8th.—2 chain, miss 2, 2 treble, 2 chain, miss 2, 6 treble, 5 chain, miss 3, 6 treble, 2 chain, miss 2, 2 treble, repeat.

9th.—(2 chain, miss 2, 4 treble, twice,) 3 chain, miss 2, 1 plain, 3 chain, miss 2, 4 treble, 2 chain, miss 2, 4 treble, repeat.

10th.—2 chain, miss 2, 6 treble, 6 chain, miss 6, 3 plain, 6 chain, miss 6, 6 treble, repeat.

11th.—4 chain, miss 4, *, 4 treble, 7 chain, miss 7, 1 plain, 7 chain, miss 7, 4 treble, 7 chain, miss 6, repeat from * and end with 2 chain instead of 7.

12th.—1 plain, 8 chain, miss 8, 4 treble, 6 chain, miss 5, 4 treble, 8 chain, miss 8, repeat.

13th.—2 plain, *, 7 chain, miss, 7, 6 treble, 2 chain, miss 2, 6 treble, 7 chain, miss 7, 3 plain, repeat from *, and end with 1 plain.

14th.—1 plain, 4 chain, miss 4, (4 treble, 2 chain, miss 2, 3 times,) 4 treble, 4 chain, miss 4, repeat.

15th.—5 chain, miss 5, *, 6 treble, (2 chain, miss 2, 2 treble twice,) 2 chain, miss 2, 6 treble 9 chain, miss 9, repeat from *, and end with 5 chain instead of 9.

16th.—1 plain, 6 chain, miss 6, 6 treble, 2 chain, miss 2, 2 treble, 2 chain, miss 2, 6 treble 6 chain, miss 6, repeat.

17th.—2 plain, *, 11 chain, miss 11, 6 treble, 11 chain, miss 11, 3 plain, repeat from *, and end with 2 plain instead of 3.

18th.—Same as 16th. 19th, same as 15th. 20th, same as 14th. 21st, same as 13th.

22d.—1 plain, 8 chain, miss 8, 4 treble, 7 chain, miss 6, 4 treble, 8 chain, miss 8, repeat.

23d.—4 chain, miss 4, *, 4 treble, 8 chain, miss 8, 1 plain, 8 chain, miss 8, 4 treble, 6 chain, miss 7, repeat from * and end with 2 chain instead of 6.

24th.—2 chain, miss 2, 6 treble, 7 chain, miss 7, 3 plain, 7 chain, miss 7, 6 treble, repeat.

25th.—(2 chain, miss 2, 4 treble, twice,) 4 chain, miss 4, 1 plain, 4 chain, miss 4, 4 treble, 2 chain, miss 2, 4 treble, repeat.

26th.—2 chain, miss 2, 2 treble, 2 chain, miss 2, 6 treble, 9 chain, miss 9, 6 treble, 2 chain, miss 2, 2 treble, repeat.

27th.—2 treble, 2 chain, miss 2, 6 treble, 6 chain, miss 6, 1 plain, 6 chain, miss 6, 6 treble, 2 chain, miss 2, repeat.

28th.—4 treble, *, 11 chain, miss 11, 3 plain, 11 chain, miss 11, 6 treble, repeat from *, and end with 4 treble instead of 6.

29th.—Same as 27th. 30th, as 26th. 31st as 25th. 32d, as 24th. 33d, as 23d.

34th.—1 plain, 8 chain, miss 8, 4 treble, 6 chain, miss 7, 4 treble, 8 chain, miss 8, repeat.

35th.—Same as 13th; and repeat to the 21st row.

44th.—1 plain, 7 chain, 1 plain; both these plain stitches are worked in one stitch, 8 chain, miss 8, 4 treble, 6 chain, miss 6, 4 treble, 8 chain, miss 8, repeat, and end with 1 plain, 7 chain, 1 plain.

45th.—1 chain, miss 1, *, 2 treble, 2 chain, 2 treble, 3 chain, 2 treble, 2 chain, 2 treble, 3 chain, 2 treble, 2 chain, 2 treble; these 12 treble stitches are all to be worked in the 7 chain of the last row, then 1 chain, miss 6, 3 plain, (5 chain, miss 4, and 1 plain twice,) 5 chain, miss 4, 3 plain, 1 chain, miss 6, repeat from *, and end with the 12 treble as at commencement.

46th.—1 chain, miss 3, *, (2 treble, 2 chain, 2 treble; these 4 treble are to be worked in the 2 chain of the last row, 3 chain, miss 3, 1 plain in the 3 chain of last row, 3 chain, miss 3, twice,) 2 treble, 2 chain, 2 treble in the 2 chain as before, miss 8, 1 plain in the 5 chain of last row, (3 chain, miss 5, and 1 plain twice,) miss 8, repeat from *.

47th.—(3 chain, miss 4, 3 treble, 2 chain, 3 treble; these 6 treble in the 2 chain of last row,) 3 chain, miss 4, 1 plain, miss 1, 1 plain, repeat.

48th.—1 plain, 3 chain, miss 5, (3 treble, 2 chain in the 2 chain of last row,) 3 chain, miss 5 1 plain, miss 3, repeat.

49th.—1 plain, miss 5, (7 treble in the 2d chain of the last row, miss 3, 3 plain, miss 2 3 plain, miss 3 twice,) 7 treble in the 2 chain as before, miss 5, 1 plain in the 3 chain of last row, miss 2, repeat, and fasten off. If the edging is required at the sides, commence the 44th row at the foundation, and work down the sides.

BAND FOR RIBBON.

Commence on the foundation.

1st row.—All treble.

2d.—3 treble, 11 chain, miss 8, repeat, and end with 3 treble.

3d.—Miss 3, 11 treble on the 11 chain, repeat.

COLLARETTE.—POINT DE NAVARRE.

*Taylor's Crochet Thread, No. 12; Needle, No. 22. Make a chain of 557 stitches, turn back and work 2 plain, *, 3 chain, miss 3, 2 plain; repeat from * to the end of the foundation chain. This forms the centre of the Collarette; and the following rounds are worked on both sides of this row:—*

1st round.—Miss 2, 1 plain, 7 chain, 1 plain, 9 chain, 1 plain, 7 chain, 1 plain; these 4 plain stitches are all worked in the 3 chain of the foundation; miss 2, 3 plain in the next 3 chain of the foundation; repeat round both sides, working the plain stitches in the same spaces as those on the other side.

2nd.—5 chain, miss 12, 3 plain in the 9 chain of last round, 5 chain, miss 12, 1 plain in the centre stitch of the 3 plain in last round; repeat all round.

3rd.—5 chain, miss 9, 1 plain in the 5 chain of last round, 3 chain, miss 3, 1 plain in the 5 chain of 2nd round; repeat 57 times (and for the corner), 5 chain, miss 1, 1 plain 3 times; then as before 56 times, and work the other corner the same.

4th.—3 chain, miss 2, 1 treble, and 3 chain 4 times, in the 5 chain of last round), miss 2, 1 plain in the 3 chain of last round; repeat all round.

5th—Miss 1, 3 plain in the 3 chain of last round; repeat all round, and then work 6 single stitches.

6th.—11 chain, and 1 plain in the 4th stitch of the 11 chain, to form a round loop, 3 chain, miss 12, 3 plain; repeat 14 times; then to draw it in for shaping the neck, work 10 chain, 1 plain in the 3rd stitch; to form a round loop, 2 chain, miss 12, 3 plain; repeat 28 times; then work as before 76 times to finish the round.

7th.—3 chain, miss 4, (1 treble, and 3 chain 4 times, 1 treble, these 5 treble are all worked in the round loop in last round,) then, 3 chain, miss 4, 1 plain in the centre stitch of the 3 plain in last round; repeat 14 times, and for the neck, miss 3 instead of 4, 28 times, the repeat as before, 76 times to finish the round.

8th. — Miss 4, (3 plain, and miss 1 4 times, in the 3 chain of last round), miss 8, repeat from *, all round, but in the patterns at each corner, work 5 plain instead of 3 plain, and end with miss 3 instead of 8, and then work 5 single stitches.

9th.—8 chain, miss 1, 1 plain, *, 7 chain, miss 10, 1 plain, 7 chain, miss 10, 1 plain, 8 chain, miss 1, 1 plain: repeat from * 32 times. For the corner, 15 chain, miss 10, 1 plain, 8 chain, miss 1, 1 plain, 15 chain, miss 10, 1 plain, 8 chain, miss 1, 1 plain, then repeat as before 33 times, and work the other corner the same, then 7 chain, miss 10, 1 plain.

10th.—For the edge, 1 plain in the 8 chain of last round, 9 chain, 1 plain in the 3d chain stitch of these 9 chain, to form a round loop, 2 plain on the 2 plain left from the 9 chain, making in all 3 plain, 1 plain in the 8 chain, 13 chain, and 3 plain on the 1st 3 stitches as before, 1 plain in the 8 chain, 15 chain, 3 plain on the 1st 3 stitches as before, 1 plain in the 8 chain, 13 chain, 3 plain on the 1st 3 stitches as before, 1 plain in the 8 chain, 9 chain, 3 plain, as before, 1 plain in the 8 chain, the 6 plain stitches are all to be worked in the same 8 chain of last round, miss 1, 15 plain, repeat.

11th.—7 plain in the 1st round loop, 9 plain in the 2d round loop, 11 plain, in the 3d round loop, 9 plain in the 4th round loop, 7 plain in the 5th loop, then 1 chain, miss 7, 1 treble, in the centre of the 15 plain in last round, 1 chain, miss 7, repeat all round.

Should this Collarette be required of coarser thread, making less work, use *Taylor's No.* 8 *Needle, No.* 20; and make a chain of 487 stitches; and working the repeats 8 times less than the number given in the direction.

EDGING FOR HANDKERCHIEF.

Taylor's Crochet Thread, No. 12; *Fine Needle, No.* 22, *Bell Gauge.—Make a chain of* 816 *stitches for each yard, or* 16 *stitches for each pattern.*

1st row.—1 plain; 8 chain, 1 plain, both these plain stitches are to be worked in the same stitch, 15 single stitches, repeat to the end, and cut off the thread, then work the same as the 10th and 11th rounds in Collarette, working rows instead of rounds.

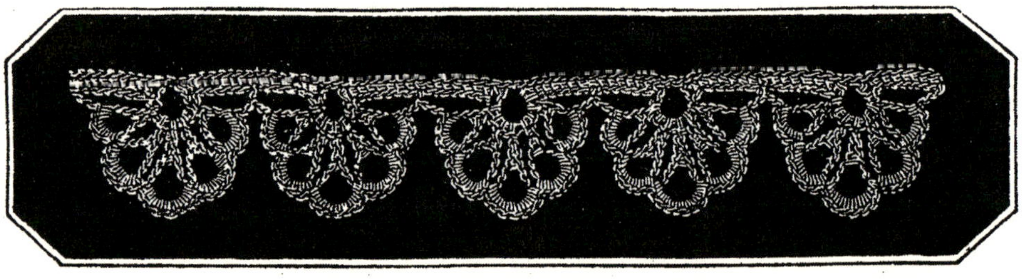

EDGING FOR VEILS.

Taylor's Crochet Thread, No. 20, *or Fine Black Netting Silk.—Needle, No.* 24, *Bell Gauge.—Work in Double Crochet, and commence with the Leaf, thus:—*

17 chain, miss 1, 2 plain, 7 treble, 2 plain, then turn the work so as to crochet on the other side of the chain, and leaving 5 chain for the *stem*, work 1 chain to cross it, then in the same stitch as those on the other side, work 2 plain, 7 treble, 2 plain, 1 plain in the 1 chain at the point, and on the other side in the same stitches, work 2 plain, 7 treble, 2 plain, and

1 plain on the stem, then work a flower, thus: 16 chain, put the needle into the 7th stitch of these 16 chain, and work 1 plain stitch in it, to form a round loop, leaving the 6 chain for the stem, then work 13 plain in the round loop, and 1 single stitch on the stem; turn back, work (9 chain, and 2 plain 7 times on the 13 plain), then 1 single stitch on the stem and turn back, miss 3, 5 plain in the 9 chain, then 5 chain, (miss 10, and 1 plain in the 9 chain

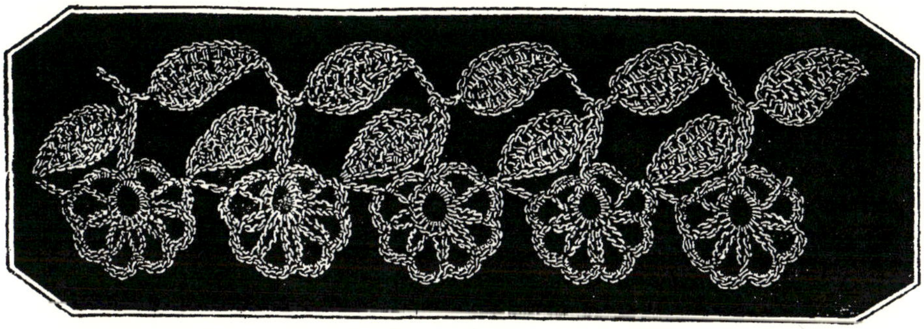

6 times), then 4 plain stitches in the same 9 chain, then miss 2, and work 5 plain down the 5 stem stitches, and 1 plain on the stem of the leaf: (2nd leaf), the same as the first, and then work 12 single stitches on it, which will bring the thread to the point of the leaf, and continue working 2 leaves and 1 flower until the required length is obtained, cut off the thread; and to join the leaves and flowers together, work a row all along the tops of the flowers, thus, commence at the point of the 1st leaf and work 1 plain stitch on it, then 3 chain, and on the flower 5 plain in the 1st 5 chain, (miss 1, and 5 plain in the 5 chain 5 times), 1 chain, and 1 plain on the point of the next leaf: repeat to the end.

CROCHET SPRIG.

Taylor's Crochet Thread, No. 20; or Black Netting Silk; Needle, No. 24, Bell Gauge.—This Sprig is to be sewn on Brussels net, for Veils, Collars, &c., and is worked in Double Crochet.

1st leaf.—24 chain, turn, miss 2, 2 plain, 7 treble, 2 plain, turn, and leaving 13 chain stitches for the stem, work 1 chain to cross it, and in the same stitches as those on the other side work 2 plain, 7 treble, 2 plain, 1 plain on the 1 chain, turn, and on the other side work 2 plain, 7 treble, 2 plain as before, 1 single stitch on the stem, and commence

The Flower.—17 chain, put the needle into the 6th stitch and work 1 plain in it to form a round loop, then leaving 5 chain for the stem, work 15 plain stitches in the round loop; turn back, and on the 15 plain work 1 plain, (5 chain, miss 1, and 1 plain 7 times,) 3 chain, turn back, and join it to the centre of the 7 *treble* of the leaf; then on the flower, (miss 1, and 5 plain in the 5 chain 7 times; then on the stem of the Flower, 5 plain, and 5 plain on the stem of the leaf, and work the

2d leaf.—13 chain, turn, miss 1, 2 plain, 7 treble, 2 plain, turn, and leaving 1 chain for the stem, work 1 chain to cross it, and in the same stitches as those on the other side, work 2 plain, 4 treble; then join it to the last 5 *plain* of the flower, and on the leaf, 3 treble, 2 plain, 1 plain in the 1 chain; turn, and on the other side, 2 plain, 7 treble, 2 plain, 1 single stitch and 7 plain on the stem of the 1st leaf. Knot the two ends together and cut them off.

THE END.

THE

CROCHET APPLIQUE FLOWER BOOK,

FORMING

THE THIRD SERIES OF THE CROCHET BOOK.

BY

MLLE. RIEGO DE LA BRANCHARDIERE.

Fifth Edition--25,000.

London:

SIMPKIN MARSHALL, AND CO.;

ACKERMANN & CO., STRAND; OLIVER AND BOYD EDINBURGH;

AND ALL THE BERLIN WAREHOUSES.

1853.

CONTENTS.

PREFACE.

In introducing this entirely New Style of Crochet *in Colored Flowers and Leaves*, I have endeavoured to make it available for all purposes to which Embroidery and Tambour are now applied; at the same time beg to assure my Patronesses that it is *simple* in detail, and so easily acquired, that I feel certain *one lesson* would perfect even the most inexperienced worker, and overcome any imaginary difficulty that at the first glance might be entertained from the appearance of the work. It is amusing, light, more interesting, and sooner executed than embroidery, being formed in separate sprigs, large pieces of material can be ornamented without experiencing any inconvenience from the *size;* and the Patterns will admit of an infinite variety in colour and arrangement, according to the taste and judgment of the worker. At all times I shall feel happy to afford any information which my experience may impart.

Gratefully acknowledging, and encouraged by the extensive patronage conferred, I beg respectfully to intimate that a Fourth Series is in preparation, consisting of a variety of articles of utility and ornament.

E. R. de la la Branchardiere.

106, *New Bond Street*,
June, 1848.

Instructions and Directions given in Point, Lacet, Crochet, Tatting, Embroidery, Lace-work, Knitting, Netting, Tambour, &c.

Ladies experiencing any difficulty in the following Directions, may communicate personally or by letter, enclosing a *directed stamped envelope,* and an *extra stamp* for a reply, to the Authoress, 106, New Bond Street.

The appearance of all articles in Crochet is so much spoiled by the use of cotton that becomes "heavy," loose, or fibrous *in the working*, that to prevent disappointment in the *result*, Mdlle. Riego particularly warns Ladies against the use of any but Messrs. I. & W. Taylor's Crochet Thread, as she cannot ensure the peculiar *lightness*, and distinctness of her patterns from any other make. This Thread is equally adapted for Point, Lacet, Knitting, Netting, and Tatting.

Post Office Orders for Eleonore Riego, to be made payable at the Post Office Old Cavendish Street.

INTRODUCTORY REMARKS.

To avoid unnecessary repetition in the heading of the following designs, the directions are given only for Silk; but as they are applicable to so many useful and ornamental purposes, the materials are varied according to the articles required, namely:—

For Collars .... Berthes .... Veils .... Lappets .... Robings .... Visites .... Coloured Net Dresses....	I particularly recommend John and William Taylor's Crochet Thread, Nos. 10, 12, or very fine No. 16; or fine Black Netting Silk; Fine Steel Crochet Needles, Nos. 20, 22, and 24, Bell Gauge.

The sprigs are to be sewn on Brussels net, the same as the Honiton; thus—tack the net on stiff paper; and with No. 20 Thread, sew the edges of the sprigs to the net; if for Collars, or Berthes, net is not used, they should be tacked on paper, and then *chained* together in the intermediate spaces.

For Dress-Trimmings ...... Sofa-Pillows .... Sachet .... Gentlemen's Waistcoats Caps .... Slippers................ Parasols................ Bags, &c................	Use Coarse or Fine Shaded Silks in *Skeins;* Needles, Nos. 20 and 22. The designs to be sewn on velvet, satin, or cloth. The colours Claret, Amber, White, or Fawn, are the most appropriate.

The Sprigs should be ironed on the wrong side, and the cloth or velvet should be framed, for small articles.

For Table Covers .... Couvre Pied............ Ottomans, &c.	Shaded Chenille, or Shaded Berlin Wools; Needles, Nos. 13 and 15 Bell Gauge.

For the centres, group the designs together, the borders for the sides, and distribute the sprigs in the corners and intermediate spaces.

On commencing a sprig, leave an end of two inches; and to fasten off draw the silk through the stitch, and knot this and the one at the commencement together.

To commence working a Flower in the Calyx or stem, insert the needle in it, and drawing the silk in a loop through, work a chain stitch.

Never cut off the silk unless directed to fasten off.

The long Stem is formed by the chain stitches first worked. The centre stem by the chain stitches left unworked, between the leaves or stems in working one side of the pattern.

All single, plain, treble, and long stitches are to be worked in Double Crochet—that is, by taking both sides of the previous stitches on the needle, except when they are worked "in the Chain." In crossing the stem, keep the silk under it, and work the chain stitch over it.

When using thread, the Sprigs can be worked without joining the thread at the Flowers, by commencing them, after working half of the Calyx.

For *Long* stitch, see "*Winter Book,*" page 18, in *Mary Stuart Hood.*

For the other terms used see 1st and 2nd Series of the "*Crochet Book.*"

SPRAY OF ROSE BUD AND LEAVES.

Material—Shaded Pink for the Flower, and shaded Yellow Green for the Leaves.

FOR THE FLOWER.

With the pink silk, commencing with the darkest shade, work a chain of 6 stitches; make it round by working 1 single stitch in the 1st chain stitch.

1st round.—(3 chain and 1 plain in the round 7 times).

2d.—(3 chain, miss 3, and 1 plain in the 3 chain of the 1st round 7 times).

3d.—Miss 1, 1 plain, 5 chain, 1 plain; both these plain stitches are to be worked in the 3 chain of last round—repeat 6 times more.

4th.—Miss 2, 1 plain, 5 treble, 1 plain; these 7 stitches are all to be worked in the 5 chain of last round—repeat 6 times more.

5th.—Five single stitches, *, 3 chain, miss 4, 3 single stitches; repeat from * 3 times more; turn back to work the 6th row; (miss 1, 1 plain, miss 1, and 7 treble in the 3 chain 4 times), miss 1, 3 single stitches; turn back to work the 7th row; (5 chain, miss 5, and 3 single stitches on the 7 treble 5 times), 7 chain, miss 7, 1 plain between the two 5 trebles of the 4th round, then 7 chain, miss 7, 1 plain.

8th round, (miss 1, 1 treble, 9 long stitches, 1 treble; these 11 stitches are all to be worked in the 5 chain; then miss 1, 1 plain in the centre stitch of the 3 single stitches; repeat 4 times more,) then 8 treble and 1 plain in the 7 chain, miss the 1 plain, 1 plain and 8 treble in the 7 chain, 1 plain, and fasten off.

FOR THE LEAVES AND STEMS.

Commence with the green, make a chain of 60 stitches, and work

The First Leaf.

Turn, miss 2, 3 plain, (2 chain, miss 2 and 1 treble 4 times), 2 chain, miss 2, 1 plain, turn, leaving the chain stitches for the stem, work 1 chain to cross it; then on the other side of the foundation, 7 chain, miss 1, 1 plain in the 2 chain of foundation, miss 1, 1 plain in the next 2 chain, turn back, and missing the 2 plain, work 5 treble and 1 plain in the 7 chain, turn back; 9 chain, 1 plain in the same 2 chain of the foundation as before, miss 1, 1 plain in the next 2 chain, turn back, and missing the 2 plain, work 7 treble and 1 plain in the 9 chain; turn back, then 7 chain, 1 plain in the 2 chain as before, miss 1, 1 plain, turn back; 5 treble and 1 plain in the 7 chain, turn back; 5 chain, 1 plain in the 2 chain, miss 1, 1 plain, turn back; 3 treble and 1 plain in the 5 chain, turn back; 1 chain, miss 1, 3 treble on the 3 plain, and in the 2 chain at the point of the leaf, (work 1 plain, 2 chain, and 1 plain), turn, and work the other side to correspond, thus: 3 treble, 5 chain, 1 plain in the 2 chain, miss 1, 1 plain, turn back, and missing the 2 plain, work 3 treble and 1 plain in the 5 chain, turn back, 7 chain, 1 plain, miss 1, 1 plain, turn back, work 5 treble and 1 plain in the 7 chain, turn back; 9 chain, 1 plain, miss 1, 1 plain, turn back; 7 treble, and 1 plain in the 9 chain, turn back; 7 chain, 1 plain, miss 1, 1 plain, turn back; 5 treble and 1 plain in the 7 chain, turn back; 7 chain, 1 single stitch on the stem—this finishes the leaf; work 5 single stitches down the long stem, then 40 chain, and work the 2d leaf the same as first, on completing it, work 4 single stitches down the stem; instead of 5 single; then 36 chain for the 3rd leaf, and work another leaf the same—when finished, work 10 single stitches down the stem.

Then work 28 chain, and work the 4th leaf the same; then 7 single stitches down the stem, and 13 plain down the long stem, work 28 chain, and work the 5th leaf, when finished, 7 single stitches down the stem, and 14 plain down the long stem.

For the stem of the flower, 28 chain; join the flower by inserting the needle in the 3rd plain stitch, and work 1 plain in it; then 28 plain stitches down the stem, and 5 plain down the long stem. For the Small Leaf 16 chain, turn, miss 1, 3 plain, (1 chain and 1 treble 5 times), 3 single stitches.

For the stem and calyx of the Bud, work 24 chain; turn, miss 1, 8 plain; turn, leaving 15 stitches for the stem, work 1 chain to cross it, and on the other side 2 plain, 5 treble, 1 plain, 8 chain; turn, miss 1, 7 plain on the 8 chain, then 1 plain at the point of calyx, 8 chain; turn, miss 1, 7 plain on the 8 chain, and down the calyx work 1 plain, 5 treble, 2 plain, and 14 single stitches down the stem, then 4 single stitches down the stem of the small leaf, and 4 plain down the long stem; then work a Small Leaf as before, working 7 single stitches on the stem, then 15 plain stitches down the long stem, 3 treble, and fasten off.

FOR THE BUD.

With the pink silk, commence in the 4th or centre stitch of the 7 plain at the calyx, work 1 treble, 1 chain, 1 treble; both these treble stitches in the centre stitch at the point of the calyx, join to the centre stitch of the other 7 plain; turn back, work 2 treble, 3 chain, 2 treble; these 4 treble in the 1 chain, then 1 plain: draw the silk through, and fasten off.

BORDER.

OAK LEAVES AND ACORNS.

Material—Shaded Yellow Green for the Leaves, and Shaded Brown Silk for the Acorns.

Commence with the green, make a chain of 17 stitches, and work a Leaf thus:—turn, miss 5 1 single stitch in the 6th, to form a loop, and leaving 11 chain for the centre stem, turn back, and in the loop work 1 plain, 7 chain, 1 plain, 9 chain, 1 plain, 7 chain, 1 plain; then 1 single stitch on the stem, turn back, miss 2, 1 plain in the 7 chain, (4 chain and 1 plain 7 times in the 7 chain), miss 1, 1 plain, (4 chain and 1 plain 7 times in the 9 chain), miss 1, 1 plain, (4 chain and 1 plain 7 times in the 7 chain), then work 5 single stitches down the stem: this finishes the leaf—and leaving 6 chain for the centre stem, work 12 chain, and join it to the centre of the *18th 4 chain of leaf*, then 15 chain, and

For the Acorn, turn, miss 4, 1 single stitch in the 5th stitch to form a round loop, 2 chain, then 6 treble in the loop, 1 chain, and down the stem 4 single stitches, and repeat the leaf and acorn until sufficient is worked, finishing with the acorn; (*the chain stitches left unworked form the centre stem*) turn and work the other side thus—8 plain, down the centre stem *.

For the Leaf 12 chain, turn, miss 5, 1 single in the 6th stitch, turn back, leaving 6 chain for the stem; work in the round loop 1 plain, 7 chain, 1 plain, 9 chain, 1 plain, 7 chain, 1 plain, then 1 single stitch on the stem, turn back, miss 2, 1 plain in the 7 chain (4 chain and 1 plain 3 times in the 7 chain), 2 chain—join it to the 1st stitch of the 8 *plain* on the centre stem; then 2 chain, 1 plain, (4 chain and 1 plain 3 times in the same 7 chain), miss 1, 1 plain, (4 chain and 1 plain in the 9 chain 7 times), miss 1, 1 plain, (4 chain and 1 plain 7 times in the 7 chain), then 5 single stitches down the stem, and 7 plain on the *centre stem.*

For the Acorn, 9 chain, turn, miss 4, 1 single stitch, 2 chain, 6 treble in the round loop, 1 chain, and 4 single stitches down the stem, then 17 plain down the centre stem; repeat from *, but joining the leaf to the 6th stitch from the acorn on the centre stem.

To finish the Acorn.—With the brown silk, commence on the 2nd treble stitch of the acorn, work 1 chain and 1 treble on the 3rd treble stitch, 3 chain; turn, miss 2, 1 single stitch in the chain stitch, to form the point, then 2 treble in the 3rd treble stitch, 1 single stitch, and fasten off.

HEART'S-EASE.

Material—Shaded Yellow Green Silk for the Leaves, and shaded Amber and Violet Silk for the Flowers.

FOR THE FLOWERS.

Commence with the amber and violet—work a chain of 6 stitches and make it round.

1st Round—10 plain in the round.

2nd Round.—8 chain, 3 plain, 8 chain, 1 plain, 5 chain, miss 1, 1 plain, 7 chain, miss 1, 1 plain, 5 chain, miss 1, 1 plain.

3rd Round.—(1 plain, 1 treble ; 12 long stitches, and 1 treble; these 15 stitches are all worked in the 8 chain of 2d round,) then miss 1 '1 plain on the 3 plain, miss 1, (1 treble, 12 long, 1 treble, and 1 plain; these 15 stitches in the 8 chain as before,) miss 1, (1 plain, 1 treble, 7 long, 1 treble, 1 plain; these 11 stitches in the 5 chain,) miss 1, (1 plain, 1 treble, 9 long, 1 treble, and 1 plain; these 13 stitches in the 7 chain,) miss 1, (1 plain, 1 treble, 7 long, 1 treble and 1 plain ; these 11 stitches in the 5 chain,) then (1 chain and 1 plain 30 times on the stitches of this round,) fasten off, and work 2 flowers more the same.

FOR THE LEAVES AND STEMS.

Commence with the green, make a chain of 44 stitches, and for the

1st Leaf, turn, miss 1, 28 plain, turn, and leaving the remaining chain for the stem, work 1 chain to cross it, and on the other side work 3 plain, 5 treble, (1 plain and 5 treble 3 times,) 2 plain, and at the point, 2 chain, turn, and on the other side, work 4 plain (5 treble and 1 plain 4 times), 2 single on the stem, and for the stems of the flowers

Work 37 chain for the 1st Stem—join on a flower by working 1 plain in it, (between the 2 largest leaves) then down the stem 29 single, and for the 2nd stem, 50 chain, join on a flower, and work 43 single down the stem.

For the 3rd Stem—25 chain, join on a flower, then 25 single down the stem, 15 single down the 2nd and 1st stems, and 4 single down the long stem.

For the 2nd Leaf, 31 chain, and work as 1st leaf. When finished, work 9 plain down the long stem, and fasten off.

GERANIUM.

Material—Yellow shaded Green Silk for the Leaf and Stem, and plain Geranium or shaded Pink Silk for the Flowers.

FOR THE LEAF AND STEMS.

Commence with the green, and make a chain of 28 stitches for the long stem, and for the LEAF, turn, miss 4, 1 single stitch in the 5th chain stitch, to form a round loop, and in this round loop work the

1st row.—1 plain, 9 chain, 1 plain, 11 chain, 1 plain, 9 chain, 1 plain; turn back.

2d.—Miss 1, 11 treble in the 9 chain, miss 1, 13 treble in the 11 chain, miss 1, 11 treble in the 9 chain, 1 plain on the stem; turn back.

3d.—Treble in every stitch of the 2d row, then 1 plain on the stem; turn back.

4th.—3 chain, 1 plain, repeat along the 3d row; this finishes the leaf. Then work 10 single stitches on the stem, then 24 chain stitches for centre stem of the flowers; turn, miss 5, 1 single in the 6th chain stitch, 5 chain; turn, miss 4, 1 plain in the 5th stitch.

For the calyx of 1st flower, 18 chain; turn, miss 5, 1 plain in the 6th stitch, 5 treble, 1 plain then 6 single stitches.

For the calyx of 2d flower, 22 chain; turn, miss 5, 1 plain in the 6th stitch, 5 treble, 1 plain, 10 single stitches, and 1 plain on the centre stem.

For the 3d calyx, 20 chain; turn, miss 5, 1 plain in the 6th stitch, 5 treble, 1 plain, then 8 single stitches. Then for the calyx of the bud, 15 chain; turn, miss 5, 5 treble, 1 plain, 4 single stitches, 1 plain on the centre stem, 5 chain, 16 plain down the centre stem, then 10 plain down the long stem, 2 treble, and fasten off

FOR THE FLOWERS.

With the Geranium Silk commence by working 1 plain in the 5 chain at the point of the 1st calyx, then 9 chain; turn, miss 2, 1 plain in the 3d chain, 5 treble, 1 plain, then 1 plain in the 5 chain of the calyx; repeat 4 times more, fasten off, and work the same in the 2d and 3d calyx. For the BUD, work 1 plain in the 5 chain, 2 treble, 3 chain, 2 treble, 1 plain, and fasten off.

ROSE, SHAMROCK, AND THISTLE.

ROSE.

Material—Shaded Yellow Green for the Leaves, and shaded Pink Silk for the Flowers.

FOR THE LEAVES AND STEMS.

Commence with the green, and make a chain of 41 stitches, and for the SMALL LEAF, turn, miss 1, 8 plain; and leaving the chain stitches for the long stem, work 1 chain to cross it and on the other side, 2 plain; 4 treble, 2 plain, 1 chain at the point; turn, and on the other side 2 plain, 4 treble, 2 plain, 1 single stitch on the stem, which finishes the leaf.

For the stem and calyx of bud, 22 chain; turn, miss 1, 8 plain down the stem; work 1 chain to cross it, and on the other side of the 8 plain, 2 plain, 5 treble, 1 plain, 8 chain; turn, miss 1, 7 plain on the 8 chain, 1 plain at the point of calyx; 8 chain, turn, miss 1, 7 plain on the 8 chain, and down the calyx, 1 plain, 5 treble, 2 plain, 11 single down the stem.

For the 2nd Small LEAF, 11 chain, and work the same as the 1st LEAF, then 8 single stitches down the stem.

For the stem and CALYX of the FLOWER, 40 chain, turn, miss 1, 10 plain down the stem; turn, work 1 chain to cross it; and on the other side, 2 plain, 6 treble, 2 plain, 3 chain at the point; turn, and on the other side 2 plain, 6 treble, 2 plain, 20 plain stitches down the stem. Then 20 chain, and work the 1st Small LEAF, the *stem* and calyx of the *bud,* and then the 2nd Small LEAF the same as at the commencement; when finished, work 10 single stitches down the stem, and 30 plain down the long stem, and fasten off.

FOR THE FLOWER.

With the darkest shade of pink, commence in the 3 chain at the point of the calyx.

1st row.—Work 5 chain, and 1 plain 5 times in the 3 chain; turn back.

2d row.—(5 chain, miss 3, and 3 plain in the 5 chain, 5 times), 5 chain, and 1 plain on the calyx; turn back.

3rd row.—(Miss 1, 1 treble, 9 long stitches, and 1 treble; these 11 stitches are all to be worked in the 5 chain), then miss 1, 1 plain in the centre of the 3 plain. Repeat 5 times more, and fasten off.

For the Buds, work the same as in the Spray of Rose and Leaves.

SHAMROCK.

Material—Shaded Yellow Green Silk.

Make a chain of 37 stitches, and for the 1st Leaf, turn, miss 4; 1 plain in the 5th stitch to form a round loop, turn back (then 5 chain, and 1 plain 3 times in the round loop,) turn back; (miss 1, 1 plain, 5 treble, 1 plain; these 7 stitches are all to be worked in the 5 chain, repeat twice more), then 5 single stitches down the stem—this finishes the Leaf.

15 chain, and work the 2d Leaf the same as the 1st; then 10 chain, and work the 3d Leaf as before; then 17 single stitches down the centre stem.

For the 2d *Spray*, 24 chain, and work the 1st, 2nd, and 3rd leaves; then 19 single down the stem, and 15 plain down the long stem—fasten off.

THISTLE.

Material—Shaded Blue Green for the Leaves, and Shaded Lilac Silk for the Flowers.

FOR THE LEAF AND STEMS.

Commence with the green. Make a chain of 56 stitches, and for the calyx of the 1st *bud*, turn, miss 3, 1 single stitch in the 4th chain stitch, to form a round loop; 1 chain, 7 treble in the round loop, 1 plain on the stem, and for the uneven stem, work down the chain stitches, thus—(2 chain, 2 single, miss 2, and 2 single 4 times), leaving the remaining stitches for the long stem.

Then 29 chain for the stem of the 2nd *bud*, and work the calyx and uneven stem, the same as for the 1st *bud*, then 3 plain down the long stem.

For the Stem of 1st Thistle, 38 chain, turn, and for the calyx, miss 5, 1 single stitch in the 6th chain stitch to form a round loop, (then 1 chain and 1 treble, 7 times in the round loop), 1 chain, 1 plain on the stem, turn back, and work 16 treble stitches on the stitches last worked; then 1 plain, and down the stem, work (2 chain, 2 single, miss 2, 2 single, 5 times,) then 1 plain down the long stem.

38 chain for the stem of the 2nd Thistle, and work the calyx and stem, the same as the 1st Thistle; when finished, work 4 plain down the long stem,

And for the Leaf—25 chain, turn, miss 1, 5 plain, 16 treble, 2 plain; turn, and leaving one chain for the stem, work 1 chain to cross it, and on the other side 2 plain, 2 chain, 5 long stitches, 2 chain, 1 plain, 2 chain, 5 long stitches, 2 chain, 1 plain, 1 chain, 5 treble, 5 single, 1 chain; turn, and on the other side, work 5 single, 5 treble, 1 chain, 1 plain,

2 chain, 5 long, 2 chain, 1 plain, 2 chain, 5 long, 2 chain, 2 plain; this finishes the LEAF Then down the long stem 1 plain, (2 chain, 2 plain, miss 2, and 2 plain 3 times)—fasten off.

FOR THE BUDS.

With the lilac silk commence in the centre treble stitch of the calyx, work 5 chain, 1 long stitch, 2 chain, I long stitch, 5 chain, 1 single; these stitches are to be worked in the centre stitch of the calyx. Fasten off, and work the other bud the same.

For the FLOWERS—Commence in the 7th treble stitch of the calyx, work 6 chain, 1 long stitch, 1 chain, 1 long stitch; both these stitches in the 7th stitch of the calyx, (1 chain and 1 long stitch, 3 times in the 8th stitch), turn back, (5 chain, miss 1, and 1 plain in the 1 chain 5 times), 5 chain, 6 single down the6 chain, and fasten off.

SNOW-DROP.

Material—Shaded Blue Green for the Leaves, and plain White Silk for the Flowers.

FOR THE FLOWERS.

Commence with the white silk, and make a chain of 10 stitches; turn, miss 1, 8 plain; turn, and leaving 1 chain, work 1 chain to cross it; on the other side, work 2 plain, 5 treble, 1 plain; then in the 1 chain at the point (1 plain, 3 chain and 1 plain); turn, and on the other side work 1 plain, 5 treble, 2 plain, 1 single stitch on the 1 chain; then 10 chain, turn, miss 1, 8 plain, turn, work 1 chain to cross the 1 chain, and on the other side work 2 plain 3 treble, join to the 3rd treble stitch of the other leaf; then 2 treble, 1 plain, and in the 1 chain at the point, (1 plain, 3 chain, 1 plain), turn, and on the other side work 1 plain, 5 treble, 2 plain; fasten off, and work 3 more flowers the same.

FOR THE LEAVES AND STEMS.

Commence with the Green Silk. Make a chain of 39 stitches.

1st Leaf.—Turn, miss 1, 3 plain, 19 treble, 2 single, (the remaining chain stitches are for the stem) then 26 chain, and for the 2nd leaf work the same as 1st.

Then 28 chain for the stem of the 1st flower; insert the needle at the fastening off in one of the flowers, and work 1 plain, then down the stem 3 treble, 3 single stitches, 8 chain.

For the Small Leaf, turn, miss 1, 2 single, 5 plain; then down the stem 18 single stitches.

25 chain for the 3d leaf, and work as 1st leaf; at the end work 4 single stitches down the stem of 1st flower; 27 chain for the stem of the 2d flower, work the small leaf; then 6 chain, and join on a flower as before; then down the stem 3 treble, 22 single stitches.

For the stem of 3d flower, 23 chain; work the small leaf, then 6 chain, join on a flower as before, and down the stem 3 treble 18 single stitches, 1 plain down the stem of 1st flower, and 1 plain down the stem of the 2d leaf.

25 chain for the 4th leaf, and work as 1st leaf; then 4 plain down the stem of 1st leaf; 15 chain for the stem of the 4th flower; work the small leaf; then 6 chain, join on a flower as before, and down the stem 3 treble 10 single stitches: then 10 plain down the stem of 1st leaf, and fasten off.

FORGET-ME-NOT.

Material—Shaded Yellow Green Silk for the Leaves, plain Blue Silk, and 6 Gold Beads for the Flowers.

FOR THE LEAVES AND STEMS.

Commence with the green, make a chain of 25 stitches, and for the first Leaf, turn, miss 3, 1 plain, 2 chain, miss 2, 1 treble, 2 chain, miss 2, 1 treble, 2 chain, miss 2, 1 plain, turn, and leaving the remaining chain for the long stem, work 1 chain to cross it, and on the other side, (miss 1, 1 plain and 4 treble; these 5 stitches are all worked in the 2 chain. Repeat 3 times more), turn, and in the same spaces as those on the other side, (miss 1, 1 plain, and 4 treble 3 times,) then 2 single on the stem and for the *Stems of the Flowers,* 15 chain, turn, miss 3, 3 single, 12 chain, turn, miss 3, 3 single 12 chain, turn, miss 3, 3 single, 10 chain, turn, miss 2, 3 single, 7 chain, turn, miss 2, 2 single, 4 chain, turn, miss 2, 2 single, turn, and work down the other side to correspond, thus—(6 single down the centre stem, 6 chain, turn, miss 3, and 3 single 3 times), then 7 single down the centre stem, and for the 2d *Leaf,* 15 chain and work as 1st leaf, theu 14 plain down the long stem, and fasten off.

FOR THE FLOWERS.

Thread the beads on the blue, and commence in one of the round loops at the stem, work 1 plain in it, 5 chain, turn, miss 2, 1 single in the 3d chain stitch, 2 chain, 1 plain in the round loop, 5 chain, turn, miss 2, 1 single, 2 chain, pass a bead down, and bring it through the round loop to the right side, then 1 plain (5 chain, turn, miss 2, 1 single, 2 chain, and 1 plain 3 times,) fasten off, and work the same, for 3 Flowers on each side of the stem.

BORDER.

ROSE-BUDS AND LEAVES.

Material—Shaded Pink Silk for the Buds, and shaded Yellow Green for the Leaves.

FOR THE BUDS.

Commence with the pink silk, and make a chain of 11 stitches; turn, miss 1, 3 singles stitches, 7 plain; turn, and on the other side, work 2 plain, 5 treble, 3 plain, and 1 plain at the point; turn, and on the other side 3 plain, 5 treble, 2 plain, fasten off; repeat until sufficient buds are made for the length required.

FOR THE LEAVES AND STEM.

With the green silk make a chain of 18 stitches, and work a *Small Leaf* thus:— turn, miss 1, 1 single, 3 treble, 2 plain, then 29 chain,

For the 1st *Large Leaf,* turn, miss 1, 4 plain, 6 treble, 2 plain; turn, and leaving the remaining chain for the centre stem, work 1 chain to cross it; and on the other side 2 plain, 8 treble, 2 plain, 1 plain at the point; turn, and on the other side 2 plain, 8 treble, 2 plain, and 3 single stitches on the stem.

Then 22 chain for the 2d *Leaf;* work another leaf the same; when finished, work 4 single stitches on the stem.

17 chain for the 3rd *Leaf,* and work another leaf the same; then 3 single stitches down the stem, and 9 single stitches down the centre *stem,* which finishes the spray.

Then 38 chain; join on a *bud* by inserting the needle in the fastening off, and work 1 plain in it. For the calyx, 8 plain down the stem; turn, work 1 chain to cross it, and on the other side 2 plain, 5 treble, 1 plain; then work 2 plain up the side of the *bud,* 4 chain; turn, miss 1, 3 single on the 4 chain, then 5 single up the *bud,* 5 chain; turn, miss 1, 4 single on the 5 chain, 3 single up the *bud,* 5 chain; turn, miss 1, 4 single on the 5 chain, 4 single down the *bud,* 4 chain; turn, miss 1, 3 single on the 4 chain, 6 single down the *bud,* 4 chain; turn, miss 1, 3 single on the 4 chain, 1 plain down the *bud;* and down the calyx 1 plain, 5 treble, 2 plain, then 10 single down the stem; repeat until sufficient is worked for the length required. (The chain stitches left unworked form the centre or foundation stem).

For the other side of pattern work 11 plain down the centre stem (that is, from the 10 single on the stem of the *bud*), *, then 22 chain, and work the spray of 3 leaves the same as on the other side; when finished, work 22 plain down the centre stem, then 19 chain, join on a *bud,* and work the calyx and stem the same as on the other side; then 7 plain on the centre stem, then 7 chain for the small leaf, turn, miss 1, 1 single, 3 treble, 2 plain, 9 plain down the centre stem; repeat from *, and fasten off.

JASMINE.

Material—Shaded Yellow Green Silk for the Leaves, and plain White Silk for the Flowers.

Commence with the white. Work a chain of 6 stitches, and make it round.

1st Round—Work 8 plain stitches in the round.

2d Round—6 chain, turn, miss 2, 1 single in the 3d chain stitch, 3 chain, miss 1, and 1 plain on the 1st round; repeat 3 times more, and fasten off. Work 2 flowers more the same.

FOR THE LEAVES AND STEMS.

Commence with the Green. Make a chain of 54 stitches, and for the

1st *Leaf*, turn, miss 1, 8 single, turn, and leaving the remaining chain for the stem, work 1 chain to cross it, and on the other side, work 1 plain, 3 treble, 2 plain, 2 single, 1 chain at the point, turn, and on the other side, work 2 single, 2 plain, 3 treble, 1 plain, 3 single.

For the 2d *Leaf*, 19 chain, and work as 1st leaf.

For the 3d *Leaf*, 13 chain, and work as 1st leaf, when finished, work 3 single down the centre stem.

For the 4th *Leaf*, 13 chain, work as 1st leaf; when finished, work 6 single down the centre stem.

For the 5th *Leaf*, 13 chain, work as 1st leaf, then 10 single down the centre stem, which finishes the 1st spray of leaves, and for the

Stems of the flowers, 15 chain, join on a flower by working 1 plain in it, then down the stem 8 single. For the 2d stem, 11 chain, join on a flower, work 11 single down the stem and 1 single on the centre stem. For the 3d stem, 5 chain, join on a flower, work 5 single down the stem, and 18 single down the centre stem.

For the 2d spray of leaves, 23 chain, and work the 5 leaves as in 1st spray; when finished work 16 plain down the long stem; and fasten off

HYACINTH.

Material—Shaded Yellow Green for the Leaves, and shaded Lilac, Amber, or Blue for the Flowers.

FOR THE LEAVES AND STEMS.

Commence with the green. Make a chain of 45 stitches, and for the

HYACINTH.

1st *Leaf*, turn, miss 1, 3 plain, 4 treble, 22 long stitches, 4 treble, 2 plain, 2 single, this finishes the leaf; leaving the remaining chain for the long stem.

For the *Stems of the Flowers*, 16 chain; turn, miss 3, 4 single, (13 chain, turn, miss 3, and 4 single 4 times,) 9 chain, turn, miss 3, 4 single, 7 chain, turn, miss 3, 4 single, turn and work down the other side, thus: (6 single stitches down the centre stem, 7 chain, turn, miss 3, and 4 single 4 times), then 7 plain down the centre stem, and for the

2d *Leaf* 38 chain, and work as 1st leaf, then 11 plain down the long stem, and fasten off.

FOR THE FLOWERS.

With the Lilac Silk, commence in one of the round loops at the stems, work 9 chain; turn, miss 1, 3 single, 3 treble, 1 plain, and 1 plain in the round loop, then 4 chain, 1 single stitch in the 1st treble stitch of the other leaf, 4 chain, turn, miss 1, 3 single stitches, 3 treble, 1 plain, and 1 plain in the round loop. Fasten off,, and work the same in each stem.

CARNATION.

Material—Shaded Blue Green for the Leuves, and P nk and White Chenée Silk for the Flowers.

FOR THE LEAVES AND STEMS.

Commence with the green. Make a chain of 40 stitches, and for the

1st *Leaf,* turn, miss 1, 3 plain, 3 treble, 18 long stitches, 3 treble, 2 single; this finishes the leaf, and leaving the remaining chain for the stem, for the 2d *Leaf,* 35 chain, and work as 1st leaf, then 30 chain, and for the *Calyx of* 1*st Flower,* turn; miss 1, 8 plain, turn, work 1 chain to cross the stem, and on the other side, work 2 plain, 5 treble, 1 plain, 7 chain at the point, and on the other side of the 8 plain, work 1 plain, 5 treble, 2 plain, then down the stem 5 single stitches.

For the *Calyx of* 2*d Flower,* 18 chain; work the same as 1st Calyx; when finished, work 8 single stitches down the stem, and 4 single stitches down the centre stem.

For the Calyx of the bud, 15 chain, and work as 1st Calyx; when finished, 5 single stitches down the stem and 9 single down the centre stem,

For the 3d *Leaf,* 30 chain, and work as 1st leaf; when finished, work 6 single down the centre stem.

For the 4th *Leaf,* 30 chain, and work as 1st leaf; then 11 plain down the stem, and fasten off.

FOR THE FLOWERS.

With the Pink and White Silk commence in the 7 chain at the point of the calyx, and work (5 chain, and 3 plain in the calyx 5 times), turn back, (work 1 chain, miss 3, and 4 treble in the 5 chain 5 times), one single stitch on the calyx, turn back, (6 chain, miss 4, and

1 plain in the 1 chain 5 times), turn back, miss 1, 1 plain, (3 chain, and 1 plain in the 6 chain 4 times). Repeat 4 times more, and fasten off; work the other flower the same.

For the Bud—Commence in the 3rd calyx, work 2 treble, 3 long stitches, 2 treble, 1 plain, and fasten off.

THE END.

THE

CROCHET BOOK,

FOURTH SERIES,

BY

Mdlle. RIEGO DE LA BRANCHARDIERE.

FOURTH EDITION.—20,000.

LONDON:

SIMPKIN, MARSHALL, AND CO;

ACKERMANN, STRAND; OLIVER AND BOYD, EDINBURGH;

ALL BOOKSELLERS, AND BERLIN WAREHOUSES.

1849.

CONTENTS.

*** All The terms used are illustrated and explained in the 1st, 2nd, and 3rd Series.

PREFACE.

It was my intention that this Series should have comprised D'Oyley's and Anti-Macassars, but at the request of many ladies who have honored me with their patronage, I have been induced to present Collars, &c. in this the Fourth Series, and defer the publication of the other articles to the Fifth, which will appear shortly. Sincerely acknowledging the approbation and support received from my numerous correspondents, I shall be most happy in return to afford all the information in my power, and elucidate difficulties, should any arise in the following directions.

Eleonore Riego de la Branchardiere.

106, *New Bond Street.*

N.B.—All communications must enclose a stamp for reply.

*** Lessons in Point, Lacet, Crochet. Knitting, Netting, Embroidery, &c.

COLLAR—Le Bouquet de Fleurs.

Taylor's Crochet Thread, No. 12; *Needle No.* 23, *Bell Gauge.—All stitches that are not worked in the chain are to be worked in* Double Crochet.

FIRST SMALL LEAF—Make a chain of 10 stitches, turn, miss 4, and work 1 single in the 5th stitch to form a round loop, turn back; leaving the chain for the stem, work in the round loop 7 chain, 1 plain, 9 chain, 1 plain, 7 chain, 1 plain, turn back; miss 1, (4 chain, and 1 plain 7 times in the 7 chain), miss 1, 1 plain in the 9 chain, (4 chain, and 1 plain 7 times in the 9 chain), miss 1, 1 plain in the 7 chain, (4 chain and 1 plain in the 7 chain 7 times); this finishes the Leaf; work 5 single stitches down the stem. and for the

SECOND SMALL LEAF—10 chain, turn; miss 4, 1 single in the 5th stitch, turn back, and work in the round loop 7 chain, 1 plain, 9 chain, 1 plain, 7 chain, 1 plain, turn back; (4 chain, and 1 plain 3 times in the 7 chain, 2 chain, join it to the centre stitch of the *18th* 4 *chain* of 1st leaf, 2 chain, and in the same 7 chain work 1 plain, then 4 chain, and 1 plain 3 times in the same 7 chain), miss 1, 1 plain in the 9 chain, (4 chain, and 1 plain 7 times in the 9 chain), miss 1, 1 plain in the 7 chain, (4 chain and 1 plain 7 times in the 7 chain); this finishes the leaf; then 5 single stitches down the stem; and for the centre stem 5 chain, join it to the *20th* 4 *chain* of the 2d leaf, 5 chain, join it to the *17th* 4 *chain* of the 2d leaf, 10 chain, join it to the centre or *11th* 4 *chain* of the 2d leaf, 6 chain, join it to the *6th* 4 *chain* of the 2d leaf; and for the

FIRST LARGE LEAF—29 chain, turn, miss 2, 3 plain, (2 chain, miss 2, and 1 treble 4 times), 2 chain, miss 2, 1 plain, turn, leaving the chain stitches for the stem, work 1 chain to cross it; then on the other side of the foundation, 7 chain, miss 1, 1 plain in the 2 chain of foundation, miss 1, 1 plain in the next 2 chain, turn back, and missing the 2 plain, work 5 treble and 1 plain in the 7 chain, turn back; 9 chain, 1 plain in the same 2 chain of the foundation as before, miss 1, 1 plain in the next 2 chain, turn back, and missing the 2 plain, work 7 treble and 1 plain in the 9 chain, turn back; join it to the 12th 4 *chain* of the 1st small leaf, then 7 chain, 1 plain in the 2 chain as before, miss 1, 1 plain, turn back; 5 treble and 1 plain in the 7 chain, turn back; 5 chain, 1 plain in the 2 chain, miss 1, 1 plain, turn back; 3 treble and 1 plain in the 5 chain, turn back; 2 chain, miss 1, 3 treble on the 3 plain, and in the 2 chain at the point of the leaf, (work 1 plain, 2 chain, and 1 plain), turn, and work the other side to correspond, thus—3 treble, 5 chain, 1 plain in the 2 chain, miss 1, 1 plain, turn back, and missing the 2 plain, work 3 treble and 1 plain in the 5 chain, turn back; 7 chain, 1 plain, miss 1, 1 plain, turn back, work 5 treble and 1 plain in the 7 chain, turn back; 9 chain, 1 plain, miss 1, 1 plain, turn back; 7 treble, and 1 plain in the 9 chain, turn back; 7 chain, 1 plain, miss 1, 1 plain, turn back; 5 treble and 1 plain in the 7 chain, turn back, 7 chain, 1 plain; this finishes the leaf; work 6 plain down the stem; and for the

CALYX AND FIRST FLOWER—14 chain, turn, miss 1, 8 plain, turn, work 1 chain to cross the stem, and on the other side work 2 plain, 5 treble, 1 plain, 7 chain, 1 single stitch at the point, turn back, and work 16 plain in the 7 chain, turn back; (7 chain, miss 1, and 1 plain on the 16 plain 8 times), turn back; 4 chain, miss 4, 1 plain in the 7 chain, (4 chain, miss 7, and 1 plain in the 7 chain 7 times), 4 chain, miss 4, 1 plain on the 1st stitch of the calyx, turn back; miss 1, (1 plain, and 3 treble in the 4 chain, join it to the *3d division* or open space of the large leaf, always counting from the point; then 3 treble 1 plain, these 8 stitches are all worked in the same 4 chain), miss 1, (1 plain, 6 treble and

1 plain in the next 4 chain), and before finishing the flower, work the spray of 3 leaves thus—

THIRD SMALL LEAF—13 chain, and work the same as the 2d small leaf, joining it to the

[SECTION OF COLLAR.]

1st division of the large leaf; when finished, work 4 single stitches down the stem and for the

FOURTH SMALL LEAF—15 chain, and work as the 2d small leaf, joining it to the centre of the 18*th* 4 *chain* of the 3d leaf; when finished work 6 single down the stem; and for the

FIFTH SMALL LEAF—9 chain, and work as the 2d small leaf, joining it to the centre of the 18*th* 4 *chain* of the 4th small leaf; when finished work 4 single down the stem, and 8 single down the centre stem; and on the *flower*, miss 1, (1 plain, 6 treble and 1 plain in the 4 chain), miss 1, (1 plain, 3 treble; join it to the centre of the 18*th* 4 *chain* of the 5th small leaf; then 3 treble, 1 plain, these 8 stitches in the same 4 chain), miss 1, (1 plain, 6 treble and 1 plain in the 4 chain); and commence the

SECOND FLOWER and CALYX—14 chain, turn, miss 1, 8 plain, turn, work 1 chain to cross the stem, and on the other side 2 plain, 5 treble, 1 plain, 6 chain, 1 single at the point, turn back; work 14 plain in the 6 chain, turn back; (7 chain, miss 1, and 1 plain 7 times on the 14 plain), turn back; 4 chain, miss 4, 1 plain in the 7 chain, (4 chain, miss 7, and 1 plain in the 7 chain 6 times) 4 chain, miss 4, 1 plain on the 1st stitch of the calyx, turn back; miss 1, (1 plain, 3 treble in the 4 chain, join it to the centre 4 *chain* of the 5th small leaf; then 2 treble, 1 plain, these 7 stitches in the same 4 chain), (miss 1, 1 plain, 5 treble, and 1 plain in the 4 chain 7 times); then down the calyx, 1 plain, 5 treble, 2 plain; and down the stem, 4 plain; and to finish the 1st flower, (miss 1, 1 plain, 6 treble and 1 plain in the 4 chain 4 times); then down the calyx, 1 plain, 5 treble 2 plain, 4 plain down the stem, 6 plain down the centre stem; and for the

SECOND LARGE LEAF—22 chain, work the same as the 1st large leaf, joining it to the centre of the last 6 *treble* of the 1st flower; when the leaf is finished work 2 plain down the stem, and 7 plain down the centre stem, turn back; work 3 chain and 1 plain in each of the 5 divisions of the leaf; then 3 chain, and 1 plain at the point. This finishes the First Pattern: but in repeating it the directions are altered so that the 1st part of the pattern may join to that already worked, the shape and position of the leaves and flowers remaining the same.

SECOND PATTERN.

FIRST SMALL LEAF—10 chain, turn, miss 4, 1 single, turn back, and in the loop work 7 chain, 1 plain, 9 chain, 1 plain, 7 chain, 1 plain, turn back; (4 chain and 1 plain in the 7 chain twice, 2 chain; join it to the *2d division* of the 2d large leaf, 2 chain, 1 plain; then 4 chain, and 1 plain 4 times, all in the same 7 chain), miss 1, 1 plain in the 9 chain, (4 chain and 1 plain twice in the 9 chain, 2 chain: join it to the centre of the *7th 6 treble* of the 1st flower; 2 chain, 1 plain, then 4 chain and 1 plain 4 times in the same 9 chain), miss 1, 1 plain in the 7 chain, (4 chain and 1 plain 7 times in the 7 chain); 5 single down the stem, then

Work the *2d small leaf* and centre stem as in the First Pattern; and for the

FIRST LARGE LEAF—29 chain, turn, miss 2, 3 plain, (2 chain, miss 2, and 1 treble 4 times) 2 chain, miss 2, 1 plain, turn, and leaving the chain stitches for the stem, work 1 chain to cross it; then on the other side of the foundation, 7 chain, miss 1, 1 plain in the 2 chain of foundation, miss 1, 1 plain in the next 2 chain, turn back, and missing the 2 plain, work 5 treble and 1 plain in the 7 chain, turn back; then 9 chain, 1 plain in the same 2 chain of the foundation as before, miss 1, 1 plain in the next 2 chain, turn back, and missing the 2 plain, work 7 treble and 1 plain in the 9 chain, turn back; join it to the centre of the *12th 4 chain* of the 1st small leaf; then 7 chain, 1 plain in the 2 chain as before, miss 1, 1 plain, turn back, 5 treble and 1 plain in the 7 chain, turn back; join it to the 6th 6 treble of the 1st flower; then 5 chain, 1 plain in the 2 chain, miss 1, 1 plain, turn back; 3 treble and 1 plain in the 5 chain, turn back, 1 chain, miss 1, 3 treble on the 3 plain, and in the 2 chain at the point of the leaf, (work 1 plain, 1 chain, join it to the last 5 treble of the 2d flower, 1 chain and 1 plain), turn, and work the other side to correspond, the same as in 1st large leaf of the 1st pattern, work 6 plain down the stem, repeat the calyx and 1st flower, to the 3d small leaf, the same as in First Pattern.

THIRD SMALL LEAF—13 chain, turn; miss 4, 1 single in the 5th stitch, turn back, and work in the round loop 7 chain, 1 plain, 9 chain, 1 plain, 7 chain, 1 plain, turn back; (4 chain, and 1 plain 3 times in the 7 chain, 2 chain: join it to the *1st division* of the 1st large leaf, 2 chain, and in the same 7 chain work 1 plain, then 4 chain, and 1 plain, 3 times in the same 7 chain), miss 1, 1 plain in the 9 chain, (4 chain, and 1 plain 3 times in the 9 chain, 2 chain; join it to the centre of the *6th 5 treble* of the 2d flower, 2 chain, 1 plain; then 4 chain and 1 plain 3 times in the same 9 chain), miss 1, 1 plain in the 7 chain, (4 chain and 1 plain 7 times in the 7 chain), then 4 single down the stem—repeat the 4th and 5th *small leaves*, the *2d flower* and *calyx*, and the *2d large leaf*, as in the

First Pattern. Work this pattern 10 times more, making in all 12 patterns; but in working the last pattern to form the corner, omit the 2nd flower, finish the pattern, then work the 2 first small leaves, and the *1st* large leaf, joining the point to the *5th* small leaf, then, work 20 plain down the centre stem, and

For the Band.—1st row, work 3 chain and 1 treble in each of the chains along the sides of the 1st small and large leaves.

2nd. row,—3 chain, miss 3, 1 treble in the 3 chain of last row, repeat and fasten off.

COLLAR.—La Rose.

Taylor's Crochet Thread, No. 12; Needle, No. 23, Bell Gauge.

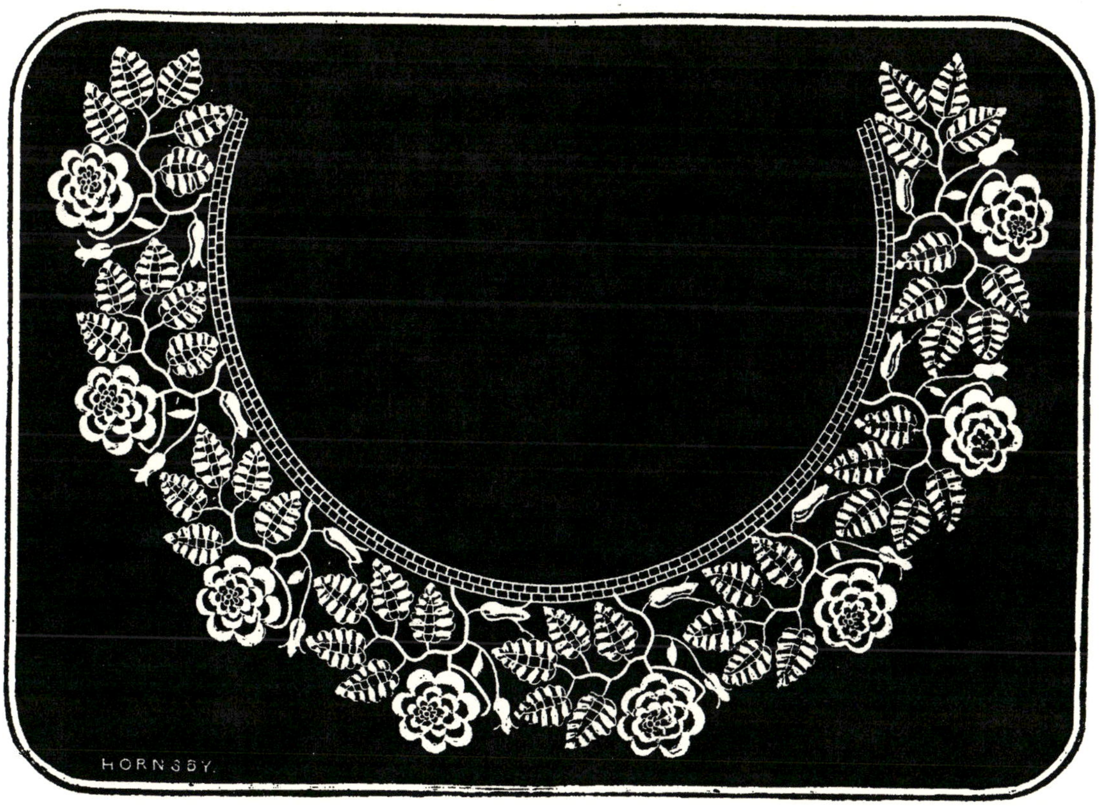

FOR THE ROSE.

Work a chain of 6 stitches, and make it round by working 1 single stitch in the 1st chain stitch.

1st round.—(3 chain and 1 plain in the round 7 times).

2d.—(3 chain, miss 3, and 1 plain in the 3 chain of the 1st round 7 times).

3d.—Miss 1, 1 plain, 5 chain, 1 plain; both these plain stitches are to be worked in the 3 chain of last round—repeat 6 times more.

4th.—Miss 2, 1 plain, 5 treble, 1 plain; these 7 stitches are all to be worked in the 5 chain of last round—repeat 6 times more.

5th.—5 single stitches, *, 3 chain, miss 4, 3 single stitches; repeat from * 3 times more, turn back to work the 6th row; (miss 1, 1 plain, miss 1, and 7 treble in the 3 chain 4 times), miss 1, 3 single stitches; turn back to work the 7th row; (5 chain, miss 5, and 3 single stitches on the 7 treble 5 times), 7 chain, miss 7, 1 plain between the two 5 trebles of the 4th round, then 7 chain, miss 7, 1 plain.

8th.—(Miss 1, 1 treble, 9 long stitches, 1 treble; these 11 stitches are all to be worked in the 5 chain; then miss 1, 1 plain in the centre stitch of the 3 single stitches; repeat 4 times more,) then 8 treble and 1 plain in the 7 chain, miss the 1 plain, 1 plain and 8 treble in the 7 chain, 1 plain, and fasten off. Work 8 of these Roses.

FOR THE LEAVES AND STEMS.

Make a chain of 80 stitches for the long stem.

First Leaf—Turn, miss 2, 3 plain, (2 chain, miss 2, and 1 treble 4 times), 2 chain, miss 2, 1 plain, turn, leaving the chain stitches for the stem, work 1 chain to cross it; then on the other side of the foundation, 7 chain, miss 1, 1 plain in the 2 chain of foundation, miss 1 1 plain in the next 2 chain, turn back; and missing the 2 plain, work 5 treble and 1 plain in the 7 chain, turn back; 9 chain, 1 plain in the same 2 chain of the foundation as before, miss 1, 1 plain in the next 2 chain, turn back, and missing the 2 plain, work 7 treble and 1 plain in the 9 chain; turn back, and join it to the 29*th chain stitch* of the long stem, counting from the commencement; then for the leaf, 7 chain, 1 plain in the 2 chain as before, miss 1, 1 plain, turn back; 5 treble and 1 plain in the 7 chain, turn back; 5 chain, 1 plain in the 2 chain, miss 1, 1 plain, turn back; 3 treble and 1 plain in the 5 chain, turn back; 2 chain, miss 1, 3 treble on the 3 plain, and in the 2 chain at the point of the leaf, (work 1 plain, 1 chain; join it to the 17th chain stitch of the long stem, and on the Leaf, 1 chain, and 1 plain). Work the other side to correspond, thus:— 3 treble, 5 chain, 1 plain in the 2 chain, miss 1, 1 plain, turn back, and missing the 2 plain, work 3 treble and 1 plain in the 5 chain, turn back; 7 chain, 1 plain, miss 1, 1 plain, turn back; work 5 treble and 1 plain in the 7 chain, turn back; 9 chain, 1 plain, miss 1, 1 plain, turn back; 7 treble, and 1 plain in the 9 chain, turn back; 7 chain, 1 plain, miss 1, 1 plain, turn back; 5 treble and 1 plain in the 7 chain, turn back; 5 chain, 1 plain; this finishes the Leaf. (The 5 leaves are all worked in the same manner, the difference being in the joining). Work 5 single stitches down the stem: and for the

SECOND LEAF—38 chain, and work the same as the 1st leaf: but instead of joining it to the 29*th chain* of the long stem, join it to the 2d division or open space of the 1st leaf, always counting from the point of the leaf; and in the 2d joining at the point of the leaf, join it to the 1st stitch of the long stem.

THIRD LEAF—34 chain, turn, miss 2, 3 plain, (2 chain, miss 2, and 1 treble 4 times), 2 chain, miss 2, 1 plain, turn; leaving the chain stitches for the stem, work 1 chain to cross it; then on the other side of the foundation, 7 chain, miss 1, 1 plain in the 2 chain of foundation, miss 1, 1 plain in the next 2 chain, turn back, and missing the 2 plain, work 5 treble and 1 plain in the 7 chain, turn back, join it to the 2d division of the 2d leaf; then 9 chain, 1 plain in the same 2 chain of the foundation as before, miss 1, 1 plain in the next 2 chain, turn back, and missing the 2 plain, work 7 treble and 1 plain in the 9 chain; turn back, then 7 chain, 1 plain in the 2 chain as before, miss 1, 1 plain, turn back, 5 treble and 1 plain in the 7 chain, turn back; 5 chain, 1 plain in the 2 chain miss 1, 1 plain, turn back; 3 treble and 1 plain in the 5 chain, turn back; 1 chain, miss 1, 3 treble on the 3 plain, and in the 2 chain at the point of the leaf; (work 1 plain, 2 chain, and 1 plain), turn, and work the other side to correspond, the same as in 1st leaf; when finished, work 8 single stitches down the stem, and for the

FOURTH LEAF—25 chain, and work the same as the 3d leaf, joining it to the 4th division of the 3d Leaf; when finished, work 5 single stitches down the stem, and 13 plain down the centre stem; and for the

FIFTH LEAF—25 chain, turn, miss 2, 3 plain, (2 chain, miss 2 and 1 treble 4 times), 2 chain, miss 2, 1 plain, turn; leaving the chain stitches for the stem, work 1 chain to cross it; then on the other side of the foundation, 7 chain, miss 1, 1 plain in the 2 chain of foundation, miss 1, 1 plain in the next 2 chain, turn back, and missing the 2 plain, work 5 treble and 1 plain in the 7 chain, turn back; 9 chain, 1 plain in the same 2 chain of the foundation as before, miss 1, 1 plain in the next 2 chain, turn back, and missing the 2 plain, work 7 treble and 1 plain in the 9 chain, turn back; then 7 chain, 1 plain in the 2 chain as before, miss 1, 1 plain, turn back; 5 treble and 1 plain in the 7 chain, turn back; 5 chain, 1 plain in the 2 chain, miss 1, 1 plain, turn back; 3 treble, and 1 plain in the 5 chain, turn back; join it to the 4th division of the 4th Leaf; 2 chain, miss 1, 3 treble on the 3 plain, and in the 2 chain at the point of the leaf, (work 1 plain, 2 chain, and 1 plain), turn, and work the other side to correspond, thus—3 treble, 5 chain, 1 plain in the 2 chain, miss 1, 1 plain, turn back, and missing the 2 plain, work 3 treble and 1 plain in the 5 chain, turn back; 7 chain, 1 plain, miss 1, 1 plain, turn back; work 5 treble and 1 plain in the 7 chain, turn back; 9 chain, 1 plain, miss 1, 1 plain, turn back; 7 treble, and 1 plain in the 9 chain, turn back; join on a rose at the centre stitch of the 1*st* 8 *treble*; then for the leaf, 7 chain, 1 plain, miss 1, 1 plain, turn back; 5 treble and 1 plain in the 7 chain, turn back; 5 chain, 1 plain, 5 single down the stem, and 14 plain down the centre stem; then

FOR THE STEM OF THE ROSE—9 chain; join it to the rose by working a single stitch in the 22d stitch from the last joining; then 9 chain, and join it to the 12th stitch from the last joining, 10 chain, join it to the 6th stitch from the last joining, turn, and work 28 plain down the stem, and 5 plain down the centre stem.

For the Small Leaf—16 chain, join it to the 15th plain stitch of the stem of the rose, turn, work 3 plain, 5 treble, 2 plain, 2 single, leaving 3 chain for the stem; then work 26 chain for the stem of the bud; and to form the

Calyx and Bud—Turn, miss 4, 8 plain, turn, work 1 chain to cross the stem; and on the other side, 2 plain, 3 treble; join it to the 5th stitch of the stem of the rose, then 2 treble 1 plain; and in the round loop, 1 plain, 9 chain, turn, miss 1, 8 plain on the 9 chain, 1 plain in the round loop, turn back; (1 chain, 1 treble, 2 chain, and 1 treble: these 2 treble in the last 1 plain); then 1 single in the 4th stitch of the 8 plain, turn back; (1 chain, miss 1, 2 treble, 3 chain, and 2 treble, 1 chain: these 4 stitches in the 2 chain), 3 single down the side of the 1 treble, and 1 plain in the round loop, 3 chain, 1 single in the 1 chain stitch 5 chain, turn; miss 1, work 8 plain down the chain stitches, and 1 plain in the round loop; then down the calyx, 1 plain, 5 treble, 2 plain, 13 single down the stem, 3 single down the stem of the small leaf, and 6 plain down the centre stem; then 13 chain; for the

Second Bud—Work a bud and calyx as before, *not* joining it; when finished, work 5 plain, and 3 treble down the centre stem, turn back; work 5 chain, miss 9, and 15 single stitches on the side of the bud. This finishes one pattern of the Collar, and is to be repeated, with the following variation:—

[SECTION OF COLLAR.]

SECOND PATTERN.

80 chain for the long stem, and work the 1st 2d and 3rd leaves the same as in 1st pattern, but after joining the 3d leaf to the 2d leaf, also join the 3d leaf to the 2d bud at the 8 plain, and then join the point of this leaf to the stem of the small leaf; work the 4th leaf, joining the point to the top of the calyx of the 1st bud; then work the 5th leaf, the rose, and the bud, exactly the same as in the First Pattern, and work the same for 8 patterns: but in working the *last pattern*, to form the corners to correspond with the other side, after working the 13 single down the stem of the 1st bud, work 40 chain, and a leaf the same as the 1st leaf, joining it only to the calyx of the bud; then work 3 leaves as the 3d, 4th, and 5th leaves, and when finished work 8 plain down the centre stem; finish the 8th pattern by working the 3 single down the stem of the small leaf; then 6 plain down the centre stem; then the 2d bud, joining the 9 chain to the stem of the 4th leaf, and after working the 15 single on the side of the bud, work 12 single on the side of the 4th leaf, and turning back, work the band along the remaining chain stitches of the long stem and sides of the buds.

1st row.—3 chain, miss 3, 1 treble: repeat to the end.

2d.—3 chain, miss 3, 1 treble in the 3 chain of last row; repeat.

3d.—Miss 2, 2 plain in the 3 chain; repeat, and fasten off.

MANCHETTE.

Taylor's Crochet Thread, No. 12; Fine Black Silk; Needle, No. 23, Bell Gauge.—Make a chain of 136 stitches, and cut off the thread at the end of each row. The plain

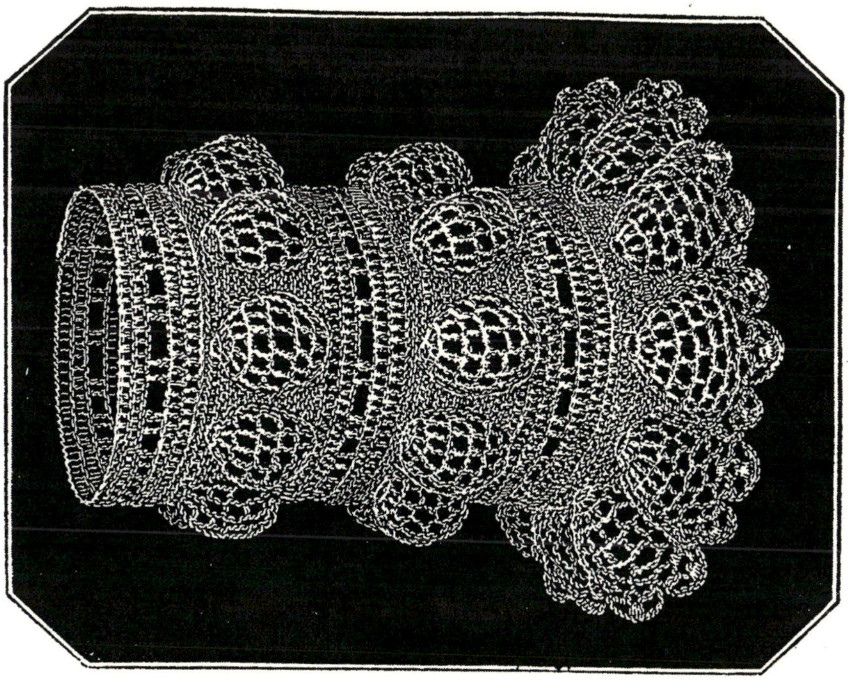

*stitches are all to be worked in Double Crochet;—(see Instructions—*SECOND SERIES,*) and in working the treble rows, put the needle* between *the stitches in the preceding row.*

1st and 2d rows.—Treble.

3d.—1 treble, *, 4 chain, miss 4, 2 treble: repeat from *, and end with 1 treble.

4th and 5th.—Treble. 6th and 7th.—Plain.

8th.—6 plain, *, 5 chain, miss 1, 11 plain; repeat from *, and end with 6 plain, instead of 11.

9th.—5 plain, *, miss 1, (1 chain, and 1 treble 5 times in the 5 chain of the 8th row,) 1 chain, miss 1, 9 plain; repeat from *, and end with 5 plain.

10th.—4 plain, *, (2 chain, miss 1, and 1 treble in the 1 chain 6 times,) 2 chain, miss 1, 7 plain: repeat from *, end with 4 plain.

11th.—3 plain, *, (2 chain, miss 2, and 1 treble in the 2 chain 7 times,) 2 chain, miss 2, 5 plain; repeat from *, end with 3 plain.

12.—2 plain, *, (2 chain, miss 2, and 1 treble in the 2 chain 8 times,) 2 chain, miss 2, 3 plain: repeat from *, and end with 2 plain.

13th.—Same as the 11th.

14th.—4 plain, *, (2 chain, miss 2, and 1 treble in the 2 chain 6 times), 2 chain, miss 2, 7 plain: repeat from *, and end with 4 plain.

15th.—5 plain, *, (1 chain, miss 2, and 1 treble in the 1 chain 5 times,) 1 chain, miss 2, 9 plain; repeat from *, end with 5 plain.

16th.—6 plain, *, (miss 1, and 1 treble in the 1 chain 4 times), miss 1, 11 plain, repeat from *, end with 6 plain.

17th.—6 plain, *, 1 chain, miss 4, 11 plain; repeat from *, end with 6 plain.

18th and 19th.—Plain: repeat those 19 rows once more, and then work the 1st 12 rows; and for

THE EDGING,

51st.—1 plain, (2 chain, miss 2, and 1 treble in the 2 chain 9 times), 2 chain, miss 2, repeat, end with 1 plain.

52d.—3 chain, miss 2, 1 plain in the 2 chain of the last row: repeat to the end.

53d.—1 chain, miss 2, (2 treble, 3 chain, 2 treble, these 4 treble are worked in the 3 chain of the last row,) 1 chain, miss 2, 1 plain in the 3 chain—repeat.

54th.—1 plain in the 1 chain of the last row, 3 chain, miss 2, 5 treble, in the 3 chain of the last row, 3 chain, miss 2, 1 plain in the 1 chain of last row, miss 1; repeat to the end, and fasten off; knot the ends together, and work a plain row down each side.

CHEMISETTE.

Taylor's Crochet Thread, No. 12*; Needle, No.* 22*; if wished coarser, No.* 8*; Needle, No.* 20*, Bell Gauge.—Make a chain of* 14 *stitches for the Point. The round loop in*

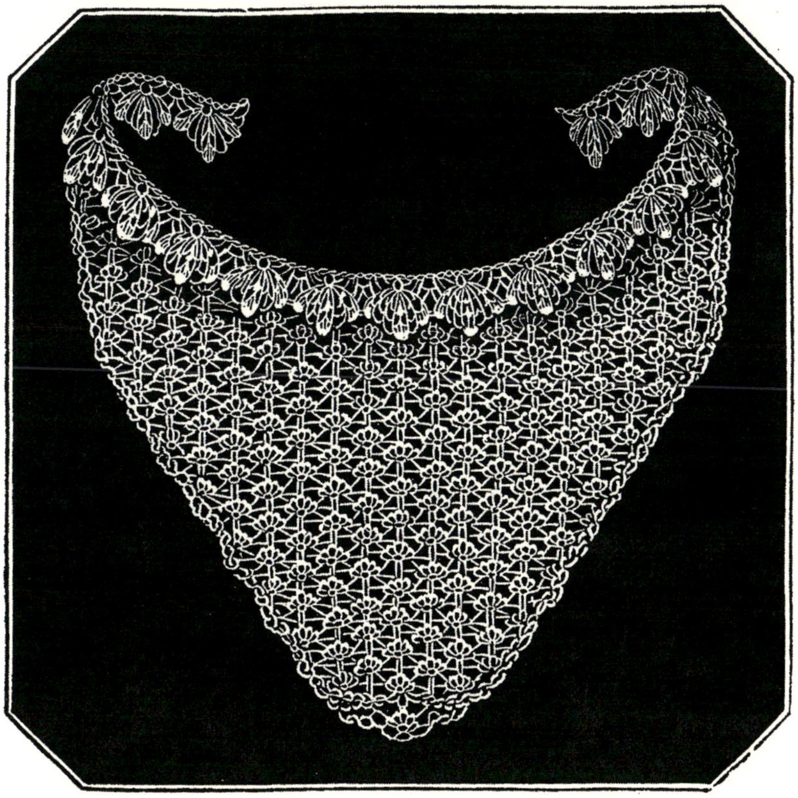

*this Pattern is always worked thus—*13 *chain,* 1 *plain in the* 3*d stitch,* 2 *chain,* 1 *plain in the same stitch as the last stitch in the direction—(See Instructions—*SECOND SERIES).

1st row.—Miss 4, (2 treble, 1 chain, 2 treble: these 4 treble in 1 stitch of the foundation), then 3 chain, 1 plain, 3 chain, miss 2, 1 plain, work a round loop, then 3 chain, miss 2 1 plain, 3 chain, (2 treble, 1 chain, 2 treble, these 4 treble in 1 stitch,) turn back.

2d.—2 chain, miss 2, (2 treble, 1 chain, 2 treble : these 4 treble stitches are to be worked in the 1 chain, between the 2 trebles, of the preceding row; this is for the Edge.) 5 chain, miss 4, 1 plain in the 3 chain, miss 1, 1 plain in the next 3 chain, 3 chain, miss 5, 11 plain in the round loop, 3 chain, miss 5, 1 plain, miss 1, 1 plain, 5 chain, miss 4; and for the edge, work (2 treble, 1 chain, 2 treble—these 4 treble in 1 stitch as before) the stitches forming the edge are to be repeated at the beginning and end of every row.

3d.—Work the edge; 3 chain, miss 2, 1 plain, work a round loop, then 5 chain, miss 10, 1 plain; then (5 chain, miss 1, and 1 plain 5 times on the 11 plain), 5 chain, miss 10, 1 plain, work a round loop, then 3 chain, miss 2, and edge.

4th.—Edge; 3 chain, miss 2, 1 plain, 3 chain, miss 7, 11 plain in the round loop, 3 chain, miss 7, 1 plain in the 5 chain, (miss 3, and 3 plain in the 5 chain 5 times), miss 3 1 plain in the 5 chain, 3 chain, miss 7, 11 plain in the round loop, 3 chain, miss 7, 1 plain, 3 chain, miss 2, and edge.

5th.—Edge; 5 chain, miss 10, 1 plain, (5 chain, miss 1, and 1 plain 5 times), 5 chain miss 11, 1 plain, work a round loop, 5 chain, miss 11, 1 plain, (5 chain, miss 1, and 1 plain 5 times) 5 chain, miss 10, and edge.

SECTION OF CHEMISETTE.

6th.—Edge; **3 chain, miss 5, 1 plain in the 5 chain, (miss 3, and 3 plain in the 5 chain 5 times), miss 3, 1 plain in the 5 chain, 3 chain, miss 7, 11 plain in the round loop, 3 chain, miss 7, 1 plain in the 5 chain, (miss 3, and 3 plain 5 times as before), miss 3, 1 plain in the 5 chain, 3 chain, miss 5, edge.**

7th.—Edge; 3 chain, miss 2, 1 plain, 5 chain, miss 11, 1 plain, work a round loop, 5 chain, miss 11, 1 plain, (5 chain, miss 1, and 1 plain 5 times), 5 chain, miss 11, 1 plain, work a round loop, 5 chain, miss 11, 1 plain, 3 chain, miss 2, edge.

8th.—Edge; 5 chain, miss 4, 1 plain in the 3 chain, miss 1, 1 plain in the 5 chain, 3 chain, miss 7, 11 plain in the round loop, 3 chain, miss 7, 1 plain in the 5 chain, (miss 3, and 3 plain in the 5 chain 5 times), miss 3, 1 plain, 3 chain, miss 7, 11 plain as before, 3 chain, miss 7, 1 plain, miss 1, 1 plain, 5 chain, miss 4, edge; these 8 rows form the point, and are not to be repeated.

9th.—Edge; 3 chain, miss 2, *, 1 plain, work a round loop, 5 chain, miss 11, 1 plain, (5 chain, miss 1, and 1 plain 5 times), 5 chain, miss 11: repeat from *, end with 1 plain, work a round loop, 3 chain, miss 2, and edge.

10th.—Edge: 3 chain, miss 2, 1 plain, *, 3 chain, miss 7, 11 plain in the round loop, 3 chain, miss 7, 1 plain in the 5 chain, (miss 3, and 3 plain in the 5 chain 5 times), miss 3, 1 plain in the 5 chain; repeat from *, and end with 3 chain, miss 7, 11 plain as before, 3 chain, miss 7, 1 plain, 3 chain, miss 2, and edge.

11th.—Edge, *, 5 chain, miss 11, 1 plain, (5 chain, miss 1, and 1 plain 5 times), 5 chain, miss 11, 1 plain, work a round loop: repeat from *, and end with 5 chain, miss 11,

1 plain, (5 chain, miss 1, and 1 plain 5 times as before), 5 chain, miss 11, and edge.

12th.—Edge; 3 chain, miss 5, 1 plain in the 5 chain, *, (miss 3, and 3 plain in the 5 chain 5 times), miss 3, 1 plain in the 5 chain, 3 chain, miss 7, 11 plain in the round loop, 3 chain, miss 7, 1 plain in the 5 chain; repeat from *, and end with (miss 3, and 3 plain 5 times), miss 3, 1 plain, 3 chain, miss 5, and edge.

13th.—Edge; 3 chain, miss 2, 1 plain,*, 5 chain, miss 11, 1 plain, work a round loop, 5 chain, miss 11, 1 plain, (5 chain, miss 1, and 1 plain 5 times): repeat from *, and end with 5 chain, miss 11, 1 plain, work a round loop, 5 chain, miss 11, 1 plain, 3 chain, miss 2, and edge.

14th.—Edge; 5 chain, miss 3, 1 plain in the 3 chain, miss 3, *, 1 plain in the 5 chain, 3 chain, miss 7, 11 plain in the round loop, 3 chain, miss 7, 1 plain in the 5 chain, (miss 3, and 3 plain in the 5 chain 5 times), repeat from *, and end with miss 3, 1 plain, 3 chain, miss 7, 11 plain as before, 3 chain, miss 7, 1 plain, miss 3, 1 plain, 3 chain, miss 3, and edge. Repeat the last 6 rows 6 times more; and to shape the Neck, decrease thus:—

1st row.—Work the pattern as the 11th row 3 times, then 3 chain, miss 11, (2 treble, 1 chain, 2 treble in one, for the edge,) turn back, leaving the remaining stitches for the other side.

2d.—Work as the 10th row; end with 3 chain, miss 2, and edge.

3d.—Work as the 13th row: end with 5 chain, miss 9, and edge.

4th.—Work as the 12th row; end with miss 3, 1 plain, 3 chain, miss 2, and edge.

5th.—Work as the 11th row; at the end omit the last round loop, and work 1 chain, miss 13, and edge.

6th.—Work as the 12th row; and end the same as that row.

7th.—Work as the 13th row; end with 5 chain, miss 11, 1 plain, 1 chain, miss 13, and edge.

8th.—Work as the 12th row; and end with miss 3, 1 plain, 3 chain, miss 2, and edge: repeat these 8 rows twice more, working one pattern less each repeat. For the other side, commence in the 78th stitch from the 1st side—that is, in the side of the round loop, and decrease thus:—

1st.—2 treble, 1 chain, 2 treble, for the edge; then work as the 13th row 3 times, and end with 5 chain, miss 11, and edge.

2d.—Work as the 12th row, end with 5 chain, miss 7, and edge.

3d.—Work as the 11th row, end with 5 chain, miss 11, 1 plain, 3 chain, miss 2, and edge.

4th.—Work as the 14th row, and end with miss 3, 1 plain, 3 chain, miss 3, and edge.

5th.—Edge; 1 chain, miss 13, 1 plain, *, then work as the 11th row, and end the same as that row.

6th.—Work as the 12th row, and end the same as that row.

7th.—Edge; 1 chain, miss 13, 1 plain, *, work as the 11th row, end with 5 chain, miss 11, 1 plain, 3 chain, miss 2, and edge.

8th.—Work as the 14th row; end with miss 3, 1 plain, 3 chain, miss 5, and edge: repeat these 8 rows twice more, working 1 pattern less each repeat. Then work 50 chain stitches turn, and on the chain stitches work 50 plain and along the neck work 5 chain, and 1 plain in the 2 chain at the beginning and end of the rows, repeating to the other point, and at the end work 50 chain to correspond with the other side.

FOR THE EDGING.—1st. row—4 chain, miss 4, 2 treble, repeat.

2nd, 3d, and 4th rows—1 chain, miss 1, 1 treble, repeat.

5th row—12 plain, *, 7 chain, 21 plain, repeat from * and end with 7 chain, 12 plain.

6th row—5 chain, miss 2, 1 plain, 5 chain, miss 3, 3 plain, 1 chain, miss 3, (2 treble, 2 chain, 2 treble, 3 chain, 2 treble, 2 chain, 2 treble, 3 chain, 2 treble, 2 chain, 2 treble ; these 12 treble stitches are all to be worked in the 7 chain of the last row,) then 1 chain, miss 3, 3 plain, 5 chain, miss 2, 1 plain, repeat, and end with 5 chain, miss 2, 1 plain.

7th row—1 chain, miss 3, 1 plain,*, 3 chain, miss 5, 1 plain, in the 5 chain, miss 8, (2 treble, 2 chain, 2 treble ; these 4 treble are to be worked in the 2 chain of the last row,) 3 chain miss 3, 1 plain in the 3 chain of last row, 3 chain, miss 3 (2 treble, 2 chain, 2 treble in the 2 chain as before), 3 chain, miss 3, 1 plain in the 3 chain, 3 chain, miss 3, (2 treble, 2 chain, 2 treble in the 2 chain as before,) miss 8, 1 plain in the 5 chain of the last row, 3 chain, miss 5, 1 plain, in the 5 chain, repeat from *.

8th row—miss 1, 1 plain, 3 chain, miss 4, (3 treble, 2 chain, 3 treble ; these 6 treble in the 2 chain of last row,) 3 chain, miss 4, 1 plain, repeat, end miss 1, 1 plain.

9th row—miss 2, 1 plain, 3 chain, miss 5, (3 treble, 2 chain, 3 treble in the 2 chain of last row,) 3 chain, miss 5, 1 plain, repeat, end, miss 1, 1 plain.

th row—miss 2, 3 plain, miss 3, 7 treble in the 2 chain, miss 3, 3 plain, repeat.

CROCHET EDGING.

Taylor's Crochet Thread, No. 10, *or* 12; *Needle, No.* 22, *Bell Guage.—Make a chain of* 792 *stitches per yard, or* 33 *for each pattern. This Edging is worked backwards and forwards, and will be one inch and a half deep.*

1st row.—3 chain, miss 2, 1 plain : repeat, and end with 2 plain.

2d and 3d.—3 chain, miss 3, 1 plain in the 3 chain of the last row : repeat.

4th.—Miss 1, 3 plain in the 3 chain of the last row—repeat, and end 1 plain.

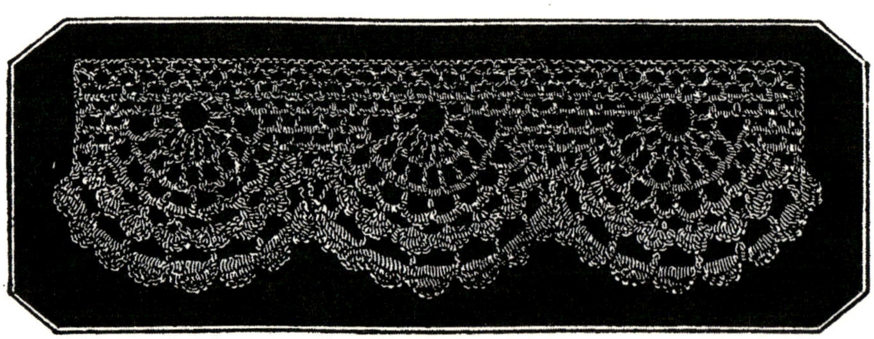

5th.—(3 chain, miss 2, 1 plain 5 times), 7 chain, miss 2, 1 plain, (3 chain, miss 2, 1 plain 5 times) ; repeat.

6th.—(Miss 1, 3 plain in the 3 chain 4 times), miss 2, 1 plain in the 3 chain, miss 2, (3 chain, and 1 treble 7 times in the 7 chain of the 5th row), 3 chain, miss 2, 1 plain in the 3 chain miss 2, (3 plain, and miss 1, 4 times in the 3 chain) : repeat.

7th.—2 plain, *, (3 chain, miss 2, 1 plain 3 times,) (3 chain, miss 3, and 1 treble in the 3 chain 8 times), 3 chain, miss 3, 1 plain, (3 chain, miss 2, and 1 plain 4 times); repeat from*.

8th.—Miss 1, and 3 plain in the 3 chain : repeat, and end with 1 plain.

9th.—(3 chain, miss 2, and 1 plain twice), 3 chain, miss 5, 1 plain, (5 chain, miss 2, and 1 plain 8 times), 3 chain, miss 5, 1 plain, (3 chain, miss 2, and 1 plain twice) : repeat.

10th.—(Miss 1, and 3 plain in the 3 chain twice), miss 2, 1 plain in the 3 chain, miss 2, (5 plain, and miss 1 in the 5 chain 8 times), miss 2, 1 plain in the 3 chain, miss 2, (3 plain, and miss 1 in the 3 chain twice): repeat.

11th.—2 plain, *, 3 chain, miss 3, 1 plain, (2 chain, miss 3, 1 plain, 4 chain, and 1 plain 8 times), 2 chain, miss 3, 1 plain, (3 chain, miss 2, and 1 plain twice): repeat from *.

12.—(Miss 1, 3 plain in the 3 chain twice), (miss 2, 1 plain in the 2 chain, miss 2, 4 treble in the 4 chain 8 times), miss 2, 1 plain in the 2 chain, miss 2, 3 plain in the 3 chain, repeat, end with 2 plain.

13th.—5 chain, miss 5, 1 plain, (5 chain, miss 4, 1 plain in the centre of the 4 treble in the 12th row 8 times), 5 chain, miss 5, 1 plain—repeat.

14th.—Miss 1, 1 plain, 6 treble, 1 plain : these 8 stitches are worked in the 5 chain of the 13th row: repeat, and fasten off.

CROCHET COLLAR
THE BRITISH EMBLEMS.
W.D. HORNSEY
LONDON

THE

CROCHET BOOK,

FIFTH SERIES,

BY

MDLLE. RIEGO DE LA BRANCHARDIERE.

Second Edition---10,000.

LONDON:
SIMPKIN, MARSHALL, AND CO;
ACKERMANN, STRAND; OLIVER AND BOYD, EDINBURGH;
ALL BOOKSELLERS, AND BERLIN WAREHOUSES.
1849.

CONTENTS.

PREFACE.

I FEEL it is requisite to give some explanation why this series of designs appears *first*, contrary to my announcement. The cause of this change has been owing to the many infringements of my *works*, particularly the Crochet Flower Books, which, from their novelty, have recently furnished to *others* a source for unacknowledged adaptation. For some time past I have been anxious to prove how easy it is for the unprincipled to take credit for originality, and to *vary* and *re-arrange* a design. I have been led by this idea to form the first collar in this series from my APPLIQUÉ FLOWER BOOK, for the directions therein contained to form the collars in *thread*, being but secondary to the object of the work; I have long felt dissatisfied with those sprigs worked in detached portions for that *purpose*, and with the difficulty a lady must experience in producing, without instruction, an effective and elegant arrangement. Fully aware of this, from the many inquiries I have had for more elaborate directions, I have taken great pains to give a new design and receipt for working the Patterns in an entire piece, at the same time preserving the character of the Flowers and Leaves.

Sincerely grateful for the extensive patronage I have received, I beg respectfully to intimate that "The Crochet D'Oyley and Anti-Macassar Book" is in the press.

E. R. DE LA BRANCHARDIERE.

106, *New Bond Street.*
March, 1849.

Instructions and Directions given in Point, Lacet, Crochet, Embroidery, Lace-work, Knitting, Netting, Tambour, &c.

Ladies experiencing any difficulty in the following Directions, may communicate personally, or by Letter, enclosing a stamp for a reply.

Prices of Collars:

	s.	d.		s.	d.
Emblem	7	6	La Rose	5	6
Lily of the Valley	6	0	Le Bouquet de Fleurs	5	6
Honiton	6	0	La Reine des Fleurs	5	0

And the other Collars in the 1st and 2nd Series, from 2*s.* 6*d.* to 3*s.* 6*d.*

POINT-LACET COLLARS 7*s.* 6*d.*, 10*s.* 6*d.*, and 15*s.* each.

THE CROCHET BOOK.

Fifth Series.

COLLAR—THE BRITISH EMBLEMS.

Jno. and Wm. Taylor's Crochet Thread, No. 12. Needle, No. 23, Bell Guage.

FOR THE ROSES.

Work a chain of 6 stitches; make it round by working 1 single stitch in the 1st chain stitch.

1st round.—(3 chain and 1 plain in the round 7 times).

2nd—(3 chain, miss 3, and 1 plain in 3 chain of the 1st round 7 times).

3rd—Miss 1, 1 plain, 5 chain, 1 plain; both these plain stitches are to be worked in the 3 chain of last round—repeat 6 times more.

4th—Miss 2, 1 plain, 5 treble, 1 plain; these 7 stitches are all to be worked in the 5 chain of last round—repeat 6 times more.

5th round—5 single stitches, *, 3 chain, miss 4, 3 single stitches; repeat from * 3 times more; turn back to work the 6th row; (miss 1, 1 plain, miss 1, and 7 treble in the 3 chain, 4 times), miss 1, 3 single stitches; turn back to work the 7th row; (5 chain, miss 5, and 3 single stitches on the 7 treble, 5 times), 9 chain, miss 7, 1 plain between the two 5 trebles of the 4th round, then 9 chain, miss 7, 1 plain.

8th round, (miss 1, 1 treble, 9 long stitches, 1 treble; these 11 stitches are all to be worked in the 5 chain; then miss 1, 1 plain in the centre stitch of the 3 single stitches; repeat 4 times more,) then 8 treble and 1 plain in the 9 chain, miss the 1 plain, 1 plain and 8 treble in the 9 chain, 1 plain, and fasten off. Work 4 more Roses.

FOR THE 1st PATTERN.

Make a chain of 21 stitches, turn, miss 1, 20 single on the chain, then 72 chain for the long stem, and for the

First Rose Leaf—Turn, miss 2, 3 plain, (2 chain, miss 2, and 1 treble 4 times), 2 chain, miss 2, 1 plain, turn, leaving the chain stitches for the stem, work 1 chain to cross it; then on the other side of the foundation, 7 chain, miss 1, 1 plain in the 2 chain of foundation, miss 1, 1 plain in the next 2 chain, turn back; and missing the 2 plain, work 5 treble and 1 plain in the 7 chain, turn back; 9 chain, 1 plain in the same 2 chain of the foundation as before, miss 1, 1 plain in the next 2 chain, turn back; and missing the 2 plain, work 7 treble and 1 plain in the 9 chain, turn back; then join it to the 32nd *chain stitch* of the long stem, counting from the commencement; then for the Leaf, 7 chain, 1 plain in the 2 chain as before, miss 1, 1 plain, turn back; 5 treble and 1 plain in the 7 chain, turn back, join it to the 25th *chain stitch* of the long stem; then 5 chain, 1 plain in the 2 chain, miss 1, 1 plain, turn back; 3 treble and 1 plain in the 5 chain, turn back; 2 chain, miss 1, 3 treble on the 3 plain, and in the 2 chain at the point of the Leaf, (work 1 plain, 1 chain, join it to the 4th *chain stitch* of the long stem, and on the Leaf, 1 chain, and 1 plain). Work the other side to correspond, thus:—3 treble, 5 chain, 1 plain in the 2 chain, miss 1, 1 plain, turn back; and missing the 2 plain, work 3 treble and 1 plain in the 5 chain, turn back; 7 chain, 1 plain, miss 1, 1 plain, turn back; work 5 treble and 1 plain in the 7 chain, turn back; 9 chain, 1 plain, miss 1, 1 plain, turn back; 7 treble, and 1 plain in the 9 chain, turn back; 7 chain, 1 plain, miss 1, 1 plain, turn back; 5 treble and 1 plain in the 7 chain, turn back; 5 chain, 1 plain, and 5 single down the stem, this finishes the Leaf.

Second Rose Leaf—32 chain, turn, miss 2, 3 plain, (2 chain, miss 2, and 1 treble 4 times), 2 chain, miss 2, 1 plain, turn, and leaving the chain stitches for the stem, work 1 chain to cross it; then on the other side of the foundation, 7 chain, miss 1, 1 plain in the 2 chain of foundation, miss 1, 1 plain in the next 2 chain, turn back, and missing the 2 plain, work 5 treble, and 1 plain in the 7 chain, turn back; join it to the *last* 5 *chain* of the 1st Leaf, 9 chain, 1 plain in the same 2 chain, miss 1, 1 plain, turn back; 7 treble, and 1 plain in the 9 chain, turn back; then 7 chain, 1 plain in the 2 chain as before, miss 1, 1 plain, turn back; 5 treble and 1 plain in the 7 chain, turn back; 5 chain, 1 plain in the 2 chain, miss 1, 1 plain, turn back; 3 treble, and 1 plain in the 5 chain, turn back; 2 chain, miss 1, 3 treble on the 3 plain, and in the 2 chain at the point of the Leaf, (work 1 plain, 2 chain, and 1 plain,) turn, and work the other side to correspond as in the first Leaf.

[SECTION OF COLLAR.]

3rd Leaf.—25 chain, turn, miss 2, 3 plain, (2 chain, miss 2 and 1 treble, 4 times), 2 chain miss 2; plain, turn, leaving the chain stitches for the stem, work 1 chain to cross it, join it to the *last 5 chain* of the 2nd Leaf; then on the other side of the foundation, 7 chain, miss 1, 1 plain in the 2 chain of foundation, miss 1, 1 plain in the next 2 chain, turn back, and missing the 2 plain, work 5 treble and 1 plain in the 7 chain, turn back; 9 chain, 1 plain in the same 2 chain of the foundation as before, miss 1, 1 plain in the next 2 chain, turn back, and missing the 2 plain, work 7 treble and 1 plain in the 9 chain, turn back; then 7 chain, 1 plain in the 2 chain as before, miss 1, 1 plain, turn back; 5 treble and 1 plain in the 7 chain, turn back; 5 chain, 1 plain in the 2 chain, miss 1, 1 plain, turn back; 3 treble, and 1 plain in the 5 chain, turn back; 2 chain, miss 1, 3 treble on the 3 plain, and in the 2 chain at the point of the Leaf, (work 1 plain, 2 chain, and 1 plain), turn, and work the other side to correspond, thus * *—3 treble, 5 chain, 1 plain in the 2 chain, miss 1, 1 plain, turn back, and missing the 2 plain, work 3 treble and 1 plain in the 5 chain, turn back; 7 chain, 1 plain, miss 1, 1 plain, turn back; work 5 treble and 1 plain in the 7 chain, turn back; join on a Rose at the centre stitch of the *last 9 long stitches* of the Flower, then for the Leaf, 9 chain, 1 plain, miss 1, 1 plain, turn back; 7 treble, and 1 plain in the 9 chain, turn back; 7 chain, 1 plain, miss 1, 1 plain, turn back; 5 treble and 1 plain in the 7 chain, turn back; 5 chain, 1 plain, 5 single down the stem, and 19 plain down the centre stem; then for the

STEM of the ROSE 15 chain, join it to the 4th *stitch* of the 19 plain, worked down the centre stem of the leaves; then 9 chain, join it to the Rose in the 17th *stitch* from where it was joined to the Leaf; turn, work 24 plain down the stem, and 15 plain down the long stem of the leaves.

FOR THE SMALL LEAF.—16 chain, join it to the 21st *plain* stitch of the stem of the Rose, turn, 3 plain, 6 treble, 2 plain, 1 single, and leaving 3 chain for the stem, work 26 chain for the stem of the Bud; and to form the

CALYX and BUD—Turn, miss 4, 8 plain, turn, work 1 chain to cross the stem; and on the other side, 2 plain, 3 treble, join it to the 16th *plain* stitch of the stem of the Rose; then 2 treble, 1 plain, and 1 plain in the round loop, 9 chain, join it to the Rose in the 6th *stitch* from where the stem joins, turn, miss 1, 8 plain on the 9 chain, 1 plain in the round loop, turn back; (1 chain, 1 treble, 2 chain, and 1 treble, these 2 treble, in the last 1 plain), then 1 single in the 4th stitch of the 8 plain, turn back; (1 chain, miss 1, 2 treble 3 chain, and 2 treble, these 4 treble stitches in the 2 chain), 1 chain, 3 single down the side of the 1 treble, and 1 plain in the round loop; 3 chain, 1 single in the 1 chain stitch, 5 chain, turn, miss 1, work 8 plain down the chain stitches, and 1 plain in the round loop; then down the calyx, 1 plain, 5 treble, 2 plain, 13 single down the stem, 3 single down the stem of the small Leaf, and 8 plain down the long stem.

SECOND SMALL LEAF,—16 chain, join it to the 11th *single stitch* of the stem of the Bud, turn, 3 plain, 7 treble, 2 plain, 3 single for the stem; then 22 plain down the long stem, join it to the 3 *single* of the stem of the 2nd small Leaf, then 8 plain down the long stem; and for the

FIRST THISTLE LEAF—38 chain, turn, miss 1, 5 plain, 16 treble, 2 plain, turn, work 1 chain to cross the stem, and on the other side, 2 plain, 2 chain, 3 long, join it to the 4th *single* stitch of the stem of the Bud; then 2 long, 2 chain, 1 plain, 2 chain, 5 long, 2 chain 1 plain, 1 chain, 5 treble, join it to the top of the *outer point* of the Bud, then 5 single, join it to the 12th stitch of the Rose from the last joining; turn, and on the other side of the Leaf, work 4 single, and before finishing the Leaf, work the

First Thistle—12 chain, and to form the calyx, turn, miss 5, 1 single in the 6th stitch, 1 chain to cross the stem.

1st round—10 treble in the round loop, 1 chain, to cross the stem.

2nd round—2 treble in each stitch of the 1st round, 11 times, 1 chain to cross the stem.

3rd round—13 plain on the treble stitches of the 2nd round, and to form the top of the Thistle, turn back; 16 chain, 1 single on the last or 13th *plain* stitch of the calyx, turn back; work 7 single on the 16 chain, turn back; 9 chain, 1 single in the same plain stitch of the calyx as before, turn back; work 7 single on the 9 chain, * turn back; 9 chain, 1 single in the 12th plain stitch of the calyx, turn back; work 7 single on the 9 chain; repeat from * twice more, join it to the 1st *long* stitch of the Rose, then (5 chain, miss 1, and 1 plain in the 2 chain, between the bars of the Thistle, 5 times), 5 chain and 7 single down the 7 chain left at the side; and to finish the calyx, work 10 plain on the remaining treble stitches of the 2nd *round*—then 3 plain down the stem; and to finish the Leaf, 1 single, 5 treble, 1 chain, 1 plain, 2 chain, 5 long, 2 chain, 1 plain, 2 chain, 5 long, 2 chain, 2 plain; and down the stem, 1 plain, 2 chain, 2 plain, miss 2, 3 plain, and for the stem of the

2nd Thistle—12 chain, join it to the centre of the last 5 long of the Leaf; 14 chain, join it to the centre of the next 5 long of the Leaf; 12 chain, join it to the centre of the 5 treble of the Leaf; and to form the calyx of the 2nd Thistle, 13 chain, turn, miss 5, 1 single in the 6th stitch, 1 chain to cross the stem.

1st. round—10 treble in the round loop, 1 chain to cross the stem.

2nd round—2 treble in each stitch of the 1st round, 11 times; 1 chain to cross the stem.

3rd round.—4 plain, join it to the *8th plain* of the calyx of the 1st Thistle, 5 plain, and before finishing this Thistle, work 10 chain to form the

1st Small Thistle—Turn, and for the calyx, miss 4, 1 single in the 5th stitch, 1 chain to cross the stem.

1st round—8 plain in the round loop, 1 chain to cross the stem.

2nd round—2 treble in one stitch 5 times, turn back; and to form the top of the Thistle, 12 chain, 1 single in the last treble stitch, turn back; work 5 single on the 12 chain, (turn back; 6 chain, 1 single in the same treble stitch as before, turn back; and 5 single on the 6 chain 3 times), join it to the 3rd single stitch at the side of the top of 1st Thistle, (then 3 chain, miss 1, and 1 plain, 4 times in the 1 chain between the bars of the Thistle), 3 chain, 5 single down the side of the 5 chain, and to finish the calyx, 2 treble in one stitch 4 times; 1 single, 3 plain down the stem, and 4 plain on the calyx of the 2nd Large Thistle; and to form the Top, turn back; 16 chain, 1 single in the last plain stitch, turn back; 7 single on the 16 chain, turn back; 9 chain, 1 single in the same plain stitch of the calyx, turn back; 7 single on the 9 chain, (turn back; 9 chain, 1 single on the 12th plain stitch of the calyx, turn back; and 7 single on the 9 chain, 3 times), join it to the *5th treble* stitch of the calyx of the 1st Small Thistle, 5 chain, 1 plain in the 2 chain, and before finishing the Thistle, work the sprig of Shamrock, thus—12 chain for the

1st Shamrock Leaf,—Turn, miss 4, 1 single in the 5th stitch, turn back; (5 chain and 1 plain, 3 times in the round loop, turn back); miss 1, (1 plain, and 3 treble in the 5 chain, join it to the *3rd treble* stitch of the calyx of the small Thistle, then 2 treble and 1 plain in the same 5 chain,) (miss 1, 1 plain, 5 treble, and 1 plain in the 5 chain, twice), this finishes the Leaf; work 5 single down the stem, then 15 chain for the

2nd Shamrock Leaf,—Work as the 1st Leaf, joining it to the centre of the 3rd division of the 1st Leaf; when finished, work 5 single down the stem, then 10 chain for the

3rd Shamrock Leaf,—Work as the 1st Leaf, joining it to the centre of the 3rd division of the 2nd Leaf; when finished, work 5 single down the stem, 7 single down the centre stem, and to finish the top of the Thistle, (5 chain, miss 1, and 1 plain 4 times in the 2 chain 1,) 5 chain, 7 single down the side; then 29 chain for the stem of the

4th Leaf,—Turn, miss 4, 1 single in the 5th stitch, turn back; work (5 chain and 1 plain, 3 times in the round loop, turn back); miss 1, (1 plain, and 3 treble in the 5 chain, join it to the last 5 *chain* of the top of the Thistle, 2 treble, and 1 plain in the same 5 chain), (miss 1, 1 plain and 3 treble in the next 5 chain, join it to the centre of the 3rd division of the 3rd Shamrock Leaf, 2 treble, and 1 plain in the same 5 chain), miss 1, (1 plain, 5 treble, and 1 plain in the next 5 chain), then 5 single down the stem; and 16 chain for the

5th Leaf,—Turn, miss 4, 1 single in the 5th stitch, turn back; (5 chain and 1 plain in the round loop, 3 times, turn back); miss 1, (1 plain, and 3 treble in the 5 chain, join it to the centre of the 3rd division of the 4th Leaf, 2 treble, and 1 plain in the same 5 chain,) miss 1, 1 plain, and 3 treble in the next 5 chain, and before finishing the Leaf, work 12 chain for the

6th Leaf,—Work as the 1st Leaf, joining it to the centre of the 2nd division of the 3rd Leaf; when finished, work 3 single down the stem; then 14 chain for the

7th Leaf,—Work as the 1st Leaf, joining it to the centre of the 2nd division of the 6th Leaf; when finished, work 3 single down the stem; then 14 chain for the

8th Leaf,—Work as the 1st Leaf, joining it to the centre of the 3rd divison of the 7th Leaf; when finished, work 5 single down the stem; then 8 chain for the

9th Leaf,—Work as the 1st Leaf, joining it to the centre of the 3rd division of the 8th Leaf; when finished, work 3 single down the stem and 13 single down the centre stem; then 8 chain for the

10th Leaf,—Work as the 4th Leaf, joining it first, to the 7th *stitch* of the 13 single worked down the centre stem, and secondly, to the centre of 3rd division of the 9th Leaf; when finished, work 3 single down the stem, 1 single on the centre stem; and to finish the 5th Leaf, work 2 treble and 1 plain in the same 5 chain as before, miss 1, (1 plain, 5 treble and 1 plain in the next 5 chain), 5 single down the stem; then 8 chain for the

11th Leaf,—Work as the 1st Leaf, joining it to the centre of the 3rd division of the 5th Leaf; when finished, work 3 single down the stem, and 11 single down the centre stem; then 10 chain for the

12th Leaf,—Turn, miss 4, 1 single, turn back; (5 chain and 1 plain 3 times, in the round loop), turn back; (miss 1, 1 plain, 3 treble in the 5 chain, join it to the 3rd stitch of the 11 single, worked down the centre stem, 2 treble and 1 plain, in the same 5 chain), miss 1, 1 plain, and 3 treble in the next 5 chain, and before finishing this Leaf; work 12 chain for the

13th Leaf,—Work as the 12th Leaf, joining it to the centre of the 3rd division of the 11th Leaf, before finishing this Leaf; work for the stem of the next Leaf, 9 chain, turn, miss 1, 8 single on the 9 chain, then 12 chain for the

14th Leaf,—Miss 4, 1 single, turn back; (5 chain and 1 plain 3 times in the round loop), turn back; (miss 1, 1 plain, 5 treble, and 1 plain in the 5 chain, 3 times), 5 single down the stem; then 15 chain for the

15th Leaf,—Work as the 1st Leaf, joining it to the centre of the 3rd division of the 14th Leaf; when finished, work 5 single down the stem; then 10 chain for the

16th LEAF,—Work as the 1st Leaf, joining it to the centre of the 3rd division of the 15th Leaf; when finished, work 5 single down the stem, 7 single down the centre stem, and to finish the 13th Leaf, work 2 treble and 1 plain in the same 5 chain as before, miss 1, (1 plain, and 3 treble in the next 5 chain join it to the centre of the 3rd division of the 16th Leaf, then 2 treble, and 1 plain in the same 5 chain), 4 single down the stem; then 15 chain for the

th LEAF—Work as the 1st Leaf, joining it to the 1st treble stitch of the 3rd division of the 16th Leaf; when finished, work 5 single down the stem; then 10 chain for the

18th LEAF—Work as the 14th Leaf, when finished, work 5 single down the stem, and 8 single down the centre stem; and to finish the 12th Leaf, 2 treble and 1 plain in the same 5 chain as before, miss 1, (1 plain and 3 treble in the 5 chain, join it to the centre of the 3rd division of the 18th Leaf, 2 treble and 1 plain in the same 5 chain), then 5 single down the stem, 14 single down the long stem; and to finish the caylx of the Thistle, 10 plain, and 4 plain down the stem; then down the chain stitches attached to the Thistle Leaf, to form the uneven stem, work (2 plain, miss 2, 2 plain, 2 chain, 4 times), 2 plain, and for the

2nd SMALL THISTLE,—18 chain, and for the caylx, turn, miss 4, 1 single in the 5th stitch, 1 chain to cross the stem.

1st round.—8 plain in the round loop, 1 chain to cross the stem

2nd round.—(2 treble in 1 stitch 5 times), turn back; and to form the top of the Thistle, 12 chain, and 1 single in the last treble stitch, turn back; 5 single on the 12 chain, (turn back; 6 chain, 1 single in the same treble stitch as before, turn back; and work 5 single on the 6 chain 3 times), join it to the 1st 2 *chain* worked down the uneven stem of the large Thistle; (3 chain, miss 1, and 1 plain, 4 times in the 1 chain, between the bars of the Thistle); join to the 4th plain stitch of the calyx of the large Thistle; then 3 chain and 5 single down the side of the Thistle; to finish the calyx, (work 2 treble in 1 stitch 4 times), 1 single, and down the stem 4 single.

3rd SMALL THISTLE—15 chain, and for the calyx, turn, miss 4, 1 single in the 5th stitch, 1 chain to cross the stem.

1st round—8 plain in the round loop, 1 chain to cross the stem.

2nd round—(2 treble in 1 stitch twice), join it to the 3rd treble stitch of the calyx of the 2nd *small Thistle*, (2 treble in 1 stitch 3 times), turn back; and to form the top of the Thistle, 12 chain, 1 single in the last treble stitch, turn back; 5 single on the 12 chain (turn back; 6 chain, 1 single in the same treble stitch as before, turn back; and work 5 single on the 6 chain 3 times), join it to the 6th single stitch of the 14 single, worked down the long stem of the Shamrocks; then (3 chain, miss 1, and 1 plain 4 times in the 1 chain, between the bars of the Thistle); join it to the centre of the 2nd division of the 18th Shamrock; then 3 chain, 5 single down the side of the Thistle; and to finish the calyx (work 2 treble in 1 stitch 4 times), 1 single, and down the stem, 2 single, miss 2, 2 single.

4th SMALL THISTLE—17 chain, turn, and for the Calyx, miss 4, 1 single in the 5th stitch, 1 chain to cross the stem.

1st round—8 plain in the round loop, 1 chain to cross the stem.

2nd round—(2 treble in 1 stitch twice), join it to the 3rd treble stitch of the calyx of the 3rd Small Thistle, (2 treble in 1 stitch 3 times), turn back; and to form the top of the Thistle; 12 chain; 1 single in the last treble stitch, turn back; and work 5 single on the 12 chain, (turn back; 6 chain, 1 single in the same treble stitch as before, turn back; 5 single on the 6 chain 3 times), join it to the *centre* of the 1st *division* of the 18th shamrock; then 3 chain, 1 plain in the 1 chain, join it to the *centre* of the 3rd *division* of the 17th Shamrock; (then 3 chain, miss 1, and 1 plain 3 times, in the 1 chain between the bars of the Thistle) 3 chain, 5 single down the side of the 5 chain, and to finish the calyx, 2 treble in 1 stitch 4 times, 1 single, and down the stem, 2 single, 2 chain, 2 single, miss 2, 2 single, 2 chain, 2 single, then 3 single down the stem of the 3rd small Thistle; and down the stem of the 2nd small Thistle, 2 single, 2 chain, 2 single, miss 2, 2 single, and down the stem of the 2nd large Thistle, 2 plain, miss 2, 2 plain, 2 chain, 2 plain, miss 2, 2 plain, and 2 plain on the stem of the 1st Thistle Leaf; and for the

2nd Thistle Leaf—28 chain, turn, miss 1, 5 plain, 16 treble, 2 plain, turn, work 1 chain to cross the stem, and on the other side, work 2 plain, 2 chain, 3 long stitches, join it to the 4th plain stitch worked down the stem of the 2nd large Thistle; then 2 long, 2 chain, 1 plain, 2 chain, 3 long, join it to the 2 chain worked down the stem of the 2nd small Thistle; then 2 long, 2 chain, 1 plain, 1 chain, 5 treble, join it to the last 2 chain worked down the stem of the 4th small Thistle; 5 single, join it to the 1st 2 chain of the stem of the 4th small Thistle; turn, and down the other side of the Leaf, work 5 single (1 chain, 5 treble, 1 chain, and 1 plain 3 times), then 3 plain on the stem, 3 plain down the stem of the 1st Leaf, and 2 plain on the long stem, turn back; 3 chain, miss 11, 3 single on the wrong side of the treble stitches of the 2nd Leaf, 3 chain, miss 5, 3 single on the Leaf as before; 3 chain, miss 5, 3 single on the Leaf; 7 chain, 1 treble on the calyx of the 4th small Thistle; 7 chain, 1 plain in the last 3 chain at the top of the 4th small Thistle; 7 chain, 1 plain on the 2nd division of the 17th Shamrock; 7 chain, 1 plain on the 2nd division of the 16th Shamrock; 7 chain, 1 plain on the 2nd division of the 15th Shamrock, this finishes the 1st pattern.

SECOND PATTERN.

Make a chain of 21 stitches, turn, miss 1, 20 single on the chain, then 72 chain for the long, stem, and for the

First Rose Leaf—Turn, miss 2, 3 plain, (2 chain, miss 2, and 1 treble 4 times), 2 chain miss 2, 1 plain, turn, leaving the chain stitches for the stem, work 1 chain to cross it; then on the other side of the foundation, 7 chain, miss 1, 1 plain in the 2 chain of foundation, miss 1, 1 plain in the next 2 chain, turn back, and missing the 2 plain, work 5 treble and 1 plain in the 7 chain, turn back; 9 chain, 1 plain in the same 2 chain of the foundation as before, miss 1, 1 plain in the next 2 chain, turn back, and missing the 2 plain, work 7 treble, and 1 plain in the 9 chain, turn back; then join it to the 32nd *chain stitch* of the long stem, counting from the commencement; then for the Leaf, 7 chain, 1 plain in the 2 chain as before, miss 1, 1 plain, turn back; 5 treble and 1 plain in the 7 chain, turn back; join it to the 25th *chain stitch* of the long stem, then 5 chain, 1 plain in the 2 chain, miss 1, 1 plain, turn back; 3 treble and 1 plain in the 5 chain, turn back; 2 chain, miss 1, 3 treble on the 3 plain, and in the 2 chain at the point of the Leaf, (work 1 plain, 1 chain, join it to the 4th *chain stitch* of the long stem, and on the Leaf, 1 chain, and 1 plain). Work the other side to correspond, thus :—3 treble, 5 chain, 1 plain in the 2 chain, miss 1, 1 plain, turn back; and missing the 2 plain, work 3 treble and 1 plain in the 5 chain, turn back; 7 chain, 1 plain, miss 1, 1 plain, turn back; work 5 treble and 1, plain in the 7 chain, turn back; join it to the *centre* of the 2nd *division* of the 14th Shamrock, 9 chain, 1 plain, miss 1, 1 plain, turn back; 7 treble, and 1 plain in the 9 chain, turn back; 7 chain, 1 plain, miss 1, 1 plain, turn back; 5 treble and 1 plain in the 7 chain, turn back; 5 chain, 1 plain, and 5 single down the stem, this finishes the Leaf.

SECOND ROSE LEAF—32 chain, turn, miss 2, 3 plain, (2 chain, miss 2, and 1 treble 4 times), 2 chain, miss 2, 1 plain, turn, and leaving the chain stitches for the stem, work 1 chain to cross it; then on the other side of the foundation, 7 chain, miss 1, 1 plain in the 2 chain of foundation, miss 1, 1 plain in the next 2 chain, turn back, and missing the 2 plain, work 5 treble, and 1 plain in the 7 chain, turn back; 9 chain, 1 plain in the same 2 chain miss 1, 1 plain, turn back; 7 treble, and 1 plain in the 9 chain, turn back; join it to the *centre* of the 1st *division* of the 14th Shamrock, then 7 chain, 1 plain in the 2 chain as before, miss 1, 1 plain, turn back; 5 treble and 1 plain in the 7 chain, turn back; 5 chain, 1 plain in the 2 chain, miss 1, 1 plain, turn back; 3 treble, and 1 plain in the 5 chain, turn back; join it to the stem of the 14th Shamrock; 2 chain, miss 1, 3 treble on the 3 plain, and in the 2 chain at the point of the Leaf, (work 1 plain, 1 chain, join it to the *centre* of the 2nd *division* of the 11th Shamrock, then 1 chain, 1 plain), and to work the other side, turn, 3 treble, join it to the *centre* of the 3rd *division* of the 10th Shamrock, 5 chain, 1 plain in the 2 chain, miss 1, 1 plain, turn back, and missing the 2 plain, work 3 treble and 1 plain in the 5 chain, turn back; 7 chain, 1 plain, miss 1, 1 plain, turn back; work 5 treble and 1 plain in the 7 chain, turn back; join it to the *centre* of the 3rd *division* of the 9th Shamrock, 9 chain, 1 plain, miss 1, 1 plain, turn back; 7 treble, and 1 plain in the 9 chain, turn back; 7 chain, 1 plain, miss 1, 1 plain, turn back; 5 treble and 1 plain in the 7 chain, turn back; 5 chain, 1 plain, and 5 single down the stem.

3rd LEAF.—25 chain, turn, miss 2, 3 plain, (2 chain, miss 2 and 1 treble 4 times), 2 chain miss 2, 1 plain, turn, and leaving the chain stitches for the stem, work 1 chain to cross it, join it to the *last 5 chain* of the 2nd Leaf; then 7 chain, miss 1, 1 plain in the 2 chain, miss 1, 1 plain in the next 2 chain, turn back, and missing the 2 plain, work 5 treble and 1 plain in the 7 chain, turn back; 9 chain, 1 plain in the same 2 chain as before, miss 1, 1 plain in the next 2 chain, turn back, and missing the 2 plain, work 7 treble and 1 plain in the 9 chain, turn back; joinit to the *centre* of the 2nd *division* of the 9th Shamrock; 7 chain, 1 plain in the 2 chain as before, miss 1, 1 plain, turn back; 5 treble and 1 plain in the 7 chain, turn back; 5 chain, 1 plain in the 2 chain, miss 1, 1 plain, turn back; 3 treble and 1 plain in the 5 chain, turn back; 2 chain, miss 1, 3 treble on the 3 plain, and in the 2 chain at the point of the Leaf, (work 1 plain, 2 chain, and 1 plain), turn, and work the other side to correspond as in the 3rd Rose Leaf of the 1st Pattern, commencing from the * * and work the Small Leaf, Bud, Thistles, and Shamrocks to the end of the 1st pattern.

Repeat this pattern 3 times more, but in the *last pattern* to form the side, after the working half of the 5th Shamrock Leaf; omit the 6th, 7th, 8th, 9th, and 10th Leaves. Finish the 5th Leaf as directed at the end of the 10th Leaf, repeat as the 11th, 12th, and 13th Leaves; but after working the half of that Leaf, omit the 14th, 15th, and 16th Leaves; finish the 13th Leaf as directed at the end of the 16th, *without joining* it; then work the 17th Leaf, joining it to the 13th Leaf, and the remainder of the pattern; when finished, work a row along the chain stitches for the Band, thus—miss 1, 7 treble, repeat to the end, and fasten off.

COLLAR.—LILY OF THE VALLEY.

Jno. & Wm. Taylor's Crochet Thread, No. 12; *Needle, No.* 24, *Bell Gauge.*

1st LEAF—Make a chain of 41 stitches, turn, miss 4, 1 plain, 2 chain, miss 2, 1 plain, 2 chain, miss 2, 1 treble, (2 chain, miss 2, and 1 long stitch 7 times), 2 chain, miss 2, 1 treble, 2 chain, miss 2, 1 plain, turn, and leaving 6 chain for the stem, work 1 chain to cross it, and on the other side, (miss 1, 1 treble, 3 long, 1 treble and 1 plain, these 6 stitches are all to be worked in the 2 chain of the foundation, repeat 9 times more), then (miss 1, 5 treble and 1 plain in the 2 chain twice), turn, and work the other side to correspond, thus—(miss 1, 5 treble and 1 plain in the 2 chain), (miss 1, 1 treble, 3 long, 1 treble and 1 plain, all in the 2 chain 10 times); then 2 plain on the stem, this finishes the Leaf.

For the 1st FLOWER—20 chain, turn, miss 5, 1 single in the 6th stitch to form a round loop, 1 chain to cross the stem, (5 chain and 1 plain twice in the round loop), 2 chain, join it to the centre of the 10th *division* of the Leaf counting from the point, 2 chain, 1 plain in the round loop, (5 chain and 1 plain 3 times in the round loop) 2 single down the stem, leaving 12 chain for the centre stem.

2nd FLOWER—14 chain, turn, miss 5, 1 single, 1 chain to cross the stem, (5 chain and 1 plain twice in the round loop), 2 chain, join it to the centre of the *8th division* of the Leaf, 2 chain, 1 plain in the round loop, (5 chain and 1 plain 3 times in the round loop), 2 single down the stem, leaving 6 chain for the centre stem.

Repeat as the 2nd Flower 3 times more, joining them to every other division of the Leaf.

6th FLOWER—11 chain, turn, miss 5, 1 single, 1 chain to cross the stem, 2 chain, join it to the last 5 *chain* of the 5th Flower; 2 chain, 1 plain in the round loop, (5 chain and 1 plain in the round loop 5 times), 3 single down the stem, leaving 1 chain for the centre stem.

7th FLOWER—8 chain, work as the 6th Flower, joining it to the last 5 *chain* of the 6th Flower, then 2 single down the stem, and 5 single down the centre stem.

8th FLOWER—8 chain, turn, miss 5, 1 single, 1 chain to cross the stem, (5 chain and 1 plain in the round loop 6 times), 2 single down the stem, and 6 single down the centre stem. Work 3 Flowers more as the 8th; and leaving 8 chain for the band, work the

2nd LEAF—47 chain, turn, miss 4, 1 plain, 2 chain, miss 2, 1 plain, 2 chain, miss 2, 1 treble, (2 chain, miss 2 and 1 long 7 times), 2 chain, miss 2, 1 treble, 2 chain, miss 2, 1 plain, turn, work 1 chain to cross the stem; and on the other side, *, miss 1, (1 treble, 3 long, 1 treble and 1 plain, these 6 stitches are all worked in the 2 chain of the foundation), miss 1, (1 treble, 2 long in the next 2 chain, join it to the 4th 5 *chain* of the 11th, or last Flower; then 1 long, 1 treble, and 1 plain in the same 2 chain as before); repeat from * 4 times more, joining every other division of the Leaf to the opposite Flower; (miss 1, 5 treble and 1 plain in the 2 chain twice), turn, and work the other side to correspond, thus—miss 1, 5 treble and 1 plain in the 2 chain, (miss 1, 1 treble, 3 long, 1 treble and 1 plain, all in the 2 chain 10 times); then 2 plain on the stem.

Repeat the Flowers and 2nd Leaf 17 times more; then 3 chain, join it to the centre of the last division of the Leaf.

BAND FOR RIBBON.

1st row—3 plain on the chain stitches, 12 chain, turn, (miss 4, 1 plain, 2 chain, miss 2, 1 treble, 2 chain, miss 2, 1 plain on the 12 chain), turn, 1 chain to cross the stem; and on the other side 10 chain, miss 7, 1 plain in the 4 chain at the point, turn, 10 chain, miss 7, 1 single on the stem; turn, miss 1, (1 treble, 15 long, 1 treble and 1 plain in the 10 chain), turn, miss 1, (1 plain, 1 treble, 15 long and 1 treble in the 10 chain), and 1 single on the stem *, then 15 plain on the chain stitches left at the Flowers and Leaves; 12 chain, turn, miss 4, 1 plain, 2 chain, miss 2, 1 treble, 2 chain, miss 2, 1 plain, turn, 1 chain to cross the stem, 10 chain, miss 7, 1 plain in the 4 chain, turn, 10 chain, miss 7, 1 single on the stem, miss 1, (1 treble and 8 long in the 10 chain; join it to the 8th *long* stitch of the other pattern; 7 long, 1 treble and 1 plain in the same 10 chain), turn, miss 1, (1 plain, 1 treble, 15 long and 1 treble in the 10 chain); 1 single on the stem; repeat from *, end with 1 plain, join it to the 1st division of the 1st Leaf; turn back, work 19 single up the side of the last pattern to the top.

2nd row—14 chain, 1 plain on the 2 plain at the top of the patterns in the 1st row; repeat.

3rd row—Plain, on the chain stitches of the 2nd row. Fasten off. The ribbon should be run in this band, so as only to cover the stripe in the centre of each pattern.

BABY'S CAP.

HEAD PIECE.

Jno. and Wm. Taylor's Crochet Thread, No. 12; Needle, No. 23, Bell Gauge, or to make a larger size, Crochet Thread, No. 10; Needle, No. 22.

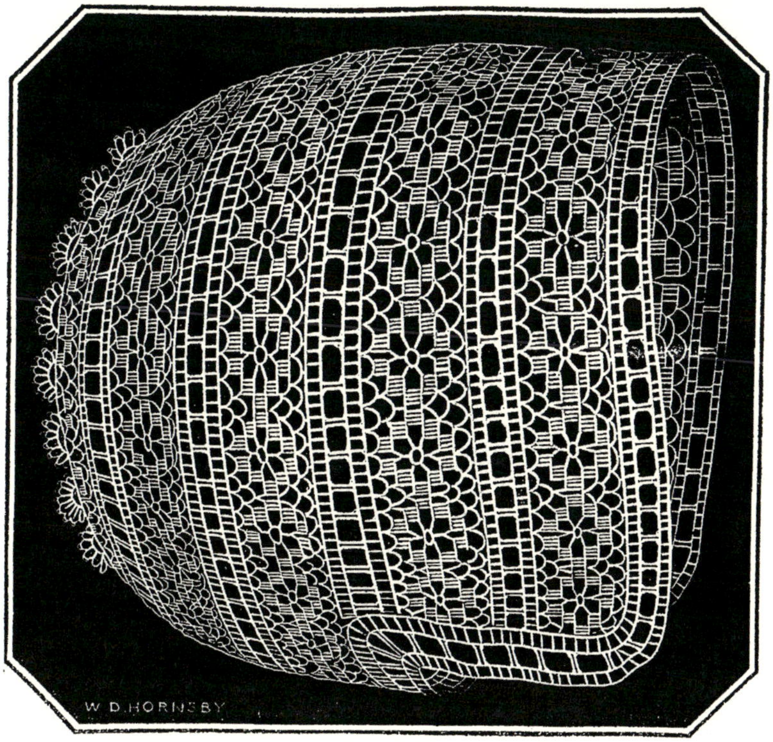

Make a chain of 258 stitches, cut off the thread at the end of each row. [The proper method to commence and end a row—*See 2nd Series.*]

1st row—3 chain, 1 plain in the 1st chain stitch *, 5 chain, miss 3, 1 plain, repeat from *; end with 3 chain. Cut off the thread and draw it through.

2nd—1 plain in the 1st stitch of the 3 chain worked at the commencement of the 1st row * 5 chain, miss 5, 1 plain in the 5 chain, 3 chain, miss 3, 5 treble in the 5 chain, 1 chain miss 1, 5 treble in the 5 chain, 3 chain, miss 3, 1 plain in the 5 chain; repeat from *, end with 3 chain, miss 5, 1 plain in the last stitch of the 3 chain worked at the end of the 1st row.

3rd—1 chain, 1 plain in the 5 chain, *, 3 chain, miss 3, 5 treble in the 3 chain, 3 chain, miss 5, 1 plain in the 1 chain, 3 chain, miss 5, 5 treble in the 3 chain, 3 chain, miss 3, 1 plain in the 5 chain, repeat from *, end with 1 chain.

4th—1 plain in the 1st chain stitch, *, 1 chain, miss 1, 5 treble in the 3 chain, 5 chain, miss 7, 1 plain in the 3 chain, 1 chain, miss 1, 1 plain in the 3 chain, 5 chain, miss 7, 5 treble in the 3 chain, repeat from *, end 1 chain, miss 1, 1 plain.

5th—3 chain, 1 plain in the 1 chain *, 3 chain, miss 5, 5 treble in the 5 chain, 3 chain, miss 3, 1 plain in the 1 chain, 3 chain, miss 3, 5 treble in the 5 chain, 3 chain, miss 5, 1 plain in the 1 chain, repeat from *, end 3 chain.

6th—1 plain in the 1st stitch of the 3 chain *, 5 chain, miss 5, 1 plain in the 3 chain, 3 chain, miss 5, 5 treble in the 3 chain, 1 chain, miss 1, 5 treble in the 3 chain, 3 chain, miss 5, 1 plain in the 3 chain, repeat from *, end 3 chain, miss 5, 1 plain.

7th—3 chain, 1 plain in the 5 chain, *, 5 chain, miss 5, 1 plain in the 3 chain, 5 chain, miss

5, 1 plain in the 1 chain, 5 chain, miss 5, 1 plain in the 3 chain, 5 chain, miss 5, 1 plain in the 5 chain, repeat from *, end 3 chain.

8th—1 plain in the 1st stitch of the 3 chain, *, 3 chain, miss 5, 1 plain in the 5 chain, repeat.

9th—1 treble on the 1st stitch, *, 1 chain, miss 1, 1 treble, repeat from *.

10th—3 treble, *, 6 chain, miss 6, 2 treble, repeat from *

11th—Same as the 9th row, repeat from 1st row, once more; then for the

BACK.

Work 110 chain, make it *round* by working 2 single on the 1st 2 stitches of the last *row*, and repeat the pattern in rounds, with the following variations, thus—

1st round—5 chain, miss 3, 1 plain, repeat, at the end 2 stitches will be left.

2nd—Repeat the Pattern from * in the 2nd row; at the end 5 chain, miss 5, 1 plain in the 5 chain.

3rd—As the 3rd row, from *, omitting the 1 chain at the end.

4th—As the 4th row, from *, ending the same.

5th—As the 5th row, from *, omitting the end stitches.

6th—As the 6th row, from *, end with 5 chain, miss 4, 1 plain in the 5 chain.

7th—As the 7th row, from *, omitting the end stitches.

8th—3 chain, miss 5, 1 plain in the 5 chain, repeat, end with 3 chain, miss 3, 1 single in the 1st 3 chain.

9th—2 chain, 1 treble, *, 1 chain, miss 1, 1 treble; repeat from *, end with 1 chain, miss 1 1 single in the 1st 2 chain.

10th—3 chain, 1 treble *, 6 chain, miss 6, 2 treble; repeat from *, end with 8 chain, miss 8, 1 single in the 1st 3 chain.

11th—Same as 9th round; repeat these 11 rounds once more; then repeat the first 7 rounds, making in all 29 rounds.

30th—2 chain, miss 5, 1 plain in the 5 chain, repeat, and fasten off.

Then commencing at the foundation chain, work 3 rounds, thus—

1st round—1 chain, miss 1, 1 treble, along the front, sides, and back.

2nd—As the 10th round.

3rd—As the 11th round. Fasten off, and run narrow ribbon through each of the open rows.

BABY'S CAP CROWN.

Jno. and Wm. Taylor's Crochet Thread No. 12 ; *Needle, No.* 23, *Bell Gauge.*

Work a chain of 10 stitches and make it round.

1st round—5 chain, and 1 plain in the foundation chain, 16 times.

2nd—5 chain, miss 5, and 1 plain in the 5 chain, repeat.

3rd—6 chain, miss 11, (1 plain, 5 chain, 1 plain, both these plain stitches in the same 5 chain), repeat 7 times more.

4th—5 chain, miss 8, (3 treble, 3 chain and 3 treble, these 6 treble in the 5 chain), repeat.

5th—5 chain, miss 5, 1 plain in the 5 chain, 5 chain, miss 5, (3 treble, 3 chain and 3 treble, these 6 treble, are all to be worked in the 3 chain), repeat.

6th—5 chain, miss 5, 1 plain in the 5 chain, 5 chain, miss 5, 1 plain in the 5 chain, 5 chain, miss 5, (3 treble, 3 chain and 3 treble, these 6 treble in the 3 chain), repeat.

7th—1 chain, miss 5, 1 plain in the 5 chain, 3 chain, miss 3, 9 treble in the 5 chain, 3 chain, miss 3, 1 plain in the 5 chain, 1 chain, miss 5, (3 treble, 3 chain and 3 treble in the 3 chain as before), repeat.

8th—3 chain, miss 5, 6 treble in the 3 chain, 4 chain, miss 4, 1 plain in the centre of the 9 treble, 4 chain, miss 4, 6 treble in the 3 chain, 3 chain, miss 5, (3 treble, 3 chain and 3 treble in the 3 chain as before), repeat.

9th—1 chain, miss 3, 6 treble in the 3 chain, 3 chain, miss 7, 1 plain in the 4 chain, 3 chain, miss 3, 1 plain in the 4 chain, 3 chain, miss 7, 6 treble in the 3 chain, 1 chain, miss 3, 7 treble in the 3 chain, repeat; at the end 1 chain, miss 3, 1 plain in the 1st 1 chain.

10th—6 chain, miss 6, 1 plain in the 3 chain, 6 chain, miss 4, 1 plain in the 3 chain, 6 chain, miss 4, 1 plain in the 3 chain, 6 chain, miss 6, 1 plain in the 1 chain, 6 chain, miss 3, 1 plain in the centre of the 7 treble, 6 chain, miss 3, 1 plain in the 1 chain, repeat.

11th—7 chain, miss 3, 1 plain in the 6 chain, * 7 chain, miss 6, 1 plain in the 6 chain repeat from * end 7 chain, miss 7, 1 plain in the 1st 7 chain.

12th —5 chain, miss 7, 1 plain in the 7 chain, 3 chain, miss 4, 7 treble in the 7 chain, 3 chain, miss 4, 1 plain in the 7 chain, repeat, end with 5 chain, miss 7, 1 plain in the 5 chain.

13th—3 chain, miss 3, 5 treble in the 3 chain, 3 chain, miss 3, 1 plain in the centre of the 7 treble, 3 chain, miss 3, 5 treble in the 3 chain, 3 chain, miss 3, 1 plain in the 5 chain, repeat.

14th—1 chain, miss 1, 5 treble in the 3 chain, 5 chain, miss 7, 1 plain in the 3 chain, 1 chain, miss 1, 1 plain in the 3 chain, 5 chain, miss 7, 5 treble in the 3 chain, repeat, end 1 chain, miss 1, 1 plain in the 1 chain.

15th—3 chain, miss 5, 5 treble in the 5 chain, 3 chain, miss 3, 1 plain in the 1 chain, 3 chain, miss 3, 5 treble in the 5 chain, 3 chain, miss 5, 1 plain in the 1 chain, repeat.

16th—5 chain, miss 5, 1 plain in the 3 chain, 3 chain, miss 5, 5 treble in the 3 chain, 1 chain, miss 1, 5 treble in the 3 chain, 3 chain, miss 5, 1 plain in the 3 chain; repeat.

17th—5 chain, miss 5, 1 plain in the 5 chain, 5 chain, miss 5, 1 plain in the 3 chain, 5 chain, miss 5, 1 plain in the 1 chain, 5 chain, miss 5, 1 plain in the 3 chain; repeat.

18th—6 chain, miss 5, 1 plain in the 5 chain, repeat.

19th—3 chain, miss 6, 1 plain in the 6 chain, 7 chain, turn, miss 6, 1 single in the 1st stitch of the 7 chain to form a round loop, miss 4, 1 treble in the 6 chain of the 18th round, (7 chain, turn, miss 6, 1 single in the 1st stitch of the 7 chain, 1 treble in the same 6 chain as before, 5 times), 7 chain, turn, miss 6, 1 single as before, miss 4, 1 plain in the next 6 chain, 3 chain, miss 6, 1 plain in the next 6 chain, repeat.

20th—3 chain, miss 3, 1 plain in the 3 chain, (3 chain, miss 3, 1 plain, 5 chain and 1 plain, both the plain stitches in the round loop of the 19th round, 3 chain, miss 3 and 1 plain on the 1 treble 6 times), (3 chain, miss 3, 1 plain, 5 chain and 1 plain both in the round loop as before), 3 chain, miss 3, 1 plain in the 3 chain, repeat, fasten off, and sew it to the Head piece at the 18th round.

EDGING FOR CAP.

Jno. & Wm. Taylor's Crochet Thread. No. 12; Needle, No. 23, Bell Gauge.

Make a chain of 801 stitches for each yard, or 16 stitches for each pattern.

1st row—3 chain, 1 plain in the 1st stitch of the foundation *, 5 chain, miss 3, 1 plain; repeat from *, end with 3 chain. Cut off the thread.

2nd row—1 plain in the 1st stitch of the 3 chain, *, 5 chain, miss 5, 1 plain in the 5 chain; repeat from *, ending with the plain stitch in the last stitch of the 3 chain.

3rd row—3 chain, 1 plain in the 5 chain, *, 5 chain, miss 5, 1 plain in the 5 chain; repeat from *, end with 3 chain. Repeat the 2nd, 3rd, 4th, 5th, 6th, and 7th rows as in the Head Piece of the Cap.

10th row—4 chain, 1 plain in the 1st stitch of the 3 chain, *, 6 chain, miss 5, 1 plain in the 5 chain; repeat from *, end with 4 chain.

11th row—2 chain, 1 plain in the 1st stitch of the 4 chain, *, 7 chain, turn, miss 6, 1 single in the 1st stitch of the 7 chain to form a round loop, miss 4, 1 treble in the 6 chain, (then 7 chain, turn, miss 6, 1 single in the 1st stitch of the 7 chain, 1 treble in the same 6 chain as before 5 times); 7 chain, turn, miss 6, 1 single in the 1st stitch of the 7 chain as before, miss 4, 1 plain in the next 6 chain of the 10th round; 3 chain, miss 6, 1 plain in the next 6 chain, 3 chain, miss 6, 1 plain in the next 6 chain, repeat from *, and end with working the 7 round loops to finish the pattern.

12th row—1 plain on the 2 chain, *, (3 chain, miss 3, 1 plain, 5 chain and 1 plain; both these plain stitches in the round loop of the last row, 3 chain, miss 3, 1 plain on the 1 treble 6 times), (3 chain, miss 3, 1 plain, 5 chain and 1 plain; both these plain stitches in the round loop as before), 3 chain, miss 3, 1 plain, in the 3 chain, 3 chain, miss 3, 1 plain in the 3 chain; repeat from * to the end.

CROCHET HONITON COLLAR.

Jno. & Wm. Taylor's Crochet Thread, No. 12; Needle, No. 24, Bell Gauge.

To form this Collar, work 9 of the following Sprigs and 34 Flowers of the Border; and for the band, make a chain of about 290 stitches, and work a treble row along it. After they are worked, cut the shape of a Collar in coloured paper, and tack the Band, Sprig, and

Border on it; the right side facing the paper, in the form as shown in the engraving. Then place Brussels net over the work, and with a fine needle and thread, run the edges of the Sprigs and Band to the net; but in running the net to the Border, it should be attached only by the Leaves and *half* or lower portion of the Flowers, which will leave the other part to form the edge of the Collar. When finished, take it off the paper, and carefully cut off the edges of the net close to the Band and Border.

HONITON SPRIG.

CORN-FLOWER.

Jno. & Wm. Taylor's Crochet Thread, No. 12 *or* 16; *Needles, No.* 24, *Bell Gauge.*

Make a chain of 14 stitches for the

1st LEAF—Turn, miss 1, 1 plain, 3 treble, 2 single, then 19 chain for the

2nd LEAF—Turn, miss 1, 1 single, 2 plain, 1 treble, 4 long, 1 treble, 1 plain, 2 single; then 17 chain for the

FLOWER—Turn, miss 5, 1 single in the 5th stitch to form a round loop, 1 chain to cross the stem.

1st *row*—*1 plain in the round loop, 8 chain, turn, miss 5, 1 single in the 6th stitch to form a round loop, 2 chain,1 plain in the round loop; repeat from * 4 times more, then 7 plain down the stem to form the calyx; 1 chain to cross the stem, and on the other side 1 plain, 4 treble, 1 plain, 1 single.

2nd *row* of the FLOWER—*3 chain, miss 3, 1 plain in the round loop of the 1st row, (4 chain and 1 plain, 4 times in the same round loop), 3 chain, miss 3, 1 plain, between the 2 plain in the 1st row; repeat from * 4 times more; then down the calyx, 1 single, 1 plain, 4 treble, 1 plain. This finishes the Flower—3 single down the stem, 4 single down the stem of the Leaf, and for the

3rd LEAF—13 chain, and work as the 2nd Leaf; when finished work 2 single down the stem of the 2nd Leaf, and 7 single down the stem of the 1st Leaf. Fasten off.

BORDER FOR COLLARS, HANDKERCHIEFS, VEILS, &c.

CORN-FLOWER PATTERN.

Jno. & Wm. Taylor's Crochet Thread, No. 12 *or* 16; *Needle, No.* 24, *Bell Gauge.*

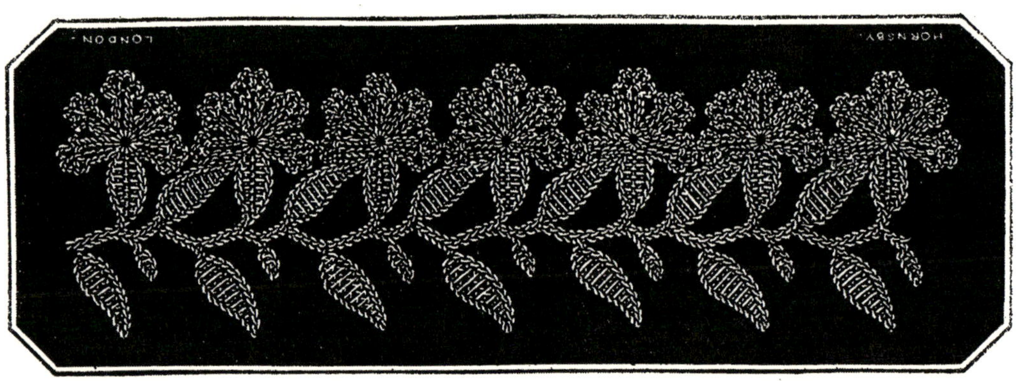

Make a chain of 21 stitches, and for the

1st FLOWER—Work as the Flower and calyx in the Honiton sprig, when finished, work 2 single down the stem, and for the

The LEAF—*23 chain, join it to the *last* 3 *chain* of the Flower, turn, miss 1, 1 single, 2 plain 1 treble, 4 long, 1 treble, 1 plain, 2 single, leaving 10 chain for the centre stem.

2nd FLOWER—21 chain, turn, miss 5, 1 single in the 6th stitch, 1 chain to cross the stem.

1st row—(1 plain in the round loop, 8 chain, turn, miss 5, 1 single in the 6th stitch, 2 chain 1 plain in the round loop, repeat 4 times more); then 7 plain down the stem for the calyx; 1 chain to cross it, and on the other side, 1 plain, 4 treble, 1 plain, 1 single.

2nd row of the flower, 3 chain, miss 3, 1 plain in the round loop of the 1st row, (4 chain and 1 plain twice in the same round loop, 2 chain, join it to the 2nd 4 *chain* worked in the last round loop of the 1st Flower; then 2 chain, 1 plain in the same round loop of the 2nd Flower, 4 chain, 1 plain in the same round loop), 3 chain, miss 3, 1 plain between the 2 plain of the 1st row, (3 chain, miss 3, 1 plain in the next round loop, 4 chain and 1 plain in the same round loop, 3 chain, miss 3, 1 plain between the 2 plain; repeat 3 times more); then down the calyx, 1 single, 1 plain, 4 treble, 1 plain and 2 single down the stem, leaving 5 chain for the centre stem; repeat from * until the required length is worked; then work 7 chain for the centre stem, turn, miss 1, 1 plain **; and for the

2nd LEAF—13 chain, turn, miss 1, 1 single, 2 plain, 1 treble, 4 long, 1 treble, 1 plain, 2 single; then 8 single down the centre stem, and for the

SMALL LEAF—6 chain, turn, miss 1, 1 plain, 3 treble, 1 single; then 7 single down the centre stem; repeat from ** to the end.

EDGING.—No. 1.

Jno. & Wm. Taylor's Crochet Thread, No. 4, or No. 6. Needle, No. 20 or 21, Bell Gauge.

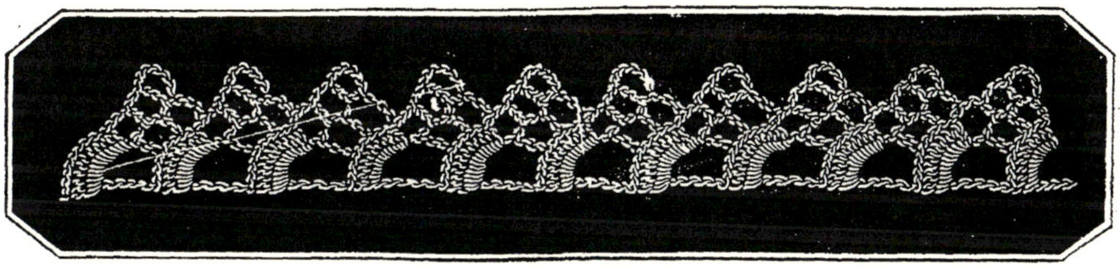

This edging is worked backwards and forwards the depth of the Pattern. Make a chain of 11 stitches, and work 1 plain in the 1st chain stitch to make it round, then work 11 treble in the round, turn back.

1st—10 chain, miss 4, 1 treble, 3 chain, miss 2, 1 treble, 3 chain, miss 2, 1 treble, turn back.

2nd—5 chain, miss 2, 1 treble in the 3 chain, 3 chain, miss 3, 1 treble in the next 3 chain, 3 chain, miss 2, 11 treble in the 10 chain. Repeat these 2 rows, until sufficient is worked.

EDGING.—No. 2.

Jno. & Wm. Taylor's Crochet Thread, No. 4, or No. 6; Needle, No. 20, or 21, Bell Gauge.

This edging is worked backwards and forwards the depth of the Pattern. Make a chain of 13 stitches.

1st row.—Miss 6, 1 plain, 5 chain, miss 4, 3 treble in one stitch, 3 chain, 3 treble in one stitch, this row forms the foundation, and is not repeated.

2nd—5 chain, miss 3, (3 treble in the 3 chain of last row, 5 chain, turn, miss 4, 1 single in the 1st stitch of the 5 chain to form a round loop, then 3 treble in the same 3 chain as before), 1 chain, miss 5, 1 plain in the 5 chain, 2 chain, miss 3, (1 treble, 1 chain, and 1 treble, both these treble stitches in the 6 chain.)

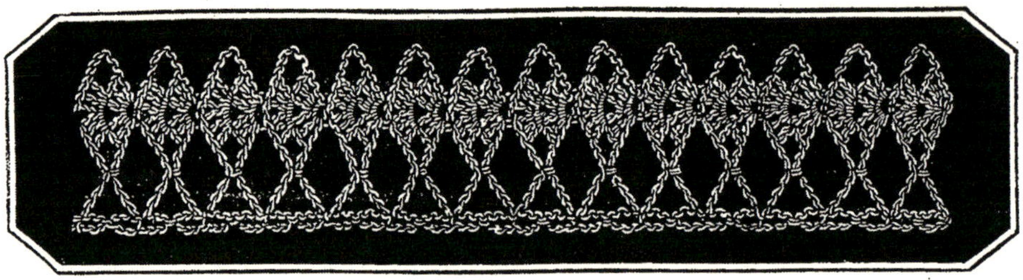

3rd row—6 chain, miss 1, 1 plain in the 1 chain, 5 chain, miss 8, (3 treble, 3 chain, 3 treble, these 6 treble in the round loop of 2nd row.) Repeat the 2 last rows, until sufficient is worked.

INSERTION FOR SHIRT FRONTS, ETC.

Jno. & Wm. Taylor's Crochet Thread, No. 16; *Needle, No.* 23, *Bell Gauge.*

Make a chain 1267 stitches for each yard, or 14 stitches for each Pattern, and 7 over for the Edge.

1st row.—1 single stitch,* 4 chain, miss 4, 3 single stitches; repeat from *, end with 4 chain miss 4, 1 single stitch. This forms the centre of the Insertion, and the following rows are worked on each side of it; turn, and on the other side of the foundation work the

2nd.—(5 chain, and 1 plain in the 4 chain 5 times), *, miss the 3 single stitches, 5 plain in the 4 chain, miss the 3 single, 1 plain in the 4 chain, (5 chain and 1 plain in the same 4 chain 5 times); repeat from * to the end, turn, and repeat this row on the other side, working in the same spaces.

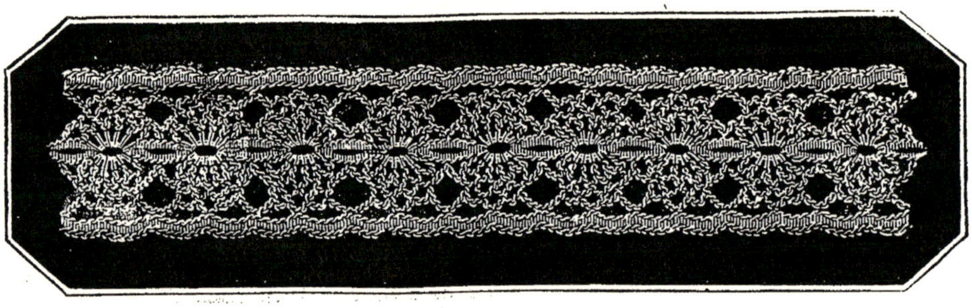

3rd.—(3 chain, miss 5 and 1 plain in the 5 chain 5 times),* 3 chain, miss 5, 1 plain in the centre stitch of the 5 plain in the last row, (3 chain, miss 5, and 1 plain in the 5 chain 5 times); repeat from *, and work the other side the same.

4th.—5 chain, miss 7, 1 plain in the 3 chain of the last row, (3 chain, miss 3 and 1 plain in the 3 chain 3 times,) *, 5 chain, miss 11, 1 plain in the 3 chain, (3 chain, miss 3, and 1 plain in the 3 chain 3 times); repeat from *, and work the other side the same.

5th.—7 chain, miss 3, 1 plain in the 5 chain of the last row, *, 7 chain, miss 8, 1 plain in the 3 chain of last row, 7 chain, miss 8, 1 plain in the 5 chain; repeat from *, and work the other side the same.

6th.—Miss 1, and 7 plain on the 7 chain of last row; repeat, and work the other side the same. Fasten off.

FINIS.

THE CROCHET BOOK,

SIXTH SERIES:

CONTAINING

D'OYLEYS AND ANTI-MACASSARS.

BY

MDLLE. RIEGO DE LA BRANCHARDIERE.

Second Edition--10,000.

LONDON:
SIMPKIN, MARSHALL, AND CO;
ACKERMANN, STRAND; OLIVER AND BOYD, EDINBURGH;
ALL BOOKSELLERS, AND BERLIN WAREHOUSES.
1849.

CONTENTS.

INTRODUCTORY REMARKS.

THE single stitches at the *end* of the rounds in the following directions, are to be worked through both sides of the chain stitches of the preceding round. This is necessary to be observed for it makes the work neater, preventing the *beginning* and *ends* of the Pattern from being perceived. Also when directed—" To turn back and work 3 or more single on the last stitches of the round ;" that is done to bring the thread to the centre of the chain stitches, its proper place to commence the next round.

TO MAKE VARIOUS SIZED D'OYLEYS, ETC.

1st Size—7½ inches in diameter—Use Jno. and Wm. Taylor's Crochet Thread, No. 000; Needle, No. 16, Bell Gauge.

2nd Size—6½ inches in diameter—Taylor's Crochet Thread, No. 0; or Taylor's Drab Mecklenburgh, No. 1; Needle, No. 18, Bell Gauge.

3rd Size—5 inches in diameter—Taylor's Crochet Thread, No. 2; Needle, No. 20, Bell Gauge.

For Baby's Cap Crowns—Taylor's Crochet Thread, No. 12; Needle, No. 23, Bell Gauge.

For Ornamental Mats, 8 inches in diameter—Crochet Twist, Colours as directed.

For Table Covers, &c.—Work the Anti-macassar Patterns in Crochet Floss, or Single Berlin Wool.

For the Terms used—See the 1st, 2nd, and 3rd SERIES.

THE CROCHET BOOK.

SIXTH SERIES.

CONTAINING

D'OYLEYS AND ANTI-MACASSARS.

D'OYLEY—No. 1.

Jno. and Wm. Taylor's Crochet Thread, No. 000; *Needle, No.* 17, *Bell Gauge.*

Work a chain of 7 stitches, and make it round.

1st round—11 chain and 1 plain in the foundation chain 7 times, then 5 single stitches on the 1st 11 chain.

2nd—(1 plain, 11 chain, 1 plain : both these plain stitches are to be worked in the 11 chain of the 1st round), 3 chain, miss 10 ; repeat, end 1 single stitch.

3rd—11 plain, 3 chain, miss 5 : repeat, and end with 1 single stitch.

4th—14 chain, miss 13, 1 plain in the 3 chain of last round : repeat.

5th—Miss 1, 7 plain, 5 chain, 7 plain : repeat, end with 6 single stitches.

6th—7 plain, 9 chain, miss 12: repeat, and end with 3 single stitches.

7th—(1 plain, 9 chain, 1 plain: both these plain stitches in the centre stitch of the 7 plain in 6th round), 7 chain, miss 7, (1 plain, 9 chain, 1 plain: both these plain stitches in the centre stitch of the 9 chain in 6th round), 7 chain, miss 7; repeat, end with 2 single stitches.

8th—(1 plain, 7 chain, 1 plain, 9 chain, 1 plain, 7 chain, 1 plain: these 4 plain stitches are worked in the 9 chain of 7th round); 5 chain, miss 4, 1 plain in the centre of the 7 chain in 7th round, 5 chain, miss 4, repeat, and end with 1 single stitch.

9th—7 plain, miss 1, 9 plain, miss 1, 7 plain, 3 chain, miss 13: repeat, and end with 4 single stitches.

10th—13 chain, miss 15, 1 plain, 3 chain, miss 9, 1 plain: repeat, at the end turn back, work 2 single on the last 3 chain; turn back.

11th—6 chain, 9 plain, 7 chain, 9 plain: repeat.

12th—(1 plain, 11 chain, 1 plain, 13 chain, 1 plain, 11 chain, 1 plain: these 4 plain stitches in the 6 chain of 11th round); 3 chain miss 9, 5 plain in the 7 chain of the 11th round 3 chain, miss 9: repeat, and end with 1 single.

13th—9 plain, miss 3, 11 plain, miss 3, 9 plain, 3 chain, miss 7, 1 plain in the centre of the 5 plain, 3 chain, miss 7; end 1 single stitch: repeat, and fasten off.

D'OYLEY—No 1, IN COLOURS.

Amber and Dark Green—Commence with the Amber, and work the 1st, 2nd, and 3rd rounds—Green, 4th, 5th, and 6th rounds—Amber, 7th, 8th, and 9th rounds—Green, 10th and 11th rounds—Amber, 12th and 13th rounds.

D'OYLEY.—No. 2.

Jno. and Wm. Taylor's Crochet Thread, No. 000; *Needle, No.* 17, *Bell Gauge.*

Work a chain of 8 stitches, and make it round.

1st round—7 chain, and 1 plain 8 times in the foundation chain, then 3 single stitches upon the 1st 7 chain.

2nd—(1 plain, 5 chain, 1 plain: both these plain stitches in the 7 chain of 1st round), 1 chain, miss 6: repeat 7 times, end with 1 single stitch.

3rd—1 chain, miss 1, 5 treble in the 5 chain of 2nd round, 1 chain, miss 1, 1 plain in the 1 chain of 2nd round—repeat, at the end work 3 single stitches.

4th—(1 plain, 6 chain, 1 plain: both these plain stitches in the centre of the 5 treble in 3rd round), 5 chain, miss 7: repeat, at the end work 3 single stitches.

5th—(1 plain, 7 chain, 1 plain: both these plain stitches in the 6 chain of the 4th round), 3 chain, miss 5, 1 plain in the 5 chain of 4th round, 3 chain, miss 5; repeat, and end with 2 single stitches.

6th—1 plain in the 7 chain, (5 chain, and 1 plain in the same 7 chain 5 times), 5 chain, miss 9; repeat, and end with 1 single stitch, turn back, and work 3 single stitches on the last 5 chain, turn back.

7th—6 chain, miss 11, 1 plain in the 5 chain of 6th round: repeat all round, end with 2 single on the 1st 6 chain.

8th—8 single stitches, 5 chain, 8 single, (7 chain, put the needle into the 2nd stitch of these 7 chain, and work a plain stitch in it to form a round loop), 1 chain, miss 5; repeat and end with 3 single.

9th—3 chain, miss 5, (1 plain, 7 chain, 1 plain: both these plain stitches in the round loop of the 8th round), 3 chain, miss 5, 1 plain, in the centre of the 8 single; repeat, and end with 3 single stitches.

10th—1 chain, miss 2, 7 treble in the 7 chain of the 9th round, 1 chain, miss 2, 1 plain in the 3 chain, 1 chain, miss 3, 1 plain in the 3 chain: repeat, and end with 6 single stitches.

11th—13 chain, put the needle into the 4th stitch and work a plain stitch in it to form a round loop, 3 chain, miss 9, 3 single stitches: repeat, and end with 3 single stitches more.

12th—1 plain in the round loop, (5 chain, and 1 plain 5 times in the same round loop), 5 chain, miss 11; repeat, end 1 single; turn back, work 3 single on the last 5 chain, turn back.

13th—Same as 7th.

14th—Same as 8th, working plain stitches instead of single stitches.

15th—1 chain, miss 4 (1 plain, 5 chain, 1 plain, 7 chain, 1 plain, 9 chain, 1 plain, 7 chain, 1 plain, 5 chain, 1 plain: these 6 plain stitches are all to be worked in the 5 chain of 14th round), 1 chain, miss 4, 1 plain: repeat, and work 1 plain stitch. Fasten off.

D'OYLEY—No. 2, IN COLOURS.

Pink and Slate—Commence with the Pink, and work the 1st, 2nd, and 3rd rounds—Slate, 4th, 5th, and 6th rounds—Pink, 7th, 8th, 9th, and 10th rounds—Slate, 11th and 12th rounds —Pink, 13th, 14th, and 15th rounds.

D'OYLEY.—No. 3.

Jno. and Wm. Taylor's Crochet Thread, No. 000; *Needle, No.* 17, *Bell Gauge.*

Work a chain of 8 stitches, make it round.

1st round—5 chain and 2 plain 8 times in the foundation chain.

2nd—2 chain, miss 1, (2 treble, 3 chain, and 2 treble, these 4 treble in the 5 chain), 2 chain, miss 1, 1 single between the 2 plain of the 1st round; repeat.

3rd—3 chain, miss 4, (2 treble in the 3 chain, 5 chain, turn, miss 4, 1 single in the 5th chain stitch, 2 treble in the same 3 chain as before), 3 chain, miss 4, 1 single on the 1 single of last round; repeat, end 5 single.

4th—7 plain in the round loop, and for the 1st Flower, 15 chain, turn, miss 7, 1 single, in the 8th stitch to form a round loop, turn, and leaving 7 chain for the stem, work 1 chain to cross it, 1 plain in the round loop, 6 chain, join it to the 4th *stitch* of the 7 plain worked in the round loop of the 3rd round; turn, and on the 6 chain, miss 1, 1 plain, 3 treble, 1 single, 1 plain in the round loop, (then 6 chain, turn, miss 1, 1 plain, 3 treble, 1 single, and 1 plain in the round loop 5 times), and to form the 7th division of the Flower, work 1 single 3 treble, and 1 single down the stem, leaving 2 chain, *, then 2 chain, miss 11 stitches of the 3rd round, 3 plain in the round loop, join it to the point of the 6th *division* of the Flower, then 4 plain in the same round loop.

For the 2nd *Flower*—15 chain, turn, 1 single in the 8th stitch, 1 chain to cross the stem, 1 plain in the round loop, 6 chain, join it to the 4th *stitch* of the 7 plain, worked in the last round loop; turn, miss 1, 1 plain, 3 treble, 1 single, 1 plain in the round loop, 6 chain, join it to the point of the 5th *division* of the 1st Flower, turn, miss 1, 1 plain. 3

treble, 1 single, 1 plain in the round loop, (then 6 chain, turn, miss 1, 1 plain, 3 treble, 1 single, and 1 plain in the round loop, 4 times), and for the 7th division of the Flower, work 1 single, 3 treble, and 1 single down the stem, leaving 2 chain, repeat from *, 6 times more, then 2 chain, miss 11, 3 single on the 1st 7 plain of the round, join it to the 6th *division* of the 8th Flower; then 11 single up the sides of the 2 1st divisions of the 1st Flower and join it to the 5th *division* of the 8th Flower.

5th—6 chain, miss 11, 1 plain in the point of the 3rd division of the 1st Flower; 6 chain, miss 11, 1 plain in the point of the 4th division of the Flower; 6 chain, miss 11, 1 plain in the point of the 5th *division* of the Flower; repeat, end 4 single.

6th—17 plain, and for the 1st LEAF—16 chain, turn, miss 4, 1 plain, 2 chain, miss 2, 1 plain, 2 chain, miss 2, 1 plain, 1 chain to cross the stem; and on the other side, miss 1, 1 plain and 2 treble in the 2 chain, join it to the 12th *stitch of the* 17 plain, then 1 treble and 1 plain in the same 2 chain of the Leaf as before; then (miss 1, 1 plain, 3 treble and 1 plain in the 2 chain), miss 1, 1 plain and 2 treble in the 4 chain; and before finishing this Leaf, work 13 chain for the

1st FLOWER—Turn, miss 7, 1 single in the 8th stitch, turn, 1 chain to cross the stem; 1 plain in the round loop, (6 chain, turn, miss 1, 1 plain, 3 treble, 1 single on the 6 chain and 1 plain in the round loop 6 times); then to form the 7th division, work 1 single, 3 treble and 1 single down the stem; and to finish the Leaf, work 1 treble and 1 plain in the same 4 chain as before, (miss 1, 1 plain, 3 treble, and 1 plain in the 2 chain twice) then 2 single down the stem, and for the

2nd FLOWER.—15 chain, turn, miss 7, 1 single in the 8th stitch, 1 chain to cross the stem, 1 plain in the round loop, 6 chain, join it to the *centre treble* stitch of the 1st Leaf, turn, miss 1, 1 plain, 3 treble, 1 single, 1 plain in the round loop, 6 chain, join it the 6th *division* of the 1st Flower, turn, miss 1, 1 plain, 3 treble, 1 single, 1 plain in the round loop (6 chain, turn, miss 1, 1 plain, 3 treble, 1 single, and 1 plain in the round loop 4 times), and down the stem 1 single, 3 treble, 3 single; and 1 plain on the stem of the 1st Leaf.

2nd LEAF—13 chain, turn, miss 4, 1 plain, 2 chain, miss 2, 1 plain, 2 chain, miss 2, 1 plain, 1 chain to cross the stem, and on the other side miss 1, (1 plain, 3 treble, and 1 plain in the 2 chain), miss 1, 1 plain and 2 treble in the next 2 chain; join it to the point of the 6th *division* of the 2nd Flower, 1 treble, and 1 plain in the same 2 chain, miss 1 (1 plain, 3 treble, and 1 plain in the 4 chain), turn, and down the other side, (miss 1, 1 plain, 3 treble, and 1 plain in the 2 chain twice), 2 single down the stem, and 2 plain down the stem of the 1st Leaf; then 4 plain on the 5th round, join it to the centre of the last *division* of the 2nd Leaf, * *, 17 plain on the 5th round; and for the

3rd LEAF—16 chain, turn, miss 4, 1 plain, 2 chain, miss 2, 1 plain, 2 chain, miss 2, 1 plain, 1 chain to cross the stem; and on the other side, miss 1, 1 plain and 2 treble in the 2 chain, join it to the 12th *stitch of the* 17 plain, then 1 treble and 1 plain in the same 2 chain of the Leaf as before; then (miss 1, 1 plain, 3 treble and 1 plain in the 2 chain), miss 1, 1 plain and 2 treble in the 4 chain; join it to the *point* of the 2nd Leaf; and before finishing this Leaf, work 13 chain for the

3rd FLOWER—Turn, 1 single in the 8th stitch, 1 chain to cross the stem, 1 plain in the round loop, 6 chain, join it to the point of the 5th *division* of the 2nd Flower, turn, miss 1, 1 plain, 3 treble, 1 single, 1 plain in the round loop, (then 6 chain, turn, miss 1, 1 plain, 3 treble, 1 single, and 1 plain in the round loop 5 times), and for the 7th division of the Flower, work 1 single, 3 treble, and 1 single down the stem; and to finish the Leaf, work 1 treble and 1 plain in the same 4 chain as before; (miss 1, 1 plain, 3 treble, and 1 plain in the 2 chain twice), then 2 single down the stem; and for the

4th FLOWER—15 chain, turn, miss 7, 1 single in the 8th stitch, 1 chain to cross the stem, 1 plain in the round loop, 6 chain, join it to the *centre treble* stitch of the 3rd Leaf, turn, miss 1, 1 plain, 3 treble, 1 single, 1 plain in the round loop, 6 chain, join it to the 6th *division* of the 3rd Flower, turn, miss 1, 1 plain, 3 treble, 1 single, 1 plain in the round loop; (6 chain, turn, miss 1, 1 plain, 3 treble, 1 single, and 1 plain in the round loop 4 times), and down the stem, 1 single, 3 treble, 3 single; and 1 plain on the stem of the 3rd Leaf.

4th LEAF—13 chain, turn, miss 4, 1 plain, 2 chain, miss 2, 1 plain, 2 chain, miss 2, 1 plain, 1 chain to cross the stem, and on the other side, miss 1, (1 plain, 3 treble, and 1 plain in the 2 chain), miss 1, 1 plain, 2 treble, in the 2 chain; join it to the point of the 6th *division* of the 4th Flower, 1 treble and 1 plain in the same 2 chain, miss 1, (1 plain, 3 treble and 1 plain in the 4 chain), turn, (miss 1, 1 plain, 3 treble and 1 plain in the 2 chain twice), 2 single down the stem, and 2 plain down the stem of the 3rd Leaf; then 4 plain on the 5th round, join it to the *centre of the last division* of the 4th Leaf; repeat from * *, and when the round is finished, work 11 single up the side of the last Leaf; join it to the point of the 1st Leaf, then 12 single up the 1st Flower, joining it to the 5th *division* of the last Flower. Fasten off.

D'OYLEY—No. 3, IN COLOURS.

Pink and Green—Commence with the Green, and work 1st, 2nd, and 3rd rounds—Pink, 4th round—Green, 5th round—Pink and Green are used in the 6th round, thus—work the plain stitches and half of the 1st Leaf with the Green, carrying the Pink under it. Work the 1st Flower with Pink, finish the Leaf with Green, carrying the Pink under it. Work the 2nd Flower with Pink, leave it, and work the 2nd Leaf with Green; and then the plain stitches on the 5th round with Green, carrying the Pink under: repeat.

D'OYLEY—No. 4.

Jno. and Wm. Taylor's Crochet Thread, No. 000; *Needle, No.* 17, *Bell Gauge.*

Work a chain of 8 stitches, and make it round.

1st round—13 chain and 1 plain 7 times in the foundation chain, end 1 single on the 1st 13 chain.

2nd—11 plain, miss 3: repeat, end with 6 single stitches on the 1st 11 plain.

3rd—8 chain, miss 9, 2 plain: repeat.

4th—3 plain, and 2 plain in the 4th stitch; repeat, and end with 1 single stitch.

5th—5 chain, miss 2, 3 plain: repeat, and end with 3 single stitches on the 1st 5 chain.

6th—6 chain, miss 6, 2 plain: repeat.

7th—3 chain, miss 1, 1 plain: repeat.

8th—6 chain, miss 7, 1 plain in the 3 chain: repeat.

D'OYLEY.—No. 4.

9th—3 chain, miss 5, (2 treble, 4 chain, 2 treble: these 4 treble are all to be worked in the 6 chain of the last round); 3 chain, miss 5, 1 plain in the 6 chain: repeat.

10th—3 chain, miss 5, (2 treble, 4 chain, 2 treble; these 4 treble are to be worked in the 4 chain of 9th round), 3 chain, miss 5, 1 plain on the 1 plain of last round: repeat.

11th—Same as 10th round, and at the end work 5 single stitches.

12th—(1 plain, 5 chain, 1 plain: both these plain stitches in the 4 chain of last round), 7 chain, miss 11; repeat, end 1 single, turn back, and work 3 single on the last 7 chain, turn back.

13th—2 chain, miss 4, 1 treble in the 5 chain, (4 chain and 1 treble 4 times in the same 5 chain of the last round), 2 chain, miss 4, 1 plain in the 7 chain of last round: repeat.

14th—1 chain, miss 3, 1 plain in the 2 chain, (miss 1, 1 plain, 4 treble and 1 plain in the 4 chain 4 times), miss 1, 1 plain in the 2 chain: repeat, and fasten off.

D'OYLEY—No. 4, IN COLOURS.

Blue and White—Commence with the Blue, and work the 1st and 2nd rounds, then with White, work the 3rd and 4th rounds—Blue, 5th, 6th, and 7th rounds—White, 8th, 9th, 10th, 11th rounds—Blue, 12th, 13th, and 14th rounds.

D'OYLEY.—No. 5.

Jno. and Wm. Taylor's Crochet Thread, No. 000; *Needle, No.* 17, *Bell Gauge.*

Work a chain of 8 stitches, make it round.

1st round—6 chain, 1 plain in the foundation chain, 10 chain, turn, miss 5, 5 plain on the 10 chain, 1 plain in the foundation chain; repeat 7 times more, turn back; work 5 single up the last 5 plain, turn back.

2nd—3 chain, miss 18, 1 plain in the round loop of the 1st round; (5 chain and 1 plain 5 times in the same round loop): repeat, and end with 2 single on the 1st 3 chain.

3rd—13 chain, miss 32, 1 plain in the 3 chain: repeat, end with 2 single.

4th—11 plain on the 13 chain, 9 chain, turn, miss 5, 4 plain on the 9 chain, miss 3: repeat, end with 5 single.

5th—1 plain in the centre stitch of the 11 plain, and for the 1st Leaf, 11 chain, turn, miss 1, 1 single, 1 plain, 4 treble, 1 single. 2nd Leaf—8 chain, turn, miss 1, 1 single, 1 plain, 4 treble, 1 single. 3rd Leaf—8 chain, turn, miss 1, 1 single, 1 plain, 4 treble, 1 single, 3 single down the stem, and 1 plain in the same centre stitch of the 11 plain of the 4th round as before, and for the FLOWER—3 chain, miss 9, 1 plain in the round loop, (5 chain and 1 plain 5 times in the same round loop), 3 chain, miss 9: repeat, end with 11 single up the stem and 1st Leaf to the Point.

6th—7 chain, miss 14, 1 plain in the point of the 2nd Leaf; 7 chain, miss 14, 1 plain in the point of the 3rd Leaf; 3 chain, miss 29, 1 plain in the centre 5 chain of the Flower; 3 chain, miss 29, 1 plain in the Point of the next Leaf: repeat, end with 6 single.

7th—14 plain, 12 chain, and for the 1st Leaf, turn, miss 4, 1 single in the 5th stitch, turn back; (5 chain and 1 plain 3 times in the round loop), turn back; 1 plain in the 5 chain, (4 chain and 1 plain twice in the same 5 chain, 2 chain, join it to the 5th *stitch* of the 14 plain, 2 chain, 1 plain in the same 5 chain, 4 chain and 1 plain twice in the same 5 chain), miss 1, 1 plain in the next 5 chain, (4 chain and 1 plain 5 times in the same 5 chain), miss 1, 1 plain in the next 5 chain, (4 chain and 1 plain 5 times in the same 5 chain), 4 single down the stem—this finishes the Leaf—and for the 2nd Leaf, 9 chain and work as the 1st Leaf, joining it to the *centre* 5 chain of the 3rd division of the 1st Leaf—*, and for the 3rd Leaf, 9 chain, and work as the 1st Leaf, joining it to the *centre* 5 chain, of the 3rd division of the 2nd Leaf, when finished, work 3 plain down the stem of the 1st Leaf and 10 plain on the 6th round, join it to the centre 5 *chain* of the 3rd division of the 3rd Leaf; then 14 plain, 12 chain, and for the 4th Leaf, turn, miss 4, 1 single in the 5th stitch, turn back; (5 chain and 1 plain 3 times in the round loop), turn back; 1 plain in the 5 chain, (4 chain and 1 plain twice in the same 5 chain, 2 chain, join it to the 5th *stitch* of the 14 plain, 2 chain, 1 plain in the same 5 chain, 4 chain and 1 plain twice in the same 5 chain), miss 1, 1 plain in the next 5 chain, (4 chain and 1 plain twice in the same 5 chain, 2 chain, join it to the *centre* 5 chain of the 2nd division of the 3rd Leaf, 2 chain, 1 plain, 4 chain and 1 plain twice in the same 5 chain), miss 1, 1 plain in the next 5 chain, (4 chain and 1 plain 5 times in the same 5 chain), then 4 single down the stem; and for the

5th Leaf—9 chain, and work as the 2nd Leaf, then repeat from*, and for the *last* Leaf—9 chain and work as the 4th Leaf, joining it 1st to the centre 5 chain of the last Leaf worked; and 2ndly to the centre 5 chain of the 1st Leaf worked; when finished work 3 plain down the Stem, and 10 plain on the 6th round, join it to the centre 5 chain of the 3rd division of the last Leaf. Fasten off.

D'OYLEY—No. 5, IN COLOURS.

Ponceau and Gold—Commence with the Ponceau, and work the 1st and 2nd rounds—Gold, the 3rd and 4th rounds—Ponceau, 5th round—Gold, 6th and 7th rounds.

D'OYLEY—No. 6.

Jno. and Wm. Taylor's Crochet Thread, No. 000; *Needle, No.* 17, *Bell Gauge.*

Work a chain of 8 stitches, make it round.

1st round—12 chain, turn, miss 5, 2 single, and 5 treble on the 12 chain, 1 plain in the foundation chain; repeat 7 times more, end with 7 single up the first 12 chain.

2nd—1 plain in the round loop of the 1st round (5 chain and 1 plain 3 times in the same round loop as before), 3 chain, miss 15; repeat, end 1 single.

3rd—9 chain, turn, miss 1, 1 single, 1 plain, 1 treble and 2 long on the 9 chain, 3 chain, miss 19, 1 plain in the 3 chain of the 2nd round, 8 chain, turn, miss 5, 1 single in the 6th stitch, 2 chain, 1 plain in the same 3 chain of the 2nd round; repeat, end with 9 single up the 1st 9 chain.

4th—5 chain, miss 13, 1 plain in the round loop of the 3rd round; and for the 3 *small Leaves,*

D'OYLEY.—No. 6.

(5 chain, turn, miss 2, 2 treble and 1 single on the 5 chain, 1 plain in the same round loop as before, repeat twice more); then 5 chain, miss 13, 1 single in the 1 chain at the point of the star in the 3rd round; repeat.

5th—8 chain, miss 17, 1 plain in the 2 chain at the top of the 2nd small Leaf in the 3rd round; 8 chain, miss 17, 1 single on the 1 single at the point of the star in last round; repeat, end 4 single on the 1st 8 chain.

6th—14 plain, and for the 1st Flower, 11 chain, turn, miss 4, 1 single in the 5th stitch, turn, 1 chain to cross the stem, 2 chain; join it to the 11th *stitch* of the 14 plain; then 2 chain, 1 plain in the round loop, (5 chain and 1 plain 4 times in the same round loop), 3 single down the stem; and for the 2nd Flower, 9 chain, turn, miss 4, 1 single, 1 chain to cross the stem; 2 chain, join it to the *last 5 chain* of the 1st Flower, 2 chain, 1 plain in the round loop, (5 chain and 1 plain 4 times in the same round loop), 4 single down the stem, and 1 single down the stem of the 1st Flower; and for the 3rd Flower, 8 chain, turn, miss 4, 1 single, 1 chain to cross the stem, 2 chain, join it to the last 5 *chain* of the 2nd Flower, 2 chain, 1 plain in the round loop, (5 chain and 1 plain 4 times in the round loop), 3 single down the stem, and 2 single down the stem of the 1st Flower; then miss 1, and work 3 plain on the 5th round, join it to the last 5 *chain* of the 3rd Flower; repeat, at the end work 5 single on the 1st 14 plain.

7th—5 chain, miss 15, 1 plain in the centre 5 chain of the 1st Flower, 8 chain, miss 23, 2 plain in the centre 5 chain of the 2nd Flower, 8 chain, miss 23, 1 plain in the centre 5 chain of the 3rd Flower, 5 chain, miss 15, 2 plain on the centre of the plain stitches; repeat, end 5 single on the 1st 5 chain.

8th—5 plain on the 7th round, and for the 1st *Leaf,* 10 chain, turn, miss 2, 4 treble, and 2 single on the 10 chain, leaving 2 chain for the stem, work 8 chain, (miss 2, 4 treble and 2 single on the 8 chain), 8 chain, turn, (miss 2, 4 treble and 2 single on the 8 chain); then 2 single down the stem, this finishes the Leaf; * 6 plain on the 7th round, and for the 2nd Leaf—9 chain; join it to the *point* of the 3rd *division* of the last Leaf, 1 chain, miss 1, 4 treble and 2 single, leaving 2 chain for the stem, (8 chain, turn, miss 2, 4 treble and 2 single twice), 2 single down the stem; then 6 plain on the 7th round, and work the 3rd Leaf the same as the 2nd Leaf; then 5 plain and 5 single on the 7th round; and for the 4th Leaf, 9 chain, join it to the last stitch of the 5 plain, 1 chain, turn, miss 1, 4 treble, and 2 single on the 9 chain, and leaving 2 chain for the stem, work 7 chain; join it to the *point* of the 3rd *division* of the 3rd Leaf, 1 chain, miss 1, 4 treble, 2 single, 8 chain, turn, miss 2, 4 treble and 2 single; then 2 single down the stem, and 5 single on the 7th round; join it to the *point* of the last *division* of the 4th Leaf, 5 plain—5th Leaf same as the 2nd, joining it to the *point* of the 2nd *division* of the 4th Leaf: repeat from *, and fasten off.

D'OYLEY—No. 6, IN COLOURS.

Gold colour and Dark Blue—Commence with the Gold colour, and work the 1st and 2nd rounds—Blue, 3rd and 4th rounds—Gold, 5th and 6th rounds—Blue, 7th round—Gold, and Blue, 8th round, working the leaves with the Gold; and the plain stitches on the 7th round with the Blue, working the gold under them.

ANTI-MACASSAR, OR COUVRE PIED.

DIAMOND AND STAR PATTERN.

Jno. & Wm. Taylor's Crochet Thread, No. 2, or O.; Needle, No. 20, Bell Gauge; and for the Couvre Pied, Taylor's Knitting Cotton, No. 12; Needle, No. 16, Bell Gauge.

FIRST DIAMOND—Work a chain of 8 stitches, and make it round.

1st round—(1 treble, 3 chain, 1 treble, and 1 plain 4 times, in the foundation chain.)

2nd—1 chain, miss 1, (3 treble, 3 chain, 3 treble; these 6 treble in the 3 chain of the last round), 1 chain, miss 1, 1 plain on the 1 plain of the last round; repeat 3 times more; then work 4 single stitches.

3rd—(1 plain, 8 chain, 1 plain, 9 chain, 1 plain, 8 chain, 1 plain; these 4 plain stitches in the 3 chain of the last round), 7 chain, miss 9; repeat 3 times more, and end with 1 single, turn back; and work 3 single on the last 7 chain, turn back.

4th—Miss 4, 8 treble and 1 plain in the 8 chain of the last round, miss 1, (1 plain, 10 treble, and 1 plain in the 9 chain of the last round), miss 1, 1 plain and 8 treble in the 8 chain of the last round, miss 4, 1 plain in the 7 chain; repeat 3 times more, and fasten off neatly at the back, by running this end down to the end left at the commencement, and knot them together. All the Diamonds are worked in the same manner; the variations of the direction being caused by the joining of the patterns.

2nd DIAMOND—Commence by working a chain of 8 stitches as before; and work the first 3 rounds of the pattern as in the 1st Diamond; then work the pattern as in the 4th round, *repeating it only twice,* and to finish this round, miss 4, 8 treble and 1 plain in the 8 chain,

No. I.

miss 1, (1 plain and 5 treble in the 9 chain; then 3 chain, and join it to the centre of the 2nd 10 treble of the 1st Diamond; turn, and work 3 plain on the 3 chain, then 1 single in the top of the last treble stitch; and to finish the Diamond—work 5 treble, and 1 plain in the same 9 chain as before); miss 1, 1 plain, and 8 treble in the 8 chain, miss 4, 1 plain, in the 7 chain. Fasten off, and repeat the 2nd Diamond pattern as many times as may be required, always joining it to the *last* Diamond pattern worked.

STAR PATTERN.

Work a chain of 10 stitches, and make it round.

1st round—16 plain in the foundation round.

2nd—8 chain, turn, miss 5, 1 single in the 3rd stitch of the 8 chain to form a round loop; then 2 chain, 2 plain on the 16 plain; repeat 7 times more, and end with 2 single up the first 2 chain.

3rd—7 plain in the round loop, 1 chain, miss 7; repeat 7 times more, and end with 1 single.

4th—8 chain, miss 7, 2 plain in the 1 chain of the last round; repeat 7 times more.

5th—(Miss 2 1 plain, 1 treble, 7 long, 1 treble, and 1 plain; these 11 stitches in the 8 chain of the last round, repeat 3 times more); then miss 2, (1 plain, 1 treble, and 4 long in the next 8 chain; join it to the centre of the 1st 8 *treble* in the last Diamond Pattern worked; then 3 long, 1 treble, and 1 plain in the same 8 chain of the Star Pattern), miss 2, (1 plain, 1 treble, and 3 long in the next 8 chain; join it to the centre of the last 8 *treble* of the same Diamond pattern; then 4 long, 1 treble, and 1 plain in the same 8 chain), miss 2, (1 plain, 1 treble and 4 long in the next 8 chain; join it to the centre of the 3rd 8 *treble* of the next Diamond Pattern; then 3 long, 1 treble, 1 plain in the same 8 chain), miss 2, (1 plain, 1 treble and 3 long in the next 8 chain; join it to the centre of the 2nd 8 *treble* of the Diamond Pattern; then 4 long, 1 treble, 1 plain in the same 8 chain), and fasten off. Repeat the Star Pattern, always joining them between the Diamond Patterns.

2nd. STRIPE OF DIAMOND PATTERN.

1st DIAMOND—Work the first 3 rounds as in first Stripe, then work the pattern as in the 4th round repeating it only once, and to finish the round, miss 4, 8 treble, and 1 plain in the next 8 chain, miss 1, (1 plain and 5 treble, in the 9 chain, 3 chain, join it to the centre of the 1*st* 10 *treble* of the last Diamond of the first Stripe worked, turn, 3 plain on the 3 chain, and 1 single on the top of the last treble stitch, then 5 treble and 1 plain in the same 9 chain), miss 1, (1 plain, and 4 treble in the 8 chain, join it to the centre of the 4th *division* of the first Star; then 4 treble in the same 8 chain), miss 4, 1 plain in the 7 chain, miss 4, (4 treble in the 8 chain, join it to the centre of 3rd *division* of the Star pattern, 4 treble and 1 plain in the same 8 chain), miss 1, (1 plain, 10 treble, and 1 plain in the 9 chain), miss 1, 1 plain and 8 treble in the 8 chain, miss 4, 1 plain in the 7 chain. Fasten off.

2nd DIAMOND—Work the first 3 rounds as before.

4th round—Miss 4, 8 treble and 1 plain in the 8 chain, miss 1, (1 plain, 10 treble and 1 plain in the 9 chain), miss 1, 1 plain, and 8 treble in the 8 chain, miss 4, 1 plain in the 7 chain, miss 4, 8 treble and 1 plain in the 8 chain, miss 1, (1 plain and 5 treble in the 9 chain, 3 chain, join it to the centre of the *last* 10 treble in the 1st Diamond of this stripe, turn, 3 plain on the 3 chain, 1 single in the top of the last treble stitch, then 5 treble and 1 plain in the same 9 chain), miss 1, (1 plain and 4 treble in the 8 chain, join it to the centre of the 2nd *division* of the Star; then 4 treble in the same 8 chain), miss 4, 1 plain in the 7 chain, miss 4, (4 treble in the 8 chain, join it to the centre of the 1st *division* of the Star, then 4 treble and 1 plain in the same 8 chain), miss 1, (1 plain and 5 treble in the 9 chain, 3 chain, join to the *top* of the Diamond in the 1st stripe, turn, 3 plain on the 3 chain, 1 single in the top of the treble stitch, then 5 treble and 1 plain in the same 9 chain), miss 1 (1 plain and 4 treble in the 8 chain, join it to the centre of the 4th *division* of the 2nd Star pattern, then 4 treble in the same 8 chain), miss 4, 1 plain in the 7 chain, miss 4, (4 treble in the 8 chain, join it to the centre of the 3rd *division* of the Star, then 4 treble and 1 plain in the same 8 chain), miss 1, (1 plain, 10 treble and 1 plain in the 9 chain), miss 1, 1 plain and 8 treble in the 8 chain, miss 4, 1 plain in the 7 chain. Fasten off.

Repeat this 2nd Diamond until the Stripe is finished, and work alternately the Star and 2nd Diamond Stripe until sufficient is made. Finish with a tassel between each Diamond.

ANTI-MACASSAR, OR COUVRE-PIED.

FLOWER PATTERN.

Jno. and Wm. Taylor's Knitting Cotton, No. 12; Needle, No. 16, Bell-Gauge for a Couvre Pied. Crochet Thread, No. 2, or O, for an Anti-Macassar.

Make a chain of 17 stitches, and for the calyx of the Flower, turn, miss 6, 7 plain down the stem; work 1 chain to cross it and on the other side, 2 plain, 3 treble, 2 single, and

FOR THE FLOWER—work 10 plain in the round loop, turn back; (5 chain, miss 1, and 1 plain 5 times on the 10 plain), turn back; (miss 1, 1 plain, 5 treble, 1 plain, these 7 stitches are worked in the 5 chain, repeat 4 times more), then 2 single, 3 treble, 2 plain down the calyx, and 1 single on the stem, leaving 3 chain for the *centre* stem; then 9 chain, join it to the centre of the last 5 treble of the Flower.

FOR THE LEAF—* 15 chain, turn, miss 4, 1 single in the 5th stitch, turn back; (7 chain, and 1 plain 3 times in the round loop), turn back; (miss 1, 1 plain, 1 treble and 3 long stitches in the 7 chain, join it to the centre of the 4th 5 *treble* of the Flower, and in the same 7 chain of the Leaf work 6 long, 1 treble, and 1 plain), then (miss 1, 1 plain, 1 treble, 9 long, 1 treble, and 1 plain in the 7 chain twice), 5 single down the stem, which finishes the Leaf, and leaving 5 chain for the centre stem, work 9 chain, join it to the 7th long stitch of the 3rd *division* of the Leaf, and for the

2nd FLOWER and CALYX—19 chain, turn, miss 6, 7 plain, turn, work 1 chain to cross the stem, and on the other side, 2 plain, 3 treble, 2 single, 10 plain in the round loop, turn back; (5 chain, miss 1, and 1 plain 5 times on the 10 plain), turn back; miss 1, (1 plain,

No. 2.

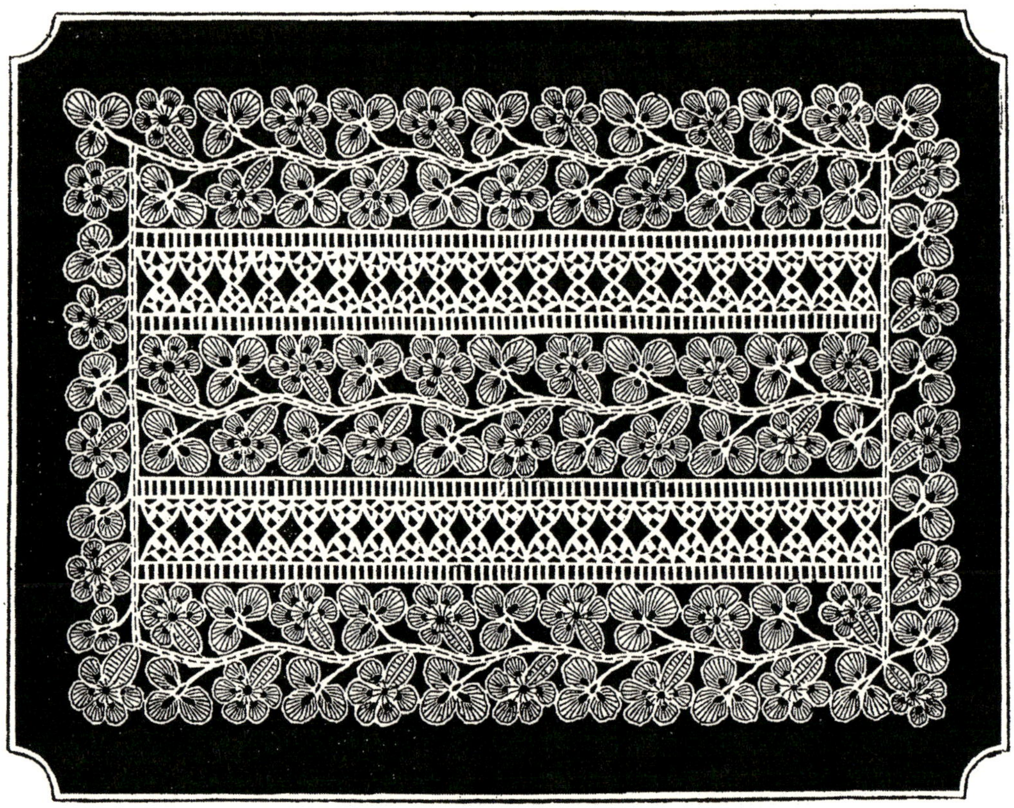

and 3 treble in the 5 chain, join it to the 7th long stitch of the 2nd *division* of the Leaf, and in the same 5 chain as before, work 2 treble and 1 plain,) then (miss 1, 1 plain, 5 treble and 1 plain in the 5 chain, 4 times), and down the calyx, 2 single, 3 treble, 2 plain, and 1 single on the stem, leaving 5 chain for the centre stem; work 9 chain, join it to the centre of the last 5 *treble* of the Flower; repeat from * until the required length is made (with the Knitting Cotton, 15 patterns, or with the Crochet Thread, 18 patterns for one yard.) To form the

SECOND SIDE

Work 3 chain, turn, miss 1, 2 plain on the 3 chain, and 12 plain down the centre stem which will be 9 on the 9 chain, and 3 on the 5 chain.

1st LEAF—10 chain, and work a Leaf as directed on the other side, but *joining* it to the 6th *stitch* of the 14 plain worked down the centre stem, * * then 14 plain down the centre stem, and for the

FLOWER—14 chain, turn, miss 6, 7 plain down the stem, work 1 chain to cross it, and on the other side, 2 plain, 3 treble, 2 single, then 10 plain in the round loop, turn back; (5 chain, miss 1, and 1 plain, 5 times), turn back; (miss 1, 1 plain, and 3 treble in the 5 chain, join it to the 6th *stitch* of the 14 plain worked down the centre stem, then 2 treble and 1 plain in the same 5 chain), (miss 1, 1 plain and 3 treble in the next 5 chain, join it to the 7th long stitch of the 3rd *division* of the Leaf, then 2 treble and 1 plain in the same 5 chain), (miss 1, 1 plain, 5 treble and 1 plain in the 5 chain 3 times), and down the calyx, 2 single, 3 treble, 2 plain, and 1 single on the stem; then 14 plain down the centre stem; and for

2nd LEAF—10 chain, turn, miss 4, 1 single, turn back; (7 chain and 1 plain 3 times in the round loop), turn back; (miss 1, 1 plain, 1 treble, and 3 long in the 7 chain, join it to the 6th *stitch* of the 14 plain worked down the centre stem; and in the same 7 chain, 6 long, 1 treble, and 1 plain), then miss 1, (1 plain, 1 treble, and 3 long in the next 7 chain, join it to the centre of the *last* 5 treble of the Flower, and in the same 7 chain, 6 long, 1 treble, and 1 plain), (miss 1, 1 plain, 1 treble, 9 long, 1 treble, and 1 plain in the 7 chain); then 5 single down the stem; repeat from * *, until the length is worked, and to form the INSERTION between the Stripes, work 14 single up the calyx and side of the *first* Flower worked, and along the edge of the Flowers and Leaves to form the foundation for the 1st side of the insertion, thus:—

1st row—4 chain, miss 6, 1 plain on the centre of the 2nd 5 treble of the Flower *, 6 chain, miss 6, 1 plain on the centre of the 3rd 5 treble of the Flower, 5 chain, miss 8, 1 plain on the 7th long stitch of the 1st division of the Leaf, 6 chain, miss 7, 1 plain on the 2nd division of the Leaf, 5 chain, miss 3, 1 plain on the 2nd division of the Leaf, 5 chain, miss 8, 1 plain on the centre of the 2nd 5 treble of the next Flower; repeat from *, end with 6 chain, miss 6, 1 plain on the 3rd division of the Flower. Cut off the thread at the end of each row, and commence at the other end.

2nd—1 treble on the 1st chain stitch of the 1st row *, 1 chain, miss 1, 1 treble, repeat from *.

3rd—1 plain in the 1st chain stitch, *, 1 chain, miss 3, (2 treble, 3 chain, 2 treble, these 4 treble in the 1 chain of the last row), 1 chain, miss 3, 1 plain in the 1 chain; repeat from *.

4th—miss 1, 1 plain in the 1 chain, 2 chain, miss 2, (2 treble, 3 chain, 2 treble in the 3 chain of the last row), 2 chain, miss 2, 1 plain in the 1 chain, repeat and fasten off the ends. This finishes the 1st Stripe.

The edging not being required on *both sides* of the *first* and *last* Stripes.

SECOND STRIPE.

Work the same as the 1st Stripe, and

For the Edging on the other side—Commence by working 1 plain in the 5th long stitch of the 2nd division of the *first Leaf* of the 2nd side.

1st row—5 chain, miss 3, 1 plain on the 2nd division of the Leaf, 6 chain, miss 7, 1 plain on the 3rd division of the Leaf, 5 chain, miss 8, 1 plain on the centre of the 3rd 5 treble of the Flower, 6 chain, miss 6, 1 plain on the centre of the 4th 5 treble of the Flower, 5 chain, miss 8, 1 plain on the Leaf, repeat, end with 5 chain, miss 3, 1 plain, 4 chain, miss 7, 1 plain. Cut off the thread and commence as before.

2nd—1 treble on the 1st plain stitch *, 1 chain, miss 1, 1 treble; repeat from *.

3rd—1 plain in the 1st chain stitch, *, 1 chain, miss 3, (2 treble, 3 chain, 2 treble, these 4 treble in the 1 chain of the last row), 1 chain, miss 3, 1 plain in the 1 chain; repeat from *.

4th—In this row, the 2 Stripes worked are joined together, thus:—miss 1, 1 plain in the 1 chain, 2 chain, miss 2, (2 treble in the 3 chain, 1 chain, join it to the centre of the *last* 3 chain of the edging of the first Stripe worked; then 1 chain and 2 treble in the same 3 chain of the 2nd Stripe as before), 2 chain, miss 2, 1 plain in the 1 chain, repeat, joining to the opposite point each time. Fasten off. Continue working the 2nd Stripe until sufficient width is made.

BORDER FOR THE TOP.

Commence by working 1 plain in the top of the centre stem of the last Stripe worked.

1st row—5 chain, miss 7, 1 plain in the 7th long stitch of the 1st division of the Leaf, 7 chain, miss 8, 1 plain on the 2nd division of the Leaf, 5 chain, 1 plain in the side of the 3rd row of the edging between the Stripes; 13 chain, 1 plain in the side of the 3rd row of the other side of the edging; 7 chain, 1 plain on the 3rd 5 treble of the Flower; 5 chain, miss 6, 1 plain on the 4th 5 treble of the Flower, 7 chain, miss 8, 1 plain on the centre stem of the next Stripe; repeat to the centre stem of the 1st Stripe. Cut off the thread.

2nd—Commence on the 1 plain worked at the beginning of the 1st row, 10 chain and work a Leaf the same as the Leaf in the 2nd side of the stripe: when finished work 3 plain on the 1st row, *, and for the FLOWER, 15 chain, and work a Flower the same as the 2nd Flower in the 1st side of the Stripe: when finished work 9 plain on the 1st row; join it to the *last* 5 treble of the Flower; then 5 plain on the 1st row, and for the 2nd LEAF 10 chain, and work as the Leaf on the 1st side of the stripe: when finished work 9 plain on the 1st row, join it to the 7th long stitch of the 3rd *division* of the Leaf; then 5 plain on the 1st row: repeat from *, but end with 1 plain instead of 5 on the 1st row: then 15 chain, and work a Flower the same, joining the last division to the third long stitch of the Leaf at the side before finishing it. Fasten off.

BORDER FOR THE BOTTOM.

1st—Commence by working 1 plain on the end of the centre stem of the 1st Stripe; 5 chain, miss 6, 1 plain on the 1st treble stitch of the calyx of the 1st Flower, 7 chain, miss 9,

1 plain on the centre of the 1st 5 treble of the Flower, 5 chain, 1 plain in the side of the 3rd row of the edging, 13 chain, 1 plain in the side of the 3rd row of the other side of the edging, 7 chain, 1 plain on the centre of the 3rd division of the Leaf, 5 chain, miss 5, 1 plain on the same division of the Leaf, 7 chain, miss 7, 1 plain on the centre stem; repeat to the centre stem of the last Stripe. Cut off the thread.

2nd—Commence on the 1 plain worked at the beginning of the 1st row; then 15 chain, and work a Flower the same as the 2nd Flower in the 1st side of the Stripe, joining it to the centre of the 3rd division of the Leaf at the side; when finished, work 3 plain on the 1st row, and for the Leaf, 10 chain, and work a Leaf the same as in the 1st side of the Stripe, joining it to the centre of the last 5 treble of the Flower, *; when finished, work 9 plain on the 1st row, join to the 7th long stitch of the 3rd division of the Leaf; then 5 plain on the 1st row; and for the FLOWER, 15 chain: work as the 2nd Flower in the 1st side of the Stripe; when finished work 9 plain on the 1st row, join it to the centre of the last 5 treble of the Flower, then 5 plain on the 1st row; and for the next LEAF, 10 chain; and work the Leaf in the 1st side of the Stripe; repeat from *, but before working the last Leaf, work 2 plain instead of 5 on the 1st row, and in working the Leaf, join the centre of the last division to the 1st 5 treble of the Flower at the side. Fasten off.

ANTI-MACASSAR, OR TOILET-COVER.

Jno. and Wm. Taylor's Crochet Thread, No. 00; Needle, No. 16, Bell Gauge.

Make a chain of 415 stitches for ¾ of a yard, or 23 stitches for each pattern; the thread is cut off at the end of each row.—*See 2nd Series.*

1st row—1 treble *, 5 chain, miss 5, 4 treble, 4 chain, miss 4, 4 treble, 5 chain, miss 5, 1 treble: repeat from * to the end.

2nd—4 treble, *, 3 chain, miss 3, 2 treble, 2 chain, miss 2, 2 treble, 2 chain, miss 2, 2 treble, 3 chain, miss 3, 7 treble: repeat from *, end with 4 treble instead of 7 treble.

3rd—1 treble, *, 2 chain, miss 2, 3 treble, 4 chain, miss 4, 4 treble, 4 chain, miss 4, 3 treble 2 chain, miss 2, 1 treble: repeat from *.

4th—2 treble, *, 2 chain, miss 2, 4 treble, 3 chain, miss 3, 2 treble, 3 chain, miss 3, 4 treble: 2 chain, miss 2, 3 treble: repeat from *, end with 2 treble instead of 3 treble.

5th—3 treble, *, 2 chain, miss 2, 4 treble, 6 chain, miss 6, 4 treble, 2 chain, miss 2, 5 treble repeat from *, end with 3 treble instead of 5 treble.

6th—Same as the 4th row—7th row, same as the 3rd row—8th row, same as the 2nd row: this finishes one pattern. Repeat, and work 24 patterns for the Anti-macassar or one yard; and to make the last pattern perfect, repeat as the 1st row, and without cutting off the thread commence

THE EDGING.

1st round—Work a plain row down the side, working 3 stitches on the side of every treble stitch; then work along the foundation chain, thus—(2 plain in 1 stitch, and 22 plain:

No. 3.

repeat to the other corner), and work a plain row up the other side, working 3 stitches to every treble stitch as before; and along the last side work 2 stitches in one and 22 plain. Repeat.

2nd—To form the corner—1 chain, 5 long in 1 stitch, 1 chain, 1 single, *, 1 chain, miss 2, 5 long in 1 stitch, 1 chain, miss 2, 1 single; repeat from * down the 1st side, then work the corner, and repeat as before along the 2nd, 3rd, and 4th sides, working the corner at the beginning of each side: at the end work 3 single on the 1st 3 stitches of the round.

3rd—For the corner—(9 chain, turn, 1 single in the 1st stitch of the 9 chain to form a round loop, 5 times), miss 1, 1 plain on the 5 long, 5 chain, miss 6, 1 plain in the centre of the 5 long, *, 5 chain, miss 7, 1 plain, (9 chain, turn, 1 single in the 1st stitch of the 9 chain to form a round loop, 5 times), miss 7, 1 plain, 5 chain, miss 7, 1 plain, 5 chain, miss 7, 1 plain; repeat from * down the side, then work the corner. Repeat as before along the other sides, working the corners at the end of each side; at the end, turn back and work 3 single on the last 5 chain, turn back.

4th—For the corner—(9 chain, turn, 1 single in the 2nd stitch of the 9 chain to form a round loop; 1 chain, miss 9, 1 plain in the round loop of the last round; repeat 5 times), 9 chain, 1 single in the 2nd stitch as before, 1 chain, miss 9, 1 plain in the 5 chain *, 3 chain, miss 5, 1 plain in the 5 chain, (9 chain, turn, 1 single in the 2nd stitch as before, 1 chain, miss 9, 1 plain in the round loop of the last round, 5 times), 9 chain, turn, 1 single in the 2nd stitch as before, 1 chain, miss 9, 1 plain in the 5 chain, 3 chain, miss 5, 1 plain in the 5 chain; repeat from * along the sides, working the corners as before.

5th—For the corner—(miss 3, 1 plain, 5 treble and 1 plain; these 7 stitches in the round loop of last round, 6 times), *, miss 3, 1 plain in the 3 chain, (miss 3, 1 plain, 5 treble and 1 plain in the round loop, 6 times), miss 3, 1 plain in the 3 chain; repeat from * along the sides, working the corners as before. Fasten off.

TO WORK THE ANTI-MACASSARS IN COLOURS.

THE DIAMOND OR STAR PATTERN.

This can be worked in two colours that contrast well, by making the Star with one colour, and the Diamonds with another.

THE FLOWER PATTERN.

Work the Stripes of Flowers and Leaves in Pink, and the Insertion White or Drab, or in any two colours that contrast.

FINIS.

THE CROCHET BOOK,

SEVENTH SERIES,

BY

MDLLE. RIEGO DE LA BRANCHARDIERE.

FIRST EDITION.

LONDON:
SIMPKIN, MARSHALL, AND CO.;
ACKERMANN & CO., STRAND; OLIVER AND BOYD, EDINBURGH;
AND ALL THE BERLIN WAREHOUSES.

1849.

CONTENTS

RULES.

Plain Crochet, in two or more colors.—Place the color not used along the stitches of the previous row, and crochet over it. *To change the colors,* when the two loops are on the needle, draw the other color through them to finish the stitch: in reckoning these stitches, it is best to count the lower or first loop of the stitches.

Bead Crochet—Pass a bead down, and work a plain stitch. This work is always on the wrong side of the crochet.

To Decrease—Take two stitches of the previous row on the needle, and work as one stitch.

For the other Terms used—*See First and Second Series.*

To My Patronesses.—As the beauty and effect of the following designs depend greatly upon a judicious selection of the materials and colors, I shall be happy to assist my Correspondents by forwarding samples for their guidance; or afford any information in my power, on the receipt of a "*directed stamped envelope and an extra stamp,*" which has become really necessary from the great labour and expense entailed upon me, by my anxious desire to facilitate, and *instruct,* the uninitiated in the art.

Sincerely acknowledging the kind commendations received, I beg to announce that it is my intention shortly to publish the Eighth Series of the Crochet Book, which will contain Mottoes, Alphabets, and Tablets, arranged for Purses, Handkerchiefs, Sachets, &c.

E. R. DE LA BRANCHARDIERE.

106, *New Bond Street.*

The Designs of the Pen-wiper and Bag are registered under the Act 5 and 6 Vict., cap. 100.

Ladies are respectfully informed that these articles cannot be purchased without the *registered* mark being affixed; and parties wishing to manufacture them for the purposes of sale, must have the Authoress's permission.

The Trade supplied with samples of the work on application, and are requested to observe the above notice.

Prices of Collars:

	s.	*d.*		*s.*	*d.*
Emblem	7	0	La Rose	5	0
Lily of the Valley	6	0	Le Bouquet de Fleurs	5	0
Honiton	6	0	La Reine des Fleurs	5	0

And the other Collars in the 1st and 2nd Series, from 2*s.* 6*d.* to 3*s.* 6*d.*

Point-Lacet Collars 7*s.* 6*d.*, 10*s.* 6*d.*, and 15*s.* each.

THE CROCHET BOOK.

SEVENTH SERIES.

ESSUIE-PLUME; OR PEN-WIPER,

GERANIUM LEAF, AND BUTTERFLY.

FOR THE BUTTERFLY.

Materials—1 *skein of shaded Violet, in short shades,* 1 *skein of plain Abricot or Gold colour,* 1 *skein of shaded Light Brown, and* 4 *yards of fine Silk Wire; Needle, No.* 20, *Bell Gauge.*

THE SUPERIOR OR FRONT WINGS.

The plain and single stitches are to be worked in double crochet. Commence with the lightest part of the shade of violet, work 23 chain, turn.

1st row—miss 1, 4 plain, 2 single, turn back.

2nd—1 single, 4 plain, 2 plain in one, turn back.

3rd—2 plain, 2 plain in one, 2 plain, 2 plain in one, 1 plain, and on the foundation chain, 2 plain, 2 single, turn back.

4th—1 single, 11 plain, 2 plain in one, turn back.

ESSUIE-PLUME.

Registered Design.

5th—Gold and violet—(violet, 2 plain, and 2 plain in one, 4 times,)—gold, 2 plain, and on the foundation chain, 2 plain, 2 single, turn back. Before working single stitches the other colour must be left in *front*, that it may be worked under the plain stitches in the next row.

6th—Gold, 1 single, 7 plain—violet, 14 plain, turn back.

7th—Violet, (4 plain, and 2 plain in one, twice,)—gold, (3 plain, and 2 plain in one, 3 times,) and on the foundation chain, 2 plain, 2 single, turn back.

8th—Gold, 1 single, 7 plain—violet, 5 plain—gold, 6 plain—violet, 12 plain, turn back.

9th—Violet, miss 1, 17 plain—gold, 13 plain, and on the foundation chain, 2 plain, 2 single, turn back. In the 4 following rows the wire is to be worked under, as in 2 colours. Commence by leaving an end of 3 inches to form a leg.

10th—Gold, 19 plain—violet, 15 plain, turn back.

11th—Violet, miss 1, 4 plain, 2 plain in one, 4 plain, 2 plain in one, 1 plain—(gold, 4 plain, and 2 plain in one, 3 times,) 6 plain, turn back.

12th—Gold, 25 plain—violet, 12 plain, turn back.

13th—Violet, miss 1, 8 plain—gold, 27 plain, leave 3 inches of the wire, turn back.

14th—Gold, 1 single, 26 plain, violet, 6 plain; miss 1, 1 plain, turn back.

15th—Violet, miss 1, 6 plain, 1 single, turn back.

16th—Violet, 1 single, 6 plain, turn back.

17th—Violet, 2 plain in one, 6 plain, and on the 14th row, 3 plain, 1 single, turn back.

18th—Violet, 1 single, 10 plain, 2 plain in one, turn back.

19th—Violet, (2 plain in one, and 2 plain, 4 times), 1 plain, then on the 14th row, 1 plain—gold, 3 plain, 1 single, turn back.

20th—Gold, 1 single, 7 plain—violet, 13 plain, 2 plain in one, turn back.

21st—Violet, (2 plain in one, and 3 plain, 4 times)—Gold, 7 plain, and on the 14th row, 5 plain, and 1 single, turn back.

22nd—Gold, 1 single, 1 plain—violet, 19 plain—gold, 3 plain—violet, 8 plain, 2 plain in one, turn back.

23rd—Violet, 2 plain in one, 8 plain—gold, 5 plain—violet, 20 plain, and on the 14th row, 3 plain, 1 single, turn back.

24th—Violet, 1 single, 24 plain—gold, 3 plain—violet, 11 plain, turn back.

25th—Violet, miss 1, 30 plain—gold, 8 plain, 6 plain on the 14th row. Fasten off, twist the 2 ends of wire for an inch and a half. Cut it off. Work another wing the same.

THE POSTERIOR WINGS.

With the gold silk work 19 chain, turn.

1st row—Miss 1, 6 plain, 2 single, turn back. 2nd row—1 single, 6 plain, turn back.

3rd—Violet and gold—gold, miss 1, 2 plain—violet, 2 plain in one—gold, 3 plain, and on the foundation chain, 1 plain, 2 single, turn back.

4th—Gold, 1 single, 4 plain—violet, 4 plain—gold, 1 plain, turn back.

5th—Gold, miss 1, 1 plain—violet, 2 plain—gold, 3 plain—violet, 3 plain, and on the foundation chain, 2 single, turn back.

6th—Violet, 1 single, 6 plain—gold, 4 plain, turn back.

7th—Gold, 2 plain—violet, 9 plain, and on the foundation, 2 single. turn back.

8th—Violet, 1 single, 7 plain—gold, 2 plain—violet, 1 plain—gold, 2 plain, turn back.

9th—Gold, 1 plain—violet, 1 plain—gold, 4 plain—violet, 7 plain, and on the foundation, 2 single. In the 4 following rows the wire is to be worked under; commence by leaving an end of 3 inches for the leg.

10th—Violet, 10 plain—gold, 2 plain—violet, 2 plain—gold, 2 plain in one, turn back.

11th—Gold, 2 plain, (violet 2 plain in one, and 3 plain, 3 times,) and on the foundation, 2 plain, turn back.

12th—Violet, 15 plain—gold, 2 plain—violet, 2 plain—gold, 2 plain in one, turn back.

13th—Gold, 1 plain—violet, 2 plain in one, 1 plain—gold, 4 plain—violet, (2 plain in one, and 2 plain, 3 times,)—gold, 2 plain—violet, 3 plain, turn back, leave 3 inches of the wire.

14th—Violet, 7 plain—gold, 2 plain—violet, 9 plain—gold, 2 plain—violet, 4 plain—gold, 2 plain in one, turn back.

15th—Gold, 4 plain—violet, 4 plain, 2 single, turn back.

16th—Violet, 1 single, 1 plain—gold, 8 plain, turn back.

17th—Gold, miss 1, 3 plain—violet, 2 plain—gold, 2 plain—violet, 2 plain, and on the 14th row, 5 plain, 2 single, turn back.

18th—Violet, 1 single, 5 plain—gold, 4 plain—violet, 4 plain—gold, 2 plain, turn back.

19th—Gold, miss 1, 2 plain—violet, 2 plain—gold, 3 plain—violet, 8 plain, and on the 14th row, 4 plain, 2 single, turn back.

20th—Violet, 1 single, 9 plain—gold, 9 plain, miss 1, 1 plain, turn back.

21st—Gold, miss 1, 17 plain—violet, 2 plain, and 3 plain on the 14th row. Fasten off, twist the wire, and work another wing the same.

FOR THE BODY.

Thread 2 gold beads upon the brown silk, and commence with the lightest part of the shade, work 4 chain, make it round; then work in *plain* crochet, (1 plain, and 2 plain in one, 5 times,) (2 plain, and 2 plain in one, 3 times,) 25 plain, (3 plain, and 2 plain in one, 6 times,) 54 plain, (decrease 1, and 4 plain, 10 times,) stuff the body with wool; and to form the head, 8 plain, 2 single, (2 plain in one, 6 times,) 2 plain, 1 single, 1 plain; pass a bead down, bring it through a stitch to the right side, 1 plain; and to form the antennæ, take a piece of gold twist or wire, tie two knots in it, 2 inches apart, cut off the ends close to the knots; then place the centre of this piece along the head, and keeping one of the ends in front, fasten it in, by working it under for 3 plain stitches; then bring the other end in front, work 1 plain; then 1 bead stitch as before, 2 plain, (miss 1, and 1 single, 10 times,) 5 chain, turn, miss 1, and 4 single on the 5 chain, 2 single on the head, 5 chain, turn, miss 1, and 4 single on the 5 chain, 1 single on the head. Fasten off; draw the end through the body.

Sew the wings to the body, and taking a piece of wire to form the centre legs, pass it through the middle of the body, leaving the wire sufficiently long to be attached to the following Leaf.

GERANIUM LEAF.

Material—Coarse Netting Silk, or German Wool, 4 shades of Green, 1 shade of Red-brown; Needle, No. 18, Bell Gauge.

The Double Stitches are formed by taking both sides of the stitch in the previous row, and working as a plain stitch.—*See 2nd Series.* The silk is cut off at the end of every row, drawing it through to fasten it; the ends are always to be worked under.

To Commence a Row—Put the needle in the stitch indicated in the direction, draw a loop through, and work 1 chain stitch. This counts as one stitch.

Commence with the 2nd shade of green, make 7 chain.

1st row—1 chain, (3 plain in one stitch of the foundation, 6 times), 1 single. Cut off the silk.

2nd—Commence in the 1 chain stitch of the 1st row, 1 plain, (1 double, and 2 plain in one stitch, 8 times), 1 double, (1 plain, and 1 single in one stitch).

3rd—Commence in the 1st stitch, 2 plain in one, 1 double, 1 plain. Repeat 8 times more; end 1 plain and 1 single in one stitch.

4th—Commence in the 1st stitch, 1 plain, *, 2 plain in one, 1 double, 2 plain. Repeat from *, 8 times more; end 1 plain and 1 single in one stitch.

5th, 6th, and 7th—Commence in the 1st stitch, 3 plain, (1 double, and 4 plain, 8 times), 1 double, 3 plain, 1 single.

8th—3rd shade of green—Commence in the 4th stitch of the last row, 1 double, (1 plain and 1 double both in one stitch), 3 plain. Repeat 7 times more; end 1 double, (1 plain and 1 single in one stitch), leaving 3 stitches unworked.

9th—Commence in the 3rd stitch of the 7th row, and on the 8th row, work 1 plain, 1 double, 1 plain, 1 double, 1 plain, 2 plain in one. Repeat 7 times more; end 1 plain, 1 double, 1 plain, 1 double, then 1 single on the 7th row.

10th—Commence in the 2nd stitch of the 7th row, and on the 9th row, work 1 plain, 1 double, (1 plain and 1 double both in one stitch), 1 plain, 1 double, 2 plain. Repeat 7 times more; end 1 plain, 1 double, (1 plain and 1 double in one stitch), 1 plain, 1 double, 1 plain; then 1 single on the 7th row.

11th—With the 4th shade of green—Commence in the 24th stitch of the 10th row, 2 plain, 1 double, 1 plain, 1 double, 2 plain in one, 1 double 1 plain. Repeat twice more; end 1 single, leaving 24 stitches unworked.

12th—Commence in the 16th stitch of the 10th row, 2 plain, 1 double, (2 plain in one, and 1 double, twice); then on the 11th row, *, 3 plain, 1 double, 2 plain in one, 1 double, 2 plain 1 double. Repeat from *, twice more; then 2 plain, and on the 10th row, 1 plain, 1 double, 2 plain in one, 1 double, 2 plain in one, 1 double, 2 plain, 1 single.

13th—Commence in the 8th stitch of the 10th row, 2 plain, 1 double, (2 plain in one, and 1 double, twice); then on the 12th row, *, 3 plain, 1 double, 2 plain, 1 double, 2 plain, 1 double. Repeat from *, 4 times more; then 3 plain, and on the 10th row (1 double, and 2 plain in one, twice), 1 double, 2 plain, 1 single.

14th—Commence in the one stitch left at the beginning of the 8th row, and on the 10th row, 2 plain, 1 double, (2 plain in one, and 1 double, twice); then on the 13th row, *, 3 plain, 1 double, 2 plain, 1 double, 2 plain, 1 double. Repeat from *, 6 times more; then 3 plain, and on the 10th row, (1 double, and 2 plain in one, twice), 1 double, 2 plain; then 1 single on the 7th row.

15th—Brown and green—Commence with the brown in the 1st stitch of the last row, 1 plain, *,—green, 1 plain, 1 double—brown, 1 plain—green, 1 plain, 1 double, 2 plain, 1 double—brown, 2 plain—green, 1 plain, 1 double, 2 plain, 1 double, 1 plain—brown, 1 plain—green, 1 double—brown, 2 plain. Repeat from *, 3 times more; end green, 1 plain, 1 double—brown, 1 plain—green, 1 plain, 1 double, 2 plain, 1 double—brown, 2 plain, 1 single.

16th—With the brown, commence in the 9th stitch of the last row, 1 double, 3 plain, *,—green, 1 double—brown, 2 plain—green, 1 double, 1 plain—brown, 1 plain, 1 double, 3 plain. Repeat from *, 6 times more; end 1 single, leaving 9 stitches unworked.

17th—Brown, commence in the 5th stitch of the 15th row, 1 plain—green, 1 double—brown, 1 plain, and on the 16th row, 1 plain, *,—brown, 1 double, 3 plain, 1 double, 2 plain—green, 1 double—brown, 2 plain. Repeat from *, 6 times more; then brown, 1 double, 3 plain, 1 double, and on the 15th row, 2 plain—green, 1 double—brown, 1 plain, 1 single.

18th—Brown and 2nd shade of green—brown, commence in the 3rd stitch of the 15th row—1 plain; then on the 17th row, *,—brown, 2 plain, 1 double, 2 plain, 1 double—green, 2 2 plain—brown, 1 plain, 1 double. Repeat from *, 7 times more, 2 plain, 1 double, 2 plain and on the 15th row, 1 plain and 1 single.

19th—Green—Commence in the 2nd stitch of the 15th row, and on the 18th row, 1 plain, 1 double, 2 plain, 1 double, *,—brown, 2 plain—green, 1 double, 3 plain—brown, 1 double, 1 plain—green, 1 plain, 1 double. Repeat from *, 7 times more; then brown, 2 plain—green, 1 double, 1 plain, and 1 single on the 15th row.

20th—Green—Commence in the 1st stitch of the 15th row, and on the 19th row, (2 plain, and 1 double, 3 times), *, 3 plain, 1 double, 1 plain, (2 treble in one stitch, 3 times), 1 plain, 1 double. Repeat from *, twice more, and for the centre, 3 plain, 1 double, (2 treble in one stitch, 5 times,) 1 double, then repeat, as between the *, 3 times, end 3 plain, (1 double, and 2 plain, 3 times), then 1 single on the 15th row.

21st—1st shade of green—Commence in the 5th stitch of the last row. *All the stitches* in this, and the following row, are to be worked in double crochet—6 plain, *, 1 single, 1 plain, 3 treble, (2 treble in one, 4 times), 3 treble, 1 plain. Repeat from *, twice more; and for the centre, 1 single, 1 plain, 4 treble, (2 long in one, 4 times), 4 treble, 1 plain; work as between the *, 3 times, end 1 single, 6 plain, 1 single.

22nd—Commence in the 1st stitch of the foundation, and work 2 chain and 1 plain 7 times up the side of the 1st 7 rows, 1 plain, (2 chain and 2 plain, twice), and on the 20th row (2 chain and 2 plain, twice), on the 21st row, 1 plain, *, 2 chain, 1 plain, 1 single, 2 chain, 2 treble in one, 1 plain, 1 single. Repeat from *, 26 times more, 1 plain, and on the 20th row 1 single, 2 chain, 1 plain, 1 single, and down the side of the rows (2 chain and 2 plain, twice), (2 chain and 1 plain, 7 times), and for the stem, work 7 plain on the foundation, turn back; make it round, and work 12 rounds plain on these 7 stitches; then 2 single, and fasten off; then pass the wire left at the body of the Butterfly through the Leaf to the wrong side and fasten; cut 6 or 8 pieces of green velvet or cloth the shape of the Leaf, and sew them to the wrong side of the work.

SOVEREIGN PURSE.

Material—Fine Netting Silk; Beads, No. 4; Needle, No. 22, Bell Gauge.

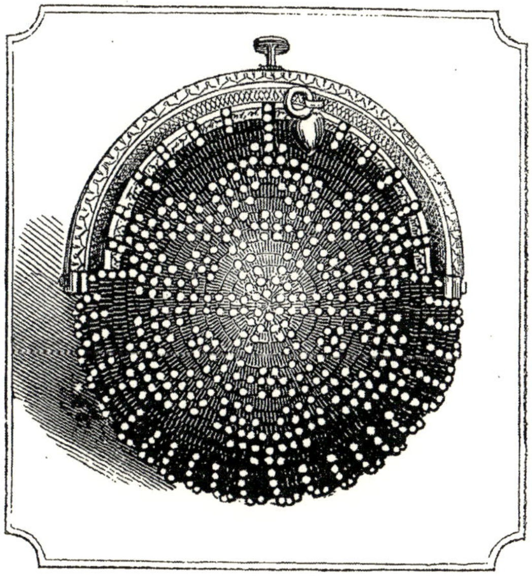

Thread 3 rows of beads upon the silk; and if shaded silk is used, commence with the lightest part. Work 6 chain, passing a bead down at each titch, and make it round.

1st round—2 bead stitches in each chain stitch, 6 times.

2nd—2 bead, 1 plain in the same stitch as the last bead stitch. Repeat 5 times more.

3rd—2 bead, 2 plain in one. Repeat.

4th—2 bead, 2 plain in one, 2 plain in the 4th stitch. Repeat.

5th—2 bead, 2 plain in one. Repeat 11 times.

6th—2 bead, 1 plain, 4 bead, 1 plain. Repeat 4 times more; then 2 bead, 1 plain, 4 bead, 1 plain in the same stitch as the last bead stitch.

7th—4 bead, 2 plain in one, 2 bead, 2 plain in one. Repeat 5 times.

8th—6 bead, 4 plain. Repeat 5 times.

9th—4 bead, 1 plain in the same stitch as the last bead stitch, 4 bead, 2 plain. Repeat times more, then 1 plain in the same stitch as the last plain stitch.

10th—5 bead, 2 plain in one, 5 bead, 1 plain in the same stitch as the last bead stitch. Repeat 5 times; then 5 bead stitches.

11th—6 plain, 7 bead. Repeat.

12th—2 plain in one, 8 plain, 2 plain in one, 3 bead. Repeat, end 10 plain and fasten off; then work the other side the same, ending with 2 plain instead of 10; then place the first side worked in front (the right side outside), at the fastening off; and to join them together work 54 plain stitches, putting the needle in a stitch of each side, and working them as one stitch. To form the edge, with a needle and silk, thread 8 beads, and sew it in every alternate stitch of the joining row. Then sew the purse firmly to the clasp; and in sewing it the last time round, when the needle is passed at the right side, thread 4 beads to each hole of the clasp which will hide the stitches.

PERSIAN PURSE.

Material—Gold Thread, 5 Skeins; Fine Netting Silk, 3 shades of Red, 3 shades of Green, 2 shades of Violet, 2 shades of Amber, and 3 Shades of Blue, one Skein of each, 2 Skeins of White and 2 of Black; Needle, No. 22, Bell Gauge.

Work a chain of 108 stitches with the gold thread, and make it round. This end of the purse is worked in plain crochet. With the black and gold work the

1st round—3 gold, 3 black, 18 times.

2nd—Darkest shade of red—2 gold, *, 3 red, 3 gold. Repeat from *, 16 times. Then 3 red.

3rd—2nd shade of red—3 red, 3 gold, 18 times, end with 1 gold.

4th—Lightest shade of red—3 red, 3 gold, 18 times.

5th—Gold, 108 plain.

6th—Black, gold, and darkest shade of green—1 gold, 13 black, 3 green, 2 black, 6 gold, 2 black. Repeat 3 times more.

7th—2nd shade of green—1 gold, 2 black, 7 green, 3 black, 3 green, 3 black, 1 gold, 4 black, 1 gold, 2 black. Repeat.

8th—1st shade of green—1 gold, 1 black, 5 green, 3 black, 5 green, 4 black, 1 gold, 4 black. 1 gold, 2 black. Repeat.

9th—Darkest shade of violet—1 gold, *, 1 violet, 3 black, 3 violet, 1 black, 8 violet, 2 black, 3 gold, 4 black, 4 gold. Repeat from *.

10th—2nd shade of violet—5 black, 3 violet, 2 black, 8 violet, 2 black, 1 gold, 6 black. Repeat, end 5 black instead of 6.

PERSIAN PURSE.

11th—1st shade of violet—7 black, 3 violet, 11 black, 3 gold, 3 black. Repeat.

12th—3 black, 3 gold, 1 black, 4 gold, 2 black, 4 gold, 6 black, 1 gold, 3 black. Repeat.

13th—White silk—2 black, 1 white, 1 black, 2 white, 1 black, 3 white, 2 black, 8 white, 3 black, 3 gold, 1 black. Repeat.

14th—Darkest shade of blue—2 black, 1 blue, 3 black, 3 blue, 3 black, 10 blue, 3 black, 1 gold, 1 black. Repeat, end 1 black.

15th—2nd shade of blue—1 black, 6 blue, 4 black, 10 blue, 3 black, 3 gold. Repeat.

16th—Darkest shade of amber—2 black, 4 amber, 6 black, 10 amber, 4 black, 1 gold. Repeat, end 2 black.

17th—1st shade of amber—12 black, 8 amber, 4 black, 3 gold. Repeat.

18th—1st shade of red—16 black, 4 red, 6 black, 1 gold. Repeat.

19th—5 gold, 3 black, 3 gold, 2 black, 2 gold, 1 black, 3 gold, 7 black, 1 gold. Repeat.

20th—2nd shade of red—4 black, 1 gold, 5 black, 1 gold, 2 black, 1 red, 1 black, 4 red, 2 black, 3 gold, 2 black, 1 gold. Repeat.

21st—1st shade of red—4 black, 1 gold, 5 black, 1 gold, 2 black, 5 red, 5 black, 1 gold, 2 black, 1 gold. Repeat.

22nd—1st shade of green—4 black, 7 gold, 3 black, 3 green, 6 black, 4 gold. Repeat.

23rd—Gold, 105 plain; then repeat the first 5 rows, working the shades of blue instead of the red, and for the 2nd stripe of pattern, work the 6th, 7th, 8th, 9th, 10th, 11th, and 12th rounds, using the white silk for the ground, instead of the black.

24th—As the 13th, using the darkest red instead of white.

25th—As 14th, 2nd shade of red instead of blue. 26th—As 15th, black instead of blue.

27th and 28th—As 16th and 17th rounds. 29th—As 18th, 2nd shade of blue instead of red.

30th—As 19th. 31st—As 20th, darkest shade of blue instead of red.

32nd—As 21st, light blue instead of red. 33rd—As 22nd, light red instead of green.

34th—Gold, 105 plain; then repeat the first 5 rounds, end 2 single, and fasten off. And to form the opening, with the darkest shade of blue, work in the 25th stitch from the fastening off. (To commence in treble crochet—*See 2nd Series.*)

1st row—1 treble, *, 1 chain, miss 1, 1 treble. Repeat from *; cut off the silk. The following rows are worked in the same manner.

2nd—2nd shade of blue, same as the last row, the ends of the silk at the beginning and end of the rows must be firmly knotted together.

3rd—Lightest blue as before; then work 3 rows with the shades of red, the same.

4th—White as before. 5th—Gold as before.

6th—White as before; then work 3 rows with the shades of violet, and 3 rows with the shades of green. 7th—Gold as before; then 3 rows with the shades of red.

8th—White as before; then make it round by commencing with the black silk in the 27th stitch of the last row, work a plain round, joining it together at the opening. Should a motto and name be required (see crochet motto and Alphabet Book); the pattern in the 8 following rounds must be omitted, and the letters worked in gold and black.

1st round—5 black, 4 gold, 12 times, end 1 black. 2nd—3 black, 6 gold, 12 times.

3rd—2 black, 2 gold, 4 black, 1 gold. Repeat 11 times more.

4th—1 black, 2 gold, 2 black, 2 gold, 1 black, 1 gold. Repeat, end 1 black, 2 gold.

5th—1 black, 4 gold, 2 black, 2 gold. Repeat, end 1 black.

6th—2 gold, 3 black, 2 gold, 2 black. Repeat.

7th—6 gold, 3 black. Repeat, end 1 black.

8th—4 gold, 5 black. Repeat.

9th—Black, plain.

10th—Gold, plain.

11th—Gold, 1 chain, miss 1, 1 treble. Repeat.

12th, 13th, and 14th—3 shades of red, 1 chain, miss 1, 1 treble, repeat.

15th—Dark green, miss 1, 1 treble, 1 chain, miss 1, 1 treble. Repeat.

16th—2nd shade of green, 1 chain, miss 2, 1 treble. Repeat.

17th—1st shade of green, same as 11th. 18th—Dark violet, same as 15th.

19th—2nd shade of violet, same as 16th. 20th—1st shade of violet, same as 15th.

21st—Gold, miss 2, 1 treble. Repeat. Draw up the remaining stitches, finish with tassel to correspond; and to join it at the square end with the gold thread, commence at the beginning of the foundation chain, and work a row of plain crochet, putting the needle in a stitch of both sides, working it as one stitch, turn back.

2nd row—1 chain, miss 1, 1 treble. Repeat along the joining row.

3rd—5 chain, miss 3, 1 plain. Repeat.

4th, 5th, and 6th—3 single *, 5 chain, miss 5, 1 plain. Repeat from *, and fasten off; finish with 2 small gold tassels at each side, and rings to correspond.

BAG; FUCHSIA PATTERN.

Material—1 *Skein of shaded Blue,* 1 *shaded Violet,* 1 *shaded Scarlet, and* 4 *shaded Green; the Silk to be used is the middle sized, and in short shades;* 12 *Skeins of Fine Gold Twist, or* 3 *Skeins of Abricot Silk; Needle, No.* 20, *Bell Gauge.*

For the Stripe of FLOWERS and LEAVES—1st SIDE, commence with the shaded green, and for the

1st LEAF—11 chain, turn, miss 4, 1 single in the 5th stitch to form a round loop, turn back; 5 chain and 1 plain, 3 times in the round loop, turn back; (miss 1, 1 plain, 7 treble and 1 plain; these 9 stitches in each 5 chain, 3 times), 4 single down the stem, 7 chain; join it to the 7th *stitch* of the 3rd division of the Leaf, *, 15 chain, and for the calyx of the FLOWER, turn, miss 6, 2 treble, 1 plain and 1 single on the 15 chain, leaving 5 chain for the centre stem, leave the green silk; and for the

FLOWER, with the Scarlet, work 1 plain and 1 treble in the 6 chain at the top of the calyx, 3 chain, join it to the 7th *stitch* of the 2nd division of the Leaf, 2 chain, miss 2, 1 plain on the 1st stitch of the 3 chain, 1 treble and 1 plain in the 6 chain, (1 treble in the 6 chain, 5 chain, turn, miss 4, 1 plain, on the 1st stitch of the 5 chain, 1 treble and 1 plain in the 6 chain, as before, 4 times): knot this end and the one at the commencement firmly together; then with the green silk left at the calyx work 7 chain; join it to the point of the *last division* of the Flower; then 13 chain, and for the

2nd LEAF—Turn, miss 4, 1 single in the 5th stitch, turn back; 5 chain and 1 plain in the round loop 3 times, turn back; miss 1, (1 plain and 2 treble in the 5 chain, join it to the

BAG.

Registered Design.

point of the 4th *division* of the Flower, 5 treble and 1 plain in the same 5 chain), (miss 1, 1 plain, 7 treble, and 1 plain in the next five chain, twice), 4 single down the stem, leaving 5 chain for the centre stem, 7 chain, and join it to the 7th stitch of the 3rd *division* of the Leaf. Repeat from *, 8 times more, working the 2nd Flower with the blue, the 3rd, scarlet, 4th, violet, 5th, scarlet, 6th, blue, 7th, scarlet, 8th, violet, 9th, scarlet, and after ending with the " 7 chain joined to the Leaf," work 3 chain.

For the 2nd side of the STRIPE, turn, miss 1, 2 plain on the 3 chain, and on the chain stitches left for the centre stem, work 7 plain on the 7 chain, and 3 plain on the 5 chain, in all 12 plain; then 10 chain, and for the calyx of the Flower, turn, miss 6, 2 treble, 1 plain, 1 single. Leave the green silk, and with the blue, work a Flower the same as the other side, joining it to the 6th stitch of the 12 plain worked down the centre stem * *; then with the green, work 12 plain down the centre stem, 9 chain, and for the

LEAF—turn, miss 4, 1 single, turn back; 5 chain and 1 plain, 3 times in the round loop, turn back; miss 1, (1 plain and 2 treble in the 5 chain, join it the 6th *stitch* of the 12 plain worked down the centre stem, 5 treble and 1 plain in the same 5 chain), miss 1, (1 plain and 2 treble in the next 5 chain, join it to the point of the *last* division of the Flower, 5 treble and 1 plain in the same 5 chain), miss 1, (1 plain, 7 treble and 1 plain in the next 5 chain), 4 single down the stem, 12 plain down the centre stem; then 10 chain for the calyx of the 2nd Flower, turn, miss 6, 2 treble, 1 plain, 1 single, and with the scarlet, work as the 1st Flower; then repeat from * *, 8 times, varying the colours as the other side. Fasten off. Work 3 stripes more.

STAR PATTERN INSERTION.

With the gold twist, work 2 chain; then commence by working 1 plain on the 6th stitch of the 1st division of the 1st Leaf of one of the Stripes, work along the Leaves and Flowers, thus—

1st row—3 chain, miss 6, 1 plain on the 2nd division of the Leaf, 3 chain, miss 9, 1 plain on the point of the 4th division of the Flower, 3 chain, miss 7, 1 plain on the point of the 3rd division, 3 chain, miss 10, 1 plain on the 1st division of the next Leaf. Repeat along the 1st side of the Stripe, ending with 3 chain, miss 6, 1 plain on the 2nd division of the Leaf, 3 chain. Cut off the twist.

2nd—Commence on the 1st chain stitch of the last row, 5 plain; and to form the 1st Star, 10 chain, turn, miss 6, 1 single in the 7th stitch to form a round loop, leaving 3 chain, turn, (4 chain and 1 plain, 11 times in the round loop), 2 chain, miss 2, 1 single in the 1st stitch of the 3 chain, (2 chain, miss 4 and 1 single in the 4 chain, 12 times), *; 4 plain on the 1st row, 4 chain, turn, miss 3, 1 single in the 1st stitch of the 4 chain, (3 chain and 1 single in the same stitch as the last single, twice); then 4 plain on the 1st row, and for the 2nd Star, 10 chain, turn, miss 6, 1 single, (4 chain and 1 plain, 11 times, in the round loop), (2 chain, miss 4, 1 single in the 4 chain, 3 times); join it to the 9th *single* stitch of the 1st Star, (2 chain, miss 4, and 1 single, 9 times). Repeat from *, ending with 5 plain. Fasten off, and knot the ends together. Repeat these two rows upon two more of the Stripes; the 4th Stripe, which forms the outside of the Bag, does not require the Star Pattern. Then on the 2nd side of the 4th Stripe, work the following row, which will form the 3rd row of the Insertion.

3rd—2 chain, commence on the point of the 3rd division of the 1st Flower of the 2nd side of the Stripe, work 3 chain, miss 7, 1 plain on the 4th point of the Flower, 3 chain, miss 10, 1 plain on the 2nd division of the Leaf, 3 chain, miss 6, 1 plain on the 1st division of the Leaf, 3 chain, miss 10, 1 plain in the 3rd point of the next Flower. Repeat, and end 3 chain, miss 7, 1 plain on the 4th point of the Flower, 3 chain. Cut off. Repeat this row on the 2nd and 3rd Stripes, and to join these Stripes together—

4th—Commence on the 1st chain stitch of the last row, 5 plain, *, join it to the 6th *single* stitch of the last Star worked in one of the Stripes, then 4 plain on the 3rd row, 4 chain, turn, miss 3, 1 single in the 1st stitch of the 4 chain, (3 chain and 1 single in the same stitch as the last single, twice), 4 plain on the 3rd row. Repeat from *, joining to every star along the Stripe, ending with 1 plain. Fasten off, and work the same on the other two Stripes.

To join the sides of the Bag, commence on the 1st Stripe, double it, and placing the edges together, work as the 1st *row* of the insertion, putting the needle through both sides of the pattern working it as one stitch. Repeat to the corner, turn back.

2nd—2 chain, miss 1, (2 treble, 3 chain, 2 treble, these 4 treble in one stitch), 2 chain, miss 1, 1 plain, repeat along the joining row, and fasten off. Then commence on the edge of the 4th Stripe, and join it by working the 3rd row of insertion, then work the 2nd row as directed for the other edge.

BAND FOR THE TOP.

1st round—With the green silk, commence upon the 2nd division of the Leaf at the top of the

1st Stripe, 4 chain, miss 6, 1 plain on the 3rd division of the Leaf, 4 chain, miss 4, 1 plain on the centre stem, 4 chain, miss 12, 1 plain on the 2nd point of the Flower, 4 chain, miss 7, 1 plain on the 4th row of the insertion, 6 chain, 1 plain on the 9th single stitch of the star, 6 chain, 1 plain on the 1st row of the insertion. Repeat all round.

2nd and 3rd rounds—4 chain, miss 1, 1 treble, *, 1 chain, miss 1, 1 treble. Repeat from *, end 1 chain, miss 1, 1 single in the 4 chain, worked at the commencement.

4th—Gold, 2 chain, miss 2, (2 treble, 3 chain, 2 treble, these 4 treble in one stitch), 2 chain, miss 2, 1 plain. Repeat and fasten off. Line the Bag with white satin, fasten with cord and slides to correspond.

FUCHSIA TASSEL.

Material—Same as the Bag.

For the FLOWER—Commence with the shaded scarlet, 4 chain, make it round, and work the plain stitches in *double crochet.*

1st round—Two plain in one of the foundation, 4 times. 2nd—Two plain in one, 8 times.

3rd and 4th—16 plain. 5th—Decrease one stitch and 2 plain, 4 times.

6th—Decrease one and 1 plain, 4 times, 1 single. 7th—3 chain and 2 plain, 4 times.

8th—1 chain, miss 1, (2 treble, 3 chain, 2 treble, these 4 treble in the 3 chain of the last round), then 1 chain, miss 1, 1 plain between the 2 plain. Repeat 3 times more.

9th—3 chain, miss 2, (2 treble in the 3 chain of the last round, 3 chain, turn, miss 2, 1 plain in the 3 chain, 2 treble in the same 3 chain as before), 3 chain, miss 2, 1 plain in the 1 chain, miss 1, 1 plain in the next 1 chain. Repeat 3 times more, and fasten off. Work 3 Flowers more the same ; then 2 with the shaded violet, and 2 with the shaded blue.

FOR THE STEM AND SMALL LEAVES.

With the shaded green commence upon the top of a red Flower, work 17 chain for the Leaf turn, miss 2, 6 single, 1 chain to cross the stem, and on the other side, 1 plain, 4 treble, 2 plain, 1 chain, turn, and down the other side 2 plain, 4 treble, 1 plain, 1 single on the stem, which finishes the Leaf ; then 26 chain and work another Leaf ; when finished, 8 chain, join it to the top of another red Flower, work 7 plain on the 8 chain, then 10 chain, work a 3rd Leaf ; then 16 plain down the stem, 10 chain, and work a 4th Leaf ; when finished, 8 plain down the stem, and fasten off, bringing the ends through the Flower. Then join 2 violet, and 2 blue Flowers in the same manner.

FOR THE CENTRE STEM AND LEAVES.

With the shaded green silk make a chain of 28 stitches, and for the Leaf, turn, miss 1, 3 plain, 12 treble, 3 plain, turn, 1 chain to cross the stem, and on the other side 3 plain, 2 treble, 9 long, 2 treble, 2 plain, 1 plain at the point, and on the other side 2 plain, 2 treble, 9 long, 2 treble, 2 plain, 2 single on the stem, then 79 chain, draw the silk and loop through the centre of a 3rd Red Flower and pass it up the stem, then work a *small Leaf* as before ; when finished, 8 chain, join to the top of the 4th red Flower, turn, and down the stem, 7 plain, 10 chain, work a 2nd *small Leaf,* 20 plain on the stem, take the stem of the 2 blue Flowers and fold it in half, lay it across the *centre* stem, and work 1 plain on it to fasten it in, then 14 plain on the centre stem, take the stem of the 2 red *Flowers,* and join it to the centre stem as before, 14 plain, then join the 2 violet, 8 plain on the centre stem, and bring the loop and silk through the red Flower first placed upon the stem, 8 plain, then 22 chain, and work a large Leaf the same as at the commencement. When finished work 8 plain upon the centre stem, and fasten off. Make a small tuft with gold thread, about an inch long, sew it in the centre of each Flower.

TASSEL FOR ANTI-MACASSARS, ETC.

The Flower of the preceding direction forms an appropriate ornament for many articles of crochet, in wool for sofa pillows, blinds, &c., and in thread and cotton, for Anti-macassars. After working the Flower make the tuft, and with the end left work 20 chain, join it to the tuft, and fasten off, then draw the loop of chain stitches through the centre of the Flower.

CARRIAGE BAG.

Material—Shaded Single German Wool; colours the same as directed for the Bag, and for the Insertion, use Grey Crochet Twine; or Gold coloured Crochet Silk, and work as directed for the Bag, line with Black Velvet or Cloth.

FOR SOFA PILLOW.

Material as above, working 7 Flower Stripes; and in shaded Shetland Wool, it can be adapted for a variety of ornamental purposes.

BEAD PURSE,

ARABESQUE PATTERN.

Material—Fine Netting Silk, 1 skein of shaded Green, and 1 of shaded Violet; 3 skeins of Gold Colour, 2 of French Blue, and 1 skein of shaded Ponceau; 4 Bunches of Steel Beads, No. 5; Needle, No. 22, Bell Gauge. The Gold colour must be of the Abricot shade.

In working the shaded silk, always commence with the darkest part of the shade.

Thread one row of beads on the blue silk, work a chain of 10 stitches, and make it round.

1st round—2 plain in one, 1 bead, 2 plain in one, 2 bead, 2 plain in one, 1 bead, 2 plain in one, 2 bead. Thread two rows of beads on the gold silk, and join it.

2nd—Work with the blue, 2 plain in one twice—gold, 1 bead—blue, 2 plain in one twice, 2 bead. Repeat once more. The two bead stitches at the sides which divide the pattern, are always to be worked *over* those of the preceding round.

3rd—Blue, 2 plain in one 3 times—gold, 3 bead—blue, 2 plain in one 3 times, 2 bead. Repeat.

4th—Blue, 4 plain—gold, 7 bead—blue, 4 plain, 2 bead. Repeat.

5th—Blue, 2 plain in one, 1 plain, 2 plain in one—gold, 9 *bead.* Then reverse the direction for this round; that is, reading it from left to right, omitting the stitches in *italics* as they form the centre of the pattern, which will be seen by the section. For example—blue, 2 plain in one, 1 plain, 2 plain in one; end with 2 bead, always repeat the whole of the pattern for the other side.

6th—Blue, 2 plain in one twice, 3 plain—gold, 4 bead, 1 *plain,* reverse as before, end 2 bead.

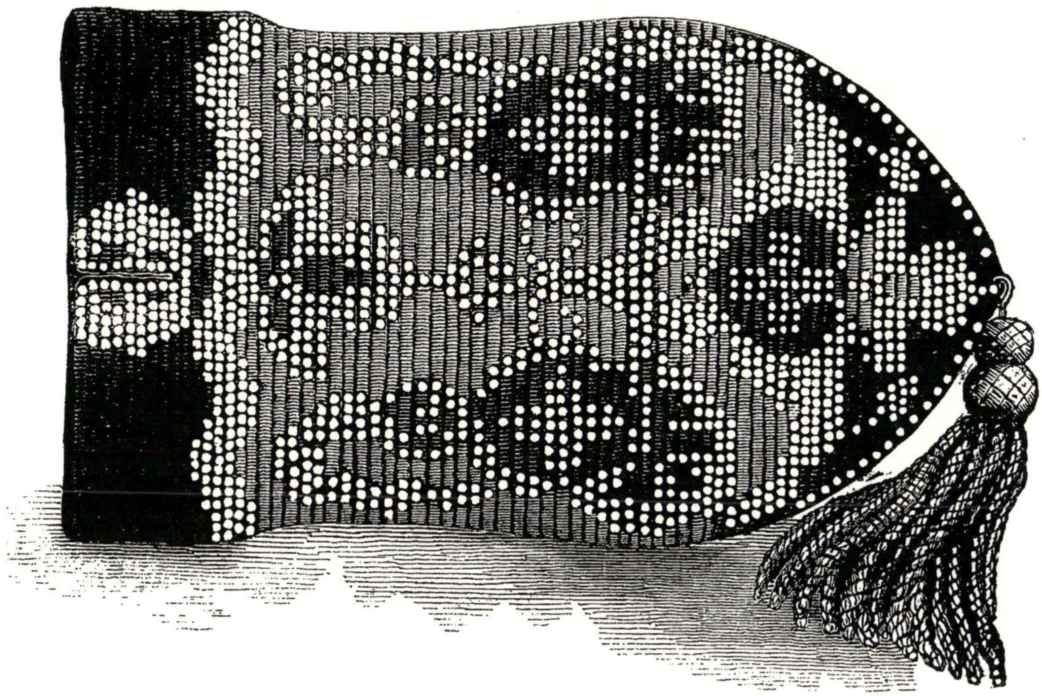

[SECTION OF PURSE.]

7th—Blue, 4 plain, 2 plain in one 3 times—gold, 4 bead, 1 *plain,* reverse, and end 2 bead.

8th—Blue, 2 plain in one—gold, 2 bead—blue, 4 plain, 2 plain in one, 3 plain—gold, 2 bead, 3 *plain,* reverse, and end 2 bead.

9th—Blue, 2 plain in one—gold, 4 bead—blue, 3 plain—gold, 7 bead, 3 *plain,* reverse, and end 2 bead.

10th—Blue, 2 plain in one, 1 plain—gold, 4 bead—blue, 3 plain—gold, 7 bead, 3 *plain,* reverse, and end 2 bead.

11th—Blue, 4 plain—gold, 2 bead—blue, 4 plain—gold, 8 bead, 1 *plain,* reverse, end 2 bead.

12th—Blue, 3 plain—gold, 1 bead—blue, 7 plain—gold, 2 bead, 4 plain, 3 *bead,* reverse, end 2 bead.

13th—Blue, 4 plain—gold, 1 bead—blue, 7 plain—gold, 2 bead, 4 plain, 1 *bead* reverse, end 2 bead. Cut off the gold silk, and thread 4 rows of beads on the ponceau, join it.

14th—Blue, 2 plain in one—red, 2 bead—blue, 1 plain, 2 plain in one—red, 12 bead, 3 *plain,* reverse, end 2 bead.

15th—Blue, 1 plain—red, 1 bead—blue, 3 plain—red, 12 bead, 2 plain, 3 *bead,* reverse, end 2 bead.

16th—Blue, 1 plain—red, 1 bead—blue, 1 plain—red, 12 bead, 4 plain, 3 *bead,* reverse, end 2 bead. Cut off the blue, thread 2 rows of beads on the gold silk, join it.

17th—Red, 9 bead—gold, 2 plain—red, 4 bead, 4 plain, 3 *bead,* reverse, end gold, 2 plain.

18th—Red, 7 bead—gold, 2 plain, 2 plain in one—red, 4 bead, 2 plain, 3 bead, 1 plain, 1 *bead,* reverse, end gold, 2 plain.

19th—Red, 5 bead—gold, 2 plain in one, 4 plain—red, 6 bead, 1 plain, 9 *bead,* reverse, end gold, 2 plain.

20th—Red, 3 bead—gold, 8 plain, 2 plain in one—red, 4 bead, 2 plain, 3 bead, 1 plain, 1 *bead,* reverse, end gold, 2 plain.

21st—Red, 3 bead—gold, 11 plain—red, 4 bead, 4 plain, 3 *bead,* reverse, end gold, 2 plain.

22nd—Red, 2 bead—gold, 11 plain, 2 plain in one—red, 4 bead, 4 plain, 3 *bead,* reverse, end gold, 2 plain. Thread 2 rows of beads on the green silk.

23rd—Red, 2 bead—gold, 2 plain—green, 7 bead—gold, 4 plain—red, 2 bead, 1 plain, 2 bead, 3 plain, 3 *bead,* reverse, end gold, 2 plain.

24th—Red, 1 bead—gold, 2 plain—green, 9 bead—gold, 7 plain—red, 2 bead, 7 *plain,* reverse, end gold, 2 plain.

25th—Gold, 2 plain—green, 6 bead, 2 plain, 3 bead—gold, 6 plain—red, 4 bead, 3 *plain,* reverse, end gold, 2 plain. Cut off the red silk.

26th—Gold, 2 plain—green, 2 bead, 2 plain, 2 bead, 2 plain, 4 bead—gold, 3 plain, 5 bead, 1 plain, 3 *bead,* reverse, end gold 2 plain.

27th—Gold, 1 plain—green, 3 bead, 3 plain, 1 bead, 2 plain, 1 bead, 1 plain, 3 bead—gold, 2 plain, 5 bead, 2 plain, 1 *bead,* reverse, end gold, 2 plain.

28th—Gold, 1 plain—green, 4 bead, 2 plain, 1 bead, 2 plain, 1 bead, 2 plain, 2 bead—gold, 3 plain, 2 bead, 1 plain, 2 bead, 3 *plain,* reverse, end gold, 2 plain.

29th—Green, 6 bead, 7 plain, 3 bead—gold, 2 plain, 1 bead, 2 plain, 3 bead, 1 *plain,* reverse, end gold, 2 plain. Thread 3 rows of beads on the violet silk.

30th—Green, 3 bead, 4 plain—violet, 6 bead—green, 2 plain, 1 bead—gold, 1 plain, 3 bead, 2 plain, 5 *bead,* reverse, end gold, 2 plain.

31st—Green, 3 bead, 2 plain—violet, 3 bead, 4 plain, 2 bead—green, 1 plain, 1 bead—gold, 1 plain, 2 bead, 1 plain, 1 bead, 1 plain, 5 *bead,* reverse, end gold, 2 plain.

32nd—Green, 3 bead, 2 plain—violet, 2 bead, 3 plain, 1 bead, 3 plain, 1 bead—gold, 6 plain, 1 bead, 1 plain, 3 *bead,* reverse, end gold, 2 plain.

33rd—Gold, 1 plain—green, 2 bead, 1 plain—violet, 2 bead, 3 plain, 3 bead, 3 plain, 2 bead —gold, 5 plain, 5 *bead,* reverse, end gold, 2 plain.

34th—Gold, 1 plain—green, 1 bead, 2 plain—violet, 2 bead, 3 plain, 3 bead, 3 plain, 2 bead —gold, 5 plain, 1 bead, 1 plain, 1 *bead,* reverse, end gold, 2 plain.

35th—Gold, 2 plain—green, 1 bead, 1 plain—violet, 1 bead, 2 plain, 7 bead, 2 plain, 1 bead —gold, 2 plain, 2 bead, 2 plain, 1 bead, 1 *plain,* reverse, end gold, 2 plain. Cut off the green silk.

36th—Gold, 4 plain—violet, 1 bead, 1 plain, 9 bead, 1 plain, 1 bead—gold, 1 plain, 1 bead, 1 plain, 1 bead, 2 plain, 1 bead, 1 *plain,* reverse, end gold, 2 plain.

37th—Gold, 4 plain—violet, 1 bead, 2 plain, 7 bead, 2 plain, 1 bead—gold, 1 plain, 1 bead, 3 plain, 2 bead, 1 *plain,* reverse, end gold, 2 plain.

38th—Gold, 4 plain—violet, 2 bead, 3 plain, 3 bead, 4 plain, 1 bead—gold, 1 plain, 5 bead, 1 plain, 1 *bead,* reverse, end gold, 2 plain.

39th—Gold, 5 plain—violet, 2 bead, 2 plain, 3 bead, 3 plain, 2 bead—gold, 2 plain, 3 bead, 2 plain, 1 *bead,* reverse, end gold, 2 plain.

40th—Gold, 6 plain—violet, 2 bead, 2 plain, 1 bead, 3 plain, 2 bead—gold, 7 plain, 1 bead 1 *plain,* reverse, end gold, 2 plain.

41st—Gold, 3 plain—violet, 1 bead—gold, 3 plain—violet, 2 bead, 3 plain, 3 bead—gold, 7 plain, 2 bead, 1 *plain,* reverse, end gold, 2 plain.

42nd—Gold, 3 plain—violet, 2 bead—gold, 3 plain—violet, 4 bead—gold, 9 plain—2 bead, 3 *plain*, reverse, end gold 2 plain. Cut off the violet, thread one row of beads on the green.

43rd—Gold, 3 plain—green, 2 bead—gold, 4 plain—green, 2 bead, 1 plain, 2 bead—gold, 8 plain, 2 bead, 1 *plain*, reverse, end gold, 2 plain.

44th—Gold, 2 plain—green, 2 bead—gold, 4 plain—green, 2 bead, 3 plain, 2 bead—gold, 8 plain, 3 *bead*, reverse, end gold, 2 plain.

45th—Gold, 2 plain—green, 1 bead—gold, 5 plain—green, 1 bead, 1 plain, 2 bead, 1 plain, 2 bead—gold, 9 plain, 1 *bead*, reverse, end, gold, 2 plain. Thread 3 rows of beads on the ponceau.

46th—Gold, 2 plain—green, 1 bead, 1 plain, 1 bead—gold, 3 plain—green, 1 bead, 1 plain, 2 bead, 2 plain, 1 bead—gold, 9 plain—red, 1 *bead*, reverse, end gold, 2 plain.

47th—Gold, 1 plain—green, 1 bead, 1 plain, 2 bead—gold, 3 plain—green, 2 bead, 4 plain, 1 bead—gold, 8 plain—red, 3 *bead*, reverse, end gold, 2 plain.

48th—Gold, 1 plain—green, 3 bead—gold, 5 plain—green, 3 bead, 1 plain, 1 bead—gold, 7 plain,—red, 7 *bead*, reverse, end gold, 2 plain. Cut off the green silk.

49th—Gold, 1 plain—red, 1 bead, 1 plain, 1 bead—gold, 6 plain—red, 3 bead—gold, 7 plain red, 9 *bead*, reverse, end gold, 2 plain.

50th—Gold, 1 plain—red, 1 bead, 1 plain, 2 bead—gold, 4 plain—red, 1 bead, 1 plain, 3 bead—gold, 6 plain—red, 4 bead, 1 *plain*, reverse, end gold, 2 plain.

51st—Gold, 2 plain—red, 3 bead—gold, 4 plain—red, 2 bead, 1 plain, 2 bead—gold, 6 plain —red, 4 bead, 1 *plain*, reverse, end gold, 2 plain.

52nd—Gold—2 plain—red, 2 bead—gold, 5 plain—red, 2 bead, 1 plain, 2 bead—gold, 7 plain—red, 2 bead, 3 *plain*, reverse, end gold, 2 plain.

53rd—Gold, 1 plain—red, 1 bead, 2 plain, 2 bead—gold, 2 plain—red, 1 bead, 1 plain, 3 bead, —gold, 3 plain—red, 7 bead, 3 *plain*, reverse, end gold, 2 plain.

54th—Gold, 1 plain—red, 1 bead, 1 plain, 3 bead—gold, 2 plain—red, 1 bead, 1 plain, 2 bead, —gold, 4 plain—red, 7 bead, 3 *plain*, reverse, end gold, 2 plain.

55th—Gold, 2 plain—red, 3 bead—gold, 3 plain—red, 3 bead—gold, 5 plain—red, 8 bead, 1 *plain*, reverse, end gold, 2 plain.

56th—Gold, 3 plain—red, 1 bead—gold, 3 plain—red, 3 bead—gold, 7 plain—red, 2 bead, 4 plain, 3 *bead*, reverse, end gold, 2 plain.

57th—Gold, 4 plain—red, 4 bead—gold, 10 plain—red, 2 bead, 4 plain, 1 *bead*, reverse, end gold, 2 plain. Cut off the red, thread 6 rows of beads on the blue silk.

58th—Gold, 18 plain—blue, 5 bead, 1 plain, 5 bead—gold, 40 plain—blue, 5 bead, 1 plain, 5 bead—gold, 22 plain.

59th—Gold, 9 plain—blue, 4 bead—gold, 8 plain—blue, 5 bead—gold, 8 plain—blue, 4 bead —gold, 8 plain—blue, 6 bead—gold, 8 plain—blue, 4 bead—gold, 8 plain—blue, 5 bead—gold, 8 plain—blue, 4 bead—gold, 8 plain—blue, 6 bead—gold, 2 plain.

60th—Gold, 4 plain—blue, 8 bead—gold, 4 plain—blue, 9 bead—gold, 4 plain—blue, 8 bead gold, 4 plain—blue, 10 bead. Repeat once more. Cut off the gold silk.

61st—Blue, 102 bead. 62nd—Work 100 bead.

63rd—8 bead, 4 plain, 8 bead, 5 plain, 8 bead, 4 plain, 8 bead, 6 plain. Repeat.

64th—2 plain, 4 bead, 8 plain, 4 bead, 9 plain, 4 bead, 8 plain, 4 bead, 8 plain. Repeat, then

2 single, fasten off the silk; and to form the opening, commence in the centre stitch of the 9 plain, or 21 stitches from the fastening off.

65th—5 bead, 91 plain, 5 bead; draw the silk through to fasten it; then lay the silk round the work, and commence in the 1st stitch of the last row; work the loose silk under it. Observe this rule in the following rows.

66th—1 bead, 1 plain, 5 bead, 87 plain, 5 bead, 1 plain, 1 bead. Draw the silk through.

67th & 68th—1 bead, 3 plain, 4 bead, 85 plain, 4 bead, 3 plain, 1 bead.

69th & 70th—1 bead, 1 plain, 2 bead, 1 plain, 4 bead, 83 plain, 4 bead, 1 plain, 2 bead, 1 plain, 1 bead.—71st & 72nd—Same as 67th.—73rd—As the 66th.

74th, as the 65th—Repeat the last 10 rows, 3 times more; and to make it round, commence on the 79th stitch of the last row, work as the 64th round, joining it at the opening; then work as 63rd and 62nd rounds. Leave this part of the purse, and for the other end, commence at the 1st round, working to the 62nd round; then place the two parts of the purse together, joining them on the wrong side by taking a stitch of each part and working it as one stitch. The rings should be put on before the ends are joined together.

BAG, ARABESQUE.

The above pattern forms a beautiful Bag of three sides, using Coarse Netting silk, and No. 9 Beads; Needle, No. 18, Bell Gauge, commence by making a chain of 15 stitches, work it round.

1st round—2 plain in one, 1 bead, 2 plain in one, 2 bead. Repeat twice more; then work the 2nd and following rounds to the 64th round, always repeating the *pattern twice.*

ROUND PURSE.

Material—Steel, Gold, or Silver Beads, No. 6; Fine Netting Silk, shaded Green, Violet, and Red; or in plain colours—Blue, Brown, and White. Needle, No. 22, Bell Gauge.

Thread 3 rows of beads on the green silk, commence with the light part of the shade, and work a chain of 4 stitches, make it round.

1st round—2 plain in one stitch of the foundation, 4 times. 2nd—2 plain in one stitch, 8 times.

3rd—1 bead, and 2 plain in one stitch. Repeat 7 times.

4th—2 bead, 2 plain in one. Repeat 7 times.

5th—3 bead, 2 plain in one. Repeat 7 times.

6th—3 bead, 1 plain and 2 plain in one. Repeat 6 times; then 3 bead, 1 plain in the same stitch as the last bead stitch, 2 plain in one.

7th—5 bead, 2 plain in one. Repeat 7 times; then 1 plain.

8th—5 bead, 2 plain in one, 1 plain. Repeat 7 times.

9th—7 bead, 2 plain in one. Repeat 7 times.

10th—72 bead stitches, thread 6 rows of beads on the violet, commence with the light part.

11th—2 plain, 2 plain in one stitch, 6 bead. Repeat 7 times.

12th—1 plain, 2 plain in one, 2 bead, 2 plain in one, 1 plain, 4 bead. Repeat 7 times.

13th—3 plain, 4 bead, 3 plain, 2 bead. Repeat, end 2 plain.

14th—3 plain, 2 bead, 3 plain, 4 bead. Repeat, end 3 plain.

15th—2 plain in one, 3 plain, 8 bead. Repeat, end 4 plain.

16th—12 bead, 2 plain in one. Repeat. Thread one row of beads on the green.

17th — Green, 120 bead stitches. Fasten off. Work the other side the same, using the red silk instead of the violet; when it is finished work 4 bead stitches more; and to join it; place the first side worked in front at the fastening off, the right side outside, work 66 plain stitches, putting the needle into a stitch of *each* side and working it as one stitch. For the fringe, with a sewing needle and silk, thread 15 beads, and missing 2 stitches, sew it in the 3rd stitch of the joining row; pass the needle and the silk through the loop, formed by the beads-bring it in front again; work another loop the same, and for the 3rd and 4th loops, thread 20 beads; 5th and 6th loops, thread 25 beads; then 10 loops, threading 30 beads; 17th and 18th loops, thread 25 beads; 19th and 20th, thread 20 beads; 21st and 22nd, thread 15 beads. Fasten off, and sew it firmly to the clasp.

BEAD PURSE.

Material—Middle-sized Netting Silk, 2 Skeins of Light Blue, 1 White, and 3 of Claret, 3 Bunches of Gold Beads, No. 6; Needle, No. 20, Bell Gauge; or Ponceau, French Blue and White, with Steel Beads, using the Ponceau instead of the Claret.

Thread 5 rows of beads upon the claret silk, work 4 chain, and make it round.

1st round—2 plain in one stitch of the foundation chain, 4 times.

2nd—1 bead and 1 plain in one stitch, 8 times. 3rd—1 bead and 1 plain, 8 times.

4th—2 bead in 1 stitch and 1 plain, 8 times. 5th—2 bead and 1 plain, 8 times.

6th—1 bead, 2 bead in one, and 1 plain, 8 times. 7th—3 bead and 1 plain, 8 times.

8th—2 bead in one, 2 bead, and 1 plain, 8 times. 9th—4 bead, and 1 plain, 8 times.

10th—2 plain in one, 2 bead, 2 plain, 8 times. 11th—4 plain, 2 plain in one, 1 bead, 8 times.

12th—2 plain in one, 3 plain, 3 bead, 8 times. 13th—4 plain, 2 plain in one, 3 bead, 8 times.

14th—7 plain, 1 bead, 2 plain in one, 8 times. 15th and 16th—5 plain, 5 bead, 8 times.

17th—6 plain, 2 plain in one, 1 bead, 1 plain, 2 plain in one, 8 times; end 2 plain.

18th—1 bead and 5 plain, 15 times; end 1 bead, 4 plain. 19th—3 bead and 3 plain, 16 times.

20th—3 bead, 2 plain, 5 bead, 2 plain, 8 times. Thread 3 rows of beads on the white silk.

21st—Brown and white—brown, 1 plain, *, 1 bead, 2 plain, 2 bead—white, 3 plain—brown, 2 bead, 2 plain. Repeat from * 7 times more.

22nd—Brown, 1 bead, 1 plain, 2 bead—white, 5 plain—brown, 2 bead, 1 plain, 8 times. Cut off the brown.

BEAD PURSE.

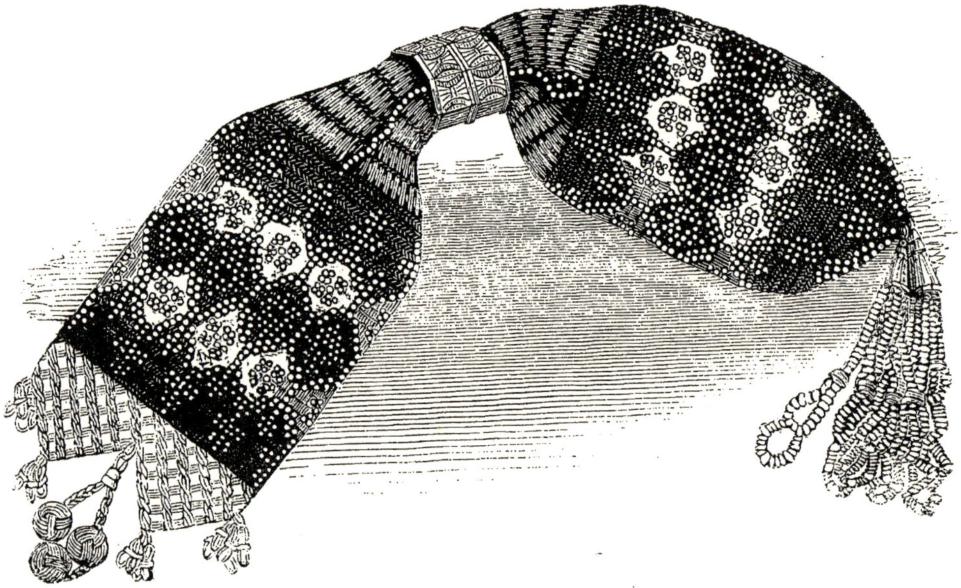

23rd—White, 3 bead, *, 1 plain, 2 bead, 1 plain, 2 bead, 1 plain, 5 bead. Repeat from * 6 times more, then 1 plain, 2 bead, 1 plain, 2 bead, 1 plain; end 2 bead single stitches.

24th—White, 2 bead, *, 2 plain, 2 bead, 1 plain, 2 bead, 2 plain, 3 bead. Repeat from * 6 times more, then 2 plain, 2 bead, 1 plain, 2 bead, 2 plain; end 1 bead single stitch.

25th—White, 1 bead and 5 plain, 16 times.

26th—Same as 24th. 27th—Same as 23rd. Thread 5 rows of beads on the blue.

28th—Blue and white—blue, 2 plain, 2 bead—white, 5 plain—blue, 2 bead—1 plain. Repeat 7 times more.

29th—Blue, 3 plain, 2 bead—white, 3 plain—blue, 2 bead, 2 plain. Repeat 7 times more.

30th—Blue, 1 bead, 3 plain, 5 bead, 3 plain. Repeat 6 times more; end 1 bead, 3 plain, 5 bead.

31st—Blue, (1 plain and 1 bead, 3 times), 2 plain, 3 bead, 1 plain. Repeat 7 times more.

32nd—Blue, 7 bead, 2 plain, 1 bead, 2 plain. Repeat 7 times more.

33rd—Brown and blue—blue, 1 plain, 2 bead—brown, 1 plain—blue, 2 bead, 3 plain, 1 bead, 2 plain. Repeat, 7 times more.

34th—Blue, 2 bead—brown, 3 plain—blue, 2 bead, 1 plain, 3 bead, 1 plain. Repeat 7 times more.

35th—Same as 33rd row. 36th—Same as 32nd. 37th—Same as 31st, end 3 plain.

Then repeat as the 30th, 29th, 28th, 27th, 26th, 25th, 24th, 23rd, and 22nd rounds.

47th—Brown, 1 bead, 2 plain, 2 bead—white, 3 plain—brown, 2 bead, 2 plain. Repeat 7 times more, end 1 plain instead of 2. 48th—As 20th. 49th—As 19th.

50th—1 plain, 1 bead, and 4 plain, 16 times. 51st—7 plain, 1 bead, and 4 plain, 8 times.

52nd and 53rd—5 plain, 5 bead, and 2 plain, 8 times.

54th—As 51st. 55th and 56th—6 plain, 3 bead, and 3 plain, 8 times.

57th—As 51st, end 5 plain, 2 single. Fasten off; and to form the opening of the Purse, turn back; and with the brown commence in the 27th stitch from the fastening off. [To commence, see Geranium Leaf.]

1st row—4 chain, miss 1, 1 treble, *, 1 chain, miss 1, 1 treble. Repeat from *, 46 times more; at the end draw the silk through to fasten it, do not cut it off, but lay it along the work to the beginning of the row, that it may be worked under in the next row. This rule must be observed every row.

2nd—Blue—commence in the 4 chain of last row; then 1 chain, miss 1 and 1 plain in the 1 chain, 47 times; end 1 chain, 1 plain. Draw the silk through, &c.

3rd—White—commence in the 1st chain stitch of last row; then 1 chain, miss 1 and 1 plain in the 1 chain, 47 times.

4th—Blue—commence on the 1st stitch of the 2nd row, 1 chain, miss 1, and 1 plain in the 1 chain, 47 times; end 1 chain, miss 1, and 1 plain on the last stitch of the 2nd row.

5th—Brown—commence in 1st stitch of the last row; then 4 chain, 1 treble in the 1st chain stitch, *, 1 chain, miss 1 and 1 treble in the 1 chain. Repeat from *, 46 times more; then repeat the last 4 rows, 10 times; make it round and fasten off, and to form the other side of the purse, thread 5 rows of beads on the brown silk, turn back; and commence in the 28th stitch from the opening. The Purse should be 96 stitches round.

1st round, as 51st. 2nd and 3rd rounds, as 55th. 4th, as 51st. 5th and 6th, as 52nd. 7th, as 51st; end 1 plain; then repeat as the 18th and following rounds to the 57th round. Join the ends by working a plain row, taking a stitch of each side; work 2 rows of beads plain round the opening. Finish with a fringe at the square end, and a tassel at the other.

GREEK PURSE.

Material—Fine Netting Silk, 1 *Skein of Shaded Green,* 1 *of Violet,* 1 *of Scarlet, in short shades,* 1 *Skein of Scarlet in long shades,* 3 *Skeins of Fine Gold Twist, Needle No.* 22.

Work with the gold 5 chain and make it round.

1st round—2 plain in one 4 times, 1 plain. 2nd—plain in one, 9 times.

3rd—2 plain in one and 1 plain, 9 times.

4th—2 plain in one and 2 plain, 9 times; there will now be 36 stitches.

5th—Green and gold—Green, 1 plain—Gold, 2 plain in one, 2 plain. Repeat 8 times more.

6th—Green, 2 plain in one—gold, 4 plain. Repeat.

7th — Scarlet in short shades, green and gold—gold, 1 plain—green, 1 plain, 2 plain in one—gold, 2 plain in one, scarlet 2 plain. Repeat, end gold, 2 plain.

8th—Green, 2 plain—gold, 1 plain—scarlet, 4 plain—gold, 1 plain. Repeat.

9th—Gold, 2 plain in one—green, 1 plain—gold, 2 plain in one, 1 plain — scarlet, 2 plain — gold, 2 plain. Repeat; cut off the scarlet.

10th—Green, 2 plain in one, 3 plain, 2 plain in one, 4 plain. Repeat; end 1 single.

11th—Violet, green and gold—1 green, 2 plain—gold, 3 plain—violet, 2 plain—gold, 5 plain. Repeat.

12th—3 green, 2 gold, 4 violet, 3 gold. Repeat; end 2 gold instead of 3.

13th—3 green, 4 gold, 2 violet, 3 gold. Repeat; cut off the violet.

14th—2 green, 10 violet. Repeat.

15th—Scarlet in long shades, commence with the lightest part, work 1 green, 2 gold, 1 scarlet, 5 gold, 1 scarlet, 2 gold. Repeat; end 1 gold instead of 2; cut off the green.

16th—3 gold, 3 scarlet. Repeat; end 2 gold.

17th—5 scarlet, 1 gold. Repeat. 18th—Scarlet, 108 plain.

19th—3 scarlet, 1 gold, 3 scarlet, 1 gold, 4 scarlet. Repeat.

20th—2 scarlet, 3 gold, 1 scarlet, 3 gold, 3 scarlet. Repeat; join on the green.

21st—2 scarlet, 1 gold, 1 green, 3 gold, 1 green, 1 gold, 3 scarlet. Repeat.

22nd—3 gold, 2 green, 1 gold, 2 green, 3 gold, 1 scarlet. Repeat.

23rd—1 gold, 2 green, 1 gold, 3 green, 1 gold, 2 green, 2 gold. Repeat; join on the violet.

24th—2 gold, 3 green, 1 gold, 3 green, 2 gold, 1 violet. Repeat; end 1 gold.

25th—2 gold, 1 green, 3 gold, 1 green, 2 gold, 3 violet. Repeat; end 1 gold.

26th—3 green, 1 gold, 3 green, 2 gold, 1 violet, 2 gold. Repeat 7 times more; end 3 green, 1 gold, 3 green, 2 gold, 1 violet; then repeat as the 23rd, 22nd, 21st, 20th, and 19th, rounds. 32nd—Scarlet, 107 plain.

33rd—1 gold, 5 scarlet. Repeat 16 times; end 1 gold, I scarlet.

34th—3 scarlet, 3 gold. Repeat; end 2 scarlet. 35th—5 gold, 1 scarlet. Repeat.

36th—Gold plain.

37th—With the darkest part of the shaded scarlet, work 108 plain. Fasten off.

For the lining; with the green, work 108 chain, and make it round.

1st, 2nd, and 3rd rounds—4 chain, miss 1, 1 treble, *, 1 chain, miss 1, 1 treble. Repeat. from *, end 1 chain, miss 1, and 1 single in the 4 chain at the commencement.

4th, 5th, and 6th with the short shaded scarlet, work as the 1st round.

7th, 8th, and 9th rounds—with the green, work as 1st round.

10th and 11th—Shaded violet as 1st round.

12th—6 chain, miss 1, 1 long, *, 1 chain, miss 1, 1 long. Repeat from *, end 1 chain, miss 1, 1 single in the 6 chain.

14th—Green, same as 12th. Fasten off. Turn the purse on the wrong side, and sew the foundation chain of the lining to the 12th round of the Purse.

For the Tassel, (see page 28) work 2 Flowers with the scarlet; join them together as directed for working the *small* leaves and stem; then work one violet Flower, and for the centre stem, with the green, make 25 chain; work a small Leaf; then 6 chain; join it to the top of the violet Flower; 5 chain on the 6 chain; then 10 chain; work another Leaf the same; then 22 chain on the stem, lay the stem of the red Flowers across the centre stem, work 1 plain to fasten it, then 3 plain; join it to the purse, and fasten off.

For the strings, gold or silk cord run in the 2 last rounds of the lining, work 2 violet Flowers, and attach one at each end of the cord; then place a small tuft of gold twist in the centre of each Flower.

THE END.

THE

CROCHET SUMMER BOOK,

EIGHTH SERIES.

BY

MDLLE. RIEGO DE LA BRANCHARDIERE.

First Edition.

LONDON:
SIMPKIN, MARSHALL, AND CO.,
ACKERMANN & CO., STRAND; OLIVER AND BOYD, EDINBURGH;
AND ALL THE BERLIN WAREHOUSES.

1850.

CONTENTS.

NOTICE.

These Designs are registered under the Act 5 and 6 Vict. Cap. 100.

Ladies are respectfully informed that these articles cannot be purchased without the *registered* mark being affixed; and parties wishing to manufacture them for the purposes of sale, must have the Authoress's permission.

TO MY PATRONESSES.

In presenting this, my *Summer Book*, to my numerous Lady Patronesses, I feel myself bound to explain why a deviation in the Eighth Series of my publications has been made, from the programme announced in the Seventh Issue. The *Motto* and *Alphabet Book*, was prepared for the press, when the MSS. was accidentally lost, and the time to re-arrange the matter, would have precluded the possibility of its appearance in time for Ladies to complete the articles for this season. The present volume, intended to occupy a place in some subsequent part of the series of my works, was already in a state of forwardness, and rather than disappoint so many of my supporters and friends, I have diligently applied myself to its completion, and I trust that these original designs will be found equal to any others I have hitherto produced. The flowers are but the commencement of a series which I purpose giving in future Brochures, and which I have "registered," previous to their publication, to prevent them being pirated.

While on this subject, I may be allowed to observe, that I have never published any book that has not been immediately seized upon by unprincipled parties, and the designs that have cost me time, labour, money, and health, have been taken from me, not only without acknowledgment, but re-issued as the inventions of other persons. The terms, explanations, and directions (arrived at, and promulgated freely to the Public by myself, through the constant study of my art) have been stolen, mutilated and abused in more than twenty other works

To recapitulate these piracies would be tedious, but I may instance the Flower and Leaf in my Second Crochet Book, which has re-appeared in other works, with such trifling alterations, that the theft is at once perceptible to those who are at all acquainted with the Work.

I have hitherto passed over these infringements of my rights and properties, but a recent addition to the heavy losses and injuries I have sustained through the misdeeds of others compels me to announce, that, under the protection of the Act for the Registration of Designs, I shall henceforth proceed against those, no matter in what station of life they may be, who shall make use of my designs and inventions, by merely varying or adapting them either in work for the shop-keepers, or in publications for sale or distribution.

Thanking my Patronesses for the large amount of favours bestowed upon my exertions in every department of Fancy Work, and apologizing for this business intrusion in a volume of instruction and amusement,

I beg to subscribe myself their faithful servant

106, *New Bond Street*. E. Riego de la Branchardiere.

THE

CROCHET SUMMER BOOK,

EIGHTH SERIES.

CORNUCOPIA STOVE ORNAMENT.

Material—22 yards of White Cord, 1 *reel of Green Wire, No.* 23, 2 *yards of Wire, No.* 20, *Bell Gauge;* 2½ *oz. of Shaded Grey German Wool;* 6 *Shades of Scarlet,* viz., 5 *skeins of the* 2 *darkest,* 3 *skeins of the other shades, and* 9 *skeins of Gold Crochet Silk or Amber Wool; Needle, No.* 17, *Bell Gauge.*

With the grey wool work a chain of 30 stitches, and make it round. 1st round—Plain.

2nd—4 plain, 2 plain in one, 6 times. 3rd—1 chain, miss 1 and 1 treble, 18 times.

4th—(The cord is to be worked under the stitches in this round.)—Miss 1, 2 plain in the 1 chain, 18 times. Leave the cord at the back as it is used only every other round.

5th—(1 chain, miss 1, 1 treble, 12 times); then (1 chain, miss 1, 1 plain, 7 times). The last plain stitch is to be worked in the 1st chain stitch of the round to keep it even; and the stitches are to be taken in double crochet. Observe these Rules every alternate round. Repeat the 2 last rounds, 22 times.

Stove Ornament--Registered Design.

E. R. de la Branchardiere, Inven., May, 1850.

50th—(Miss 1, 2 plain, miss 1, 3 plain, 6 times); (miss 1, 2 plain, 6 times). The plain stitches are always to be worked in the 1 chain of the preceding round.

51st—(1 chain, miss 1, 1 treble, 15 times), (1 chain, miss 1, 1 plain, 7 times).

52nd—(Miss 1 and 2 plain, 21 times). Repeat the 2 last rounds, 3 times more.

59th—As 51st.

60th—(Miss 1, 2 plain, miss 1, 3 plain, 6 times), (miss 1, 2 plain, 9 times).

61st—(1 chain, miss 1, 1 treble, 18 times), (1 chain, miss 1, 1 plain, 7 times).

62nd—(Miss 1 and 2 plain, 4 times), (miss 1, 2 plain, miss 1, 3 plain, 6 times), (miss 1, 2 plain, 8 times). Leave the work, and to form the

FIRST BORDER OF LEAVES.

With the 2nd shade of scarlet wool, work 20 chain, turn, miss 1, 13 plain, 2 single. Repeat 10 times more.

2nd row—3rd shade of scarlet and fine wire, working it under, commence in the 1st chain stitch of the last row, 2 plain, miss 1, and up the side 3 plain, 2 treble, 4 long, 3 treble, 4 plain, *, and down the other side 3 plain, 3 treble, 4 long, 2 treble, 3 plain, miss 1, 2 plain on the chain stitches; miss 1, 3 plain, 2 treble, 2 long; join it to the 3rd long stitch of the other Leaf, 2 long, 3 treble, 4 plain. Repeat from * 9 times more; and to finish the last Leaf, 3 plain, 3 treble, 2 long; join to the 2nd long stitch of the 1st Leaf; then 2 long, 3 treble, 3 plain. Fasten off, twisting the ends of the wire together to secure them; and to join it to the work, turn the Leaves upon the wrong side, and placing them over the work, so that the foundation lays even with the 62nd round; with the grey wool, work a plain round, putting the needle in a stitch of each piece, working as one stitch, joining 5 stitches to each leaf.

64th—(1 chain, miss 1, 1 treble, 20 times), (1 chain, miss 1, 1 plain, 8 times.)

65th—(Miss 1, and 2 plain, 4 times), (miss 1, 2 plain, miss 1, 3 plain, 6 times), (miss 1, 2 plain, 11 times).

66th—(1 chain, miss 1, 1 treble, 22 times), (1 chain, miss 1, 1 plain, 9 times).

67th—(Miss 1, 2 plain, miss 1, 2 plain, miss 1, 3 plain, 6 times), (miss 1, 2 plain, 12 times.)

68th—(1 chain, miss 1, 1 treble, 25 times), (1 chain, miss 1, 1 plain, 9 times).

69th—(Miss 1, 2 plain, miss 1, 2 plain, miss 1, 3 plain, 8 times), (miss 1, 2 plain, 9 times.)

70th—(1 chain, miss 1, 1 treble, 29 times), (1 chain, miss 1, 1 plain, 9 times.)

71st—(Miss 1, 2 plain, miss 1, 2 plain, miss 1, 3 plain, 6 times), (miss 1, 2 plain, 19 times.)

72nd—(1 chain, miss 1, 1 treble, 32 times), (1 chain, miss 1, 1 plain, 9 times).

73rd—*, (miss 1, 2 plain, 3 times), miss 1, 3 plain. Repeat from * 7 times more; then (miss 1, 2 plain, 8 times).

74th—(1 chain, miss 1, 1 treble, 34 times), (1 chain, miss 1, 1 plain, 11 times).

75th—(Miss 1, 2 plain, 44 times). 76th—As 74th.

77th—*, (miss 1, 2 plain, 3 times), miss 1, 3 plain. Repeat from * 7 times more; then (miss 1, 2 plain, 12 times).

78th—(1 chain, miss 1, 1 treble, 37 times), (1 chain, miss 1, 1 plain, 12 times).

79th—(Miss 1, 2 plain, 48 times). 80th—As 78th.

81st—*, (miss 1, 2 plain, 3 times), miss 1, 3 plain. Repeat from * 7 times more; then (miss 1, 2 plain, 16 times).

82nd—(1 chain, miss 1, 1 treble, 42 times), (1 chain, miss 1, 1 plain, 11 times).

83rd—(Miss 1, 2 plain, 52 times).

84th—As 82nd. 85th—As 83rd. 86th—As 82nd.

87th—(Miss 1, 2 plain 7 times), miss 1, 3 plain. Repeat, leave the work; and for the

SECOND BORDER OF LEAVES.

With the shaded grey wool, work 22 Leaves as in the 1st Border, when finished, place it on the work and join it as previously directed.

88th—With the darkest shade of scarlet, work plain with the cord under. Fasten off, sewing the cord at the back.

FOR THE FEATHER PATTERN.

Commence with the amber wool, and make 37 chain, turn, miss 3, 1 treble, (1 chain, miss 1, 1 treble, 7 times), (1 chain, miss 1, 1 plain, 6 times), turn, 1 chain to cross the chain stitches; and on the other side, (miss 1 and 2 plain in the 1 chain, 7 times); then (1 chain, miss 1 and 1 treble, 7 times), then (1 chain, and 1 treble, 4 times in the same 3 chain as before); and down the other side, (1 chain, miss 1, 1 treble, 6 times); 1 chain, (miss 1, 2 plain in the 1 chain, 7 times). Repeat these 2 rows, 10 times more.

3rd—With the darkest shade of scarlet and the cord, which is worked under the stitches of the row, commence in the 2nd stitch of the 7 chain left at the 1st pattern, work 3 plain on it, miss 2; and up the 1st side work 28 plain, (2 plain in one, 7 times); and down the other side 28 plain, then miss 2 chain, and repeat round the other pattern. Cut off the cord, and sew the ends together to secure it.

4th—5th shade of scarlet, commence in the 1st stitch of last row, 23 plain, (working the stitches in double crochet), then (4 chain, miss 1, 1 plain, 15 times), working the plain stitches upon the inner edge of the stitches in the 3rd row, which leaves the other side of the stitch at the back of the work; 4 chain, miss 1, then *, 31 plain in double crochet; join it to the 13th stitch of the 31 plain, then 12 plain in double crochet, 2 chain; join it to the last 4 chain of the other pattern, 2 chain, miss 1, 1 plain, (4 chain, miss 1, 1 plain on the inner edge of the stitch, 14 times). Repeat from * 9 times more, and to finish the last pattern, join it to the 1st 4 chain of the 1st pattern; then 12 plain, join it to the 11th stitch of the 1st pattern, 8 plain, and fasten off. Join it to the other part of the work in the same manner as the leaves; and to form the upper part, with the 5th shade of scarlet, commence on the 33rd stitch of the 3rd round.

1st—Work 8 plain along the top, taking the stitches of the 3rd round that were left at the back, 10 chain; then 8 plain on the next pattern, and repeat the same all round.

2nd—Plain, working the cord under the stitches.

3rd—4th shade of scarlet, (2 chain, miss 2, 1 treble, 66 times).

4th—3rd shade of scarlet, and the cord, miss 1, 3 plain in the 2 chain. Repeat.

5th—2nd shade of scarlet, 2 chain, miss 2, 1 treble. Repeat.

6th—1st shade of scarlet, same as the 4th. Fasten off the cord.

THIRD BORDER OF LEAVES.

1st row—Shaded grey, 29 chain, turn, miss 2, 3 plain, 14 treble, 2 plain, 1 single. Repeat 24 times.

2nd—Work the wire under in this row; commence in the 1st stitch of the 7 chain left at the beginning of the 1st row, work 5 plain, then miss 1, and up the side, 3 plain, 5 treble, 5 long, 4 treble, 4 plain, 2 chain, turn; and down the other side, 4 plain, 4 treble, 5 long, 5 treble, 3 plain, miss 1, and for the

2nd Leaf—Work as the 1st, joining it to the first leaf after working the 5 long, and repeat, joining the last leaf to the first to make it round; then placing it upon the work, join it as before, but working the wire under the stitches to make it firm, working 8 stitches to each leaf. Fasten off. Then commence on the *top* of the 1st Leaf, work 10 chain, 1 plain on the top of the next leaf. The plain stitches should be worked on the wire of the leaf, leaving the chain at the point of the leaf outside, to make it firm. Repeat. Then use the thick wire, and work plain all round, working the wire under. Fasten off.

Then with the amber wool work 6 small leaves as before, and join them to the 30 chain at the beginning of the work, and to form the scroll, attach the end to the 46th round. It will require two large hooks fastened to the back, which can be made of the thick wire. Work the other cornucopia the same.

CONVOLVOLUS FLOWERS.

Material—1 reel of Green Cotton Wire, No 23, Bell Gauge, and 1 skein of Wire, No. 21; Needle, No. 16, and Berlin Wool.

For the Flowers 2 shades of violet, 2 shades of blue, 2 of pink, 2 of straw colour, 5 skeins of each shade, 44 skeins of white, 1 of black, and 6 of yellow. For the leaves, 6 shades of green, 10 skeins of each shade, and 2 shades of olive green, 4 skeins of each.

In making the Flowers and Leaves the colours are to be varied, each leaf requires two following shades, commencing with the darkest of the two; the smaller leaves with the lighter shades, and a few leaves with the olive green. The buds look best with shaded wool, and it may be introduced with good effect for the flowers.

FIRST FLOWER.

Material—2 shades of Blue and White Wool.

Commence with the white, work 8 chain and make it round.

1st, 2nd, and 3rd rounds—plain. 4th—(2 plain in 1, and 3 plain, twice).

5th—(2 plain in 1, and 2 plain, 3 times). 6th—(2 plain in 1, and 6 plain, twice).

7th—White and light blue—white, 2 plain in 1, 1 plain—blue, 1 plain. Repeat 4 times more.

8th—White, 2 plain, 2 plain in 1—blue, 1 plain. Repeat.

9th—White, 2 plain in 1, 2 plain, 2 plain in 1—blue, 1 plain. Repeat.

10th—White, 2 plain, (2 plain in 1, 3 times), 1 plain—blue, 1 plain. Repeat.

11th—White, 4 plain—blue, 2 plain in 1—white 4 plain—blue, 1 plain. Repeat, end white, 1 plain.

Convolvulus Flowers--Registered Design.

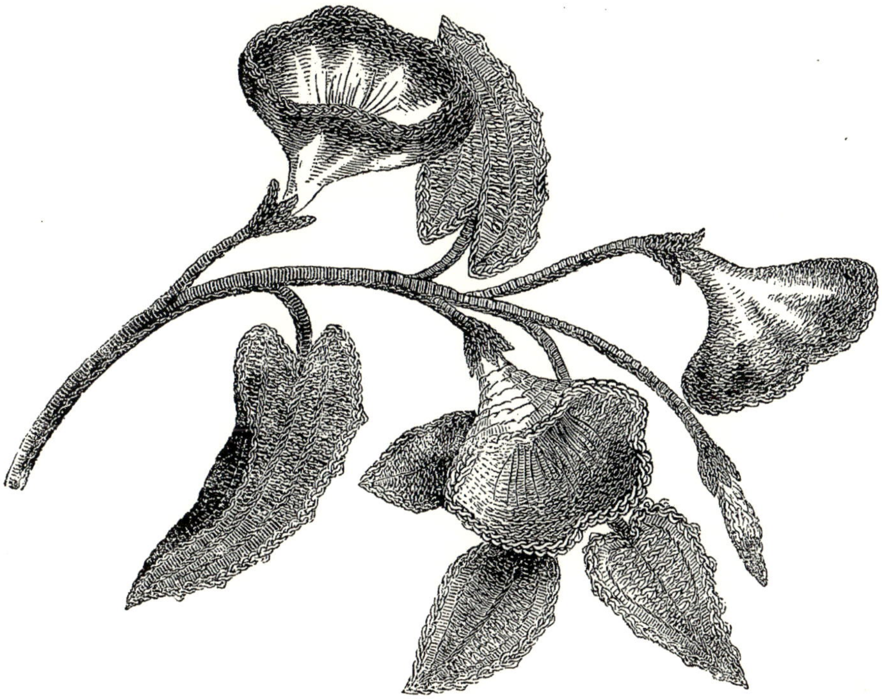

E. R. de la Branchardiere, Inven., May, 1850.

12th—White, 2 plain—blue, 3 plain, 2 plain in 1—white, 2 plain—blue, 3 plain. Repeat, end white, 1 plain.

13th—White and dark blue—white, 1 plain—blue, 6 plain—white, 1 plain—blue, 4 plain. Repeat and cut off the white.

14th—Blue, 7 treble, 2 plain, 1 single, 2 plain. Repeat, end 1 plain instead of 2.

15th—For this round, work the fine wire under. Light blue, 9 treble, 1 plain, 1 single, 1 plain. Repeat and fasten off.

PETALS AND CALYX OF THE FLOWERS.

Cut off 6 inches of the fine wire, and for the petals, take the yellow wool, wind it round two fingers about 12 times, and 1 fold of black, pass the wire through the loop of wool, fold the wire in half and twist it together to fasten the wool, cut the top of the wool and pass the ends of the wire down the centre of the flower; and for the

CALYX—With the green wool; work 17 chain, turn, miss 4, 1 single in the 5th stitch to form a round loop, turn, and on this round loop.

1st round—Work (2 plain in 1 and 1 plain, 3 times), then 3 rounds plain.

5th—4 chain, turn, and on the 4 chain, miss 1, 1 plain, 2 treble; then on the 4th round miss 1, 1 plain. Repeat 3 times more. Cut off the wool, leaving about one yard, and draw it through the calyx to the chain stitches at the commencement, then pass the ends of wire of the flower through this calyx, and to form the stem, work 12 plain on the chain stitches, working the wires under. Fasten off, leaving the ends of the wire and the wool. Work 2 more flowers the same, varying the colours.

LEAVES—LARGEST SIZE.

Commence with the darkest shade of green, work 40 chain, turn, miss 1, 30 single, turn, 1 chain to cross the stem, and for the

1st round—6 chain, (2 long in one stitch, 3 times), 8 long, 12 treble, 5 plain, 2 single, 2 chain at the point; and on the other side 2 single, 5 plain, 12 treble, 8 long, (2 long in one stitch, 3 times), 6 chain, 1 single in the same stitch as the last long. Fasten off. In the 2 following rounds the stitches should be worked in double crochet, and the ends of the wool worked under.

2nd—With the next shade of green, commence in the 1st long stitch in the 1st round; then 4 chain, (3 long in the same stitch), 16 long, 11 treble, 4 plain, 2 single, 2 chain; and on the other side 2 single, 4 plain, 11 treble, 16 long, 3 long in one stitch 4 chain, 1 single in the same stitch as the 3 long. Fasten off.

3rd—Work the wire under the stitches of this round, leaving an end of about 3 inches, commence in the 1st chain stitch of the first round, 9 plain up the side of the leaf; then (2 chain, 1 plain in the same stitch as last plain, and 5 plain, 16 times), 6 plain, 1 single down the side, and on the chain stitches for the stem, work 7 plain, working the 2 ends of the wire under. Fasten off, leaving about one inch of the wool and wire.

SECOND SIZE LEAF.

With dark green, work 28 chain, turn, miss 1, 20 single, turn, 1 chain to cross the stem.

1st round—6 chain, (2 long in one, 3 times), 6 long, 5 treble, 4 plain, 2 single, 2 chain, turn, 2 single, 4 plain, 5 treble, 6 long, (2 long in one, 3 times), 6 chain, 1 single in the same stitch as the last long. Fasten off.

2nd—With the 2nd shade, commence in the 1st long stitch, 4 chain, 3 treble in the same stitch, 15 treble, 5 plain, 3 single, 2 chain, turn, 3 single, 5 plain, 15 treble, 3 treble in one, 4 chain, 1 single. Fasten off.

3rd—With the wire—commence in the 1st chain stitch of the last round, work 10 plain up the side, (2 chain, 1 plain in the same stitch as the last, and 4 plain, 15 times); 5 plain, and 1 single down the side; then for the stem, 5 plain on the chain stitches. Fasten off, leaving the ends as before.

THIRD SIZE, SPRAY OF THREE LEAVES.

25 chain, turn, miss 1, 14 single, turn, 1 chain to cross the stem.

1st round—5 chain, (2 long in one, 3 times), 3 long, 3 treble, 3 plain, 2 single, 2 chain, turn, 2 single, 3 plain, 3 treble, 3 long, (2 long in one, 3 times), 5 chain, 1 single, 1 chain to cross the stem.

2nd—With the wire, leaving 2 inches for the stem, 5 plain, (2 chain, 1 plain, in the last plain stitch, and 4 plain, 10 times), 1 single, and down the stem 9 plain. Fasten off leaving the ends as before. Work another leaf the same, and for the 3rd Leaf

Make 58 chain, work another leaf, leaving about 3 inches of the wire at the 2nd round for the centre stem; and after working the 9 plain on the stem, join it to the last stitch of the first leaf, and placing the ends of wool and wire of both leaves together, work 15 plain down the chain stitches, working the ends under the stitches; then join the other leaf the same, working 18 plain stitches down the chain stitches as before. Fasten off, leaving an inch of the ends.

BUD.

If shaded wool is used commence with the lightest part—8 chain, make it round, work 5 rounds all treble; then (miss 1 and 1 treble, 6 times). Fasten off.

TO FORM THE BUNCH.

With the green wool make 202 chain for the centre stem, work a calyx as before. Take 40 inches of the thick wire and folding it in half, pass one of the ends through the commencement of the bud to the half, and then pass both ends of the wire through the calyx, and down the stem work 24 plain, working the wires under; join it to the last stitch of the stem of the small leaves, then down the chain stitches 10 plain, working the ends of the leaves and wire under; cut off the ends belonging to the small leaves; join to the last stitch of the stem of a *Flower*, 10 plain down the stem, working the wire as before; join on a leaf, 2nd size, 8 plain down the stem, join on another flower, 10 plain down the stem; join on a leaf of the 1st size, 10 plain down the stem; join on a flower, then 125 plain down the stem, and fasten off.

To fill the Cornucopias it will require 10 bunches, and three or more to fall between, (see engraving); and in arranging the bunches, the back ones should be attached to the Cornucopias.

NETTED CURTAINS.

Material.—1½ lb. of Knitting Cotton, No. 10. Meshes, No. 12, and 14 Bell Guage, 1 Flat Mesh, half an inch wide, and one, a quarter of an inch wide; Steel Netting Needle.

SECTION.

E. R. de la Branchardiere, Inven. May, 1850.

The foundation is 576 stitches for a curtain of 4 yards in length. Commence with No. 14 mesh, and net 4 rows plain, and for the

OPEN STRIPE.

5th row.—With the half inch mesh, work plain.

6th—Mesh, quarter of an inch, net 2 stiches together, repeat.

7th—Plain. 8th—Half inch mesh. Net 2 stitches in 1. Repeat, then for the

DIAMOND STRIPE.

With mesh No. 14, work 4 rows plain, and for the diamonds.

5th—Net 1 plain stitch, then turn the thread round the mesh, and net 1 plain stitch. Repeat these 2 stitches to the end.

SECTION OF CURTAIN.

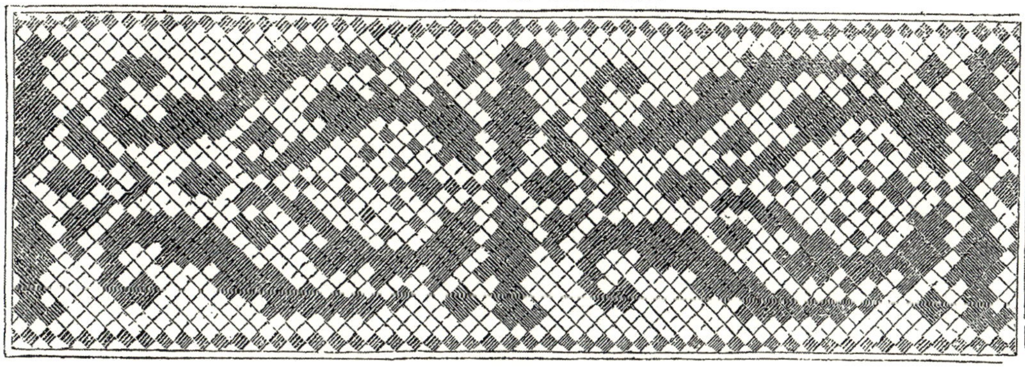

E. R. de la Branchardiere, Invent., May, 1850.

6th—All plain. 7th—Turn the thread round the mesh, net a stitch, then 1 plain stitch. Repeat these 2 stitches.

8th—Plain. Repeat the last 4 rows 5 times more, then work 3 rows plain, and then repeat the open stripe, and for the

FIRST EMBROIDERED STRIPE.

Mesh No. 14, work 36 rows plain. Then repeat the open stripe,—then the diamond stripe,—then the open stripe.

SECOND EMBROIDERED STRIPE.

Mesh No. 14.—Work 39 rows plain, then repeat the open stripe,—diamond stripe,—and open stripe, work the 3rd Embroidered Stripe the same as the 1st, then repeat the open stripe, and net 4 rows plain. This makes a curtain of one yard wide and if required wider, repeat the diamond stripe and the 2nd embroidered stripe.

VANDYCKE EDGING.

Mesh No. 12.—Net 17 plain stitches on the last row of the curtain, turn back.

2nd row—Net the 17 stitches, turn back.

3rd—Net 16 stitches, turn back, leaving one stitch.

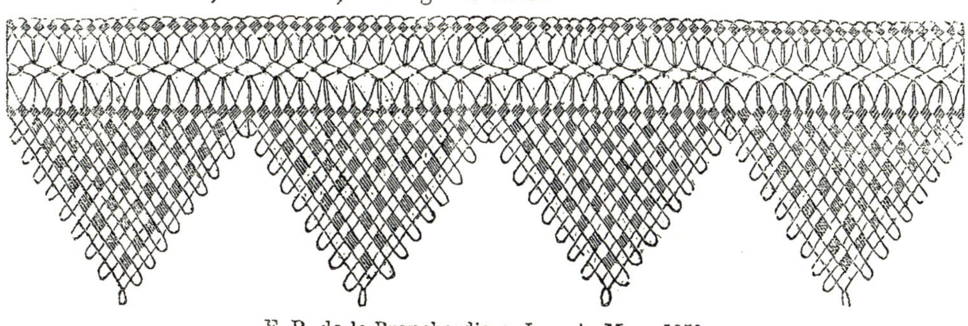

E. R. de la Branchardiere, Invent., May, 1850.

Then 15 rows, same as the last, working one stitch less each time. Cut off the thread, and commence the next Vandycke, on the 18th stitch of the curtain. Repeat the Vandyckes along one side, and at the top and bottom.

The Patterns are embroidered with the same cotton and a rug needle, in the usual manner, "that is," by passing the needle under and over the stitches of the netting about 5 times, taking care to turn the stitches the same way as marked in the *engravings*. The beading at the edge of the stripes, should also be worked on the 4 plain rows of the diamond stripes, the Vandyckes are embroidered in the same manner.

ANTIMACASSAR.

The same as the curtains. The foundation, 126 stitches; work the open stripe,—then the 1st embroidered stripe,—open stripe,—2nd embroidered stripe,—open stripe,—1st embroidered stripe; then work the open stripe along the four sides, and finish with the Vandyckes all round, and a tassel, Fuchsia Pattern, at each corner—[see 7th series].

BONNET.

Material—Drab Ficelle, or White, Black, or Grey Shetland Wool; Needle, No. 18, *Bell Gauge; or if Thread is preferred, use Taylor's Crochet, No.* 2.

This bonnet is shaped from the newest design, and as much depends upon the size of the work, it is advisable to have the shape while working, occasionally placing the work on it to regulate the stitches from being too *tight* or too *loose*. A paper pattern will be forwarded upon application.

Commence at the crown, work 6 chain and make it round.

1st round—4 chain, turn, and on the 4 chain miss 1, 1 plain, 2 treble; then 1 plain in the foundation chain. Repeat 5 times more, and work 4 single up the 1st 4 chain to the point.

2nd—8 chain, miss 7, 1 plain in the next point. Repeat; end 4 single on the 1st 8 chain.

3rd—* 13 chain, and for the

1st Leaf—Turn, and down the chain stitches miss 1, 1 single, 1 plain, 1 treble, 4 long, 1 treble, 1 plain, 2 single; then for the

Flower—12 chain, turn, miss 5, 1 single in the 6th stitch to form a round loop, 1 chain to cross the stem, 4 chain; join to the 2nd *long* stitch of the Leaf, then on the 4 chain, miss 1, 1 plain, 2 treble, 1 plain in the round loop, (4 chain, turn, miss 1, 1 plain, 2 treble, and 1 plain in the round loop 5 times), making in all 6 points or divisions; then 5 single down the stem, and for the

2nd Leaf—6 chain, join it to the last point of the flower by working a single stitch in it,

Crochet Bonnet---Registered Design.

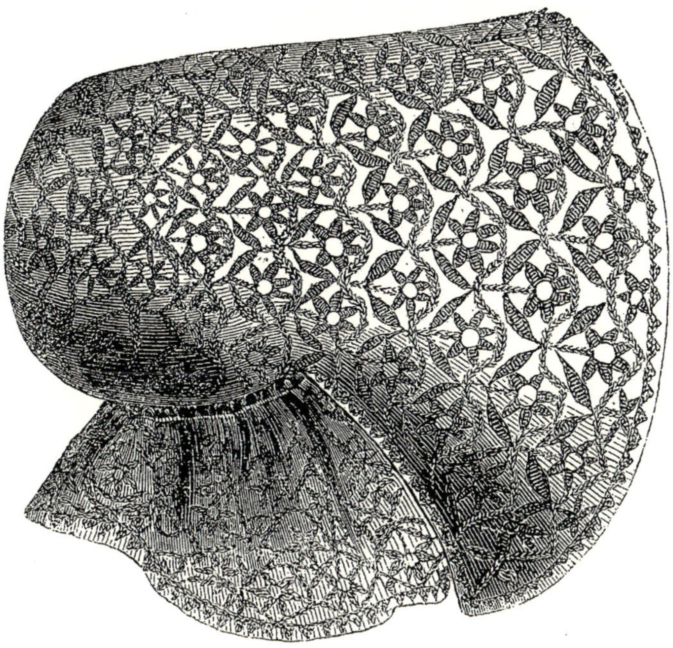

E. R. de la Branchardiere Invent., May.

then 5 chain, and work as the 1st Leaf. When finished work 2 single down the stem, and on the 2nd round 9 plain. Repeat from * 5 times more; 13 single up the side of the 1st Leaf which will bring the thread to the point.

4th—4 chain, miss 11, 1 plain in the 2nd point of the flower, 4 chain, miss 7, 1 plain in the 3rd point, 4 chain, miss 7, 1 plain in the 4th point, 4 chain, miss 7, 1 plain in the 5th point, 4 chain, miss 11, 1 plain in the point of the Leaf; then 1 plain in the point of the next Leaf. Repeat, end 6 single on the 1st stitches of the round.

5th—Same as the 3rd round, working 13 plain instead of 9 plain. In this round there will be 12 patterns.

6th—Same as the 4th round, end 7 single instead of 6.

7th—18 plain, 9 chain, join with a single stitch to the 10th stitch of the 18 plain; then 6 chain, and repeat the 1st Leaf, Flower, and 2nd Leaf as in the 3rd round. When finished work 5 single down the stem, and on the 6th round 8 plain; join it to the 4th long stitch of the last leaf. Repeat, end 14 single up the 1st leaf to the point.

8th—Same as the 6th round. 9th—as the 7th round. 10th—As the 6th round.

11th—As the 7th, but only working 11 patterns; then 18 plain, and fasten off.

12th—Commence by working 1 plain in the point of the 1st leaf of last round, (4 chain, and 1 plain in the point of the Flower 4 times as before), 4 chain, 1 plain in the point of the Leaf; 1 *chain* between the leaves. Repeat along the last row, and fasten off.

13th—Commence in the 1st stitch of the last row, 8 plain; and repeat as the 7th round, working 19 plain instead of 18 plain, and joining the 9 chain to the 11th stitch of the 19 plain.

Work the pattern 10 times, end 19 plain.

14th—As the 12th.

15th—Commence in the 1st stitch of the last row, 16 chain *, work the 1st Leaf, Flower, and 2nd Leaf as in the 3rd round. When finished 5 single down the stem, 8 plain on the last row; join it to the 4th long stitch of the Leaf, then 19 plain, 9 chain, join to the 11th stitch of the 19 plain, 6 chain, and repeat from *, 10 times more, ending with the 2nd leaf.

16th—As the 12th, working 2 chain instead of one chain, between the leaves.

17th—As the 15th, working 20 plain instead of 19, and joining the 9 chain to the 12th stitch of the 20 plain, repeat the pattern 11 times.

18th—As the 12th, working 3 chain instead of 1 chain, between the leaves.

19th—As the 15th, working 21 plain instead of 19, and joining the 9 chain to the 13th stitch of the 21 plain, repeat the pattern 12 times.

20th—As the 12th, working 4 chain instead of 1 between the leaves.

21st—As the 15th, working 22 plain instead of 19, and joining the 9 chain to the 14th stitch of the 22 plain, repeat the pattern 13 times. 22nd—Same as the 20th.

23rd—Commence in the 1st stitch of the last row, and for a *flower*, 7 chain, turn, miss 4, 1 single in the 5th stitch, 1 chain to cross, (4 chain, turn, miss 1, 1 plain, 2 treble on the 4 chain, and 1 plain on the round loop, 4 times) ;* then 2 single down the stem, 6 plain on the 22nd row, join to the 4th point of the flower, 24 plain; and for the 2nd flower, 7 chain, turn, miss 4, 1 single, in the 5th stitch, 1 chain to cross, 4 chain; join to the 18th stitch of the 24 plain, then miss 1, 1 plain, 2 treble, on the 4 chain, 1 plain in the round loop, (4 chain, turn, miss 1, 1 plain, 2 treble, and 1 plain in the round loop, 3 times). Repeat from * 13 times more, 2 single, fasten off.

24th—Commence on the 1st stitch of the 14th row, and up the sides of the leaves work (7 chain, miss 8, 1 plain, 8 times), 8 chain, miss 6, 1 plain in the 1st point of the flower in the 23rd row, 6 chain, miss 7, 1 plain in the 2nd point, *, 5 chain, miss 7, 1 plain in the 3rd point; 6 chain, miss 15, 1 plain in the centre of the plain stitches in the last row; 6 chain, miss 15, 1 plain, in the 2nd point of the next flower. Repeat from * 13 times more, then 5 chain, miss 7, 1 plain in the 3rd point, 5 chain, miss 7, 1 plain in the 4th point, and down the sides of the leaves, (7 chain, miss 8, 1 plain, 9 times). Fasten off.

25th—Commence in the 1st stitch of last row, work 1 plain, (1 treble, 1 long, and 1 treble, all in one stitch), then 1 plain, 1 single. Repeat and fasten off.

CURTAIN.

Make 81 chain, and commencing in the 1st stitch, work as the 15th row for 4 patterns. Fasten off. Then 81 chain, and work another piece the same, commence in the point of the 1st leaf, work as the 16th row, 4 times. Make 84 chain, then 1 plain on the 1st leaf of the other piece, and work on it as the 16th row, 4 times.

The pattern is now worked along the 2 pieces and chain stitches between them. Repeat as the 17th and following rows to the 25th row.

CONVOLVOLUS WREATH.

Material—1 *skein of Fine Green Wire, and* 22 *inches of Wire, No.* 21 ; *Needle No.* 20, *Bell Gauge. Fine Netting Silk, or Shetland Wool. Colours the same as directed in page* 15 ; *or the Flowers can be worked uniform in colour, if preferred.*

Work 26 flowers, as directed page 15.

Work 14 leaves of the 1st size, as page 17 ; then 18 leaves of the 2nd size, and 6 leaves of the 3rd size.

Work the petals and calyx, as directed at page 16, working only 4 stitches down the stem, join it to the last stitch of the stem of a leaf of the 2nd size ; then work the remaining stitches of the stem, working the ends of the wire and silk under the stitches ; cut off the ends of the wire and silk, belonging to the leaf, leaving those of the flower. Repeat the same for 3 other flowers. Work the petals and calyx for the other flowers, making only 9 chain for the calyx, and working 4 stitches instead of 12 down the stems, leaving the ends as before. Make 10 Buds as page 19. Cut 3 inches of the wire, pass it through the commencement of one of the buds to the half of the wire, fold it and work the calyx the same as at page 16. Repeat the same to 5 more buds.

TO MOUNT THE FIRST SPRAY.

Light Green Silk.—Work 170 chain, turn, and work a calyx, attach it to a bud, with wire as before, then down the chain stitches, which will form the centre stem, 27 plain,

E. R. de la Branchardiere, Invent, May, 1850.

working the wire from the bud under; join on a leaf, 3rd size, always joining to the last stitch of the stem, 6 plain, down the stem. In working the plain stitches, the ends of the wire and silk should be worked under, and gradually cut off when a fresh leaf or flower is joined to the stem, which makes the size uniform and even. Join on a bud, 25 plain, join on a flower, 18 plain, join on a leaf 2nd size, 24 plain, join on a flower, 18 plain, join on a leaf, 2nd size, 15 plain, join on a flower, 12 plain, join on a leaf, 2nd size, 18 plain, fasten, leaving the ends of the silk and wire. Work another spray the same.

THIRD SPRAY.

128 chain, work a calyx, join it to a bud, 20 plain, down the stem, join on a leaf, 3rd size, 16 plain, join on a bud, 28 plain, join on a flower, 20 plain, join on a leaf, 2nd size, 12 plain, join on a bud, 12 plain, join on a flower, 11 plain, fasten off. Work another spray the same.

TO FORM THE WREATH.

Make 456 chain for the centre stem, take the thick wire, and work 4 plain on the chain stitches, working the wire under, fold the end of the wire back to secure it, and join to a leaf of the 3rd size, then down the chain stitches of the centre stem, 21 plain, join on a leaf, 2nd size, 25 plain, join on a leaf, 1st size, 9 plain, join on the 1st spray, 6 plain, join on a flower, 6 plain, join on a flower, 6 plain, join on a leaf 1st size, 8 plain, join on a flower, 8 plain, join on a leaf 1st size, 6 plain, join the 3rd SPRAY—8 plain, join to the stem of one of the flowers with leaf; 6 plain, join on a flower; 8 plain, join on a leaf, 1st size; 7 plain, join on a flower with leaf; 8 plain, join on a flower, 8 plain, join on a leaf 1st size; 8 plain, join on a leaf 2nd size; 6 plain, join on a flower; 7 plain, join on a leaf 1st size; 18 plain, join on a leaf 1st size; 20 plain, join on a leaf, 2nd size; 50 plain, which forms the centre of the wreath; and for the other side, reverse the direction thus—Join a leaf of the 2nd size, 20 plain, join a leaf of the 1st size, &c. When finished make it round and fasten off.

To ornament a Ball Dress, work the bunches as page 14, and the 1st and 3rd sprays page, 32.

SERPENT-BRACELET.

Material—For the Body, 5 skeins of Fine Gold Twist, and 1 skein of Dark Green Union Cord; or 1 skein of Shaded Violet and Green Silk, and a skein of coarse Gold Twist, which is used instead of the Union Cord. If worked in imitation of Hair, *1 skein of coarse Netting Silk, 1 skein of Brown Union Cord. For the* Head, *1 skein of Fine Gold Twist; Silk same as the body, and for the Eyes, 4 Steel Beads, No. 6, and 2 large Black ones; and 1 skein of German Wool to stuff the body; Needle, No. 17, Bell Gauge.*

THE BODY.

With the gold twist, work 20 chain and make it round, keeping the wrong side of the stitches outside, take the green cord, and with the gold, work 22 stitches plain, working the cord under the stitches, still keeping the work on the wrong side; then work in *spiral crochet*, thus—it will be perceived on examining the wrong side of the plain stitches, that 2 threads of the gold lie perpendicularly across the cord of the lower part of the stitch, insert the needle in the left hand thread of the 2 perpendicular threads, and work a plain stitch in it. Repeat this stitch for 96 rounds, working the cord under the stitches, which should be worked rather loosely. Then decrease 1 by taking 2 stitches together, 37 plain, decrease 1, 35 plain, decrease 1, 33 plain, decrease 1. Repeat 12 times more, working 2 stitches less between the decreases each time. Fasten off. Double the skein of wool, and with a large rug needle, draw it through the body to the end.

THE HEAD.

Thread on the gold twist 1 steel bead, 1 black, 2 steel, 1 black, 1 steel, and commence

Serpent-Bracelet--Registered Design.

E. R. de la Branchardiere, Invent., May, 1850.

on the foundation chain of the body; work in plain crochet on the right side, working the silk under the stitches.

Gold, 9 plain, 2 plain in 1 stitch twice—(silk, 1 plain—gold, 2 plain in 1, 4 times)—gold, 2 plain in 1, 3 plain, decrease 1 by taking 2 stitches together, 3 plain, decrease 1, 3 plain, (silk, 1 plain—gold, 2 plain, 3 times)—silk, 1 plain—gold, 12 plain, (2 plain in 1, 3 times)—silk, 1 plain—gold, 2 plain in 1 and 1 plain, 3 times)—silk, 1 plain—gold, (2 plain in 1, 3 times), 15 plain—(silk, 1 plain—gold, 3 plain, 3 times)—silk, 1 plain—gold, 19 plain, (2 plain in 1 twice), (silk 1 plain, and gold 3 plain, 3 times)—silk, 1 plain, (gold, 2 plain in 1 twice), (3 plain, and decrease 1, 3 times), 4 plain, (2 plain in 1 twice), (silk, 1 plain—gold, 3 plain, 3 times), silk, 1 plain—gold, (2 plain in 1 twice), (4 plain and decrease 1, 4 times), 2 plain—silk, 1 plain—gold, decrease 1, 1 plain—silk, 1 plain—gold, 1 plain, decrease 1, 13 plain, (decrease 1 and 1 plain, 3 times), 1 bead stitch, thus—pass down 3 of the beads, and keeping the gold and beads in front, put the needle in the back of a stitch of the work, bring the gold through, and finish as a plain stitch; then decrease 1—2 plain—silk, 1 plain—gold, decrease 1,—silk, 1 plain,—gold, 2 plain, decrease 1; then 1 bead stitch as before, (decrease 1, and 1 plain, 3 times), 11 plain,—silk, 1 plain,—gold, 1 plain,—silk, 1 plain,—gold, 32 plain, (decrease 1, 3 times), 21 plain, stuff the head with wool, then (decrease 1, 3 times), 5 plain, (decrease 1, 3 times), 5 plain, (decrease 1, twice), 2 plain, (decrease 1, twice), cut off the silk, 4 plain, 2 single, miss 1, (2 treble in one stitch, twice), miss 1, 2 single, miss 1, (2 treble in 1 stitch, twice), miss 1, 1 single; and for the tongue, 1 single inside the mouth, 11 chain, turn, miss 1, 2 plain, 2 treble, 2 plain, 4 single. Fasten off.

VASE FOR FLOWERS.

Material—1 skein of shaded Green, 1 skein of shaded Scarlet German Wool, 3 skeins of gold Crochet Silk, 6 yards of White Cord, and 1 skein of Wire, No. 23; Needle, No. 17, Bell Gauge.

FOR THE STEM.

With the shaded green wool, work 70 chain, make it round, in the following rounds the cord is to be worked under the stitches. To decrease, take 2 stitches on the needle, and work as one stitch. Commence by leaving an end of the cord of 7 inches.

1st round—Plain. 2nd—Decrease 1 and 8 plain, 7 times. 3rd—Plain.

4th—Decrease 1 and 7 plain, 7 times. 5th—Plain.

6th—Decrease 1 and 6 plain, 7 times. 7th—Plain.

8th—Decrease 1 and 5 plain, 7 times.

9th—10 plain, decrease 1, 19 plain, decrease 1, 9 plain. Then work 12 rounds plain.

22nd—2 plain in 1 and 1 plain, 20 times.

23rd, 24th, 25th—Plain.

26th—2 plain in 1 and 1 plain, 30 times. 27th—2 plain in 1 and 3 plain, 22 times.

28th—2 plain in 1 and 9 plain, 11 times. 29th—2 plain in 1 and 8 plain, 14 times.

30th—2 plain in 1 and 10 plain, 13 times. 31st—2 plain in 1 and 7 plain, 19 times.

32nd—With the gold silk, gold 2 plain—green, 2 plain. Repeat. Cut off the wool and cord, 1 single.

Vase for Flowers---Registered Design.

E. R. de la Branchardiere, Invent., May, 1850.

33rd—Gold, 5 chain, miss 2, 2 plain. Repeat and fasten off.

With the green wool, work 10 leaves as directed at page 8. When finished, place them on the foundation chain of the stem, and leaving the end of cord inside, join the leaves to the stem, working 7 stitches to each leaf, leave the work; and for

THE FLOWER.

With the scarlet wool, 37 chain, turn miss 2, 4 plain, 22 treble, 3 plain, 2 single, 1 chain to cross; and up the other side, 5 plain, 6 treble, 12 long, 5 treble, 4 plain, 2 chain, turn, and down the other side, 4 plain, 5 treble, 12 long, 6 treble, 5 plain. Repeat 9 times more; then with the gold silk and the wire, which is to be worked under the stitches. Commence in the 1st chain stitch left at the 1st leaf, miss 1, and round the leaf work 66 plain, miss 1, 2 plain on the chain stitches, miss 1, and on the other leaf, 18 plain, join to the 48th stitch of the 66 plain, * then 48 plain, miss 1, 2 plain, miss 1, 18 plain, join to the 30th stitch of the 48 plain. Repeat from * 8 times more, then 28 plain; join to the 19th stitch of the 66 plain worked round the 1st leaf, then 18 plain. Fasten off, twisting the ends of the wire together; then place it along the round that joined the leaves, join it as before. When finished, work a plain round, working the cord under. Fasten off.

LONG LEAVES.

With the green wool, work 50 chain, turn, miss 2, 6 plain, 39 treble, 2 plain, 1 single, turn, 1 chain, cut off 12 inches of the wire, and work it under the following stitches, leaving an end of about 1 inch; work up the other side of the leaf, 3 plain, 5 treble, 31 long, 6 treble, 4 plain, 2 chain, turn, and down the other side, 4 plain, 6 treble, 31 long, 5 treble, 3 plain, 1 single, leave the ends.

Work 4 leaves more the same, then pass the ends of the wire of one of the leaves, through the 28th round, to the wrong side, and twisting them together, fasten off; join the other leaves the same, leaving 20 stitches of the 28th round between them, sew the top of the leaves to the stem.

For natural Flowers it is necessary to observe that a small bottle or glass is to be put down the centre.

THE END.

THE

CROCHET BOOK,

NINTH SERIES,

BY

MLLE. RIEGO DE LA BRANCHARDIERE.

Third Edition--15,000.

LONDON:
SIMPKIN, MARSHALL, AND CO.,
ACKERMANN & CO., STRAND; OLIVER AND BOYD, EDINBURGH;
AND ALL THE BERLIN WAREHOUSES.

1853.

Entered at Stationers' Hall.

CONTENTS.

RULES AND INSTRUCTIONS.

THE POLKA D'HIVER can either be worked in 8 thread German Wool, or 4 ply Fleecy 1 lb. to 1½ lb. according to the size. The *stitch* is raised crochet; that is, plain crochet, worked backwards and forwards, inserting the needle in the outer edge of the stitches in the previous row. At the *end* of every row, work 1 chain to turn back with, except when the row ends with *single* stitches, then the chain stitch is not required.

The different sizes are formed by working tighter or looser, thus—

Polka 1st size—26 to 30 inches in the waist, Walker's Penelope, No. 000; and work 5 stitches to the inch.

2nd size—22 to 26 inches, Penelope Needle, No. 00. Work 11 stitches to every 2 inches. By following these rules they may be made either smaller or larger.

PLAIN CROCHET IN TWO OR MORE COLORS.

Place the color not used along the stitches of the previous row, and crochet over it. To change the colors, when the two loops are on the needle, draw the other color through them to finish the stitch: in reckoning these stitches, it is best to count the lower or first loop of the stitches. And for the other Terms used, see my FIRST and SECOND SERIES.

E. R. DE LA la BRANCHARDIERE.

106, *New Bond Street*,
Nov. 30th, 1850.

NINTH SERIES.

POLKA D'HIVER.

[FOR MATERIALS AND INSTRUCTIONS—See page 3.]

Make a chain of 70 stitches, worked rather loose. This chain forms the length of the jacket from underneath the arm; and to shape the front and gores at the hip, commence thus—

1st row—Miss 1, 25 plain, 2 single, turn back, leaving 42 chain.

2nd—2 single, 25 plain.

3rd—24 plain, 2 single, turn back, leaving one stitch. 4th—2 single, 24 plain.

5th—23 plain, 2 single, turn back. 6th—2 single, 23 plain.

7th—22 plain, 2 single, turn back. 8th—2 single, 22 plain.

9th—24 plain. Work the one stitches left at the 7th, 5th, and 3rd rows; then on the foundation chain, 3 plain, 2 single, turn back.

POLKA D'HIVER, FOR 1852.

E. Riego de la Branchardiere, Invent., *Nov.*, 1850.

10th—2 single, 30 plain.

11th—2 plain in one, 31 plain, and on the chain, 3 plain, 2 single, turn back.

12th—2 single, 36 plain. 13th—20 plain, 2 single, turn back.

14th—2 single, 20 plain.

15th—2 plain in one, 21 plain, and on the 12th row, 1 single, turn back.

16th—2 single, 22 plain.

17th—24 plain, and on the 12th row, 1 single, turn back.

18th—2 single, 23 plain.

19th—2 plain in one, 24 plain, and on the 12th row, 1 single, turn back.

20th—2 single, 25 plain.

21st—27 plain, and on the 12th row, 13 plain; then on the foundation chain 3 plain, 2 single, turn back.

22nd—2 single, 43 plain. 23rd—2 plain in one, 23 plain, 2 single, turn back.

24th—2 single, 25 plain. 25th—24 plain, 2 single, turn back, leaving one stitch.

26th—2 single, 24 plain. 27th—2 plain in one, 22 plain, 2 single, turn back.

28th—2 single, 24 plain. 29th—23 plain, 2 single, turn back.

30th—2 single, 23 plain.

31st—2 plain in one, 24 plain. Work the one stitches left at the 29th, 27th, and 25th rows; then on the 22nd row, 19 plain; and on the chain, 3 plain, 2 single, turn back.

32nd—2 single, 51 plain. 33rd—2 plain in one, 21 plain, 2 single, turn back.

34th—2 single, 23 plain.

35th—25 plain, and on the 32nd row, 29 plain; then on the chain, 3 plain, 2 single, turn back.

36th—2 single, 57 plain, 37th—As 33rd. 38th—As 34th.

39th—25 plain, and on the 36th row, 35 plain; then on the chain, 2 plain, 2 single, turn back.

40th—2 single, 62 plain. 41st—As 33rd. 42nd—As 34th.

43rd—25 plain, and on the 40th row, 40 plain; then on the chain, 2 plain, 2 single, turn back.

44th—2 single, 67 plain. 45th—As 33rd. 46th—As 34th.

47th—25 plain, and on the 44th row, 45 plain; then on the chain, 2 plain, 2 single, turn back.

48th—2 single, 72 plain. 49th—As 33rd. 50th—As 34th.

51st—25 plain, and on the 48th row, 50 plain; then on the chain, 5 plain, turn so as to work on the other side of the foundation chain to form the back of the Polka.

52nd—Work 69 plain down the foundation chain, taking the back part of the chain stitches so as to leave the rib of the stitch in the front.

53rd—25 plain, 2 single, turn back.

54th—2 single, 25 plain.

55th—24 plain, 2 single, turn back, leaving one stitch. 56th—2 single, 24 plain.

57th—23 plain, 2 single, turn back. 58th—2 single, 23 plain.

59th—22 plain, 2 single, turn back. 60th—2 single, 22 plain.

61st—24 plain. Work the one stitches left at the 59th, 57th, and 55th rows; and on the 52nd row, 42 plain, 4 chain, turn back.

62nd—Miss 1, 3 single on the chain, and on the 61st row, 69 plain.

63rd—22 plain, 2 single, turn back. 64th—2 single, 22 plain.

65th—24 plain, and on the 62nd row, 1 single, turn back.

66th—2 single, 23 plain.

67th—25 plain, and on the 62nd row, 1 single, turn back.

68th—2 single, 24 plain.

69th—26 plain, and on the 62nd row, 1 single, turn back.

70th—2 single, 25 plain

71st—27 plain, and on the 62nd row, 45 plain, 4 chain, turn back.

72nd—Miss 1, 3 single on the chain, 72 plain.

73rd—25 plain, 2 single, turn back.

74th—2 single, 25 plain. 75th—24 plain, 2 single, turn back.

76th—2 single, 24 plain. 77th—23 plain, 2 single, turn back.

78th—2 single, 23 plain.

79th—22 plain, 2 single, turn back.

80th—2 single, 22 plain.

81st—24 plain. Work the one stitches left at the 79th, 77th, and 75th rows; then on the 72nd row, 48 plain, 4 chain, turn back.

82nd—Miss 1, 3 single on the chain, 75 plain.

83rd—23 plain, 2 single, turn back. 84th—2 single, 23 plain.

85th—25 plain, and on the 82nd row, 53 plain. Fasten off.

86th—Commence again by working 4 chain to form part of the other side of the *armhole*, and to continue the front, join the chain to the last row of the front, that is, the 51st row by working 2 stitches in the last stitch of that row, then work the remaining 79 stitches of the 51st row, plain.

87th—As 33rd. 88th—As 34th.

89th—25 plain, and on the 80th row, 57 plain; then 1 single on the chain of the armhole, turn back.

90th—83 plain. 91st—As 33rd. 92nd—As 34th.

93rd—25 plain, and on the 90th row, 59 plain, 1 single on the chain, turn back.

94th—85 plain. 95th—As 33rd. 96th—As 34th.

97th—25 plain, and on the 94th row, 61 plain, 1 single on the chain, turn back.

98th—87 plain. 99th—As 33rd. 100th—As 34th.

101st—25 plain, and on the 98th row, 63 plain, 1 single on the chain. Fasten off, and leaving the body, work the

SEELVE.

Commence with 19 chain.

1st row—Miss 1, 18 plain, 6 chain.

2nd—Miss 1, 5 single on the chain; then plain on the last row. At the end, 6 chain. Repeat the last row 10 times more.

13th—Miss 1, 5 single on the chain, the rest plain. 14th and 15th rows—Plain.

16th—Decrease one stitch, by putting the needle into the 1st and 2nd stitch, and work as one stitch, then 11 plain. Repeat 5 times more.

17th, 18th, and 19th rows—Plain.

20th—10 plain, and decrease 6 times.

21st, 22nd, and 23rd rows—Plain.

24th—Decrease, and 9 plain 6 times.

25th—2 plain in one, and the rest plain.

26th and 27th rows—Plain. Repeat the 3 last rows, 10 times more.

58th—67 plain, and leaving 4 stitches, attach this sleeve to the front of the body by work-on the 101st row, 69 plain, which will form the 102nd row.

103rd—Miss 1, 21 plain, 2 single, turn back.

104th—2 single, 21 plain. The 11 following rows are worked along the sleeve and front.

105th—Miss 1, 22 plain, and on the 102nd row, 132 plain.

106th—154 plain.

107th—Miss 1, 147 plain, 2 single, turn back, leaving 4 stitches of the sleeve.

108th—2 single, 123 plain, 3 single, turn back, leaving 21 stitches.

109th—3 single, 119 plain, 2 single, turn back.

110th—2 single, 116 plain, 3 single, turn back, 3 stitches will now be left at the front every other row.

111th—3 single, 112 plain, 2 single, turn back.

112th—2 single, 109 plain, 3 single, turn back.

113th—3 single, 105 plain, 2 single, turn back.

114th—2 single, 102 plain, 3 single, turn back.

115th—3 single, 96 plain, and leaving the remaining stitches of the sleeve, to be *sewn* to the body, work down the 85th row, which was left for the back, 78 plain.

116th—22 plain, 2 single, turn back. 117th—2 single, 22 plain.

118th—24 plain, and on the 115th row, 147 plain, 3 single, turn back. This row is worked up the back, across the shoulders, and down the front.

119th—3 single, 171 plain. 120th—As 116th. 121st—As 117th.

122nd—24 plain, and on the 119th row, 144 plain, 3 single, turn back.

123rd—3 single, 168 plain. 124th—As 116th. 125th—As 117th.

126th—24 plain, and on the 123 row, 141 plain, 3 single, turn back.

127th—3 single, 165 plain. 128th—As 116th. 129th—As 117th.

130th—24 plain, and on the 127th row, 138 plain, 3 single, turn back.

131st—3 single, 162 plain. 132nd—As 116th. 133rd—As 117th.

134th—24 plain, and on the 131st row, 135 plain, 3 single, turn back.

135th—3 single, 159 plain. 136th—As 116th. 137th—As 117th.

138th—24 plain, and on the 135th row, 132 plain, 3 single, turn back.

139th—3 single, 156 plain. 140th—As 116th. 141st—As 117th.

142nd—24 plain, and on the 139th row, 129 plain, 3 single, turn back.

143rd—3 single, 126 plain, 3 single, turn back, leaving 24 stitches.

144th—3 single, 123 plain, 3 single, turn back.

145th—3 single, 117 plain, 3 single, turn back, 6 stitches will now be left every other row.

146th—3 single, 114 plain, 3 single, turn back.

147th—3 single, 108 plain, 3 single, turn back.

148th—3 single, 105 plain, 3 single, turn back.

149th—3 single, 99 plain, 3 single, turn back.

150th—3 single, 96 plain, 3 single. 151st—3 single, 90 plain, 3 single.

152nd—3 single, 87 plain, 3 single. 153rd—3 single, 81 plain, 3 single.

154th—3 single, 78 plain, 3 single. 155th—3 single, 72 plain, 3 single.

156th—3 single, 69 plain, 3 single. 157th—3 single, 63 plain, 3 single.

158th—3 single, 60 plain, 3 single. 159th—3 single, 54 plain, 3 single.

160th—3 single, 51 plain, 3 single. 161st—3 single, 45 plain, 3 single.

162nd—3 single, 42 plain, 3 single. 163rd—3 single, 36 plain, 3 single.

164th—3 single, 33 plain, 3 single. 165th—3 single, 27 plain, 3 single.

166th—3 single, 11 plain. 167th—11 plain, turn back.

168th—5 plain, 3 single, turn back.

169th—3 single, 5 plain. Fasten off. Sew the sides of the sleeves together, and the remaining portion of the armhole.

Work another half exactly the same, and to join them, place the two sides together where the 6 stitches are left, and commencing at the 24 stitches left at the bottom of the Jacket, join them with a row of single crochet, by putting the needle in the front edge of a stitch on the one side, and the back edge of the stitch on the other, working it as one stitch. Repeat to the fastening off, or last row of the side.

BORDER (Knitting.)

Material—Single shaded Berlin Wool, Pins, No. 14, Bell Gauge.

Cast on 7 stitches.

1st row—Slip 1, put the needle in the next stitch, pass the wool between the pins from the front to the back, then round the first and second fingers to the front, pass the wool between the pins again round the fingers to the front as before; pass the wool between the pins again, which will make 3 turns of wool upon the right hand pin, two turns or loops of which are round the fingers; bring the 3 turns of wool through the stitch and take it off the left pin to finish the stitch. Work the remaining stitches the same.

2nd—Knit the 3 turns of wool together as one stitch. Repeat, knitting the last stitch plain. Repeat these 2 rows until sufficient is made.

Work 3 yards and a quarter to go round the polka, and two pieces of 20 inches each to go round the sleeve, then sew the tightest edge of the border to the polka, commencing at the left side of the neck; sew it across the neck, down the right front, across the skirt, and 9 inches up the left side of the waist; then with the shaded wool, work 2 plain rows up the remainder of the left front. Finish with 6 loops sewn to the right side, and buttons to correspond on the left.

[The Borders to the Polkas in the other WINTER BOOKS are equally applicable to this Polka.]

UNDER SLEEVE.

Material—26 Skeins of Single Berlin Wool, plain color; 1 Skein of shaded Berlin, that will contrast; Needle, No. 15, Bell Gauge, or Penelope Needle, No. 1.

Commence with the plain wool, and work a chain of 150 stitches, make it round.

1st round—2 chain, miss 2, 1 treble. Repeat.

2nd—3 chain, miss 2, 1 plain in the 2 chain. Repeat.

3rd—3 chain, miss 3, 1 plain in the 3 chain. Repeat and work 21 rows more the same.

25th—2 chain, miss 3, 1 plain. Repeat. 26th—1 chain, miss 2, 1 plain. Repeat.

27th—Miss 1, 1 plain. Repeat. 28th—Miss 1, 2 plain. Repeat.

29th—With the shaded wool, work 4 rounds plain.

34th—1 chain, miss 1, 1 treble. Repeat; then 4 rounds plain and fasten off. Sew the foundation chain to the last row of the sleeve of the Polka.

MANCHETTE.

Material—36 Skeins of Pink, Blue or Cerise, and 3 Skeins of Black Single Berlin Wool; 1 Skein of Black Shetland Wool; Needle, No. 16, Bell Gauge, or Walker's Penelope Needle, No. 2.

Commence with the black Berlin wool, and work 48 chain. This chain should measure 7 inches, and is the size for the wrist. Make it round.

1st round—1 chain, miss 2, (2 treble, 3 chain, 2 treble, these 4 treble in one stitch), 1 chain, miss 2, 1 plain. Repeat and join on the pink, turn, so as to work on the other side of the foundation chain.

2nd and 3rd rounds—Pink, plain.

4th—Black and pink, 4 black, 2 pink. Repeat.

5th—4 pink, 2 black. Repeat. 6th—4 black, 2 pink. Repeat.

7th and 8th rounds—pink, plain.

Leave the Sleeve, and with the Shetland wool, work 12 patterns of the following Edging, and to attach it to the sleeve, place the straight side of the Edging in front of the 8th round of the sleeve, and with the black Berlin wool, work the

9th round—plain, putting the needle in a loop of the edging and in a stitch of the 8th round and working it as one stitch, work the remainder of the sleeve with pink wool.

10th—3 chain, miss 1, 1 plain. Repeat.

11th—3 chain, miss 3, 1 plain in the 3 chain. Repeat.

12th—3 chain, miss 2, 2 plain in the 3 chain. Repeat.

13th and 14th—3 chain, miss 2, 3 plain in the 3 chain. Repeat.

15th—1 chain, miss 2, 1 plain on the 3 plain, 1 chain, miss 2, 2 treble in one. Repeat 23 times more.

16th—3 chain, miss 3, 2 plain on the 2 treble of last round. Repeat.

17th—2 chain, miss 1, 3 treble in one, 2 chain, miss 2, 1 plain between the 2 plain of last round. Repeat 23 times more.

18th—2 chain, miss 3, 3 plain on the 3 treble, *, 5 chain, miss 5, 3 plain on the 3 treble of last round. Repeat from *, 22 times more, end, 5 chain, miss 6, 1 plain on the 3 plain.

19th—2 chain, miss 3, 3 treble in one, 2 chain, miss 3, 1 plain. Repeat 22 times more, end, 2 chain, miss 3, 3 treble in one.

20th—5 chain, miss 5, 3 plain. Repeat 23 times more.

21st—2 chain, miss 2, 3 treble in one, 2 chain, miss 3, 1 plain, *, 2 chain, miss 3, 3 treble in one, 2 chain, miss 3, 1 plain. Repeat from *, 22 times more. Repeat the last 4 rounds, 10 times more.

62nd—2 chain, miss 3, 1 plain, *, 3 chain, miss 7, 1 plain. Repeat from *.

63rd—All treble.

64th—2 chain, miss 3, 2 treble. Repeat.

Fasten off and run an elastic ribbon in the last round.

COIFFURE MARIE STUART.

Material—20 Skeins of single Berlin Wool; colours, Pink, Cerise, Blue or Amber; and for the Border, 1 skein of Black Shetland Wool; Needle, No. 16, Bell Gauge, or Walker's Penelope Needle, No. 2.

With the Berlin Wool, commence at the point of the Hood, work 12 chain.

1st row—Turn, miss 7, 2 treble in one stitch, 7 chain, turn, miss 4, 1 single in the 3rd stitch of these 7 chain to form a round loop, 2 chain, then 2 treble in the same stitch as the other 2 treble, 2 chain, miss 3, 1 plain.

2nd—7 chain, turn, miss 4, 1 single in the 3rd stitch to form a round loop, 2 chain; turn the work so as to crochet on the other side of the foundation chain, 2 treble in the same stitch as the last I plain, 5 chain, turn, miss 4, 1 single in the 1st stitch to form a round loop, 2 treble in the same stitch as the last 2 treble, 2 chain, miss 3, 3 treble in one, 2 chain, miss 3, 2 treble in one, 5 chain, turn, miss 4, 1 single in the 1st stitch to form a round loop, 2 treble in the same stitch as before, turn back.

3rd—To form the Edge—7 chain, turn, miss 4, 1 single in the 3rd stitch of these 7 chain to form a round loop, 2 chain, miss 4, 2 treble in the round loop of last row between the treble stitches; then 5 chain, turn, miss 4, 1 single in the 1st stitch of the 5 chain, to form a round loop; then 2 treble in the same round loop as the other 2 treble. This edge is repeated at the *beginning* of every row. 5 chain, miss 4, 3 plain on the 3 treble of last row, 5 chain, miss 4; and for the Edge at the *end*, 2 treble in the round loop, 5 chain, turn, miss 4, 1 single in the 1st stitch to form a round loop, 2 treble in the same round loop as before. This Edge is repeated at the *end* of every row.

4th—Edge as at the commencement of the 3rd row, then 5 chain, miss 4, 3 treble in one stitch, 2 chain, miss 3, 1 plain on the 3 plain, 2 chain, miss 3, 3 treble in one, 5 chain, miss 4; then work the Edge as at the *end* of the 3rd row.

5th—Edge as the 3rd row, then 5 chain, miss 3, 3 plain in one, 5 chain, miss 3, 3 plain on the 3 treble of last row, 5 chain, miss 5, 3 plain, 5 chain, miss 3, 3 plain in one, 5 chain, miss 3, and work the Edge.

6th—Edge as before, then 5 chain, miss 4, 3 treble in one, *, 2 chain, miss 3, 1 plain, 2 chain, miss 3, 3 treble in one. Repeat from * 3 times more; then 5 chain, miss 4, and work the Edge.

COIFFURE MARIE STUART & MANCHETTE,

Adapted for 1851 & 1852.

E. Riego de la Branchardiere Invent. Nov. 1850.

7th—Edge as before, then 5 chain, miss 3, 3 plain in one, 5 chain, miss 3, 3 plain, *, 5 chain, miss 5, 3 plain. Repeat from *, 3 times more; then 5 chain, miss 3, 3 plain in one, 5 chain, miss 3, and work the Edge. Repeat the last 2 rows, 6 times more, Working 3 patterns more between these stars * *, each repeat.

20th—Edge as before, then 2 chain, miss 4, 3 treble in one, (2 chain, miss 3, 1 plain, 2 chain, miss 3, 3 treble in one, 25 times), end, 2 chain, miss 4, and work the Edge.

21st—Edge as before, then 2 chain, miss 4, 3 plain, (5 chain, miss 5, and 3 plain, 25 times), 2 chain, miss 4, and work the Edge.

22nd—Edge as before, then 2 chain, miss 5, 1 plain, (2 chain, miss 3, 3 treble in one, 2 chain, miss 3 and 1 plain, 25 times), 2 chain, miss 5, and work the Edge.

23rd—Edge as before, then 5 chain, miss 7, 3 plain, (5 chain, miss 5 and 3 plain, 24 times), 5 chain, miss 7, and work the Edge.

24th—Same as 20th. 25th—As 21st. 26th—As 22nd row.

27th—Edge as before, then 2 chain, miss 8, 1 plain, 2 chain, miss 6, 3 plain, (5 chain, miss 5 and 3 plain, 22 times), 2 chain, miss 6, 1 plain, 2 chain, miss 8, and work the Edge.

28th—Edge as before, 2 chain, miss 8, 1 plain (2 chain, miss 3, 3 treble in one, 2 chain, miss 3, 1 plain, 22 times), 2 chain, miss 8, and work the Edge.

Repeat the 2 last rows 6 times more, working 3 patterns less each repeat.

41st—Edge as before, 2 chain, miss 8, 1 plain, 2 chain, miss 6, 3 plain, 5 chain, miss 5, 3 plain, 2 chain, miss 6, 1 plain, 2 chain, miss 8, and work the Edge.

42nd—7 chain, turn, miss 4, 1 single, 2 chain, miss 2, 2 treble in the round loop of the Edge of last row, miss 8, 1 plain, 2 chain, miss 3, (2 treble in one, 7 chain, turn, miss 4, 1 single, 2 chain, 2 treble in the same stitch as before), 2 chain, miss 3, 1 plain, miss 8, 1 plain in the round loop of last row. Fasten off.

TRIMMING.

With the Berlin wool, make 270 chain, turn, and on the chain work 1 chain, miss 1, 1 treble, repeat. Then with the Black Shetland Wool, work 5 chain, miss 1, 1 plain in the foundation chain, of the Berlin Wool. Repeat all round. When finished, make it into 6 loops, with 2 ends. Work another piece the same for the other side.

For the Border.—With the Shetland Wool, work 56 patterns of the following Edging, then sew it to the treble stitches in the edge of the Hood, leaving the points outside: it should be put on nearly plain across the back to the 5th loop of the edging, then full round the lappet to the opposite side, plain to the point of the front, then one plait to bring it to a point, then plain and full round the other lappet, draw it together across the work at the 5th loop of the edging, and sew the loops of trimming to it.

EDGING.

WORKED BACKWARDS AND FORWARDS.

Material—Jno. & Wm. Taylor's Crochet Thread, No. 2 ; Needle, No. 18, Bell Gauge, or Walker's Penelope Needle, No. 3½.

1st row—17 chain, turn, miss 5, 1 single in the 6th stitch to form a round loop, turn, 1 chain to cross, and in the round loop work 9 plain, 3 single on the foundation chain, 3 chain, miss 1, 6 plain on the foundation, 3 chain, 1 plain, turn back. This row is not repeated.

2nd—4 chain, miss 1, 1 treble in the 3 chain, 5 chain, miss 6, (3 long in the 3 chain of last row, 3 chain, 3 long in the same 3 chain as before), 9 chain, turn, miss 5, 1 single in the 6th stitch to form a round loop, 1 chain to cross, and leaving 3 chain, work in in the round loop to form the leaf, 2 plain, (5 chain and 2 plain, 3 times), turn back.

3rd—2 chain, miss 2, 3 treble in the 5 chain, 1 chain, join to the 6th stitch of the 9 plain worked on the 1st round loop, 1 chain, 3 treble in the same 5 chain as before ; 2 chain, 1 single on the 2 plain, 2 chain, (and in the next 5 chain, 3 treble, 3 chain, 3 treble), 2 chain, 1 single on the 2 plain, 2 chain, and in the next 5 chain, 3 treble, 3 chain, 3 treble, 2 chain, 1 single on the 2 plain; then on the 3 chain 2 single, 1 chain, miss 4, (3 long in the 3 chain between the long stitches of the last row; 3 chain, 3 long in the same 3 chain as before); 2 chain, miss 5, 1 plain in the 5 chain, 3 chain, miss 3, 1 treble in the 4 chain, 3 chain, 1 treble in the same 4 chain, turn back.

4th—4 chain, miss 1, 1 treble in the 3 chain, 5 chain, miss 10, 1 plain in the 3 chain between the long stitches, 9 chain, turn, miss 5, 1 single in the 6th stitch to form a round loop, turn back.

E. R. de la Branchardiere, Invent., Nov., 1850.

5th—Work 4 plain in the round loop; join to the last 3 chain of the leaf; then 5 plain in the round loop, 3 single on the chain, 3 chain, miss 1, 6 plain, 3 chain, 1 plain, turn back. Repeat from the 2nd row until sufficient is worked.

THE MARIO CAP.

FOR THE BAND OF THE CAP.

Material—6 shades of Grey Single Berlin Wool, 1 skein of each. These colours should be shaded from the darkest to the lightest, 3 skeins of White, and 1 of Black. Crochet Silk—3 skeins of Ponceau, 1 of Light Green, 2 of Middle Green, 1 Dark Green, 2 of Gold colour; and for the Top of the Cap, 15 shades of Green, 2 skeins of each, and 9 skeins of Gold colour Crochet Silk; or if Wool is used, 9 skeins of Scarlet Berlin; Needle, No. 16, Bell Gauge, or Walker's Penelope Needle, No. 2.

With the gold silk, work 203 chain, make it round by working 3 single on the 1st stitches of the chain.

The foundation chain should measure 21 to 23 inches according to the size of the head. This band is worked in Plain Crochet—see page 3.

1st round—Gold and black, work 3 gold, 1 black. Repeat 49 times more, end 1 black more.

2nd—Darkest shade of grey and gold—1 gold, 3 grey. Repeat.

3rd—5th shade of grey—Plain.

4th—Lightest shade of green and 4th shade of grey—2 green, 3 grey, 1 green, 3 grey, 2 green, 3 grey, 2 green, 13 grey. Repeat 6 times more, end 12 grey instead of 13.

5th—3rd shade of grey—1 green, 2 grey over the 1st 2 green of last round, 1 green, 1 grey, 2 green, 2 grey, 3 green, 3 grey, 1 green, 1 grey, 3 green, 9 grey. Repeat.

6th—2nd shade of grey, 2nd shade of green, and ponceau—4 grey, 3 green, 2 grey, 2 green, 3 grey, 3 green, 2 grey, 3 green, 7 ponceau. Repeat, end 4 grey more.

THE MARIO CAP.

R. de la Branchardiere, Invent. Nov., 1850.

7th—1st shade of grey—2 green, 3 grey, 1 green, 1 grey, 3 green, 3 grey, 1 green, 2 grey, 3 ponceau, 2 green, 6 ponceau,2 grey. Repeat.

8th—White and 3rd shade of green—1 green, 1 white, 5 green, 3 white, 2 green, 2 white, 2 ponceau, 2 green, 3 ponceau, 2 green, 3 white, 2 ponceau, 1 white. Repeat, at the end omit the 1 white.

9th—3 green, 4 white, 2 green, 2 white, 2 green, 1 white, 6 ponceau, 1 white, 1 green, 2 white, 3 green, 1 white, 1 ponceau. Repeat; but in the last pattern omit the last 3 stitches, that is, working only 2 green.

10th—2nd shade of green—2 ponceau, 1 white, 2 ponceau, 3 green, 2 white, 3 green, 2 white, 1 green, 2 ponceau, 2 white, 2 ponceau, 2 white, 1 green, 4 white. Repeat.

11th—2 ponceau, 1 white, 2 ponceau, 1 white, 3 green, 2 white, 2 green, 2 white, 6 ponceau, 1 white, 2 green, 1 white, 1 green, 3 white. Repeat, end 2 white more, making in all 5 white.

12th—1st shade of green—1 ponceau, 3 white, 3 green, 3 white, 1 green, 1 white, 2 ponceau, 2 white, 2 ponceau, 1 white, 3 green, 1 white, 2 green, 4 white. Repeat, end, 2 white instead of 4.

13th—2nd shade of green—2 ponceau, 1 white, 2 ponceau, 2 white, 2 green, 4 white, 6 ponceau, 2 white, 2 green, 2 white, 3 green, 1 white. Repeat.

14th—2 ponceau, 1 white, 2 ponceau, 3 white, 1 green, 3 white, 2 ponceau, 2 white, 2 ponceau, 3 white, 1 green, 2 white, 1 green, 1 white, 2 green, 1 white. Repeat.

15th—3rd shade of green—2 white, 1 ponceau, 8 white, 6 ponceau, 1 white, 2 green, 3 white, 2 green, 3 white, 1 green. Repeat, end, 2 white.

16th—2 ponceau, 5 white, 3 ponceau, 2 white, 2 ponceau, 2 green, 1 white, 5 green, 1 white, 2 green, 4 white. Repeat, end, 1 white more.

17th—2nd shade of green and 1st shade of grey—7 ponceau, 1 grey, 3 ponceau, 7 grey, 1 green, 1 grey, 1 green, 1 grey, 3 green, 4 grey. Repeat, end, 2 grey more.

18th—2nd shade of grey—7 ponceau, 3 grey, 2 green, 2 grey, 3 green, 1 grey, 1 green, 2 grey, 2 green, 6 grey. Repeat.

19th—1st shade of green, and 3rd shade of grey—8 grey, *, 2 green, 2 grey, 2 green, 1 grey, 1 green, 1 grey, 1 green, 1 grey, 1 green, 2 grey, 1 green, 14 grey. Repeat from *, end 6 grey instead of 14.

20th—4th shade of grey—8 grey, *, 1 green, 6 grey, 1 green, 4 grey, 1 green, 16 grey. Repeat from *, end, 6 grey instead of 16.

21st—5th shade of grey—Plain.

22nd—Gold silk, and 6th shade of grey—1 gold, 3 grey. Repeat, end, 1 gold.

23rd—Black and gold—1 black, 3 gold. Repeat.

24th—All gold, end 2 single. This finishes the Band of the Cap.

FOR THE TOP OF THE CAP.

25th—Commencing with the darkest shade of green, work 1 chain, turn the wool round the needle, put it into the last stitch of the Band and finish the treble stitch, (see 2nd Series). "Every alternate round is commenced in the same manner;" then 1 chain, miss 1, 1 treble. Repeat all round, and at the end, work 1 single in the chain at the commencement of the round, knot the ends together, and cut them off.

26th—Gold silk—Commence with 1 chain; then 1 plain in the 1st chain stitch of last round, *, 1 chain, miss 1, 1 plain in the 1 chain of last round. Repeat, from *, ending with 1 single in the 1st chain stitch of the round. Repeat these 2 rounds 9 times more, working 3 of the treble rounds with each shade of green throughout the Cap.

45th—Commence as the 25th round; then (1 chain, miss 1, and 1 treble 19 times), and to decrease, miss 1, 1 treble. Repeat.

46th—Same as 26th missing 2 stitches instead of one at the decreasing stitches of the last round.

47th—As 25th. 48th—As 26th.

49th—Commence as 25th, (1 chain, miss 1 and 1 treble, 18 times), miss 1, 1 treble. Repeat; then repeat the last 4 rounds 4 times more, working "1 chain, miss 1 and 1 treble" less each time between the decreasing stitches; that is, every other treble round. Then repeat the 2 rounds of pattern, 13 times more, decreasing in the same manner *every* treble round, draw up the remaining stitches, and finish with a long Tassel.

PALETOT, OR OPERA CLOAK.

Material—1½lb. 4 or 6 ply Fleecy, Walker's Penelope Needle, No. 000. This Paletôt is worked in Double Crochet; that is, taking both sides of the stitch on the needle and working a plain stitch.

Make 101 chain for the length of the Front.

1st row—Miss 1; the rest plain except the last stitch, then work 2 plain in one.

2nd—2 plain in one, the rest plain.

3rd—Plain, except the last stitch, then 2 plain in one.

4th—2 plain in one, the rest plain. Repeat these 4 rows 3 times more. There will now be 113 stitches.

17th—Miss 1, the rest plain, except the last 2 stitches; then miss 1, 1 plain.

18th—Miss 1, the rest plain. 19th—Plain.

20th—Miss 1, the rest plain. Repeat the last 4 rows 4 times more. There will now be 93 stitches.

37th—As 17th row. 38th—Miss 1, 14 plain, 2 single, turn back.

39th—2 single, 14 plain.

40th—Miss 1, 15 plain, and on the 37th row, 74 plain; and to form the gore at the hip,

41st—60 plain, 2 single, turn back. 42nd—2 single, 60 plain.

43rd—56 plain, 2 single, turn back, leaving 4 stitches.

44th—2 single, 56 plain. Repeat the last 2 rows 13 times more, working 4 plain stitches less each repeat.

PALETOT, OR OPERA CLOAK
Adapted for 1851 and 1852.

E. Riego de la Branchardiere, Invent., Nov. 1850.

71st—6 plain, then work the 4 stitches left at the 69th, 67th, 65th, 63rd, 61st, 59th, 57th, 55th, 53rd, and 51st rows, making in all 46 stitches, turn back.

72nd—46 plain. 73rd—4 plain, 2 single, turn back. 74th—2 single, 4 plain.

75th—6 plain, and on the 72nd row, 2 plain, 2 single, turn back.

76th—2 single, the rest plain. Repeat the last 2 rows 9 times more, working 4 stitches more on the 72nd row each repeat. Then to shape the back of the armhole,

95th—45 plain, 2 plain in one. 96th—2 plain in one, 46 plain. 97th—48 plain.

98th—2 plain in one, 47 plain. 99th—49 plain. 100th—2 plain in one, 48 plain.

101st—49 plain, 2 plain in one. 102nd—51 plain. 103rd—50 plain, 2 plain in one.

104th—2 plain in one, 51 plain. 105th—Plain, at the end 7 chain.

106th—Miss 1, 6 plain on the chain, the rest plain. Repeat the last 2 rows twice more.

111th—71 Plain, at the end 19 chain.

112th—Miss 1, 7 plain, and 2 single on the chain, turn back.

113th—2 single, 7 plain.

114th—2 plain in one, 8 plain, and on the chain, 9 plain; then on the 111th row, 71 plain. Then to form the back,

115th—Plain. 116th—2 plain in one, the rest plain. Repeat the last 2 rows 10 times more; then 15 rows plain.

152nd—Miss 1, the rest plain. 153rd—Plain. Repeat the 2 last rows 10 times more.

174th—Miss 1, 7 plain, 2 single, turn back. 175th—2 single, 7 plain.

176th—9 plain, and on the 173rd row, 80 plain.

177th—71 plain, turn back, leaving 18 stitches. 178th—71 plain.

179th and 180th—65 plain. 181st and 182nd—59 plain.

183rd and 184th—53 plain. 185th—51 plain, miss 1, 1 plain.

186th—Miss 1, 51 plain. 187th—51 plain. 188th—Miss 1, 50 plain.

189th—48 plain, miss 1, 1 plain. 190th—Miss 1, 48 plain.

191st—48 plain. 192nd—Miss 1, 47 plain. 193rd—47 plain.

194th—Miss 1, 46 plain. 195th—40 plain, 2 single, turn back, leaving 4 stitches.

196th—2 single, the rest plain. Repeat the last 2 rows 9 times more, working 4 stitches less each repeat.

215th—6 plain, then work the 4 stitches left at the 213th, 211th, 209th, 207th, 205th, 203rd, 201st, 199th, 197th, and 195th rows.

216th—46 plain. 217th—4 plain, 2 single, turn back. 218th—2 single, 4 plain.

219th—6 plain, and on the 216th row, 2 plain, 2 single, turn back.

220th—2 single, the rest plain. Repeat the last 2 rows 9 times more, working 4 stitches more on the 216th row each repeat.

239th—46 plain, 5 chain, turn back.

240th—Miss 1, 4 single on the chain, 46 plain. Repeat the last 2 rows 3 times more, working 4 stitches more each repeat.

247th—2 plain in one, 61 plain, then 28 chain. Then for the other front.

248th—Turn, miss 1, 14 plain and 2 single on the chain, turn back.

249th—2 single, 14 plain.

250th—2 plain in one, 15 plain, then on the chain, 11 plain, and on the 247th row, 63 plain.

251—Plain, working 2 stitches in the last stitch.

252nd, 253rd, and 254th rows—2 plain in one, the rest plain. Repeat the last 4 rows 4 times more.

271st—As 251st. 272nd—Miss 1, the rest plain.

273rd—Plain, except the last two stitches, then miss 1, 1 plain.

274—Miss 1, then plain to the last stitch, 2 plain in one.

275th—Plain except the last two stitches, then miss 1, 1 plain. Repeat the last 4 rows 3 times more, and fasten off.

SLEEVE.

Work 4 chain.

1st row—Miss 1, 3 plain in one, 2 plain.

2nd—2 plain in one, the rest plain except the last stitch, then 2 plain in one.

3rd—3 plain in one, the rest plain. Repeat the last 2 rows 9 times more.

22nd—2 plain in one, the rest plain except the last stitch, then 2 plain in one.

23rd—2 plain in one, the rest plain. Repeat the last 2 rows 6 times more.

36th—Plain, at the end work 4 chain.

37th—Miss 1, 3 plain on the chain; (then 10 plain and 2 plain in one, 6 times), then 3 chain.

38th—Miss 1, 2 plain on the chain, the rest plain. 39th, 40th, and 41st—Plain.

42nd—(10 plain and 2 plain in one, 7 times).

43rd—2 plain in one, the rest plain; then work 7 rows more the same as last

51st—2 plain in one, (12 plain and 2 plain in one, 7 times); then work 10 rows plain.

62nd—93 plain, 3 single, turn back, leaving 4 stitches.

63rd—3 single, 84 plain, 3 single, turn back, leaving 6 stitches.

64th—3 single, then plain to within 7 stitches of the last row, 3 single, turn back, leaving 4 stitches more.

65th—3 single, plain to within 9 stitches of last row, 3 single, turn back, leaving 6 stitches more. Repeat the last 2 rows 6 times more.

78th—3 single, 17 plain, then work plain on all the "4 stitches" left, turn back.

79th—52 plain. Work all the "6 stitches" left, and fasten off. Work the other Sleeve the same.

Then sew up the sides of the last 53 rows; "that is," to the chain stitches at the 37th row, then place the point at the commencement of the Sleeve to the seam on the shoulder of the body, and keeping the shortest side of the Sleeve to the front, sew it to the armhole.

FOR THE BORDER.

Material—5 shades of any colour to contrast, 4 or 6 ply Fleecy.

With the lightest shade, make 664 chain and make it round.

1st round—2nd shade—1 chain, miss 1, 1 treble. Repeat.

2nd—3rd shade—1 chain, miss 1, 1 treble, 80 times; and to turn the corner, (miss 3 and 1 plain, twice); then 1 chain, miss 1, 1 treble, 164 times; and for the other corner, (miss 3 and 1 treble, twice), then 1 chain, miss 1, 1 treble, 80 times.

3rd—4th shade—1 chain, miss 1, 1 treble, 80 times; then for the corner, miss 3, 1 treble, (1 chain, miss 1, 1 treble, 163 times); and for the corner, miss 3, 1 treble, (1 chain, miss 1, 1 treble, 80 times.)

4th—5th shade—1 chain, miss 1, 1 treble, 79 times; miss 2, 1 treble, (1 chain, miss 1, 1 treble, 62 times), miss 2, 1 treble, (1 chain, miss 1, 1 treble, 79 times), 2 single, and fasten off.

Then place the foundation chain even with the edge of the Paletôt, and commencing at the neck with the lightest shade, join the Border to the Paletôt with a plain round, putting the needle in a stitch of each.

For the Sleeves—136 chain, and work 4 rounds of open crochet to correspond, and join to the sleeves as before. If preferred the Border to the Polka can be substituted.

CAPOTE OR HOOD.

Commence with the same colour as the Paletôt, work 4 chain.

1st row—Miss 1, 3 plain, 4 chain, turn back.

2nd—Miss 1 and 3 plain on the chain, then 3 plain. 3rd—Plain, at the end 4 chain.

4th—Miss 1, 3 plain on the chain, the rest plain. Repeat the last 2 rows 8 times more.

21st—Plain. Fasten off, commence again, and work another piece the same. When finished, join these 2 pieces together by continuing the last row of the second piece along the last row of the first piece. There will now be 66 stitches. This will shape the neck.

22nd—10 plain and 2 plain in one, 6 times; then 6 rows plain.

29th—2 plain in one, and 11 plain 6 times. 6 rows plain.

36th—12 plain and 2 plain in one, 6 times. 6 rows plain.

43rd—2 plain in one, 13 plain, 6 times. 6 rows plain.

50th—14 plain, 2 plain in one, 6 times. 6 rows plain.

57th—2 plain in one, 15 plain, 6 times. 27 rows plain.

85th—80 plain, 2 single, turn back. 86th—2 single, 58 plain, 2 single, turn back.

87th—2 single, 50 plain, 2 single, turn back. 88th—2 single, 42 plain, 2 single.

89th—2 single, 34 plain, 2 single. 90th—2 single, 26 plain, 2 single.

91st—2 single, 28 plain. Work the 8 plain left at the 89th and 87th rows; then on the 84th row 20 plain.

92nd—10 plain, 2 single, turn back. 93rd—2 single, 10 plain.

94th—6 plain, 2 single. 95th—2 single, 6 plain. 96th—2 plain, 2 single.

97th—2 single, 2 plain.

98th—4 plain; then work the 4 stitches left at the 96th and 94th rows, and on the 91st row, 54 plain. Work the 8 stitches left at the 90th and 88th rows; then on the 85th row, 20 plain. Repeat as the 92nd, 93rd, 94th, 95th, 96th, and 97th rows.

105th—4 plain, work the 4 stitches left at the 103rd and 101st rows; then on the 89th row 39 plain; fold the work in half, and join the 2 sides of the row together. Fasten off. Then work a plain row round the neck; and for the Border, make 200 chain, and work 4 rows of open crochet to correspond with the Paletôt, and join it to the edge of the Hood. Finish with a Cord and Tassel run through on the wrong side to the joining row of the Hood, about 3 inches from the edge, and one large Tassel at the point.

PALETOT FOR A CHILD EIGHT OR TEN YEARS OF AGE.

Materials—1 lb. *of* 2 ply. *Fleecy; Penelope Needle, No.* 0.

Work as preceding directions; and for a younger child, use Single Berlin Wool, and Penelope Needle, No. 1.

COUVRE-PIED, IRIS PATTERN.

Materials—Pink or Blue Single Berlin Wool for the Pattern, and Jno. & Wm. Taylor's Knitting Cotton, No. 10, *for the ground, Needle, No.* 16, *Bell Gauge or Walker's Penelope Needle, No.* 2. *The whole may be worked in* 4 *ply Fleecy, Penelope Needle, No.* 1.

This pattern is worked in narrow stripes of close raised crochet (see page 3.) The white thread or wool is always worked under the stitches of the coloured wool; but the coloured wool is not to be carried under the first and last stitches of the white in each row.

Commence with the white, and work 35 chain.

1st row—Miss 1, 34 plain, turn back. 2nd and 3rd rows—Plain.

4th—11 white stitches, then 2 blue, working the white under, bring the blue wool in front and leave it, then with the white, work 21 stitches, turn back.

5th—21 white, then with the blue left at the back, 2 blue, leave it in front; then 11 white.

6th—As 4th row. 7th—As 5th row.

8th—10 white, 3 blue, leave it in front, 21 white.

9th—21 white, 3 blue, leave it, 10 white.

10th—10 white, 1 blue, 1 white, 2 blue, 2 white, 5 blue, leave it, 13 white.

11th—13 white, 5 blue, 2 white, 2 blue, 1 white, 1 blue, 10 white.

12th—9 white, 1 blue, 3 white, 10 blue, leave it, 11 white.

13th—As 12th, reversing the pattern, thus—11 white, 10 blue, 3 white, 1 blue, 9 white, the alternate rows are always worked the same as the preceding row, reversing the order of the stitches, as example, "12th and 13th rows."

14th—8 white, 2 blue, 3 white, 1 blue, 1 white, 1 blue, 2 white, 6 blue, 6 white, 1 blue, 3 white. Reverse the pattern for the next row.

16th—8 white, 1 blue, 3 white, 2 blue, 1 white, 3 blue, 3 white, 5 blue, 3 white, 2 blue, 3 white. Reverse row.

18th—8 white, 1 blue, 2 white, 3 blue, 2 white, 5 blue, 2 white, 8 blue, 3 white. Reverse.

20th—9 white, 3 blue, 1 white, 1 blue, 3 white, 6 blue, 2 white, 5 blue, 4 white. Reverse.

22nd—7 white, 4 blue, 1 white, 2 blue, 5 white, 9 blue, 6 white. Reverse.

24th—6 white, 4 blue, 1 white, 2 blue, 21 white. Reverse.

26th—5 white, 4 blue, 1 white, 3 blue, 2 white, 5 blue, 14 white. Reverse.

28th—5 white, 3 blue, 1 white, 3 blue, 2 white, 1 blue, 1 white, 5 blue, 13 white. Reverse.

30th—4 white, 7 blue, 2 white, 3 blue, 1 white, 4 blue, 13 white. Reverse.

COUVRE PIED, IRIS PATTERN.

E. Riego de la Branchardiere, Inventor, Nov., 1850.

32nd—4 white, 6 blue, 3 white, 4 blue, 1 white, 3 blue, 1 white, 3 blue, 9 white. Reverse.

34th—4 white, 5 blue, 1 white, 1 blue, 2 white, 8 blue, 1 white, 3 blue, 9 white. Reverse.

36th—4 white, 4 blue, 2 white, 2 blue, 2 white, 6 blue, 1 white, 4 blue, 9 white. Reverse.

38th—4 white, 4 blue, 1 white, 1 blue, 1 white, 2 blue, 2 white, 9 blue, 10 white. Reverse.

40th—4 white, 3 blue, 2 white, 1 blue, 2 white, 4 blue, 2 white, 1 blue, 1 white, 2 blue, 12 white. Reverse.

42nd—5 white, 2 blue, 2 white, 1 blue, 6 white, 4 blue, 1 white, 6 blue, 7 white. Reverse.

44th—5 white, 2 blue, 2 white, 2 blue, 4 white, 5 blue, 1 white, 7 blue, 6 white. Reverse.

46th—6 white, 2 blue, 2 white, 2 blue, 2 white, 4 blue, 1 white, 2 blue, 1 white, 6 blue, 6 white. Reverse.

48th—11 white, 2 blue, 1 white, 3 blue, 1 white, 3 blue, 1 white, 6 blue, 6 white. Reverse.

50th—12 white, 1 blue, 5 white, 4 blue, 1 white, 5 blue, 6 white. Reverse.

52nd—5 white, 2 blue, 5 white, 1 blue, 5 white, 5 blue, 1 white, 3 blue, 7 white. Reverse.

54th—5 white, 3 blue, 3 white, 1 blue, 6 white, 5 blue, 11 white. Reverse.

56th—3 white, 5 blue, 2 white, 3 blue, 5 white, 5 blue, 11 white. Reverse.

58th—3 white, 8 blue, 1 white, 1 blue, 6 white, 3 blue, 12 white. Reverse.

60th—7 white, 2 blue, 3 white, 3 blue, 19 white. Reverse.

62nd—13 white, 2 blue, 6 white, 2 blue, 11 white. Reverse. Commence again at the 5th row, and repeat according to the length required. An even number of patterns must be worked to correspond with the Border. In working the *last* pattern omit the 62nd row, and work instead 13 white, 2 blue, 19 white. Reverse; then work 4 rows plain and fasten off. Work as many Stripes as will be required for the width.

FOR THE INSERTION BETWEEN THE STRIPES.

1st row—With the white work a single row down the side of one of the Stripes, working 2 stitches to each rib. Cut off the thread.

2nd—All treble.

3rd—1 single, 1 chain, miss 1, 4 treble in one, 1 chain, miss 1. Repeat; then work these 3 rows on a second Stripe; then work the 1st two rows on the other side of the second Stripe, and for the *joining* row.

3rd—1 single, 1 chain, miss 1, 2 treble in one, join to the centre stitch, between the 4 treble in the 3rd row of 1st Stripe; then 2 treble in the same stitch as before, 1 chain, miss 1. Repeat.

Repeat as the second Stripe to all the other Stripes, then knot the ends together.

BORDER.

1st round—With the white, work single crochet round the 4 sides of the work.

2nd—Treble, working 4 treble in one at the corners.

3rd—1 chain, miss 1, 4 treble in one, 1 chain, miss 1, 1 single. Repeat.

4th—3 chain, miss 6, 1 plain between the 4 treble of the last round. Repeat and fasten off.

5th—Commence with 1 plain in the 7th stitch of last round and up *the side*, 5 chain, miss 2, 36 plain. Repeat, and for the corner, 5 chain, miss 2, 5 plain, (3 plain in one, twice), 5 plain. Repeat the same for the other sides and corners. The corners are all worked the same as this round to the 10th round, and in the following rounds all the plain stitches are worked in double crochet.

6th—Miss 2 (1 chain and 1 treble, 5 times in the 5 chain), 1 chain, miss 2, 32 plain. Repeat, working the corners as 5th round.

7th—Miss 2 (2 chain, miss 1 and 1 treble in the 1 chain of last round, 6 times), 2 chain, miss 2, 28 plain. Repeat.

8th and 9th rounds—same as the last, working 2 chain and 1 treble more, and 4 plain less each round.

10th—Miss 2, (3 chain, miss 2 and 1 treble, 9 times), 3 chain, miss 2, 16 plain. Repeat all round.

11th—Miss 2, (3 chain, miss 3 and 1 treble, 10 times), 3 chain, miss 2, 12 plain. Repeat.

19th—Miss 2, (4 chain, miss 3 and 1 treble, 11 times), 4 chain, miss 2, 8 plain. Repeat.

13th and 14th—As the last, working "4 chain and 1 treble" more, and 4 plain less each round. Fasten off.

FRINGE.

Mesh 4 inches wide, 3 balls of white cotton, and knot the 3 ends of the cotton together, keeping one thread to crochet with, and the other two for the Fringe. With the single thread make a chain stitch; take the mesh in the left hand, holding it at the top together with the chain stitch, pass the double threads round the mesh, bringing it up between the single thread and the loop from the chain stitch; then work another chain stitch which will cross the double threads to fasten them. Then bring the double threads down again between the single thread and chain stitch, turn it round the mesh and repeat the length required. Then work a plain row on these chain stitches, putting the needle in a stitch and also through the threads of the Fringe at the back; then join it with a single row to the last round of the Border by putting the needle in a stitch of each.

TASSELS.

With the blue—work the Fuchsia Tassel in the 7th Series.

CARRIAGE BAG.

The preceding Pattern can be adapted for a Carriage Bag, using shaded Berlin Wool for the ground, and gold coloured crochet silk for the pattern.

THE END.

THE

CROCHET BOOK,

TENTH SERIES,

CONTAINING

D'OYLEYS AND ANTI-MACASSARS,

BY

MDLLE. RIEGO DE LA BRANCHARDIERE.

Fourth Edition--20,000.

LONDON:
SIMPKIN, MARSHALL, AND CO.,
ACKERMANN & CO., STRAND; OLIVER AND BOYD, EDINBURGH;
AND ALL THE BERLIN WAREHOUSES.

1852.

CONTENTS.

Instructions and Directions given in Point, Lacet, Crochet, Embroidery, Lace-work, Knitting, Netting, Tambour, &c.

NEW TERMS.

To Join with a Single Stitch—Keep the loop on the needle, then put the needle into the stitch, which is to be joined; bring the thread through and also through the loop on the needle. This mode of joining is used when a chain is to be continued. Thus, 6 chain, join with a single stitch, 4 chain, will appear as 11 chain; but if joined in the usual manner, the chain would be uneven where it is joined.

Single stitches on the top of previous stitches, are worked in the chain formed by the upper part of the stitch, and are used to prevent any space from appearing after leaving off in the middle of a leaf, or flower, to work another part of the pattern.

"4 *chain and a long with it.*"—To form this compound term, make 4 chain, put the needle into the 2nd stitch of these 4 chain, turn the thread round the needle as in commencing a treble stitch; then put the needle in the next stitch of the work, bring the thread through the stitch: there will now be 4 loops on the needle, counting the chain stitch as one; take up the thread, bring it through two of the loops, take up the thread again and bring it through the next two loops; take up the thread again and bring it through the remaining two loops, exactly the same as for a long stitch.

MATERIAL FOR D'OYLEYS.

1st Size, 7½ inches in diameter—Use J. and W. Taylor's Crochet Thread, No. 000 or 00; Needle, No. 16, Bell Gauge; or Walker's Penelope, No. 2.

2nd Size, 6½ inches in diameter—Taylor's Crochet Thread, No. 0 or 1; Needle, No. 18, Bell Gauge; or Walker's Penelope, No. 3.

For Baby's Cap Crowns—Taylor's Crochet Thread, No. 12; Needle, No. 24, Bell Gauge; or Walker's Penelope, No. 4½.

MATERIAL FOR ANTI-MACASSARS—Taylor's Crochet Thread, No. 00; Needle, No. 16, Bell Gauge; or Walker's Penelope, No. 2.

THE CROCHET BOOK,

TENTH SERIES.

CONTAINING

D'OYLEYS AND ANTI-MACASSARS.

D'OYLEY—No. 1.

For Materials, &c., see Instructions.

Work 6 chain, make it round.

1st round—5 chain, 1 treble in the foundation chain, then (2 chain and 1 treble 6 times in the foundation chain), 2 chain, 1 single in the 3rd stitch of the 5 chain at the commencement.

2nd round—1 single, and for the 1st SHAMROCK—11 chain, turn, miss 6, 1 single in the 7th stitch to form a round loop, turn, 1 chain to cross, and in the round loop work (3 chain, 3 treble, 3 chain and 1 single, 3 times), 4 single down the stem; and on the 1st round, 1 single, 1 chain, 3 treble in one, 1 chain. Repeat 7 times more, and fasten off.

3rd round—Commence in the centre treble stitch of the 2nd division of one of the Sham-

E. Riego de la Branchardiere. *Invent., May*, 1851.

rocks, work 2 single on the top of it, *, 9 chain, 5 single on the top of the 2nd division of the next Shamrock. Repeat from * 6 times more, then 9 chain, 2 single on the 1st Shamrock.

4th round—1st FLOWER—7 chain, turn, miss 5, 1 single in the 6th stitch to form a round loop, turn, 1 chain to cross; and in the round loop, (4 chain and 1 single, 5 times), 1 single on the stem, and on the 3rd round, 2 single, 1 plain, 2 treble, 2 long. Work a 2nd Flower as the 1st. When finished, work 1 single on the top of the last long stitch; then on the 3rd round, 2 long, 2 treble, 1 plain, 2 single. Repeat and fasten off.

5th round—Commence in the 2nd 4 chain of the 2nd Flower in the 4th round; and for the œillet and Vandyke, 8 chain, turn, miss 4, 1 single in the 5th stitch to form a round loop, turn, 1 chain to cross, and in the round loop, 7 plain; *, then 1 single on the 1 chain that crosses the stem, and on the chain stitches, 1 plain, 2 treble, then 1 plain in the 4th 4 chain of the 2nd Flower; and to form the 2nd Vandyke, 5 chain, turn, and on the 5 chain, miss 2, 1 plain, 2 treble, then 1 plain in the 2nd 4 chain of the next Flower, 19 chain; and for the

1st SHAMROCK—Turn, miss 7, 1 single in the 8th stitch to form a round loop, turn, 1 chain to cross, 3 chain, and in the round loop, 1 long, join to the point of the 2nd Vandyke; then in the round loop, 2 long, 3 chain, 1 single, 3 chain; join to the 5th plain stitch of the œillet, then in the round loop, 3 long, 3 chain, 1 single, 3 chain, 3 long, 3 chain, 1 single, 3 single down the stem, 12 chain; and for the

2nd SHAMROCK—Turn, miss 7, 1 single, 1 chain to cross the stem, 3 chain, join to the last long stitch of the 1st Shamrock, and in the round loop, 3 long, 3 chain, 1 single, (3 chain, 3 long, 3 chain and 1 single twice in the same round loop), 3 single down the stem, which finishes the 2nd Shamrock; 11 chain, and work the

3rd SHAMROCK—Same as the 2nd, joining it to the 2nd Shamrock; when finished work 6 single, 1 plain, 2 treble down the centre stem, 1 plain in the 4th 4 chain of the Flower. 4th Vandyke—4 chain, join to the 2nd long stitch in the 3rd division of the last Shamrock, 1 chain, miss 1, 1 plain, 2 treble on the 4 chain; then 1 plain in the 2nd 4 chain of the next Flower; and for the œillet and Vandyke, 8 chain, turn, miss 4, 1 single in the 5th stitch, turn, 1 chain to cross, 3 plain in the round loop; join to the last long stitch of the 2nd division of the 3rd Shamrock; then in the round loop, 4 plain. Repeat from * 7 times more; but in the last pattern omit the œillet, as it is not required. Work 7 single up the side of the 1st Vandyke and œillet, join to the last long stitch of the 2nd division of the last Shamrock, 1 single on the round loop, and 3 single on the long stitches of the 2nd division of the 1st Shamrock.

6th round—EDGING, 1st Small Flower—7 chain, turn, miss 4, 1 single in the 5th stitch, (4 chain and 1 single in the same stitch as the 1st single, twice), 1 single on the chain, leaving 1 chain; then work 1 chain to correspond, which finishes the 1st Flower, miss 5, 1 single on the 5th 3 chain of the 1st Shamrock in last round. Work a 2nd Flower, miss 5, 1 single on the 2nd 3 chain of the 2nd Shamrock. Work a 3rd Flower, miss 5, 1 single on the 2nd Shamrock. Work a 4th Flower, miss 3, 1 single on the 2nd Shamrock. Work a 5th Flower, miss 5, 1 single on the 2nd Shamrock. Work a 6th Flower, miss 5, 1 single on the 2nd 3 chain of the 3rd Shamrock. Work a 7th Flower, miss 5, 1 single on the 3rd Shamrock, 3 chain, miss 7, 1 single on the 4th 3 chain of the 1st Shamrock in the next pattern. Repeat and fasten off.

D'OYLEY—No. 2.

For Materials, &c., see Instructions.

Work 6 chain, and make it round.

1st round—8 plain in the chain, 1 single in the 1st stitch.

2nd—(6 chain and 2 plain in one stitch of 1st round, 8 times).

3rd—2 chain, miss 1, 2 treble in the 6 chain, 3 chain, 2 treble in the same 6 chain as before; then 2 chain, miss 1, 1 single between the 2 plain of the 2nd round. Repeat 7 times more, and end 5 single up the 1st 5 stitches of the round.

4th—12 chain, and for the 1st *Leaf*, turn, miss 2, 2 treble, 1 single. 2nd *Leaf*—6 chain, turn, miss 2, 2 treble, 1 plain, 1 single.

SMALL FLOWER—9 chain, turn, miss 4, 1 single in the 5th stitch to form a round loop, turn, (4 chain and 1 plain, 5 times in the round loop), 4 single down the stem. 3rd *Leaf*—6 chain, turn, miss 2, 2 treble, 1 plain, 1 single. 4th *Leaf*—5 chain, turn, miss 2, 2 treble, 1 single. Then 7 single down the chain stitches, 1 plain in the 3 chain of the 3rd round, 7 chain, join it to the point of the 4th Leaf, 6 chain, join with a single stitch to the point of the 3rd Leaf, 2 chain, join with a single stitch to the centre stitch of the 4th 4 chain of the small Flower. 20 chain, turn this chain round towards the

E. Riego de la Branchardiere, *Invent., May,* 1851.

right, and join it to the right hand side of the 9th stitch of these 20 chain. This will form a loop of 11 chain.

2nd FLOWER—1 chain, and on the loop of the 11 chain, miss 1, 2 treble, 1 single; then 4 chain, join to the 3rd stitch of the 20 chain, turn, 1 chain, miss 1, 2 treble and 1 single on the 4 chain; (then 5 chain, turn, miss 2, 2 treble and 1 single, 3 times), making in all 5 divisions.

* * Work down the chain stitches 15 single and 7 plain, then 6 chain for the stem; join with a single stitch to the 9th stitch of the 15 single; and for the

CENTRE LEAVES—13 chain, turn, miss 8, 1 single in the 9th stitch to form a round loop, turn, 14 plain in the round loop; cross the stem, 4 single on the 14 plain, 3 chain; join with a single stitch to the point of the 5th division of the 2nd flower, 7 chain, turn, and down the chain stitches, miss 1, 1 plain, 1 treble, (1 chain, miss 1, 1 treble, 3 times), 1 chain, miss 1, 1 plain, *, 1 single on the 14 plain, turn back, miss 1, 6 single on the treble and chain stitches, 5 chain, turn back, miss 1, plain, 1 treble, (1 chain, miss 1 and 1 treble, 3 times), 1 chain, miss 1, 1 plain. Repeat from * 5 times more, making in all 7 leaves; then 4 single on the remaining stitches of the 14 plain, and down the chain stitches 4 single, 5 plain, 1 single, 12 chain, join with a single stitch to the last stitch of the 4 single, 12 plain, join to the 7th stitch of the last leaf; and for the

3rd FLOWER—Turn, 1 chain, miss 1, 2 treble, 1 single, (5 chain, turn, miss 2, 2 treble and 1 single, 4 times), 8 single down the chain stitches; join it to the point of the last division of the flower, 5 single, join to the point of the 4th division of the flower, 1 single, 6 plain, 1 single in the same stitch as the last stitch of the 7 plain, and down the chain stitches 5 single, 3 treble, 2 chain, 1 plain in the next 3 chain of the 3rd round, which finishes the 1st Pattern; and for the

2nd PATTERN—11 chain, join it to the 4th stitch of the 5 single; and for the 1st Leaf, turn, 1 chain, miss 1, 2 treble, 1 single. 2nd Leaf—5 chain, join it to the 5th stitch of the 6 plain in last pattern, turn, 1 chain, miss 1, 2 treble, 1 plain, 1 single. For the Small Flower—9 chain, turn, miss 4, 1 single, turn, 4 chain, 1 plain in the round loop, 2 chain, (join it to the 2nd stitch of the 6 plain, 2 chain, 1 plain in the round loop, 4 chain and 1 plain 3 times in the same round loop), 4 single down the chain. 3rd Leaf—6 chain, turn, miss 2, 2 treble, 1 plain, 1 single. 4th Leaf—5 chain, turn, miss 2, 2 treble, 1 single, then 7 single down the chain stitches, 1 plain in the same 3 chain of the 3rd round as before, then 6 chain, join it to the point of the 4th Leaf, 6 chain, join with a single stitch to the point of the 3rd Leaf, 2 chain, join with a single stitch to the centre of the 4th 4 chain of the small Flower, 20 chain, turn to the right and join to the 9th stitch of these 20 chain, and for the

2nd FLOWER—1 chain, miss 1, 2 treble, 1 single, 4 chain, join to the 3rd stitch of the 20 chain, miss 1, 2 treble, 1 single, 4 chain, join to the 3rd or centre division of the 3rd Flower in the 1st Pattern, 1 chain, miss 1, 2 treble, 1 single, 4 chain, join to the 2nd division of the Flower, turn, 1 chain, miss 1, 2 treble, 1 single, then 5 chain, turn, miss 2, 2 treble, and 1 single, and to finish, repeat from * * in 1st Pattern.

Work 5 Patterns more the same as 2nd Pattern; and for the 8th Pattern, to make it round, work to the 3rd Flower. Then make the following alterations, thus—

3rd FLOWER—Turn, 1 chain, miss 1, 2 treble, 1 single, 4 chain, join to the 4th division of the 2nd Flower in 1st Pattern, 1 chain, turn, miss 1, 2 treble, 1 single, 4 chain; join to the centre division of the 2nd Flower in the 1st Pattern, turn, 1 chain, miss 1, 2 treble, 1 single, (5 chain, turn, miss 2, 2 treble and 1 single twice), then 8 single down the chain, join to the last division of the Flower, 6 single, join to the 4th division of the Flower, 1 single, 1 plain, join to the 2nd 4 chain of the small Flower in the 1st Pattern, 4 plain, join to the 2nd Leaf in the 1st Pattern, 1 plain, 1 single in the last stitch of the 7 plain, 3 single, join to the 1st Leaf in the 1st Pattern, 1 single, 3 treble, 2 chain, 1 plain on the 1st stitch of the round. Fasten off.

D'OYLEY—No. 3.

For Materials, &c., see Instructions.

FOR THE CENTRE STAR.

1st round—8 chain, turn, miss 1, 1 plain, 3 treble, 1 plain, 2 single. Repeat 7 times more, making in all 8 divisions; then to make it round, 8 single up the 1st 8 chain to the point of the 1st division.

2nd—7 chain, turn, and on the 7 chain, miss 1, 2 plain, 2 treble, 2 long; then 1 single in the point of the next division in the 1st round. Repeat 7 times more.

3rd—14 chain, turn, miss 1, 4 single, 2 plain; then 1 plain, putting the needle in the next chain stitch and also in the point of the 1st division of the 2nd round; 6 chain, 1 single on the 1 single in the 2nd round. Repeat all round.

E. Riego de la Branchardiere, *Invent., May,* 1851.

4th—Work up the side of the 1st division 6 single, 5 plain, 3 single, 3 chain, 1 single in the same stitch as the last single, turn, and down the other side, 2 single, 5 plain, 6 single; and for the *wheel,* 10 chain, turn, miss 5, 2 single, turn, 1 chain to cross the stem, and in the round loop, (2 chain and 1 treble, 6 times), 2 chain, 1 single in the 1 chain that crosses the stem, 3 single down the chain stitches, and missing the 1 single of the 3rd round. Repeat 7 times more, and fasten off.

FOR THE BORDER PATTERN.

1st SHAMROCK—31 chain, turn, miss 5, 1 single in the 6th stitch, to form a round loop, turn, and in the round loop, 3 chain. 1 treble, join to the 18th stitch of the 31 chain; then in the round loop, 1 treble, 3 chain, 1 single, 3 chain, join to the 11th stitch of the 31 chain, and in the round loop, 2 treble, 3 chain, 1 single, "3 *chain,*" 2 treble, 3 chain, 1 single; then on the chain stitches, 8 single.

FOR THE CENTRE PATTERN—6 chain, turn, miss 5, 1 single, turn, and in the round loop, 3 plain, then 7 chain, turn, and on the 7 chain, miss 1, 1 plain, 3 treble, 1 plain 1 single, (1 plain in the round loop, 3 chain, join with a single stitch to the 2nd treble stitch, 3 chain, turn, and down these 7 stitches, miss 1, 1 plain, 3 treble, 1 plain, and 1 single twice, making in all 3 divisions), 4 plain in the round loop, 1 single; then down the chain stitches, 2 single, 13 plain, 1 single, leaving 1 chain unworked, 15 chain; join to the 4th stitch of these 15 chain, turn, miss 1, 3 single; join to the 11 stitch of the 13 plain, 3 single, leaving 8 stitches unworked; and for the

DIAMOND—Make 8 chain, join to the 7th stitch of the 13 plain, 1 chain; and on the 8 chain, miss 1, 1 treble, 1 single, 5 chain, turn, miss 2, 2 treble, 1 single, 4 chain, turn, miss 2, 1 treble, 1 single, and down the chain stitches, 1 single, 2 treble, 1 single, leaving 1 chain, and to form the other side to correspond, 8 chain, turn, miss 1, 6 single, 4 chain, join with a single stitch to the 1st stitch of the 6 single, 6 chain; join with a single stitch to the 5th stitch of the 8 chain on which the 6 single were worked, 3 chain, join with a single stitch to the 3rd point of the Diamond, 7 chain; join with a single stitch to the last plain stitch worked in the round loop of centre Pattern, 14 chain, and for the

2nd SHAMROCK—Turn, miss 5, 1 single in the 6th stitch, turn, (3 chain, 2 treble, 3 chain and 1 single, 3 times in the round loop); then down the chain stitches 8 single, join to the last treble stitch of the shamrock, 2 single, 5 plain, join to the 4th treble stitch of the shamrock; then 8 plain, 1 single, leaving 8 stitches, and for the bud between the Shamrocks, 12 chain; join to the 2nd 3 chain of the shamrock, turn, miss 1, 1 single, 1 plain, 3 treble, 1 plain, 1 single; and for the 2nd division, 4 chain, join with a single stitch to the 1st treble stitch, 3 chain, turn, and down these 8 stitches, miss 1, 1 single, 1 plain, 3 treble, 1 plain, 1 single; then 3 single down the stem, which will leave 1 chain. This finishes the 1st pattern.

Work 6 patterns more the same, except that after working the "3 *chain*" marked in italics, join to the point of the 2nd division of the bud; and for the 8th Pattern, to make it round, after working the 3 chain in the 2nd division of the last bud, join to the 5th 3 chain of the 1st Shamrock, and finish the pattern. Then to attach it to the centre star, turn, so as to work on the chain stitches left *unworked* of the last pattern, thus—

Joining round—First join to one of the points of the centre star; then on the 1 chain of the Border, work 1 single, and on the 8 chain 1 single, 4 plain; join to the 13th stitch of the wheel pattern, 2 plain, 1 single on the remaining stitches of the 8 chain, 1 single on each of the 1 chains, and on the next 8 chain, 1 single, 2 plain; join to the 9th stitch of the wheel pattern, 4 plain, 1 single on the chain, 1 single on the next 1 chain, and joining to the next point of the star, repeat all round and fasten off.

D'OYLEY—No. 4.

For Materials, &c., see Instructions.

CENTRE STAR.

Work 5 chain, and make it round.

1st round—8 plain in the chain.

2nd—1 single, 2 chain, 2 long, 2 chain, 1 single. These single and long stitches are all to be worked in one stitch of the 1st round. Repeat 7 times more, and fasten off.

THE BORDER PATTERN.

1st round—20 chain, turn, miss 4, 1 single in the 5th stitch, 10 chain, turn, miss 3, 1 single in the 4th stitch to form a round loop, turn, 1 chain to cross the stem; and for the LEAF, (11 chain and 1 plain 3 times in the round loop), turn, 1 single in the 1 chain that crosses the stem, and on the 1st 11 chain to form the 1st division of the Leaf, 2 single, 1 plain, 3 treble, 4 chain, turn, and on the 4 chain, miss 1, 1 plain, 2 treble; then 1 treble in the same stitch of the 11 chain as the last of the 3 treble, and on the remaining stitches of the 11 chain, 2 treble, 1 plain, 2 single.

E. Riego de la Branchardière, *Invent May,* 1851.

For the Small Flower—*, 6 chain, join to the last treble stitch of the leaf, 1 chain, and on the 6 chain, miss 1, 1 treble, 1 single, then (4 chain, turn, miss 2, 1 treble, 1 single, 3 times), 3 single down the stem, miss 1, and on the next 11 chain, for the next division of the leaf, 2 single, 1 plain, 1 treble, join to the point of the last division of the flower; then 2 treble, 4 chain, turn, miss 1, 1 plain, 2 treble, then 1 treble in the same stitch as the last treble worked on the 11 chain, 2 treble, 1 plain, 2 single. Repeat from * once more to form the 2nd flower and 3rd division of the leaf. When finished, 1 single, and down the stem, 3 single, 2 chain, 1 single in the same stitch as the 1 single at the commencement of the pattern, 4 chain, 1 single in the same stitch as before, 3 single down the stem, leaving 12 chain unworked. Repeat from the commencement of the round 7 times more, turn so as to work on the 12 chain between the patterns.

2nd round—On the last 12 chain, work 2 single, 2 plain in 1, 1 treble, (2 long in 1 twice), 5 chain, join to the centre star between the 2 single stitches of one of the divisions, turn, miss 1, 4 single on the 5 chain, 1 single on the top of the last long stitch; then on the remaining stitches of the 12 chain, (2 long in 1, twice), 1 treble, 2 plain in 1, 2 single. Repeat 7 times more, join to the 1st single stitch of the round, and fasten off.

FOR THE STARS BETWEEN THE LEAVES.

Work 5 chain, and make it round.

1st round—8 plain in the chain.

2nd—1st division—1 single, 2 chain, 2 long, 2 chain, 1 single, these 4 stitches in on stitch of the 1st round. 2nd division—Then in the next stitch, 1 single, 2 chain, 1 long join it to the 2nd treble stitch of the 1st division of one of the leaves, and in the same stitch as before, 1 long, 2 chain, 1 single. 3rd division—Same as 2nd, joining to the centre of the 4 chain at the stem of the leaf. 4th division—Same as 1st. 5th division Same as 2nd, joining to the centre stitch of the 12 chain in the 1st round of the Border. 6th division—Same as 1st. 7th division—Same as 2nd, joining to the 4 chain at the stem of the next leaf. 8th division—Same as 2nd, joining to the last treble stitch but one in the 3rd division of the 2nd leaf. Fasten off. Repeat this star 7 times more.

FOR THE EDGING.

1st round—Commence in the point of the 1st division in one of the leaves, 5 chain, 1 plain in the 2nd division of the flower, 5 chain, 1 plain in the 3rd division of the flower, 8 chain, 1 plain in the point of the 2nd division of the leaf; 8 chain, 1 plain in the 2nd division of the 2nd flower; 5 chain, 1 plain in the 3rd division of the flower; 5 chain, 1 plain in the point of the 3rd division of the leaf; 1 plain in the point of the 1st division of the next leaf. Repeat 7 times more.

2nd—5 single on the 5 chain, and to form the 1st *point*, 1 single, 1 plain, 2 treble, 4 chain, turn; then on the 4 chain, miss 2, 1 plain, 1 treble, and 1 treble in the same stitch as the last stitch of the 2 treble, then 1 treble, 1 plain. Work 4 points more the same, then 6 single, and missing 2 stitches of the 1st round, repeat all round and fasten off.

D'OYLEY—No. 5.

For Materials, &c., see Instructions.

FOR THE STAR IN THE CENTRE.

Work 5 chain and make it round.

1st round—8 plain in the foundation chain, then 1 single in the 1st stitch.

2nd—4 chain, 1 single, taking the front part of the stitch of the 1st round, and leaving the other part at the back. Repeat 7 times more, then 1 single on the back of the 1st stitch in the 1st round.

3rd—8 chain, turn, and on these 8 chain, miss 1, 1 plain, 2 treble in 1, (2 long in 1 twice), 2 treble, 1 plain, then 1 single in the back of the next stitch in the 1st round. Repeat 7 times more, then 8 single up the 1st 8 chain to the point.

4th—1st Vandyke—5 chain, turn, miss 1, 1 single, 1 plain, 2 treble, and for the stem, 6 chain, turn, miss 1, 4 plain, 1 single. 2nd Vandyke—Same as 1st; then 1 plain in the next point of the star. Repeat the 2 Vandykes 7 times more, and fasten off.

FIRST SCROLL PATTERN.

Commence with 49 chain, turn, miss 2, (2 treble in 1 stitch, 6 times), 5 plain, 2 treble, 3 long, 2 treble, 10 plain, 2 treble, 3 long, 2 treble, 5 plain, (2 treble in 1 stitch, 6 times), 1 chain, 1 single, turn, and down the foundation chain, work 15 single; join to the 1st stitch of these 15 single, then 12 single on the foundation chain, turn back, (7 chain and 2 plain 4 times on the last single stitches), turn back, (miss 2, 1 plain, 7 treble and 1 plain; these 9 stitches in the 7 chain), miss 2, 1 plain and 5 treble in the next 7 chain; join it

E. Riego de la Branchardiere, *Invent., May*, 1851.

to the point of the 2nd Vandyke of the centre Star, then 3 treble and 1 plain in the same 7 chain as before, join it to the top of the Stem, then miss 2, 1 plain and 3 treble in the next 7 chain, join it to the point of the 1st Vandyke, 5 treble and 1 plain in the same 7 chain, "*miss* 2," (1 plain, 7 treble, 1 plain in the last 7 chain), then on the foundation chain, 20 single; join to the 5th stitch of these 20 single, turn, and on the treble and plain stitches, work 19 single.

* *, then 9 chain, turn, miss 8, 1 single on the 1st chain stitch to form a round loop, turn, 3 plain in the round loop, 10 chain, turn, miss 7, 1 single and 2 plain on the 10 chain, 1 plain in the round loop, 11 chain, turn, miss 7, 1 single, 3 plain, 1 plain in the round loop, 12 chain, turn, miss 7, 1 single, 4 plain, 1 plain in the round loop, 11 chain, turn, miss 7, 1 single, 3 plain, 1 plain in the round loop, 10 chain, turn, miss 7, 1 single, 2 plain, 5 plain in the round loop, turn, work 6 single up the side of the plain stitches to the 1st 7 chain, then 2 plain in the 7 chain; join it to the 15th stitch of the 19 single of the Scroll, 8 plain in the same 7 chain as before, (miss 8 and 10 plain in the 7 chain, 4 times), 6 single down the side, miss 24 stitches of the Scroll, work 5 single on the 5 plain; join to the 8th stitch of the last 10 plain, then 6 single; and for the

Trefoil—7 chain, join to the 3rd stitch of the 6 single, 1 chain, and on the 7 chain, miss 1, 2 treble, 1 single, (5 chain, turn, miss 2, 2 treble and 1 single, twice), 3 single down the stem, 8 single on the Scroll. Fasten off.

The 2nd Pattern will require the following alterations to join it to the 1st:—Work as the 1st Scroll Pattern to the "*miss* 2" marked in italic, joining to the 4th Vandyke, Stem and 3rd Vandyke of the centre Star; then 1 plain and 3 treble in the last 7 chain; join to the 4th stitch of the 1st 7 treble in the 1st Scroll Pattern, 4 treble and 1 plain in the same 7 chain, 20 single; join to the 5th stitch of the 20 single, and on the treble stitches, 8 single; join to the 1st stitch of the 8 single after the trefoil of the 1st Pattern, 3 single; join to the point of the last division of the trefoil, 9 single. Repeat from * * in the 1st Pattern.

Work 5 Patterns more the same as the 2nd, but in working the 8th it must be joined to the 1st Pattern, thus—join the centre stitch of the 1st 7 treble to the opposite stitch of the 1st Pattern, then work to the trefoil; and for the last division of it, 4 chain, join to the 12th stitch of the 19 single of the 1st Pattern, turn, 1 chain, miss 1, 2 treble, 1 single, 3 single down the stem; join to the 8th stitch of the 19 single in the 1st Pattern; then 8 single and fasten off.

D'OYLEY—No. 6.

For Materials, &c., see Instructions.

Work 6 chain, and make it round.

1st round—8 chain, turn, miss 4, 4 single on the chain, 1 plain in the foundation chain. Repeat 7 times more, 4 single up the side of the 1st 8 chain.

2nd—In the 1st round loop, 1 single, 1 chain, 5 treble, 1 chain, 1 single: these 7 stitches all in the round loop, 26 chain; and to form the 1st division of the cross, turn, miss 6, 1 single in the 7th stitch, 12 chain; and for the 2nd *division*—Turn, miss 6, 1 single in the 7th stitch (6 chain and 1 single twice in the same stitch as the last single), 1 single

E. Riego de la Branchardiere, *Invent.*, *May*, 1851.

on the chain; and for the 3rd *division*—11 chain, turn, miss 6, 1 single in the 7th stitch, (6 chain and 1 single twice in the same stitch as the last single), *; then 4 single down the chain; and for the 4th *division*—8 chain, turn, miss 6, 1 single in the 7th stitch, (6 chain and 1 single twice in the same stitch as last single); then 1 single, on the 1 chain, and down the chain, 4 single; and to finish the 1st division, 1 single in the same stitch in which the 1 single of the 1st division was worked, 6 chain, 1 single, in the same stitch as before, 3 chain, miss 3, 1 single, and down the chain stitches to form the

1st SMALL LEAF—1 single, 2 plain, 5 treble, 1 plain, 1 single, leaving 6 chain unworked; and for the

1st CALYX—14 chain, turn, miss 1, 7 single down the chain, turn, 1 chain to cross the stem, 1 chain, and up the other side 1 treble; join it to the 1st treble stitch of the small Leaf, 1 treble in the same stitch as the last treble, 2 long; join to the last 6 chain of the Cross, 2 long, 1 treble, 2 treble in 1, 1 chain, join with a single stitch to the centre 6 chain of the 4th division of the Cross, 3 chain, turn, and on these chain stitches to form the point of the calyx, miss 2, 1 plain, 2 treble, then 1 single in the same stitch as the 2 treble in 1, 9 chain, turn, miss 5, 1 single in the 6th stitch to form a round loop, turn, 1 chain to cross, 2 plain in the round loop, 1 chain; join with a single stitch to the point of the calyx, 4 chain; join with a single stitch to the 3rd 6 chain of the 3rd division of the Cross, 5 chain; and for the

1st LARGE LEAF—Turn, and down the chain stitches miss 1, 1 single, 1 plain, 2 treble, 4 long, 1 treble, 1 plain, 1 single, 2 plain in the round loop; and for the

1st SHAMROCK—11 chain, join to the 1st long stitch of the Leaf, turn, 1 chain, miss 1, 2 treble, 1 single; (then 5 chain, turn, miss 2, 2 treble and 1 single, twice, making in all 3 divisions), 7 single down the stem, 2 plain in the round loop, which finishes the Shamrock; then 6 chain, join with a single stitch to the 3rd division of the Shamrock, 9 chain; and for the

2nd SHAMROCK—Turn, miss 2, 2 treble, 1 single, (5 chain, turn, miss 2, 2 treble and 1 single, twice), and down the chain stitches to form the

2nd LARGE LEAF—2 single, 1 plain, 1 treble, 4 long, 1 treble, 1 plain, 1 single, 2 plain in the round loop.

3rd SHAMROCK—The same as the 1st, and for the

3rd LARGE LEAF—6 chain; join with a single stitch to the 3rd division of the last Shamrock, 5 chain, turn, miss 1, 1 single, 1 plain, "2 *treble*," 4 long, 1 treble, 1 plain, 1 single, 2 plain in the round loop, 1 single in the 1 chain that crosses the stem, 3 single down the stem; and to finish the Calyx, 1 single in the 1st stitch of the 7 single, 4 chain; join to the last plain stitch of the 3rd Leaf, turn, 1 chain, miss 1, 1 plain, 2 treble, then 2 treble in the 1st stitch of the 7 single, and down the single stitches, 1 treble, 4 long, 2 treble in 1, 2 chain, 1 single in the same stitch as the 2 treble, and down the stem 5 plain, 1 single.

2nd SMALL LEAF—6 chain, join with a single stitch to the last treble stitch of the calyx, 4 chain, turn, and down these chain stitches, miss 1, 1 single, 2 plain, 5 treble, 1 plain, 1 single; then down the remaining chain 6 single. This finishes the 1st Pattern.

The 2nd PATTERN will require the following alterations:—In the next round loop of the 1st round, (work 1 single, 1 chain, 5 treble, 1 chain, 1 single); then 15 chain; join to the point of the small Leaf; and for the 1st division of the Cross, 8 chain, join to the 2nd long stitch of the calyx, 3 chain, miss 3, 1 single, 12 chain, turn, miss 6, 1 single in the 7th stitch, 3 chain; join to the 2nd treble stitch of the calyx, 3 chain, 1 single in the same stitch as the last single, 6 chain, 1 single in the same stitch as before, 1 single, 8 chain; join to the 1st long stitch of the 3rd Large Leaf, 3 chain, miss 3, 1 single, (6 chain and 1 single twice as before). Repeat from * in the first part of the 2nd round to finish the Pattern.

Work 5 Patterns more, and for the 8th Pattern, to make it round, work only to the stitches marked in *italics*, thus—" 2 *treble*." Then make the following alterations:—Join to the 1st 6 chain of the 3rd division of the 1st Cross, then on the Leaf 4 long, 1 treble, 1 plain, 1 single, 2 plain in the round loop, 1 single on the 1 chain that crosses the stem, 3 single down the stem; and to finish the Calyx, 1 single in the 1st stitch of the 7 single, 4 chain, join to the last plain stitch of the 3rd Leaf, 1 chain, miss 1, 1 plain, 1 treble; join to the centre 6 chain of the 2nd division of the 1st Cross; then 1 treble, 2 treble in the 1st stitch of the 7 single; then 1 treble, 2 long, join to the 1st 6 chain of the 1st Cross, 2 long, 2 treble in one, 2 chain, 1 single in the same stitch as the 2 treble, and down the stem, 5 plain, 1 single.

Last SMALL LEAF—6 chain, join with a single stitch to the last treble stitch of the Calyx, 4 chain, join to the 1st stitch of the 1st small Leaf, miss 1, 1 single, 2 plain, 5 treble, 1 plain, 1 single, then 6 single down the stem, 1 single in the 1st stitch of the round, and fasten off.

ANTI-MACASSAR; MEDALLION PATTERN.

For Materials, &c., see Instructions.

FIRST MEDALLION—Commence with the *Bud* at the end of the stem, 12 chain, turn, miss 5, 1 single, turn, 1 chain to cross the stem, work 10 plain in the 5 chain, and down the stem, 3 single, then 22 chain; and for the

1st LEAF—Turn, miss 1, 4 single, (2 chain, miss 2 and 1 plain, 3 times), turn, 1 chain to cross the stem, and on the other side 2 plain, 1 treble; join to the 6th plain stitch of the Bud, then 8 treble, 2 plain, 1 single, 2 chain at the point, and down the other side 1 single, 2 plain, 9 treble, 2 plain; then on the stem 3 single, leaving 5 chain for the centre stem, then 6 chain, join with a single stitch to the last treble stitch of the Leaf, then 19 chain; and for the

1st FLOWER and CALYX—Turn, miss 5, 1 single, 7 plain, turn, 1 chain to cross the stem, and up the other side 2 plain, 3 treble, 1 plain, 2 single, 1 plain in the 5 chain; and to form the 1st *division*, 6 chain, turn, miss 3, 1 single in the 4th stitch to form a round loop, turn, 1 chain to cross, then 1 chain; join to the 1st treble stitch of the Leaf, always counting from the point, then 2 chain, 1 plain in the round loop, (4 chain and 1 plain, 3 times, in the same round loop), 2 chain, 2 plain in the 5 chain. Work 4 more divisions the same, joining to the last 4 chain of the preceding division. When finished, work down the calyx 2 single, 1 plain, 3 treble, 2 plain, and down the stem 2 single, leaving 3 chain for the centre stem, then 9 chain; join with a single stitch to the 2nd 4 chain in the last division of the Flower, 22 chain; and for the

2nd LEAF—Work as the 1st Leaf, joining it to the 2nd 4 chain in the 4th division of the

ANTI-MACASSAR; MEDALLION PATTERN. Registered Design.

E. Riego de la Branchardiere, *Invent., May,* 1851.

Flower. When finished work 4 single down the stem, leaving 3 chain, then work 23 chain; and for the

3rd Leaf—Work as the 1st Leaf, joining it to the 5th treble stitch of the 2nd Leaf. When finished 6 single down the stem, leaving 2 chain, then 19 chain; and for the

4th Leaf—Turn, miss 1, 4 single, (1 chain, miss 2, 1 plain, 3 times), turn, 1 chain to cross the stem, 2 plain, 1 treble; join to the last stitch of the 3rd Leaf, then 1 treble; and before finishing the Leaf, work for the

2nd Bud—10 chain, turn, miss 5, 1 single, 1 chain to cross, 10 plain in the 5 chain, 4 single down the stem, and to finish the Leaf, 1 single on the top of the last treble stitch; then 7 treble, 2 plain, 1 single, 2 chain, turn, 1 single, 2 plain, 6 treble, 2 plain, down the stem 4 single, and down the centre stem, 8 single, 14 plain, then 17 chain; and for the

2nd Flower—Turn, miss 5, 1 single, 7 plain, turn, 1 chain to cross, 2 plain, 3 treble, 1 plain, 2 single, 1 plain in the 5 chain; and for the 1st *division*, 6 chain, turn, miss 3, 1 single to form a round loop, turn, 1 chain to cross, (3 chain, 1 plain in the round loop, 2 chain, join to the 1st plain stitch worked down the centre stem; then 2 chain, 1 plain in the same round loop, 4 chain and 1 plain twice in the same round loop); then 2 chain, 2 plain in the 5 chain; then 6 chain, turn, miss 3, 1 single, 1 chain to cross, (1 chain, join to the last 4 chain; then 2 chain, 1 plain in the round loop, 2 chain, join to the 4th treble stitch of the 4th Leaf, 2 chain, 1 plain in the round loop, 4 chain and 1 plain twice in the same round loop); then 2 chain, 2 plain in the 5 chain. And for the 3rd *division* 6 chain, turn, miss 3, 1 single, 1 chain to cross, (1 chain, join to the last 4 chain, 2 chain, 1 plain in the round loop, 4 chain and 1 plain 3 times in the same round loop), 2 chain, 2 plain in the 5 chain. Then work 2 more divisions the same as the last. When finished, work down the Calyx, 2 single, 1 plain, 3 treble, 2 plain, 3 single on the stem, and down the centre stem 9 plain, then 19 chain; and for the

5th Leaf—Turn, miss 1, 4 single, (2 chain, miss 2 and 1 plain 3 times), turn, 1 chain to cross, 2 plain, 6 treble; join to the last treble stitch of the calyx of the 2nd Flower, 3 treble, 2 plain; join to the 2nd 4 chain of the last division of the Flower, 1 single, 2 chain, 1 single, 2 plain, 9 treble, 2 plain, 4 single on the stem, and 2 plain on the centre stem; and to form

The Oval—1st round—9 chain, 1 plain in the 4th plain stitch of the 1st Bud, 5 chain, 1 treble on the 8th treble stitch of the 1st Leaf, 5 chain, 1 plain in the point of the Leaf; 5 chain, 1 plain in the 1st 4 chain of the 2nd division of the 1st Flower, 2 chain, 1 plain in the next 4 chain, 3 chain, 1 plain in the 1st 4 chain of the next division of the Flower, 2 chain, 1 plain in the next 4 chain, 6 chain, 1 treble in the 8th treble stitch of the 2nd Leaf, 4 chain, 1 plain in the point of the Leaf, 9 chain, 1 plain in the point of the 3rd Leaf, 10 chain, 1 plain on the 6th stitch of the 2nd Bud; 9 chain, 1 plain in the point of the 4th Leaf; 5 chain, 1 plain in the 1st 4 chain of the 3rd division of the 2nd Flower; 2 chain, 1 plain in the next 4 chain, 3 chain, 1 plain in the 1st 4 chain of the next division, 2 chain, 1 plain in the next 4 chain, 5 chain, 1 plain in the point of the 5th Leaf; 7 chain, 1 treble on the 6th treble stitch of the Leaf; 8 chain, 1 single on the last plain stitch of the stem; then to form the

2nd round—119 plain, 1 single.

3rd round, 1st Scallop—1 plain, (2 treble in one twice), 1 plain, 1 single. Work 23 scallops more the same and fasten off.

2nd MEDALLION—Work as the 1st Medallion to the end of the 2nd round.

3rd round—Work 5 scallops as in the 3rd round of the 1st Medallion, then 1 plain, 2 treble in one, join to the centre of the 4 treble of the 19th scallop in the 1st Medallion; then 2 treble in one, 1 plain, 1 single, 1 plain, 2 treble in one, join to the centre stitch of the 18th scallop in the 1st Medallion, 2 treble in one, 1 plain, 1 single; then 17 scallops as before and fasten off.

3rd MEDALLION—Same as the 2nd, joining it to the 2nd instead of the 1st Medallion.

FIRST ROW OF STARS BETWEEN THE MEDALLIONS.

1st STAR—Commence with 4 chain and make it round.

1st *division*—5 chain, turn, and on these 5 chain, miss 1, 1 plain, 2 treble, leaving 1 chain; then 1 chain, 1 plain in the foundation chain. Work the 2nd *division* the same. 3rd *division*—5 chain, join to the centre of the 21st scollop in the 1st Medallion, turn, miss 1, 1 plain, 2 treble, 1 chain, 1 plain in the foundation chain. 4th *division*—Same as the 3rd, joining to the 20th scallop of the 1st Medallion. 5th *division*—Same as the 3rd, joining to the 5th scallop of the 2nd Medallion. 6th *division*—Same as the 3rd, joining to the 4th scallop of the same Medallion. Fasten off. Work another Star the same between the 2nd and 3rd Medallions.

2nd ROW OF STARS—1st STAR—4 chain, make it round.

1st *division*—5 chain, turn, miss 1, 1 plain, 2 treble, 1 chain, 1 plain in the foundation. Work 3 divisions more the same. 5th *division*—5 chain, join to the 1st scollop of the 1st Medallion, turn, miss 1, 1 plain, 2 treble, 1 chain, 1 plain in the foundation. 6th *division*—Same as 5th, joining to the last scallop of the 1st Medallion. Work 2 Stars more the same, joining them to the 2nd and 3rd Medallions. These 2 rows of Stars are repeated after every row of Medallions.

SECOND ROW OF MEDALLIONS.

1st MEDALLION—Work as the 1st Medallion to the end of the 2nd round, and for the

3rd round—Work 13 scallops as before. 14th scallop—1 plain, 2 treble in one, join to the 3rd scallop of the 1st Medallion of the 1st row; then 2 treble in one, 1 plain, 1 single. 15th scallop, as before, joining to the 2nd scallop of the 1st Medallion. 16th scallop, as before, joining to the 4th division of the next Star. 17th scallop, as before, joining to the 3rd division of the Star; then work 7 scallops without joining and fasten off.

2nd MEDALLION—Work as the 1st Medallion to the end of the 2nd round, and for the

3rd round—Work 5 scallops without joining. 6th scallop, as before, joining to the 19th scallop of the last Medallion. 7th scallop, as before, joining to the 18th scallop of the last Medallion. 8th scallop, as before, joining to the 2nd division of the Star. 9th scallop, join to the 1st division of the Star. 10th scallop, join to the 23rd scallop of the 1st Medallion of the 1st row. 11th scallop, as before, join to the 22nd scallop of the 1st Medallion. 12th scallop, join to the 2nd division of the next Star. 13th scallop, join to the 1st division of the Star. 14th scallop, join to the 3rd scallop of the 2nd Medallion in the 1st row. 15th scallop, join to the 2nd scallop of the 2nd Medallion.

16th scallop, join to the 4th division of the next Star. 17th scallop, join to the 3rd division of the Star ; then work 7 scallops without joining and fasten off.

3rd MEDALLION—Same as the last.

4th MEDALLION—Same as the last to the 11th scallop, then work 13 scallops without joining, and fasten off. Repeat the 2 rows of Stars, working one Star more to correspond with the number of Medallions.

3rd and 4th rows of MEDALLIONS—Same as last, working one Medallion more each row.

5th row of MEDALLIONS—Same as before, working 7 Medallions. Repeat the 1st row of Stars, but in working the 2nd row, omit them at the first and last Medallions, as the shape has now to be decreased.

6th row of MEDALLIONS—1st Medallion, work as before to the end of the 2nd round.

3rd round—Work 9 scallops without joining them. Repeat from the 10th scallop in the 2nd Medallion in the 2nd row.

Work 4 Medallions more the same as the 2nd Medallion in the 2nd row. 6th Medallion —Same as the last to the 15th scallop ; then work 9 scallops without joining. Repeat the Stars the same as in the 2 last rows, and then work 3 rows of Medallions the same as the 6th row ; that is, one less each time, and working the Stars between.

Should this Anti-macassar be required smaller, the 5th row of Medallions must be omitted ; if larger, work a row of 8 Medallions after the 5th row. For the Tassels, see page 28 of the Seventh Series.

ANTI-MACASSAR; OAK LEAF PATTERN.

For Materials, &c., see Instructions.

FIRST STRIPE.

Commence with 9 chain, turn, miss 1, 8 plain, 1 chain, turn, and on the other side 1 treble, 1 long, then 33 chain ;

1st LEAF, 1st row—Turn, miss 1, 8 plain, 1 chain, miss 1, 1 treble, (1 chain, miss 1, and 1 long, 4 times), 1 chain, miss 1, 1 treble, 1 chain, miss 1, 2 plain, turn, work 1 chain to cross the stem and up the other side ; and for the

2nd row—3 plain, 1 treble ; then to form the 1st division, 2 long in one, 1 long, 2 chain, 1 single on the top of the last long stitch, 1 treble, 1 plain, 2 chain. Work 2 divisions more the same, then 2 long in one, 1 long, 2 treble, 4 plain, *, turn 1 chain at the point, and down the other side, 4 plain, 2 treble, 2 long in one, 1 treble, 1 plain ; then to form the point of a division to correspond with the other side, work "4 chain and a long stitch with it," (for this term, see instructions), then 1 long, and before finishing the Leaf, work 10 chain ; and for the

1st ACORN, 1st round—To form the Cup, turn, miss 4, 1 treble in the 5th stitch, 1 chain, miss 2, 1 treble, 6 chain, turn, and on the 6 chain miss 4, 1 treble, 2 chain, 1 single in the same stitch as the 2nd treble stitch, which will make it round ; turn so as to cross the stem.

2nd round—4 plain, join to the 6th stitch of the Leaf, counting from the point, then 1 plain, 2 plain in one, 1 plain, 1 single, (1 single, 2 chain, 1 treble and 1 long, all in

ANTI-MACASSAR; OAK LEAF PATTERN. Registered Desig

E. Riego de la Branchardiere, *Invent., May,* 1851.

one stitch), (and in the next stitch, 1 long, 3 chain, turn, 1 single on the top of the last long, 1 long, both these long in one stitch), (1 long, 1 treble, 2 chain, 1 single, all in one stitch); and to finish the Cup, 1 single, 1 plain, 2 plain in one, 5 plain, 1 single, which finishes the acorn; then down the stem, 2 single, and to finish the Leaf, 1 long in the same stitch as the last long, 1 treble, 1 plain, "4 chain, and a long stitch with it," 2 long in one, 1 treble, 1 plain, "4 chain and a long with it," 2 long in one, 1 treble. then 26 chain; and for the

2nd LEAF, 1st row—Same as in the 1st Leaf.

2nd row—3 plain, 1 treble, 2 long in one, 1 long, 2 chain, 1 single on the top of the last long, 1 treble, 1 plain, 2 chain, 2 long in one, join to the 5th plain stitch of the cup of the 1st Acorn, 1 long, (2 chain, 1 single on the top of the last long, 1 treble, 1 plain, 2 chain, 2 long in one, 1 long, twice), 2 treble, 4 plain, 1 chain, turn, and down the other side, 4 plain, 2 treble, 2 long in one, 1 treble, 1 plain, ("4 chain and a long with it," 2 long in one, 1 treble, 1 plain, 3 times); 2 plain, and down the stem 2 single, then to finish the 1st Leaf, 1 single on the top of the last stitch, 3 plain, and down the stem 5 single, leaving 4 chain; then 26 chain for the

3rd LEAF, 1st row—Same as in 1st Leaf.

2nd row—3 plain, 1 treble, 2 long in one, join to the stem of the 2nd Leaf, (1 long, 2 chain, 1 single on the top of last long, 1 treble, 1 plain, 2 chain, 2 long in one, 3 times); then 1 long, 2 treble, 1 plain, and leaving the Leaf unfinished, work 18 chain for the

2nd ACORN CUP, 1st round—Same as in 1st Acorn.

2nd round—5 plain, join to the last long stitch of the 3rd Leaf, then 2 plain in one, 1 plain, 1 single, 2 chain; join to the 3rd 2 long in one of the 2nd Leaf, 2 chain, miss 3, 1 single, 1 plain, 2 plain in one, 5 plain, 1 single, then down the stem 3 single, leaving 7 chain; then 16 chain for the

3rd ACORN, 1st round—Same as in the 1st Acorn.

2nd round—5 plain, join to the 4th plain stitch of the cup of the 2nd Acorn, 2 plain in one, 1 plain, 1 single, (1 single, 2 chain, 1 treble; join to the 8th stitch of the 2nd Leaf, counting from the point, 1 long, all in one stitch), (1 long, 3 chain, 1 single on the top of the last long, 1 long, both these long in one stitch); then in the next stitch, (1 long, 1 treble, 2 chain, 1 single), 1 single, 1 plain, 2 plain in one, 5 plain, 1 single; then down the stem 3 single, leaving 5 chain; then 15 chain for the

4th ACORN—Same as the 1st Acorn, joining it to the 7th stitch of the cup of the 3rd Acorn. When finished, 3 single down the stem, leaving 4 chain; and for the

1st BRANCH at the top—5 chain, join with a single stitch to the 6th stitch of the cup of the last Acorn; then 11 chain, turn, miss 1, 6 single; 5 chain for the

2nd BRANCH—Turn, miss 1, 4 single, then 8 single down the centre stem; 10 chain for the

5th ACORN—Same as the 1st Acorn, but without joining it; when finished 2 single down the stem, and 10 single down the centre stem; then 11 chain for the

6th ACORN— Same as the 1st, joining to the 4th stitch of the cup of the 5th Acorn; when finished 3 single down the stem, and down the centre stem 5 single, join to the 7th stitch of the cup of the 6th Acorn; then 3 single down the centre stem, and on the 3rd Leaf, 3 plain, 1 chain, turn, and down the other side, 4 plain, 2 treble, 2 long in one, and leaving the Leaf to be finished when the second side is worked, make 30 chain for the

4th LEAF, 1st row—Same as in the 1st Leaf.

2nd row—3 plain, 1 treble, 2 long in one, 1 long, 2 chain, 1 single on the top of the last long, 1 treble, 1 plain, 2 chain, 2 long in one, join to the point of the 6th Acorn, then, (1 long, 2 chain, 1 single on the top of the last long, 1 treble, 1 plain, 2 chain, 2 long in one, twice), and before finishing the leaf, make 14 chain for the

3rd BRANCH—Turn, miss 1, 3 single, join to the point of the 5th Acorn, 4 single; and for the

4th BRANCH—6 chain, turn, miss 1, 5 single; then 6 *single* down the remaining chain; and make 33 chain for the

5th LEAF, forming the 1st Leaf of the 2nd Pattern, 1st row—Same as in 1st Leaf.

2nd row—3 plain, 1 treble, 2 long in one, join to the 3rd single stitch of the 4th branch, 1 long, 2 chain, 1 single on the top of the last long, 1 treble, 1 plain, 2 chain, 2 long in one, join to the 8th plain stitch of the 1st side of the cup of the 5th Acorn, 1 long, (2 chain, 1 single on the top of the long, 1 treble, 1 plain, 2 chain, 2 long in one, 1 long, twice); join to the point of the 2nd branch, 2 treble, 4 plain. Repeat from *, page 39 until the length required is made, but in working the last pattern, repeat the direction only to the 6 *single* after the 4th branch, marked in italics; then to form the

SECOND SIDE OF OAK PATTERN.

And to finish the last or 4th Leaf, work 1 single on the top of the last stitch, 1 long, 2 treble, 4 plain, 1 chain, turn, and down the other side 4 plain, 2 treble, 2 long in one, 1 treble, 1 plain, "4 chain and a long with it;" then 10 chain for the

1st ACORN of the 2nd side—Same as the 1st Acorn, joining it to the last leaf; when finished 2 single down the stem, then on the leaf (2 long in one, 1 treble, 1 plain, "4 chain and a long with it" twice); and before completing the leaf, work 26 chain for the

1st LEAF of the 2nd side—Work the same as the 2nd leaf in the 1st pattern; when finished 2 single down the stem, and on the 4th leaf, 2 long in one, 1 treble, 3 plain, then down the stem, 2 single, leaving 4 chain; then 29 chain for the

* * 2nd LEAF of this side, 1st row—Same as in the 1st leaf.

2nd row—3 plain, 1 treble, join to the stem of the 1st leaf, then (2 long in one, 1 long, 2 chain, 1 single on the top of the last long, 1 treble, 1 plain, 2 chain, twice), 1 long, and before finishing the leaf, work 10 chain for the

2nd ACORN—Work as the 1st, joining to the 3rd 2 long in one of the 1st leaf; when finished 2 single down the stem and on the leaf, 1 single on the top of the last long, 1 long in the same stitch as before, 1 long, 2 chain, 1 single on the top of the last long stitch, 1 treble, 1 plain, 2 chain, 2 long in one, 1 long, join to the 6th stitch of the cup of last Acorn; then 2 treble, 4 plain, 1 chain, turn, and down the other side 4 plain, 2 treble, 2 long in one, 1 treble, 1 plain, (" 4 chain and a long with it," 2 long in one, 1 treble, 1 plain, 3 times), 2 plain; and down the stem 5 single, then down the centre stem 4 single; and for the 1st BRANCH—8 chain, join with a single stitch to the last long stitch of the last leaf, 3 chain, turn, miss 1, 5 single.

2nd BRANCH—8 chain, turn, miss 1, 7 single, then 6 single down the remaining chain, and to complete the centre or 3rd leaf left unfinished in the 1st side, 1 single on the top of the last long stitch, (1 treble, 1 plain, " 4 chain, and a long stitch with it," 2 long in in one 3 times); then 1 treble, 3 plain, and down the stem 2 single, then 4 single on the centre stem; and on the centre or 4th leaf left unfinished on the 1st side, 1 single on the top of the last long, 1 long, 2 treble, 4 plain, 1 chain, turn, and down the other side 3 plain, and before finishing the leaf make 18 chain for the

3rd Acorn, 1st round—Same as in 1st Acorn.

2nd round—4 plain, join to the 3rd stitch of the last 18 chain, 1 plain, 2 plain in one, 1 plain, 1 single, then (1 single, 2 chain, 1 treble and 1 long, all in one stitch); (1 long, 1 chain, join to the 3rd 2 long in one of the 3rd or centre leaf of the 1st side; 1 chain, 1 single on the top of the last long, 1 long in the same stitch as before); (1 long, 1 treble, 2 chain, 1 single, all in one stitch); 1 single, 1 plain, 2 plain in one, 5 plain, 1 single, 3 single down the stem; then 20 chain for the

4th Acorn, 1st round—Same as in 1st Acorn.

2nd round—4 plain, join to the 6th stitch of the cup of the 3rd Acorn, 1 plain, 2 plain in one, 1 plain, 1 single, (1 single, 2 chain, 1 treble, 1 long, all in one stitch), (1 long, 1 chain, join to the 4th chain stitch of the 2nd branch, so that the point of the branch turns down, 1 chain, 1 single on the top of the last long, 1 long in the same stitch as before); (1 long, 1 treble, 2 chain, 1 single, all in one stitch), 1 single, 1 plain, join to the 3rd 2 long in one of the 2nd leaf, 2 plain in one, 5 plain, 1 single, then down the stem 2 single; and for the

3rd Branch—13 chain, join to the 7th stitch of the 2nd leaf, turn, miss 1, 4 single; and for the 4th Branch—7 chain, turn, miss 1, 6 single, and down the centre stem 10 single; then 11 chain for the

5th Acorn—Work as the 1st, joining to the 5th stitch of the 10 single last worked; when finished 3 single down the stem and 4 single down the centre stem; then 11 chain for the

6th Acorn—Same as the 1st, joining to the 6th stitch of the cup of the last Acorn; when finished 3 single down the stem and 5 single down the centre stem; then 11 chain for the

7th Acorn Cup, 1st round—Same as the 1st Acorn.

2nd round—4 plain, join to the 5th stitch of the cup of the 6th Acorn, 1 plain, 2 plain in one, 1 plain, 1 single, 4 chain, miss 3, 1 single, 1 plain, 2 plain in one, 5 plain, 1 single, then down the stem 3 single, and 6 single down the centre stem; then on the next unfinished leaf of the 1st side, work 1 plain, 2 treble, 2 long in one; join to the 5th stitch of the cup of the last Acorn, (1 treble, 1 plain, "4 chain and a long with it," 2 long in one, twice); 1 treble, 1 plain, "4 chain and a long with it," and before finishing the leaf, work 26 chain for the

3rd Leaf, 1st row—Same as in 1st leaf.

2nd row—3 plain, 1 treble, 2 long in one, 1 long, 2 chain, 1 single on the top of the last long, 1 treble, 1 plain, 2 chain, 2 long in one, join to the centre of the 4 chain of the 7th Acorn, (1 long, 2 chain, 1 single on the top of the last long, 1 treble, 1 plain, 2 chain, 2 long in one, twice); join to the last treble stitch in the 6th Acorn, 1 long, 2 treble, 4 plain, 1 chain, turn, and down the other side 4 plain, 2 treble, 2 long in one, 1 treble, 1 plain, ("4 chain and a long with it," 2 long in one, 1 treble, 1 plain, 3 times), 2 plain and down the stem, 2 single, and to finish the centre leaf, 2 long in one, 1 treble,

3 plain, 2 single down the stem, then 29 chain, and repeat from * * at the 2nd leaf, (this side will end on the part of a leaf worked after the 7th Acorn). Fasten off. Work 3 Stripes more the same.

INSERTION.

Commence with 10 chain, join with a single stitch to the point of the 1st branch in the last pattern of the 1st side of one of the oak stripes, *, then 45 chain; and for the

1st Trefoil—Turn, miss 6, 1 single in the 7th stitch to form a round loop, turn so as to cross the stem, work 3 chain, and in the round loop 2 long, join to the 27th stitch of the 45 chain; then 2 long, 3 chain, 1 single, 3 chain, 2 long; join to the 18th stitch of the 45 chain, then in the round loop 2 long, 3 chain, 1 single, 3 chain, 2 long, join to the 9th stitch of the 45 chain, and in the round loop 2 long, join to the point of the 4th Acorn in the last pattern of the stripe, 3 chain, 1 single in the round loop, which finishes the trefoil; then on the stem 4 single, 2 plain, join to the point of the next leaf, then 3 plain, 6 chain, join with a single stitch to the last long stitch in the 1st side of the leaf, then 45 chain; and for the

2nd Trefoil—Work as the 1st, joining it to the point of the next Acorn; when finished work on the stem 4 single, 5 plain, then 1 chain, join with a single stitch to the point of the next leaf, 4 chain, join with a single stitch to the point of the 1st branch. Repeat from *, ending with the 5 plain on the stem of the last Trefoil, join to the point of the 1st leaf; and to form the other side of the insertion, on the chain stitches work 5 plain, then 6 chain, join to the point of the 6th Acorn in the last pattern of the 2nd side of another of the oak stripes, turn, miss 1, 5 single on the 6th chain, * *, and on the chain stitches of the insertion 13 plain, then 1 chain, join with a single stitch to the point of the 5th Acorn of the 2nd stripe; then 5 chain, join with a single stitch to the point of the branch, then 8 chain; and for the

1st Trefoil of this side—Turn, miss 6, 1 single, turn so as to cross the stem, and in the round loop work (3 chain, 4 long, 3 chain, and 1 single, 3 times,) then on the stem 4 single, 5 plain, 1 single on the top of the last stitch of the 13 plain, then on the chain stitches of the 1st side, 1 plain, join to the centre stitch of the 3rd division of the Trefoil, 9 plain; join to the centre stitch of the 2nd division of the Trefoil; then 8 plain, 1 single on the top of the last plain stitch of the 1st side; then on the chain 1 plain, join to the centre stitch of the 1st division of the Trefoil, 4 plain, join to the point of the next leaf; then 13 plain, 4 chain, join with a single stitch to the point of the next Acorn, then 11 chain; and for the

2nd Trefoil—Turn, miss 6, 1 single, turn, (3 chain, 4 long, 3 chain and 1 single, 3 times in the round loop), then on the stem 4 single, 5 plain, 1 single on the top of the last stitch of the 13 plain, 1 plain; join to the 3rd division of the Trefoil, 9 plain; join to the 2nd division of the Trefoil, 8 plain, 1 single on the top of the last plain stitch of the 1st side, 1 plain, join to the 1st division of the Trefoil, then 4 plain; join to the point of the next leaf. Repeat from * *, and fasten off. Work the insertion between the other stripes.

THE END.

THE

CROCHET BOOK,

ELEVENTH SERIES.

BY

MLLE. RIEGO DE LA BRANCHARDIERE.

Fifth Edition--25,000.

LONDON:
SIMPKIN, MARSHALL, AND CO.,
ACKERMANN & CO., STRAND; OLIVER AND BOYD, EDINBURGH;
AND ALL THE BERLIN WAREHOUSES.

1853.

Entered at Stationers' Hall.

CONTENTS.

All the Terms used are illustrated and explained in the FIRST, SECOND, and THIRD SERIES.

LONDON:
Printed at the Office of E. RIEGO DE LA BRANCHARDIERE, 106, New Bond Street,

RULES TO BE OBSERVED IN THE DIRECTIONS.

THE Plain and Single stitches are all to be worked in *double crochet*, (that is, putting the needle into both edges of the previous stitches), unless directed otherwise. Be careful to observe the difference between the terms, *turn* and *turn back*. The work should be tight. For an explanation of the Terms—See the previous series.

MATERIALS.

GUIPURE COLLAR—*Taylor's Crochet Thread, No.* 10 *or* 12, *according to the size required; Walker's Penelope Needle, No.* 4½ *or* 24, *Bell Gauge.*

GUIPURE BERTHE—*Taylor's Crochet Thread, No.* 6 *or* 8; *Walker's Penelope Needle, No.* 4 *or* 22, *Bell Gauge.*

GUIPURE CHEMISETTE—*Taylor's Crochet Thread, No.* 10; *Walker's Penelope Needle, No.* 4½ *or* 24, *Bell Gauge.*

ROSE POINT COLLAR—*Taylor's Crochet Thread, No.* 10 *or* 12; *Walker's Penelope Needle, No.* 4½ *or* 24, *Bell Gauge.*

THE

CROCHET BOOK,

ELEVENTH SERIES.

GUIPURE COLLAR, AN EXACT COPY OF OLD POINT.

Materials and Rules—See Page 3.

FIRST STRIPE.

Commence with the centre scroll, work 8 chain, turn, miss 1, 7 single on the 8 chain, *, then 47 chain, turn, miss 1, 3 plain, 2 single, turn back—miss 1, 4 plain ; and for the

1st FLOWER—4 chain, 1 single in the last stitch of the 47 chain, turn back—(2 chain and 1 plain in the 4 chain, 7 times), turn back—(2 chain, miss 2 and 1 plain in the 2 chain, 7 times), turn back—(1 chain, miss 1, 3 plain in the 2 chain, 1 chain, miss 1, 6 treble in the next 2 chain 3 times); then 1 chain, miss 1, 3 plain in the last 2 chain, 1 chain, 1 plain in the 4 chain of the commencement of the flower; then down the plain stitches of the stem 4 plain, and on the 47 chain, work 2 plain and 2 single, turn back—1 single, 4 plain, 1 single, turn back—and for the

1st SCROLL—16 chain, turn, miss 1, (2 plain in one, 3 times), 1 single, turn back—1

GUIPURE COLLAR.

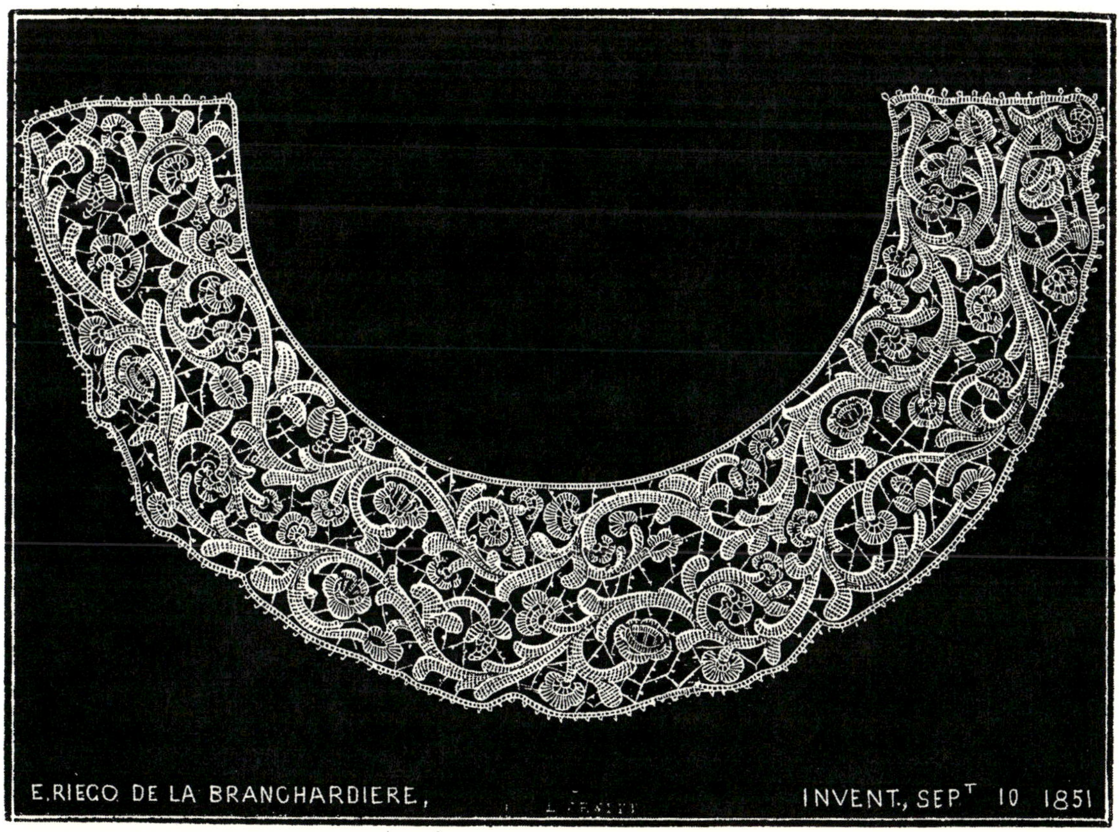

single, 5 plain, 2 plain in one, turn back—miss 1, 1 plain, (2 plain in one and 2 plain, twice); then on the chain stitches, 2 plain in one, 3 plain, 2 plain in one, 6 plain, and on the stem of the 1st flower, 6 plain; then on the chain, 1 plain, 2 single, turn back—miss 1, 4 plain, miss 1, 25 plain, turn back—miss 1, 9 plain, 2 single, then 27 chain; and for the

2nd SCROLL—Turn, miss 1, (2 plain in one, 3 times), 1 plain, 2 single, leaving 20 chain, turn back—1 single, 8 plain, turn back—miss 1, 6 plain, 1 single, leaving one stitch; and for the

1st DIVISION of the centre Scroll—17 chain, turn, miss 1, 16 plain, then 1 plain on the one stitch left at the 2nd scroll, and on the chain, 20 plain; then on the 1st scroll, 2 plain, 2 single, turn back—1 single, (4 plain and 2 plain in one, 8 times), turn back—1 chain, 18 plain, 2 single, turn back—1 single, 10 plain, (2 plain and 2 plain in one, 3 times), turn back—and for the

2nd DIVISION of the centre Scroll—19 chain, turn, miss 1, 18 plain, 1 single, turn back—1 single, (3 plain and 2 plain in one, 4 times), 2 plain, turn back—16 chain, turn, miss 1, (4 plain and 2 plain in one, 3 times); then on the plain stitches, 23 plain, and on the lower row 2 plain, 2 single, turn back—26 single, 19 plain; and for the

2nd FLOWER—4 chain, 1 single on the last stitch of the 16 chain, turn back—(2 chain and 1 plain in the 4 chain, 7 times), turn back—(2 chain, miss 2 and 1 plain in the 2 chain, 7 times), turn back—(2 chain, miss 1 and 2 plain in the 2 chain, 7 times), 2 chain, 1 plain in the 4 chain, and down the plain stitches of the stem, 4 single, then 18 chain; and for the

BUD—Turn, miss 1, 7 plain, 1 single, turn back—1 single, 4 plain, turn back—4 chain, turn, and on the 4 chain, miss 1, 1 plain, 1 treble, 1 chain, miss 1, then on the 4 plain, 1 treble, 1 chain, miss 1, 1 treble, 1 chain, miss 1, 1 single; then down the chain stitches for the stem, 9 plain, and on the centre scroll, 4 plain, 2 single, turn back—1 single, 4 plain, (miss 1 and 4 plain, twice), and to finish the bud, 1 single, 3 plain, 2 plain in one, turn back—3 chain, turn, miss 1, 2 plain on the 3 chain, then 5 plain, and down the stem, 12 single, leaving 2 stitches; and for the

STEM of the 3rd Flower—5 chain, turn, miss 1, 4 plain, 2 plain on the 2 stitches left, and on the centre Scroll, 1 plain, 2 single, turn back—1 single, 7 plain, 2 plain in one, turn back—1 chain, 2 plain in one, 1 plain, turn back; and for the

3rd FLOWER—4 chain, miss 2, 1 single, turn back—(2 chain and 1 plain in the 4 chain, 7 times), turn back—(2 chain, miss 2 and 1 plain in the 2 chain, 7 times), turn back—(2 chain, miss 1 and 2 plain in the 4 chain, 7 times), 2 chain, 1 plain in the 4 chain; then on the plain stitches of the stem, 8 plain, and on the centre scroll 13 plain, 1 single. In working these stitches, leave the rib formed by the single stitches in the front; and for the

3rd SCROLL—7 chain, turn, miss 1, (2 plain in one, 4 times), 2 plain; then on the single stitches of the centre scroll, 1 plain, 2 single, turn back—1 single, 12 plain, turn back—miss 1, (2 plain and 2 plain in one, twice), 6 plain, then on the centre scroll, "6 *plain*, 1 *single*;" and for the

3rd DIVISION of the centre Scroll—12 chain, turn, miss 1, 6 plain, 2 single, and leaving 3 chain, turn back—1 single, 5 plain, and leaving 2 stitches, turn back—then 23 chain; and for the

4th SCROLL—Turn, miss 1, 5 plain, 2 single, turn back—1 single, (2 plain and 2 plain in one, twice), turn back—1 chain, 2 plain in one, 4 plain, 2 single, and leaving 2 stitches, turn back—1 single, 7 plain, turn back—miss 1, 3 plain, 2 single, leaving 2 stitches; and for the

STEM of the 4th Flower—20 chain, turn, miss 1, 3 plain, 2 plain in one, 4 plain, 2 single, turn back—1 single, 10 plain; and for the

4th FLOWER—4 chain, 1 single, turn back—(2 chain and 1 plain in the 4 chain, 7 times), turn back—(2 chain, miss 2 and 1 plain in the 2 chain, 7 times), turn back—(2 chain, miss 1 and 2 plain in the 2 chain, 3 times); then 2 chain, miss 1, 8 treble in the next 2 chain, (2 chain, miss 1 and 2 plain in the 2 chain, 3 times), 2 chain, 1 plain in the 4 chain, and down the plain stitches of the stem, 7 plain, 1 single, leaving 3 stitches; and for the

4th DIVISION of the centre Scroll—20 chain, turn, miss 1, 19 plain, then on the 3 stitches left, 1 single, and leaving the other 2 stitches, turn back—1 single, 19 plain, turn back—6 plain, 1 single; and for the

5th DIVISION of the centre Scroll—22 chain, turn, miss 1, 21 plain, then on the plain stitches of centre scroll, 8 plain, 2 single, turn back—1 single, (4 plain and 2 plain in one, 5 times), 5 plain, turn back—miss 1, 8 plain, 1 single; and for the

5th SCROLL—30 chain, turn, miss 1, (2 plain in one, 3 times), 1 single, turn back—1 single, (1 plain and 2 plain in one, 3 times), turn back—1 chain, 10 plain, then on the chain, (2 plain in one and 4 plain, 5 times); and on the centre scroll 2 plain in one, 19 plain, 2 single, turn back—1 single, 54 plain, (2 plain in one and 3 plain, twice), turn back—miss 1, 8 plain, 2 single, then 21 chain, turn, miss 1, (3 plain and 2 plain in one, 5 times), then on the centre scroll, 2 plain, 2 plain in one, 2 single, turn back—1 single, 30 plain; then work a

PINE—4 chain, 1 single on the last stitch of the 21 chain, turn back—1 plain in the 4 chain; and to form the

1st DIVISION—9 chain, turn, miss 1, 6 plain, turn, 1 chain to cross, and up the other side for the

1st round—2 plain in one, (2 plain and 2 plain in one, twice), turn, and down the other side (2 plain and 2 plain in one, twice), 1 single.

2nd—(2 chain and 1 single, 19 times), working in the lower edge of the stitches of the 1st round, leaving the other side of the stitches at the back. This finishes the 1st division;

then 1 plain in the 4 chain, and for the centre division, turn back—and keeping the the last round down at the back, work on the back or upper edge of the plain stitches of the 1st round, miss 1, 1 single, (2 chain, miss 1 and 1 single, 4 times), 2 chain, 1 single, turn back—6 chain, turn, miss 4, 1 single on the 6 chain, (2 chain, miss 2 and 1 plain in the 2 chain, 5 times), miss 1, 1 plain in the 4 chain, turn back—(2 chain, miss 2 and 1 plain in the 2 chain, 6 times), 2 chain, 1 plain in the same chain as before, turn back—(miss 1 and 4 plain in the 2 chain, 5 times), (2 chain, miss 2 and 1 single in the 2 chain, twice), 2 chain, miss 1, 1 plain in the 4 chain; and for the

3rd DIVISION—Work as the 1st, when finished work 1 chain to cross, and to join this division to the centre, work on the back of the plain stitches of the 1st round, 2 single, join to the last 2 chain of the centre division, 2 single as before, join to the next 2 chain of the centre division, 2 single, join to the next 2 chain, 4 single, join to the 2nd stitch of the last 4 plain; then 10 single on the remaining stitches at the back, 2 plain in the 4 chain, which finishes the pine; then down the stem, 20 plain, 2 single; and for the

6th SCROLL—14 chain, turn, miss 1, 2 plain in one, 12 plain; then on the centre scroll, 2 plain, 2 single, turn back—(miss 1 and 2 plain, 5 times), miss 1, 1 plain, 2 plain in one, turn back—2 plain in one, (miss 1 and 2 plain, 4 times), and on the lower row 2 plain, 1 single, leaving 2 stitches, turn back—1 single, 12 plain, turn back—(miss 1 and 3 plain, 3 times), 1 plain, and on the 2 stitches left 2 plain; then on the lower row of the centre scroll, 1 plain, 1 single. Repeat from * at the commencement once more; then repeat half the pattern, that is, to the end of the 3rd scroll, finishing with the "6 *plain*, 1 *single* on the centre scroll;" and to form the

SECOND SIDE OF THE FIRST STRIPE.

8 chain, turn, miss 1, 7 plain on the 8 chain, and on the centre scroll, 3 plain, 2 single,

turn back—1 single, 11 plain, turn back—(miss 1 and 3 plain, 3 times), then on the centre scroll, 2 single; and for the

1st Scroll—* * 14 chain, turn, miss 1, 2 single, 4 plain, 2 single, turn back—(miss 1 and 2 plain, twice), miss 1, 2 plain in one, turn back—6 plain, then on the chain, 5 plain and 1 plain on the last single stitch of the centre scroll; and on the lower row, 2 plain, 1 single, turn back—1 single, 5 plain, (miss 1 and 2 plain, 3 times), turn back—(miss 1 and 2 plain, 4 times), thenon the centre scroll, 1 plain, 1 single; and for the

Stem of the 1st Flower—11 chain, turn, miss 1, 10 plain, then 1 single on the centre scroll, turn back—(miss 1 and 2 plain, 3 times), miss 1, 1 plain, and for the 1st flower, work the same as the 2nd flower of the 1st side. When finished, 7 single down the stem, and on the centre scroll, 12 plain, then on the lower row, 1 single; and for the

2nd Scroll—9 chain, turn, miss 1, 4 plain, 2 single, turn back—(miss 1 and 2 plain, twice), turn back—4 plain, then 2 single on the chain, and 1 single on the centre scroll, turn back—miss 1, 6 plain, turn back—(miss 1 and 2 plain, twice); then on the centre scroll, 1 single, 22 plain, 2 single; and for the

3rd Scroll—16 chain, turn, miss 1, (2 plain in one, 4 times), 2 single, turn back—1 single, (2 plain and 2 plain in one, 3 times), turn back—miss 1, 12 plain, then on the chain, 3 plain, 2 single, turn back—1 single, (3 plain and 2 plain in one, 4 times), turn back—miss 1, 12 plain, 2 single; and for the

Oval Flower—44 chain, turn, miss 5, 1 treble, 1 chain, miss 1, 1 treble, 1 chain, miss 1, 1 single, turn, 1 chain to cross; and up the other side for the

1st round—(1 plain and 2 plain in one, 7 times), 1 chain to cross.

2nd—(1 plain, 2 treble in one, 2 long in one and 1 treble, 5 times), then 1 single, and down the chain, 8 plain, 2 single, turn back—1 single, 9 plain, turn back—join to the last stitch of the flower, then down the stem, 7 single, leaving 3 stitches; and for the

Small Pine—13 chain, turn, miss 4, 1 single in the 5th stitch, turn, 1 plain in this round loop; and for the

1st Division—7 chain, turn, miss 1, 5 plain, turn, 1chain to cross, and up the other side for the

1st round—5 plain, 2 plain in one, and down the other side, 5 plain, 1 single.

2nd—(1 chain and 1 single, 12 times, working on the lower edge of the stitches of the 1st round), which finishes the division, then 1 plain in the round loop; and for the

2nd Division—15 chain, turn, and down these chain, miss 4, 1 plain, (1 chain, miss 2 and 1 plain, 3 times), turn, 1 chain to cross, and up the other side, (miss 1, 3 plain in the 2 chain, 3 times), miss 1, 5 plain in the 4 chain, and down the other side, (miss 1 and 1 plain in the 1 chain, 3 times), 1 single, and in the round loop 1 plain; then work a

3rd Division same as the 1st, when finished, 2 plain in the round loop, 1 chain to cross the stem, 1 single on the first plain stitch worked in the round loop; then on the back of the stitches of the 1st division, 9 single, 1 single in the 5th plain stitch of the centre division, and up the plain stitches, 8 single, 3 chain, 1 single in the same stitch as the last, 4 single, 1 single in the back of the 5th plain stitch of the 3rd division; and on the remaining stitches, 8 single, then 3 single on the plain stitches worked in the round loop; and down the stem, 7 plain, 3 plain on the stitches left, and on the chain, 12 plain, 2 single, turn back—(miss 1 and 5 plain, 4 times), turn back—join to the last stitch of the Pine, then down the stem, 18 single, leaving 2 stitches; and for the

4th Scroll—12 chain, turn, miss 1, 4 plain, 2 single, turn back—(miss 1 and 2 plain, twice), turn back—4 plain, then 5 plain on the chain, 2 plain on the 2 stitches left, and on the chain, 8 plain; then on the 3rd scroll, 1 plain, 2 single, turn back—(miss 1 and 3 plain, 5 times), miss 1, 1 plain, turn back—miss 1, 2 plain, miss 1, 12 plain, then 3 plain on the remaining stitches of the 3rd scroll, 4 plain on the chain, and on the 2 stitches left of the centre scroll, 2 plain; then on the lower row, 1 plain, 2 single, turn back; and for the

1st Division on this side of the centre scroll—1 single, 14 plain, 2 plain in one, turn back—17 plain, then on the lower row, 7 plain, 2 single, leaving 2 stitches; and for the

STEM of the 3rd Flower—7 chain, turn, miss 1, 6 plain, then 2 plain on the 2 stitches left, and on the chain, 30 plain, 2 single, leaving 2 chain, turn back—(miss 1 and 3 plain, 10 times); then work the 3rd flower the same as 4th flower of the 1st side, when finished work down the stem, 28 plain, 1 single, leaving 1 stitch; and for the

5th SCROLL—11 chain, turn, miss 1, 4 plain, 2 single, turn back—(miss 1 and 2 plain twice), turn back—4 plain, then on the chain, 4 plain, 1 plain on the 1 stitch left, 2 plain on the 2 chain; and on the centre scroll, 5 plain, 2 single, turn back—1 single, 3 plain, 2 plain in one, 7 plain, (miss 1 and 2 plain, twice), turn back—(miss 1 and 2 single, 3 times), 8 plain, then on the lower row, 3 single; and for the

6th SCROLL—9 chain, turn, miss 1, 2 plain in one, 2 plain, 2 single, turn back—(miss 1 and 2 plain, twice), turn back—1 chain, 4 plain, then on the chain, 3 plain, and on the centre scroll, 1 plain, 1 single, turn back—(miss 1 and 2 plain, 3 times), turn back—(miss 1 and 2 plain, twice), then on the centre scroll, 4 single, 13 plain, 2 single, turn back—and for the

2nd DIVISION of the centre scroll—1 single, 12 plain, 2 plain in one, turn back—1 chain, 2 plain in one, 14 plain, then on the centre scroll, 1 plain, 2 single, turn back—and for the

3rd DIVISION of the centre scroll—1 single, 11 plain, 2 plain in one, turn back—1 chain, 2 plain in one, 4 plain, 2 single, turn back—1 single, 6 plain, 2 plain in one, turn back—miss 1, 8 plain, then on the lower row, 7 plain, and on the centre scroll, 13 single, then on the lower row, 2 single; and for the

STEM of the 4th flower—12 chain, turn, miss 1, 9 single, leaving 2 chain, turn back—1 single, (2 plain and 2 plain in one, twice), 2 plain. Work the 4th flower the same as the 4th flower of the 1st side; when finished, 9 single down the stem, leaving 2 stitches; and for the

7th SCROLL—20 chain, turn, miss 1, (2 plain in one, 3 times), 1 single, turn back—1 single, (1 plain and 2 plain in one, 3 times), turn back—1 chain, 10 plain, then on the chain, 1 plain, 2 single, turn back—1 single, (2 plain in one and 3 plain, 3 times), turn back—miss 1, (2 plain in one and 2 plain, 4 times), 1 single, and leaving 2 stitches, work 8 chain; then leave the stripe and thread; work a

ROSE—Commence with 11 chain, worked rather tight.

1st row—Miss 1, (2 plain in one and 1 plain, 4 times), 2 plain in one, 1 single, turn back.

2nd—1 chain and 1 single 15 times, working on the lower edge of the stitches of the 1st row, leaving the upper edge in front, turn back.

3rd—This row is to be worked on the upper edge of the stitches of the 1st row, keeping the 2nd row in front—1 single, (4 chain, miss 2 and 3 single, twice), 4 chain, miss 2, 1 single, turn back.

4th—Miss 1, 8 plain in the 4 chain, miss 1, 1 single on the 3 single. Repeat twice more, making in all 3 divisions, turn back.

5th—On the 8 plain, work 1 single, 2 plain, (2 plain in one, twice), 2 plain, 1 single, miss 1. Repeat twice more, then to form the centre of the Rose, turn, and work 10 single along the chain stitches of the foundation, turn back, and on these 10 single, work (2 chain, miss 2 and 1 treble, twice), 2 chain, miss 2, 2 single, turn back—(1 chain, miss 2 and 1 plain in the 2 chain, 3 times), 1 chain, miss 2, 1 single.

6th—On the plain stitches of the 1st division, work 1 single, 3 plain, 2 plain in one, 3 plain, 1 single; then miss 2, 1 single, 6 plain, 1 single, miss 2, 1 single, 3 plain, 2 plain in one, 3 plain, 1 single; then 1 plain in the 1st 1 chain, (2 chain, miss 1 and 1 plain in the 1 chain, 3 times), 1 single. Fasten off.

Return to the stripe at the 8 chain, and join to the centre stitch of the 2nd division of the rose, turn, and down the 8 chain, miss 1, 7 plain, then 2 plain on the 2 stitches left at the 7th scroll, and down the chain, 12 plain; then on the stitches left at the stem of the 4th flower, 2 plain, then 2 plain on the 2 chain, and on the centre scroll 2 plain, 3 plain on the lower row, then 2 plain on the 2 stitches left at the stem of the 4th flower of the 1st side, and on the chain, 1 plain, 2 single, turn back—1 single. 14 plain, (miss 1 and 3 plain, 5 times), turn back—join to the next stitch of the rose—30 plain, then on the chain, 6 plain, and on the stitches left of the 4th scroll of the 1st side, 4 plain, then on the chain, 15 plain, and on the plain stitches 6 plain; then on the chain, 3 plain, and on the single stitches of the centre scroll, 3 plain, 2 single, turn back—and for the

4th DIVISION of the centre Scroll—1 single, (miss 1 and 8 plain, 5 times), 2 plain in one, turn back—1 chain, 2 plain in one, 42 plain, then on the single stitches of the centre scroll, 2 single. Repeat from * *, page 10, once more, then repeat from * * to the end of the 5th scroll, which will finish the stripe. Fasten off.

CENTRE BARS FOR THE FIRST STRIPE.

RULES.—To form a Bar, work 5 chain, turn, miss 1, 2 single on the 5 chain, which will leave 2 chain. Work thus whenever directed to work a Bar: for a Double Bar, work 5 chain, turn, miss 1, 2 single, 5 chain, turn, miss 1, 2 single.

Commence in the 1st plain stitch of the 1st scroll in the 2nd side of the stripe, 4 chain, miss 15, 1 single in the 6th chain stitch of the stem of the 1st Flower, then 4 chain; take out the needle, and passing this chain at the back of the stem of the 1st flower so as to cross it, put the needle into the opposite stitch on the other side of the stem, and bring the last stitch of the 4 chain through to join it. Work a Bar—3 chain, miss 7, 1 single on the centre scroll, then 7 chain; turn, and to work on the 1st side of the stripe, pass this chain under the centre scroll to cross it at the back, take out the needle, put it into the opposite stitch on the centre scroll, and bring the last stitch of the 7 chain through to join it. This stitch will be the 7th stitch of the 1st division of the 1st side, counting from the 2nd scroll; then work 10 single on the 1st division. Work a Bar—4 chain, and missing 4 stitches of the 2nd division of the centre scroll, work 15 single on it. Work a Bar—2 chain, miss 7, 2 single on the centre scroll. Work a Bar—3 chain, 1 single in the 2nd 2 chain of the 2nd flower, 6 chain; join to the 8th stitch of the 15 single, miss 1, 3 single on the 6 chain. Work a Bar—2 chain; join to the 2nd stitch of the 4 chain worked before the 15 single, 4 chain, 1 single in the 5th 2 chain of the 2nd flower. Work a Bar—3 chain, join to the 3rd stitch of the 10 single. Work a Bar—3 chain, 1 single in the 7th 2 chain of the 2nd flower, 3 chain; join to the 1st plain stitch of the last row of the 2nd scroll. Work a Bar—3 chain, 1 single on the 5th chain stitch of the stem of the bud. Work a Bar—6 chain; join to the 24th chain stitch of the centre scroll, counting from the 1st scroll, miss 1, 3 single on the 6 chain. Work a Bar—4 chain, turn back—and missing 10 stitches of the centre scroll, work 2 single on it; join to the point of the 1st division of the bud, 6 single on the centre scroll, turn back. Work a Bar—3 chain; join to the 7th plain stitch of the 1st scroll, then 1 single in the point of the 3rd division of the bud, and down the side of it, 12 single. Work a Bar—2 chain, 1 single in the 2nd 2 chain of the 3rd flower. Work a Bar—3 chain; join to the 1st plain stitch of the 1st scroll, turn back—4 single on the top of the 1st scroll, and down the chain stitches of it, 10 single, turn back—7 chain, turn so as to work on the 2nd side of the stripe; pass this chain at the back to cross the centre scroll; join it to the 14th plain stitch of the 1st division of the 2nd side of the centre scroll, 3 chain, 1 single in the 2nd 2 chain of the 3rd flower of the 2nd side. Work a Bar—6 chain, join to the 6th stitch of the 1st division of the centre scroll, miss 1, 4 single on the 6 chain. Work a Bar—4 chain, join to the 1st plain stitch of the 4th scroll, 4 chain, 1 single on the centre of the 8 treble of the 3rd flower. Work a Bar—6 chain, join to the 6th chain stitch of the 4th scroll, miss 1, 2 single on the 6 chain. Work a Bar—6 chain, join to the 15th stitch of the stem of the small pine, miss 1, 3 single, on the 6 chain. Work a Bar—2 chain, join to the 3rd stitch of the stem of the pine. Work a Bar—2 chain, and missing the last 2 bars, work 1 treble on the 2nd stitch of the 3 chain left after working the last 2 single. Work a Bar—2 chain, 1 single in the next 2 chain of the 3rd flower, 4 chain, join to the point of the 3rd division of the pine, always taking the stitch at the back. Work a Bar—2 chain, 1 treble on the last 2 plain of the 3rd flower. Work a Bar—1 chain, and missing 9 stitches of the centre scroll, work 6 single on it. Work a Bar—2 chain, join to the 6th single stitch of the centre division of the pine. Work a Bar—3 chain and missing 7 stitches of the centre scroll, work 3 single on it. Work a Bar—2 chain, miss 10, 1 single on the 6th chain stitch of the 5th scroll, 4 chain, join to the point of the 1st division of the pine. Work a double Bar—7 chain, join to the 3rd chain stitch of the stem of the pine, miss 1, 2 single on the 7 chain. Work a Bar—3 chain, join to the centre stitch of the 5th division of the oval flower, 4 chain, 1 treble on the 2nd 2 chain of the double bar. Work a bar—3 chain, 1 single on the 1st plain stitch of the 5th scroll, 1 chain, join to the 4th division of the oval flower. Work a Bar—2 chain, and missing 9 stitches of the 5th scroll, work 7 single on the centre scroll, which will bring it to the 6th scroll of the 2nd side.

† † then 6 chain, turn, and cross this chain under the centre scroll as before, so as to work on the 1st side of the stripe; join to the 10th stitch of the centre scroll, counting from the 5th division of the 1st side, then 3 chain; join to the 1st plain stitch of the 5th division of the centre scroll. Work a Bar—3 chain, and missing 6 stitches of the centre scroll, work 1 treble on it. Work a Bar—3 chain, miss 13, 1 single, then on the top of the 5th scroll of the 1st side, 5 single, and on the plain stitches, 5 single. Work a Bar—1 chain, miss 14, 1 single on the 9th stitch of the stem of the pine, 6 single more on the stem. Work a Bar—3 chain, 1 plain on the back of the 5th plain stitch of the 1st division of the pine, 4 chain, join to the 5th stitch of the 10 single on the 5th scroll. Work a Bar—3 chain, join to the 2nd plain stitch of the centre division of the pine. Work a Bar—join to the point of the 5th division of the centre scroll, turn back—4 single on the 5th division, turn back. Work a Bar—2 chain, 1 single on the 10th plain stitch of the centre division of the pine. Work a Bar—5 chain, join to the 10th stitch of the 5th division of the centre scroll, miss 1, 3 single on the last 5 chain, join to the point of the 4th division of the centre scroll. Work a Bar—3 chain, 1 single on the point of the 3rd division of the pine. Work a Bar—6 chain, join to the 15th stitch of the 4th division of the centre scroll, miss 1, 4 single on the 6 chain. Work a Bar—1 treble on the 5th single stitch of the 3rd division of the pine. Work a double Bar—3 chain, join to the 8th stitch of the 4th division of the centre scroll. Work a Bar—2 chain, join to the 5th plain stitch of the stem of the 4th flower. Work a Bar—2 chain, 1 treble on the 2nd 2 chain of the double bar, 2 chain, join to the last 2 plain of the 4th flower. Work a Bar—2 chain, and missing 2 stitches, work 1 treble on the pine. Work a Bar—3 chain, turn back, and work 8 single on the 8 treble of the 4th flower, turn back. Work a double Bar—5 chain, join to the 1st 2 plain of the 4th flower, miss 1, 2 single on the 5 chain. Work a Bar—5 chain, join to the 14th stitch of the stem of the 4th flower, counting from the 4th scroll, miss 1, 2 single on the 5 chain. Work a Bar—3 chain, miss 9, join to the 5th stitch of the stem, work 5 chain; turn so as to work on the 2nd side of the stripe; pass this chain under the centre scroll so as to cross it, and putting the needle into the opposite stitch, join it: this stitch will be the 12th plain stitch of the 4th division of the 2nd side of the centre scroll, turn back—work 11 single on the 4th division, turn back. Work a Bar—6 chain, join to the 14th stitch of the stem of the rose, miss 1, 3 single on the 6 chain. Work a Bar—4 chain, turn back—miss 6,

and work 4 single on the stem of the rose, turn back. Work a Bar—2 chain, join to the 6th plain stitch of the 1st division of the rose. Work a Bar—1 chain, 1 treble on the 2 chain left after working the 3 single. Work a Bar—2 chain, then 2 single on the 6th and 5th stitches of the 11 single worked on the 4th division of the centre scroll. Work a Bar—2 chain, join to the 2nd plain stitch of the 1st division of the rose. Work a Bar—2 chain, then missing 9 stitches of the centre scroll, counting from the 2 single, work 6 single on it, 6 chain, join to the centre 2 chain of the rose, miss 1, 5 single on the 6 chain, and on the centre scroll, 6 single. Work a Bar—3 chain, join to the last plain stitch of the 3rd division of the rose. Work a Bar—4 chain, and missing 5 stitches of the centre scroll, work 3 single on it. Work a Bar—3 chain, miss 17, 1 single on the 10th chain stitch of the next scroll, which is the 1st scroll of the next pattern of the 2nd side. Work a Bar—3 chain, join to the 3rd plain stitch of the 3rd division of the rose. Work a double Bar—4 chain, miss 7, join to the last chain stitch of the stem of the rose. Work a Bar—4 chain, join to the 12th plain stitch of the 7th scroll of the 2nd side. Work a double Bar—5 chain, 1 plain on the 2nd 2 chain of the 1st double bar. Work a Bar—3 chain, 1 treble on the 2 chain next the 1 single on the 1st scroll, 4 chain, 1 single on the last chain stitch of the scroll. Work a Bar—9 chain, join to the the 3rd stitch of the 5 chain worked after the last double bar, miss 1, 6 single on the 9 chain. Work a Bar—4 chain, 1 single on the 1st plain stitch of the 1st scroll. Repeat from the commencement once more, then repeat from the commencement to the end of the 5th scroll of the 2nd side, which will finish the stripe. Fasten off.

SECOND STRIPE.

Commence with part of a scroll, thus—work 23 chain, turn, miss 1, 14 plain, 2 single, turn back—16 single, turn back—6 plain, 2 single; then work from the 3rd division of the centre scroll of the 1st side of the 1st stripe, page 7, and repeat the direction to the end of the 6th scroll; then work from * at the commencement of the 1st stripe to the end of the 6th scroll twice, ending with, "on the lower row of the centre scroll, 1 plain and 1 single," which makes this stripe two patterns and a half in length; and for the

2nd Side of the Stripe—Work 7 plain and 3 single more on the centre scroll; then work from the 6th scroll in the directions for the 2nd *side* of the 1st stripe, page 12, and repeat to the end; then, commencing at the two * * in the 1st part of the 2nd side of the 1st stripe, page 10. Repeat the direction twice; and to finish the stripe, work the 1st scroll and 1st flower of the 2nd side. Fasten off.

CENTRE BARS FOR THE SECOND STRIPE.

Commence on the 1st chain stitch of the 1st scroll of the 2nd side of the stripe, then repeat from the † † marked in the centre bars for the 1st stripe, page 16, work to the end, then repeat from the commencement of the direction for the bars to the end twice. Fasten off.

BARS TO JOIN THE TWO STRIPES.

Commence in the 4th stitch of the 6 plain, worked at the commencement of the 2nd stripe, 5 chain, miss 8, 1 single on the 5th stitch of the 12 chain, worked for the division of the centre scroll. Work a double Bar—12 chain, join to the centre treble stitch of the 2nd division of the oval flower of the 1st stripe. Work a Bar—3 chain, miss 5, join to the 1st division of the flower. Work a Bar—6 chain, turn back, and missing 7 stitches of the centre scroll of the 1st stripe; work 4 single on it, turn back. Work a double Bar—3 chain, 1 treble in the 2nd stitch of the 6 chain of the last bar. Work a Bar—2 chain, 1 single on the 2nd stitch of the 12 chain, *. Work a Bar—4 chain, 1 single on the point of the division of the centre scroll of the 2nd stripe. Work a Bar —2 chain, join to the 2nd 2 chain of the double bar. Work a Bar—3 chain, and missing 7 stitches of the centre scroll of the 2nd stripe, work 4 single on it. Work a

Bar—3 chain, turn back, and missing 4 stitches of the centre scroll of the 1st stripe, work 4 single on it, turn back. Work a Bar—4 chain, miss 5 stitches of the centre scroll of the 2nd stripe, and work 8 single up the scroll. Work a Bar—2 chain, miss 5, join it to the 6th stitch of the centre scroll of the 1st stripe, counting from the 4 single. Work a Bar—4 chain, miss 14, join to the 9th plain stitch of the scroll of the 1st stripe. Work a Bar—2 chain, 1 single on the 1st plain stitch of the scroll of the 2nd stripe. Work a Bar—3 chain, 2 single on the 1st 2 chain of the bar worked after the double bar in the centre bars of 2nd stripe; then 2 single on the next 2 chain of the double bar, and 2 single on the centre 2 chain of the double bar, then work 3 chain, join to the 1st plain stitch of the scroll of the 1st stripe. Work a double Bar—5 chain, join to the 11th chain stitch of the scroll of the 1st stripe. Work a Bar—3 chain, join to the 18th plain stitch of the centre scroll, counting from the next scroll, turn back, and on the centre scroll, 5 single, 3 chain, join to the 2nd 2 chain of the double bar, miss 1, 2 single on the 3 chain, and on the centre scroll 7 single, turn back. Work a Bar—2 chain, 1 single on the 3rd treble stitch of the flower of the 2nd stripe, 4 single more on the flower. Work a Bar—4 chain, join to the last chain stitch of the next scroll of the 1st stripe. Work a Bar—2 chain, 1 treble on the 2 chain of the bar worked after the treble stitch on the pine in the centre bars. Work a Bar—3 chain, and missing 3 stitches of the stem of the pine, work 4 single on it. Work a double Bar—2 chain, join to the 5th chain stitch of the scroll of the 1st stripe. Work a Bar—3 chain, join to the 8th stitch of the centre scroll, counting from the last scroll. Work a Bar—2 chain, 1 treble on the 1st 2 chain of the double bar. Work a Bar—2 chain, miss 5, 1 treble on the stem of the pine; join to the 6th 2 chain of the flower of the 1st stripe. Work a Bar—2 chain, miss 4, 1 single on the stem of the pine. Work a Bar—3 chain, miss 9, 4 single on the next scroll of the 2nd stripe. Work a Bar—5 chain, join to the 2nd 2 *chain* of the *flower*. Work a Bar—5 chain, join to the 5th stitch of the 6 single in the centre bars of the 1st stripe, miss 1, 3 single on the 5 chain. Work a Bar—3 chain, 1 treble on the last chain stitch of the scroll of the 2nd stripe. Work a Bar—3 chain, join to the 8th plain stitch of the next scroll of the 1st stripe, turn back—work 3 single on the scroll, turn back. Work a Bar—3 chain, 1 single on the 1st plain stitch of the scroll of the 2nd stripe; work 6 single more on the scroll. Work a Bar—3 chain, miss 15, 7 single on the centre scroll of the 2nd stripe, 5 chain; join to the 4th plain stitch of the scroll of the 1st stripe, miss 1, 4 single on the 5 chain and 4 single on the centre scroll; 2 chain, join to the 1st plain stitch of the scroll of the 1st stripe. Work a double Bar—2 chain, join to the 9th stitch of the centre scroll of the 1st stripe, counting from the stem of the flower. Work a Bar—3 chain, join to the last 2 plain of the flower. Work a Bar—2 chain, 1 treble on the 2nd 2 chain of the double bar. Work a Bar—2 chain, and missing 7 stitches of the centre scroll of the 2nd stripe, work 4 single on it. Work a Bar—4 chain, join to the last treble stitch of the flower in the 1st stripe. Work a Bar—4 chain, miss 9, 1 single on the centre scroll of the 2nd stripe. Work a Bar—2 chain, 1 single on the 3rd plain stitch of the flower of the 2nd stripe. Work a Bar—3 chain, join to the 1st treble stitch of the flower of the 1st stripe. Work a double Bar—6 chain, join to the 1st plain stitch of the same flower, miss 1, 3 single on the 6 chain, 3 chain, turn back, and missing 9 stitches of the centre scroll, work 9 single on it, turn back. Work a Bar—2 chain, 1 treble on the 2nd 2 chain of the double bar. Work a Bar—2 chain, 1 single on the centre stitch of the 1st 6 treble of the flower of the 2nd stripe. Work a Bar—3 chain, join to the 6th stitch of the centre scroll of the 1st stripe. Work a Bar—4 chain, miss 10, 1 single on the 2nd 6 treble of the flower. Work a Bar—5 chain, miss 8, 1 single on the 3rd 6 treble of the flower, 2 chain, 1 single on the top of the next scroll of the 2nd stripe. Work a Bar—3 chain, 1 single in the 4th 2 chain of the next flower of the 2nd stripe, 4 chain, join to the 1st stitch of the 5 chain in the last bar but one, miss 1,

3 single on the 4 chain. Work a Bar—3 chain, join to the point of the division of the centre scroll of the 1st stripe, 3 chain, 1 treble in the 6th 2 chain of the flower. Work a Bar—3 chain, join to the point of the next division of the centre scroll of the 1st stripe. Work a Bar—3 chain, join to the 1st plain stitch of the next scroll of the 1st stripe. Work a Bar—2 chain, 1 treble on the 2 chain of the last bar but one. Work a Bar—2 chain, 1 treble on the last 2 plain of the 3rd flower. Work a Bar—1 chain, 1 single on the 8th stitch of the stem of the flower. Work a Bar—4 chain, join to the last chain stitch of the same scroll of the 1st stripe. Work a Bar—2 chain, join to the centre stitch of the oval flower. Work a Bar—3 chain, and missing 5 stitches of the centre scroll of the 2nd stripe, work 5 single on it, 2 chain, 5 single on the plain stitches of the next scroll of the 2nd stripe, 3 chain, join to the 3rd stitch of the oval flower. Work a Bar—6 chain, turn back, and missing 7 stitches of the centre scroll of the 1st stripe, work 4 single on it, turn back. Work a double Bar—3 chain, 1 treble on the 2nd stitch of the 6 chain. Work a Bar—3 chain, miss 5 stitches of the scroll of the 2nd stripe, work 4 single on it. Repeat from *, page 19, until the stripes are joined, ending at the flower marked in italics, page 20.

BARS FOR THE EDGE AND SIDES OF THE COLLAR.

Commence in the 6th plain stitch of the last scroll in the 1st side of the 1st stripe, and work down the side, 8 chain, miss 3, 1 treble, 6 chain, miss 6, 1 treble, 4 chain, 1 single on the last chain stitch of the next scroll, 3 chain, 1 single on the 1st plain stitch of the scroll, 7 chain, 1 single on the last chain stitch of the next scroll, 4 chain, 1 single on the 1st plain stitch of the scroll, 4 chain, 1 treble in the 2nd 2 chain of the flower, 6 chain, 1 single on the last plain stitch of the next scroll, 5 chain, 1 single on the 1st plain stitch of the scroll; 5 chain, miss 7, 1 treble, 9 chain, miss 7, 1 treble, 10 chain, 1 plain on the last chain stitch of the next scroll, then along the stripe for the

EDGE—*, 5 chain, 1 single on the 1st plain stitch of the same scroll; then 7 chain, 1 treble on the point of the 1st division of the centre scroll; 6 chain, 1 plain on the point of the 2nd division of the centre scroll; 8 chain, miss 6, 1 plain on the centre scroll; 16 chain, miss 8, 1 single on the centre scroll. Work a double Bar—4 chain, miss 6, 1 plain on the centre scroll. Work a Bar—3 chain, 1 single on the 6th stitch of the stem of the 1st flower, 4 chain; pass this chain under the stem and join it to the opposite side. Work a double Bar—3 chain, miss 10, 5 single on the centre scroll. Work a Bar—2 chain, 1 single in the last chain stitch of the 2nd scroll. Work a Bar—8 chain, join to the 2nd 2 chain of the double bar to the right, miss 1, 2 single on the 8 chain. Work a Bar—7 chain, turn back—work 8 single on the treble stitches of the flower, turn back. Work a Bar—4 chain, join to the 2nd 2 chain of the double bar, miss 1, 2 single on the 4 chain. Work a Bar—4 chain, join to the 7th stitch of the 16 chain; then 10 chain, 1 single on the centre of the 8 single of the flower; 7 chain, 1 plain on the 3rd stitch of the 7 chain of the next bar; 7 chain, 1 treble on the 2nd stitch of the 5 chain in the next bar; 6 chain, 1 single on the 1st plain stitch of the next scroll; 3 chain, miss 3, 1 single on the scroll; 7 chain, 1 treble on the 2nd 2 chain of the double bar; 8 chain, 1 treble on the 5th stitch of the 6 single worked in the centre bars; then 7 chain, 1 plain in the 4th 2 chain of the next flower; "6 *chain*, 1 *plain in the* 6th 2 *chain of the flower*;" 6 chain, 1 treble on the last 3 chain of the next bar; 7 chain, 1 single on the last chain stitch of the next scroll; 4 chain, 1 single on the 1st plain stitch of the scroll; 9 chain, miss 12, 1 treble on the centre scroll; 9 chain, miss 7, 4 single on the centre scroll. Work a Bar—4 chain, miss 14, 11 single up the next scroll to the 1st plain stitch of it; 3 chain, join to the 6th stitch of the 9 chain worked before the 4 single, then 8 chain, miss 4, 1 plain on the 5th plain stitch of the scroll; 5 chain, miss 4, 1 plain, 8 chain, miss 11, 1 treble on the centre scroll; 9 chain, miss 8, 1 plain, 8 chain, miss 7, 1 treble, 8 chain,

1 single on the 1st division of the oval flower; 5 chain, miss 4, 1 single on the flower; 4 chain, miss 4, 1 treble on the flower; 3 chain, 1 plain in the last chain stitch of the next scroll. Repeat from * along the stripe, ending with "6 *chain,* 1 *plain in the* 2 *chain of the* 2nd *flower,*" marked in italics; and up

The other side of the collar, 8 chain, 1 treble in the 7th 2 chain of the flower; 9 chain, 1 treble on the last stitch of the stem, 7 chain, miss 6, 1 treble on the part of the scroll worked at the commencement of the stripe; 7 chain, miss 9, 1 treble, 5 chain, miss 5, 1 plain, 4 chain, 1 single on the 6th stitch of the 12 chain, 3 chain, miss 3, 1 single more on the 12 chain, 10 chain, 1 plain on the centre stitch of the oval flower; 4 chain, 1 single on the last stitch of the stripe; and to form the

Neck—4 chain, miss 4, 1 treble on the 1st side of the centre scroll, 17 chain, miss 5, 1 single on the 1st side of the 1st stripe, turn back—miss 1, 5 single on the 17 chain, turn back—9 chain, miss 10, 1 treble on the centre scroll, (3 chain, miss 4 and 1 treble, 4 times).

* *, 8 chain, 6 single on the 1st 6 treble of the 1st flower, 6 chain, miss 9, 6 single on the flower, 2 chain, 1 treble on the top of the 1st scroll; 2 chain, 1 single, in the 5th 2 chain of the next flower; 3 chain, join to the 4th stitch of the last 6 chain, then 6 chain, 1 treble in the 7th 2 chain of the flower; 7 chain, 1 treble in the 7th stitch of the centre scroll; 5 chain, miss 5, 1 treble, 4 chain, 9 single on the plain stitches of the next scroll; 3 chain, 1 single on the point of the division of the centre scroll; 5 chain, 1 plain on the 6th stitch of the centre scroll; 8 chain, join to the 7th stitch of the last 9 single, miss 1, 7 single on the 8 chain, then 7 chain, miss 8, 1 treble on the centre scroll; 8 chain, miss 7, 4 single along the top of the next scroll; 2 chain, 1 single on the centre 2 chain of the double bar; 5 chain, 1 single on the centre stitch of the flower; 7 chain, 1 treble on the 3 chain of the next bar; 7 chain, 1 plain on the 4th stitch of the stem of the pine (4 chain, miss 5 and 1 plain, twice), 7 chain, miss 16, 1 plain on the 9th stitch of the next scroll; 4 cnain, miss 5, 1 plain, 5 chain, 1 single on the 1st plain stitch of the scroll, 6 single more on the scroll; 2 chain, 1 single on the 7th stitch of centre scroll, 4 single more on the centre scroll; 3 chain, join to the 3rd stitch of the last 5 chain, then 5 chain, miss 5, 1 treble on the centre scroll; (4 chain, miss 5 and 1 treble, twice). Repeat from * * to the end of the stripe; and to form the

Pearl Edging—Work down the side of the collar, 3 plain, 4 chain, 1 plain on the top of the last plain stitch. Repeat along the edge and up the other side; then along the neck, miss 1, 6 plain. Repeat, and fasten off.

Guipure Berthe.

Materials and Rules—See Page 3.

1st Stripe—Work as directed for the 1st stripe of the collar, making 5 patterns and a half, or 6 patterns and a half, according to the size; then work the centre bars for the 1st stripe, page 14.

2nd Stripe—Work as the 2nd stripe of the collar, page 18, making the same number of patterns as the 1st stripe; work the bars of the 2nd stripe; then work the bars to join the 1st and 2nd stripes together, page 19.

3rd Stripe—Same as 1st.

4th Stripe—Same as the 2nd, then join the 3rd and 4th stripes together the same as the 1st and 2nd stripes; and to join these two pieces together, work thus—

BARS TO JOIN THE SECOND AND THIRD STRIPES.

Commence on the 1st stitch of the 3rd stripe. Work a double bar—8 chain, miss 5, 1 treble on the centre scroll of the 1st side of the stripe. Work a double Bar—4 chain, join to

E. Riego de la Branchardiere, Inventor, *May*, 1851.

the 5th 2 chain of the last flower of the 2nd stripe. Work a Bar—5 chain, 1 treble on the 1st 2 chain of the last double bar. Work a Bar—3 chain, miss 5, 4 single on the centre scroll of the 3rd stripe. Work a Bar—4 chain, join to the 3rd stitch of the 5 chain in the last bar but one, miss 1, 2 single on the 4 chain. Work a Bar—2 chain, join to the 2nd 2 chain of the flower, *, then 6 chain, join to the 2 chain after the 6 single in the centre bars of the 2nd stripe, miss 1, 3 single on the 6 chain. Work a Bar—4 chain, 1 treble on the 1st 2 chain of the last bar worked. Work a Bar—2 chain, and missing 4 stitches of the centre scroll of the 3rd stripe, work 4 single on it. Work a double Bar—5 chain, join to the 2nd stitch of the 4 chain worked before the last treble, miss 1, 3 single on the 5 chain. Work a Bar—2 chain, join to the centre 2 chain of the double bar of the 2nd stripe. Work a Bar—2 chain, join to the 7th plain stitch of the next scroll of the 2nd stripe, 2 chain, 1 treble on the centre 2 chain of the last double bar, 5 chain, miss 4, 6 single on the centre scroll of the 3rd stripe, 2 chain, join to the 1st plain stitch of the scroll of the 2nd stripe. Work a Bar—2 chain,1 single in the 2nd treble stitch of the flower in the 3rd stripe. Work a Bar—5 chain, join to the 17th chain stitch of the scroll in the 2nd stripe, counting from the stem of the next flower, miss 1, 3 single on the 5 chain. Work a Bar—4 chain, miss 9, join to the 8th stitch of the scroll of the 2nd stripe. Work a Bar—3 chain, join to the last 2 chain of the flower of the 2nd stripe. Work a Bar—3 chain, 1 treble on the 2 chain of the bar worked after the 3 single. Work a Bar—4 chain, 2 single on the centre treble stitches of the flower in the 3rd stripe, 3 chain, join to the 6th treble stitch in the flower of the 2nd stripe. Work a Bar—3 chain, miss 9, 1 treble on the flower of the 3rd stripe, 2 chain, 2 single on the top of the next scroll of the 3rd stripe. Work a Bar—3 chain, 1 single in the 4th 2 chain of the next flower in the 3rd stripe. Work a Bar—4 chain, join to the 1st treble stitch of the flower in the 2nd stripe. Work a double Bar—3 chain, join to the 1st plain stitch of the flower of the 2nd stripe.

Work a Bar—3 chain, join to the 7th chain stitch of the stem of the flower, 4 chain, turn back, and missing 5 stitches of the centre scroll of the 2nd stripe, work 10 single on it; then 4 chain, join to the 2nd 2 chain of the last double bar, miss 1, 3 single on the 4 chain, then 6 single on the centre scroll, turn back. Work a Bar—2 chain, 1 treble on the 1st 2 chain of the same double bar, 4 chain, 1 single in the 7th 2 chain of the flower in the 3rd stripe. Work a Bar—4 chain, 1 single on the 7th plain stitch of the stem of the same flower. Work a Bar—2 chain, turn back, and missing 4 stitches of the centre scroll of 2nd stripe, work 5 single on it, turn back, and missing 2 stitches of the centre scroll of the 3rd stripe, work 6 single on it, 4 chain, 1 single on the 1st plain stitch of the next scroll of the 3rd stripe. Work a Bar—2 chain, join to the point of the next division of the centre scroll of the 2nd stripe. Work a Bar—3 chain, join to the 1st plain stitch of the next scroll of the 2nd stripe. Work a Bar—2 chain, miss 3, 5 *single on the scroll of the 3rd stripe.* Work a Bar—6 chain, join to the last chain stitch of the next scroll in the 2nd stripe, miss 1, 2 single on the 6 chain. Work a Bar—2 chain, turn back—1 single on the centre treble stitch of the oval flower, work 6 single more on the flower, turn back. Work a Bar—2 chain, 1 treble on the 2 chain worked after the 5 single on the scroll of the 3rd stripe. Work a double Bar—3 chain, miss 5, 2 single on the scroll of the 3rd stripe. Work a Bar—6 chain, miss 16, 1 single on the point of the division of the centre scroll of the 3rd stripe. Work a Bar—6 chain, join to the 2nd 2 chain of the double bar, miss 1, 3 single on the 6 chain. Work a Bar—3 chain, join to the 4th stitch of the oval flower. Work a Bar—3 chain, 1 treble on the point of the same division of the centre scroll of the 3rd stripe. Work a Bar—4 chain, turn back—miss 6, 6 single on the centre scroll of the 2nd stripe, counting from the oval flower, turn back. Work a double Bar—3 chain, 1 treble on the 2 chain of the last bar. Work a Bar—2 chain, miss 6, 12 single on the centre scroll of the 3rd stripe, 5 chain, join to the 2nd 2 chain of the double bar, miss 1, 4 single on the 5 chain, 4 single on the centre scroll, 3 chain, turn back, and missing 4 stitches of the centre scroll of the 2nd stripe, work 7 single on it, turn back. Work a Bar—2 chain, 1 single on the 1st plain stitch of the scroll of the 3rd stripe. Work a Bar—4 chain, join to the 9th plain stitch of the scroll of the 2nd stripe, miss 1, 3 single on the 4 chain. Work a Bar—3 chain, miss 9, 1 treble on the 4th stitch of the centre scroll of 3rd stripe. Work a Bar—2 chain, 2 single on the last 2 chain of the double bar in the centre bars in the 3rd stripe, 2 single on the next 2 chain of the double bar; join to the 4th plain stitch of the scroll of the 2nd stripe, then 2 single on the next 2 chain of the double bar, and 3 single on the treble stitches of the flower, 3 chain, join to the 1st plain stitch of the scroll of the 2nd stripe. Work a double Bar—6 chain, join to the 12th chain stitch of the scroll, miss 1, 3 single on the 6 chain. Work a Bar—2 chain, turn back, and missing 5 stitches of the centre scroll of the 2nd stripe, work 6 single on it. Work a double Bar—3 chain, miss 6, 4 single on the centre scroll, 5 chain, miss 8, 1 treble on the 1st plain stitch of the next scroll, turn back. Work a double Bar—4 chain, 1 single on the 2nd 2 chain of the last double bar, 4 chain, 1 treble on the centre 2 chain of the double bar that was joined to the scroll. Work a Bar—5 chain, 1 single on the last treble stitch of the flower of the 3rd stripe, 8 chain; join to the 2nd 2 chain of the last double bar, miss 1, 3 single on the 8 chain. Work a Bar—2 chain, and missing 2 stitches of the stem of the pine, work 8 single on it, 1 chain, join to the last chain stitch of the scroll of the 2nd stripe. Work a Bar—5 chain, miss 12, join to the 6th stitch of the centre scroll of the 2nd stripe, miss 1, 2 single on the 5 chain. Work a Bar—2 chain, and missing 4 stitches of the stem of the pine, work 4 single on it; 3 chain, join to the 5th 2 chain of the next flower of the 2nd stripe, 4 chain, miss 11, 8 single on the chain stitches of the next scroll of the 3rd stripe, 5 single on the top, and 7 single on the plain stitches of the scroll. Work a Bar—2 chain, miss 17, 7 single on the centre scroll of the 3rd stripe. Work a Bar—4 chain, join to the 11th single stitch of the scroll of the 3rd stripe, miss 1, 2 single on the 4 chain. Work a Bar—2 chain, join to the 2nd 2 chain of the flower in the 2nd stripe. Repeat from *, page 28, until the stripes are joined, ending with the 5 *single* marked in italics. Fasten off.

BARS FOR THE EDGE AND SIDES.

Commence on the 1st plain stitch of the last scroll of the 1st side of the 1st stripe, and for the side, 6 chain, miss 4, 1 plain, *, 8 chain, miss 3, 1 treble, 6 chain, miss 6, 1 treble, 4 chain, 1 single on the last chain stitch of the next scroll; 3 chain, 1 single on the 1st plain stitch of the scroll, 7 chain, 1 single on the last chain stitch of the next scroll; 4 chain, 1 treble on the 1st plain stitch of the scroll; 4 chain, 1 treble in the 2nd 2 chain of the flower; 6 chain, 1 single on the last chain stitch of the next scroll; 5 chain, 1 single on the 1st plain stitch of the scroll; 5 chain, miss 7, 1 treble, 9 chain, miss 7, 1 treble, 10 chain, 1 plain on the last chain stitch of the next scroll. Repeat from * once more; then to form the

EDGE—Work as directed, page 23, and continuing along the stripe, repeat as directed up the side, ending at the 10th line of page 24, and to finish the side, 9 chain, 1 plain on the centre 2 chain of the double bar; 10 chain, 1 plain on the 1st stitch of the 4 chain in the next double bar; 9 chain, 1 plain on the 7th 2 chain of the next flower; 6 chain, 1 treble on the last stitch of the stem; 7 chain, miss 6, 1 treble, 7 chain, miss 9, 1 treble, 5 chain, miss 5, 1 plain, 6 chain, 1 single on the 6th stitch of the 12 chain; 3 chain, miss 3, 1 single, 10 chain, 1 plain in the centre stitch of the flower; 4 chain, 1 single on the last stitch of the stripe. Then to form the Neck—work along the top, as directed for the neck in page 24, of the collar. When finished, to form the

Foundation Row of the edging—Work down the side, thus—miss 1, 7 plain in the

6 chain, (always work the plain stitches in each loop of the chain in the last row), †, miss 1, 11 plain in the 8 chain, miss 1, 8 plain in the 6 chain, miss 1, 5 plain in the 4 chain, miss 1, 4 plain, miss 1, 11 plain, miss 1, 5 plain, miss 1, 7 plain, miss 1, 8 plain, miss 1, 6 plain, miss 1, 7 plain, miss 1, 12 plain, miss 1, 13 plain. Repeat from † once more, then along the edge.

*, miss 1, 5 plain, (miss 1 and 8 plain, 8 times), miss 1, 4 plain, (miss 1 and 8 plain, 3 times), miss 1, 6 *plain*, miss 1, 8 plain, miss 1, 10 plain, miss 1, 5 plain, miss 1, 13 plain, (miss 1 and 6 plain, 3 times), (miss 1 and 9 plain, 4 times), (miss 1 and 6 plain, 3 times.) Repeat from *, ending with the 6 *plain* marked in italics; then up the other side (miss 1 and 12 plain, twice), (miss 1 and 10 plain, twice), (miss 1 and 7 plain, twice), miss 1, 4 plain, miss 1, 12 plain, miss 1, 4 plain, (miss 1 and 12 plain, 4 times), (miss 1 and 10 plain, twice), (miss 1 and 7 plain, twice), miss 1, 4 plain, miss 1, 12 plain, (miss 1 and 6 plain, twice), miss 1, 12 plain; then along the neck, work a plain row; and for the

Edging, 1st Scollop—Work down the side on the plain stitches of the foundation row, 27 single, always taking both edges of the stitches, 9 chain, turn, and missing the last 5 single, join to the 22nd stitch of the 27 single; and for the

1st row—2 plain in the 9 chain, (4 chain, 1 single on the top of the last plain stitch, and 3 plain in the 9 chain, 5 times); then on the foundation row, 5 single, turn back.

2nd—10 chain, 1 plain in the centre 4 chain of the 1st row; 10 chain, and missing 4 of the single stitches, work 2 single on the 16th and 15th stitches of the 27 single, turn back.

3rd—Miss 2, 3 plain in the last 10 chain, (4 chain and 7 plain in the same 10 chain, twice), 4 chain, 3 plain in the same 10 chain; then 1 plain on the plain stitch between the 10 chains, and in the next 10 chain, work 3 plain, (4 chain and 7 plain, twice), 4 chain, 3 plain; then on the foundation row, 3 single, turn back.

4th row—(7 chain, miss 8 and 3 single on the centre stitches of the 7 plain in the 3rd row, 5 times); then 7 chain, and missing 2 of the single stitches, work 2 single on the 12th and 11th stitches of the 27 single, turn back.

5th—Miss 2, (3 plain and 4 chain in the 7 chain, 3 times), 3 plain in the same 7 chain, making in all 12 plain stitches, then miss 1, 1 single on the 3 single of the last row. Repeat from the commencement of the row, 5 times more, which finishes the 1st scollop. Repeat the scollop along the edge and up the other side; and for the

Edging at the Neck—Work 10 single, then 10 chain, turn, join to the 5th stitch of the 10 single, miss 1, 2 plain in the 10 chain, (4 chain, 1 single on the top of the last plain stitch, and 3 plain in the 10 chain, 5 times.) Repeat and fasten off.

ROSE POINT COLLAR.

Materials and Rules—See Page 3.

THE FLOWERS AND LEAVES.

Commence with 21 chain; and for the

1st Small Flower—Turn, miss 7, 1 single in the 8th stitch to form a round loop, turn.

1st row—1 chain to cross, 14 plain in the round loop, turn back.

2nd—Work the single stitches in the lower edge of the stitches of the 1st row, (4 chain, miss 1 and 1 single, 7 times), turn back: this row forms a raised centre to the flower.

3rd—Work 14 plain on the upper edge of the stitches of the 1st row, keeping the 2nd row down in the front, turn back.

4th—(5 chain and 2 plain, 7 times), taking both edges of the stitches in the previous row, turn back.

5th—(Miss 1, 1 single on the 2 plain, and 6 plain in the 5 chain, 7 times); then 2 chain, 1 single in the round loop, then down the stem, 1 plain, 3 treble, 8 single, leaving 1 chain, then 27 chain; and for the

ROSE POINT COLLAR
E. RIEGO DE LA BRANCHARDIERE
INVENT.
SEPT. 1851.

1st LONG LEAF, 1st row—Turn, miss 1, (2 plain and 2 plain in one, 5 times), 1 single, turn back.

2nd—Work on the lower edge of the stitches of the 1st row, (1 chain and 1 single, 19 times), 2 single, turn back.

3rd—Work on the upper edge of the stitches of the 1st row, leaving the 2nd row in front, 2 plain, (1 chain, miss 1 and 1 treble, 8 times), 1 chain, miss 1, 2 plain; then on the stem, 4 single, leaving 6 chain; then 35 chain for the

LARGE FLOWER and CALYX—Turn, miss 7, 2 single, 8 plain, turn, 1 chain to cross the stem, and up the other side, 10 plain.

1st row—14 plain in the round loop, turn back.

2nd—Work on the lower edge of the 1st row (4 chain and 1 single, 14 times), turn back.

3rd—Work on the upper edge of the 1st row, keeping the 2nd row in front, (2 plain in one and 3 plain, 3 times), 2 plain in one, 1 single, turn back.

4th—(4 chain and 2 plain, 9 times), taking both edges of the previous row, turn back.

5th—(4 chain, miss 4, 1 plain in the 4 chain, 9 times), turn back.

6th—(Miss 1 and 5 plain in the 4 chain, 9 times), turn back.

7th—Work on the upper edge of the last row, (3 chain and 1 single, 45 times), turn back.

8th—Keep the 7th row down at the back, and work on the lower edge of the 6th row, (5 chain, miss 1 and 2 plain, 15 times), turn back.

9th—(Miss 1, 1 single on the 2 plain, and 6 plain in the 5 chain, 10 times), 1 single; and before completing the flower, repeat from the commencement 7 times more; then repeat the 1st flower, when finished, work 9 chain, turn, miss 1 and 7 plain on the 9 chain, leaving 1 chain; and for the

* SMALL LEAF—15 chain, turn, miss 2, 1 plain, (1 chain, miss 1 and 1 treble, 3 times), 1 chain, miss 1, 1 plain, turn, 1 chain to cross the stem; and for the

1st round—20 plain, 1 single, turn.

2nd—(1 chain and 1 single, 20 times), then on the stem, 3 single, and on the centre stem, 2 plain; then to finish the large flower, (1 single, miss 1, then 6 plain in the 5 chain as before, 5 times); 2 chain, 1 single in the side of the 4th row; 2 chain, 1 single in the round loop; then down the calyx, 10 plain, and down the stem 4 single, leaving 14 chain; and for the

2nd LONG LEAF—34 chain, and work the same as the 1st leaf. When finished, 13 single down the stem, leaving 4 chain; and for the

2nd SMALL FLOWER—20 chain, and work as the 1st flower. When finished, work, 4 single on the 4 chain left at the 2nd leaf, and 12 single down the stem of the large flower; then for the

ROSE LEAF—19 chain, turn, miss 3, 1 plain, (1 chain, miss 1 and 1 treble, 4 times), 1 chain, miss 1, 1 plain, turn, 1 chain to cross.

1st round—(Miss 1 and 3 plain in the 1 chain, 5 times); miss 1, 5 plain in the 3 chain at the point, turn, and down the other side, (miss 1 and 3 plain in the 1 chain, 5 times.)

2nd—1 plain, 2 treble in one, 1 plain and 1 single, 9 times; then down the stem, 4 single, and down the centre stem, 7 plain. Repeat from * 7 times more; then work another small leaf; and for the

BARS FOR THE FIRST SIDE OF THE COLLAR.

RULES to Form a Bar.—Work 4 chain, turn, miss 1, 2 single on the 4 chain, leaving 1 chain. For a double bar, 4 chain, turn, miss 1, 2 single, 4 chain, turn, miss 1, 2 single. Work thus whenever directed to work a Bar or double Bar.

Work a Bar—2 chain, 1 treble on the 6th chain stitch of the stem of the 1st flower; 3 chain, 1 single on the centre stitch of the 1st 6 plain of the flower. Work a Bar—3 chain, miss 6, 1 single on the flower. Work a double Bar—2 chain, miss 6, 1 single on the flower,*, Work a Bar—3 chain, miss 6, 1 single on the flower. Work a Bar—3 chain, miss 6, 1 treble. Work a Bar—4 chain, miss 6, 7 single on the flower. Work a double Bar—2 chain, miss 10, 2 single on the 1st single stitches of the stem of the flower. Work a Bar—1 chain, miss 10, 1 single on the 4th chain stitch of the centre stem. Work a Bar—2 chain, miss 6, 1 treble on the next leaf; 2 chain, join to the centre stitch of the double bar. Work a Bar—2 chain, and missing 5 stitches of the leaf, work 3 single up it. Work a Bar—join to the 4th stitch of the 7 single worked on the 1st flower. Work a Bar—3 chain, miss 4, 4 single up the leaf to the point of it; 5 chain, join to the 1st stitch of the bar worked before the 7 single, miss 1, 3 single on the 5 chain. Work a double Bar—4 chain, and missing 5 stitches of the leaf, work 14 single down the last row of it. Work a Bar—1 chain, miss 13, 1 single on the 7th chain stitch of the stem of the large flower. Work a double Bar—1 chain, miss 5, 1 treble on the stem of the flower. Work a Bar—2 chain, 1 single on the 2nd plain stitch of the calyx; 3 chain, 1 single on the centre stitch of the 1st 6 plain of the large flower. Work a Bar—5 chain, join to the centre stitch of the double bar; miss 1, 3 single on the 5 chain. Work a Bar—1 chain, miss 6, 1 single on the flower; 3 chain, join to the 9th stitch of the 14 single worked down the leaf. Work a Bar—1 chain, miss 6, 1 single on the flower, Work a Bar—1 chain, join to the 1st stitch of the 14 single; 1 chain, miss 6, 1 single on the flower; 4 chain, join to the centre stitch of the double bar. Work a Bar—3 chain, miss 6, 1 treble on the flower. Work a Bar—3 chain, miss 6, 1 treble. Work a Bar—3 chain, miss 6, 1 single. Work a double Bar—2 chain, miss 6, 9 single. Work a Bar—2 chain, 1 treble on the 6th chain stitch of the stem of the small flower; 3 chain, 1 single on the centre stitch of the 1st 6 plain of the small flower. Work a Bar—5 chain, join to the 4th stitch of the 9 single worked on the large flower; miss 1, 2 single on the 5 chain; 1 chain, miss 6, 1 single on the small flower; 3 chain, join to the centre stitch of the double bar. Work a Bar—3 chain, miss 6, 1 single on the flower. Repeat from * 7 times more. When finished,

Work a Bar—3 chain, miss 6, 1 single. Work a Bar—3 chain, miss 6, 1 treble. Work a Bar—4 chain, miss 6, 7 single. Work a double Bar—2 chain, miss 10, 2 single on the stem of the flower. Work a Bar—3 chain, miss 10, 2 single on the centre stem. Fasten off.

BARS FOR THE SECOND SIDE.

Commence in the 1st stitch of the last round of the last small leaf, and work a Bar—1 chain, join to the 5th plain stitch of the centre stem. Work a Bar—4 chain, 1 single in the 6th chain stitch of the small leaf; 5 chain, pass this chain under the stem of the rose leaf so as to cross it on the wrong side, take out the needle and join to the 2nd stitch of the stem of it on the other side. Work a Bar—3 chain, miss 6, join to the 6th stitch of the 12 single worked on the stem of the large flower. Work a Bar—1 chain, 1 single on the centre stitch of the 2nd division of the rose leaf. Work a Bar—2 chain, miss 6, join to the 3rd stitch of the 4 single worked on the stem of the 2nd leaf. Work a Bar—1 chain, 1 treble on the centre stitch of the 3rd division of the rose leaf; 4 chain, miss 5, join to the stem of the 2nd small flower; miss 1, 2 single on the last 4 chain. Work a Bar—1 single on the 4th division of the rose leaf. Work a Bar—1 chain, miss 3, join to the 1st single stitch of the stem of the 2nd flower; 3 chain, pass this chain under the stem as before, and join it to the 7th chain stitch of the stem on the other side. Work a Bar—1 chain, join to the 7th single stitch of the stem of the 2nd long leaf. Work a Bar—1 chain, 1 single on the 3rd plain stitch of the 2nd flower. Work a Bar—3 chain, pass this chain under the stem of the 2nd long leaf, join it to the last chain stitch but one of the stem on the other side. Work a double Bar—3 chain, miss 8 down the stem of the leaf, and join to the 6th chain stitch of it; 3 chain, join to the 7th plain stitch of the calyx of the large flower. Work a Bar—1 chain, 1 treble on the centre stitch of the double bar; 2 chain, join to the centre of the last 6 plain of the large flower; 1 chain, miss 2, 6 single on the 1st chain stitches of the 2nd long leaf; 2 chain, join to the 14th 6 plain of the large flower. Work a Bar—2 chain, miss 3, 1 single on the leaf. Work a Bar—3 chain, join to the 13th 6 plain of the flower. Work a Bar—2 chain, miss 5, 1 treble on the leaf. Work a Bar—2 chain, join to the 12th 6 plain of the flower; 1 chain, join to the 18th chain stitch of the small leaf; 7 chain, pass this chain under the leaf as before, and join to the 1st stitch of it. Repeat from the commencement (page 39) 7 times more. At the end work a Bar—2 chain, join to the 5th stitch of the centre stem, and fasten off.

EDGE—Commence in the centre stitch of the 1st double bar worked in the bars for the 1st side; and to form the neck, work a double Bar—3 chain, 1 single on the 1st stitch of the next bar †. Work a double Bar—3 chain, 1 single on the last stitch of the next bar. Work a double Bar—3 chain, 1 plain on the 1st stitch of the next Bar. (Work a double Bar, and 1 treble on the last stitch of the next bar, twice.) Work a double Bar—1 treble on the 1st stitch of the next bar but one. Work a double Bar—1 chain, 1 single on the 1st stitch of the next bar but one. Repeat from † 7 times more.

Then down the side, work a double Bar—1 single on the 1st stitch of the next bar; 7 chain, 1 treble on the 1st stitch of the next bar; 5 chain, 1 plain on the 1st stitch of the 7 single, 5 chain, miss 5, 1 plain, 5 chain, miss the double bar; 1 treble on the 1st stitch of the next bar; 5 chain, 1 treble on the centre stem, 5 chain, 1 single in the 7th chain stitch of the 1st small leaf; 5 chain, 1 single in the point of the leaf; and along the 2nd side.

† †, 1 chain, 1 plain on the point of the 2nd long leaf; (5 chain, miss 4, 1 plain, twice), 10 chain, miss 4, 4 single, 1 chain. miss 6 stitches of the flower, work 6 single on it. Work a Bar—1 chain, join to the 6th stitch of the 10 chain; 5 chain, miss 1, 1 plain on the flower; (5 chain, miss 6 and 1 plain, 3 times), 6 single on the flower. Work a Bar—2 chain, 1 single on the 2nd treble stitch of the calyx. Work a Bar—1 chain, miss 2, 1 single on the rose leaf. Work a Bar—4 chain, join to the last plain stitch on the flower; 5 chain, 1 plain in the point of the rose leaf, (5 chain, miss 4, 1 plain, 3 times); 1 chain, 1 plain on the point of the small leaf. Repeat from the † † 7 times more, and for the other side, 5 chain, 1 plain in the 15th chain stitch of the leaf; 5 chain, 1 plain in the 19th chain stitch of the leaf; 5 chain, 1 treble on the last stitch of the centre stem; 5 chain, 1 treble on the 3 chain of the 1st bar; 5 chain, 1 plain on the last stitch of the next bar; 5 chain, 1 plain on the centre stitch of the double bar, then along the neck, (6 chain and 1 plain in the centre stitch of the double bar. Repeat), at the end, 6 chain, 1 single on the 4th stitch of the 7 chain, 3 plain in the remaining stitches of the 7 chain; and for the

2nd round—(Miss 1 and 6 plain in the 5 chain, 6 times), *, miss 1, 1 plain in the 1 chain, (miss 1 and 6 plain in the 5 chain, 11 times), miss 1, 1 plain in the 1 chain. Repeat from *, 7 times more; then (miss 1, 6 plain in the 5 chain, 6 times), and along the neck, miss 1, 7 plain in the 6 chain, ending at the 3 plain worked at the end of the last round.

3rd round, 1st Scallop—8 single, taking both edges of the stitches of the 2nd row; 8 chain, turn, and missing 4 of the last single stitches, join to the 4th stitch of the 8 single, then 3 plain in the 8 chain, (4 chain and 3 plain in the 8 chain, 3 times.) Work 12 scallops more the same; and for the division between the scallop, work 12 single instead of 8; then 8 chain, and joining to the 8th stitch of the 12 single, work as the 1st scallop; then work 7 scallop as the 1st. Repeat these 8 scallops 7 times more, then 5 scallops as the 1st, and fasten off.

Guipure Chemisette.

Material and Rules, See Page 3.

1st Stripe—Work as directed for the 1st stripe of the collar, page 5, repeating the pattern 5 times, so as to make it 6 patterns and a half in length. Work the centre bars, page 14; and to form the

Edge and Neck—Commence in the 1st stitch of the stripe, and on the centre scroll of the 1st side, work (5 chain, miss 5 and 1 treble, 6 times), *; 10 chain, 1 plain on the centre of the 1st 6 treble of the 1st flower; 10 chain, miss 10, 1 plain, 5 chain, 1 single on the top of the 1st scroll, 5 chain, 1 single in the 5th 2 chain of the next flower; 5 chain, join to the 5th stitch of the last 10 chain; then 8 chain, 1 plain in the 7th 2 chain of the flower; (5 chain, miss 5 and 1 treble on the stem, 3 times); then 16 single on the plain stitches of the next scroll; 5 chain, 1 single on the point of the division of the centre scroll; 8 chain, join to the 9th stitch of the 16 single; 7 chain, 1 treble on the point of the division; (7 chain, miss 6 and 1 treble on the centre scroll, twice); 7 chain, miss 6, 1 single, 8 chain, 1 single on the 1st plain stitch of the scroll; 2 chain, 1 single on the 2nd 2 chain of the double bar; 7 chain, 1 single on the centre of the next flower; 7 chain, 1 treble on the 2 chain of the next bar; 8 chain, 1 treble on the 2nd stitch of the stem of the pine; (5 chain, miss 4 and 1 plain, 3 times); 5 chain, miss 10, 1 plain on the next scroll; 6 chain, miss 5, 1 single, 6 chain, 7 single down the plain stitches of the scroll; 4 chain, miss 13, 8 single on the centre scroll, 5 chain, join to the 3rd stitch of of the last 6 chain, then (5 chain, miss 5 and 1 treble on the centre scroll, 4 times). Repeat from * once more; and to form the neck, work from the * *, page 24 of the collar to the * * at the end, twice; then commence at the * in this page, and work to the end of the stripe.

Edge—Work on the last row, 3 plain, 4 chain, 1 plain on the top of the last plain stitch. Repeat all along, fasten off. In the following stripes, the pattern is the same as the 1st, the alteration being in the commencement and ends to form the shape.

2nd Stripe—Make 12 chain, then commencing at the 4th scroll in the 1st stripe, page 7, work to the end of the pattern; then repeat from the * at the commencement of the stripe, and work the pattern twice; then repeat from the * to the 9 plain 2 single at the end of the 1st scroll; and to form the

2nd Side—Work 4 single more on the 1st scroll, turn back; 2 single, turn back, and work from the 3rd scroll in the 2nd side of the stripe, page 10. Repeat the directions along the 1st side, ending at the 5th scroll, then 63 plain, and fasten off; and for the centre bars, work as page 14, ending with the bars between the 1st flower and scroll.

Joining Bars—Commence on the last chain stitch of the 1st scroll on the 1st side of this stripe. Work a Bar—2 chain, join to the 22nd stitch of the centre scroll of the 2nd side of the 1st stripe, counting from the last oval flower, then commencing at the 1st bar in the 5th line of page 20, work to the end of the direction; then commencing at the *, page 19, work to the end of the direction. Then repeat from the * to the 4 single in the 13th line of page 21; and to finish, join to the last treble stitch of the flower in the 1st stripe; 7 single more on the 2nd stripe, 3 chain, join to the 1st treble stitch of the same flower—4 chain, 1 single on the centre of the 1st 6 treble of the flower of the 2nd stripe, 6 chain, turn back—miss 9, 7 single on the centre scroll of the 1st stripe, join to the 2nd 6 treble of the flower of the 2nd stripe; 9 single, join to the top of the next scroll of the 2nd stripe, 3 single. Fasten off.

3rd Stripe—Make 12 chain, then commencing at the 4th scroll in the 1st stripe, work to the end of the pattern. Then repeat from * to the end of the pattern, then work from the * to the 13 plain, 1 single worked after the 3rd flower, omit the 3rd scroll, work 9 plain, 1 ingle on the centre scr oll; and for the

2nd Side—Work as directed, page 9, to the end of the pattern, then repeat from the * * to the end of the 5th scroll, work 63 plain and fasten off.

GUIPURE CHEMISETTE.

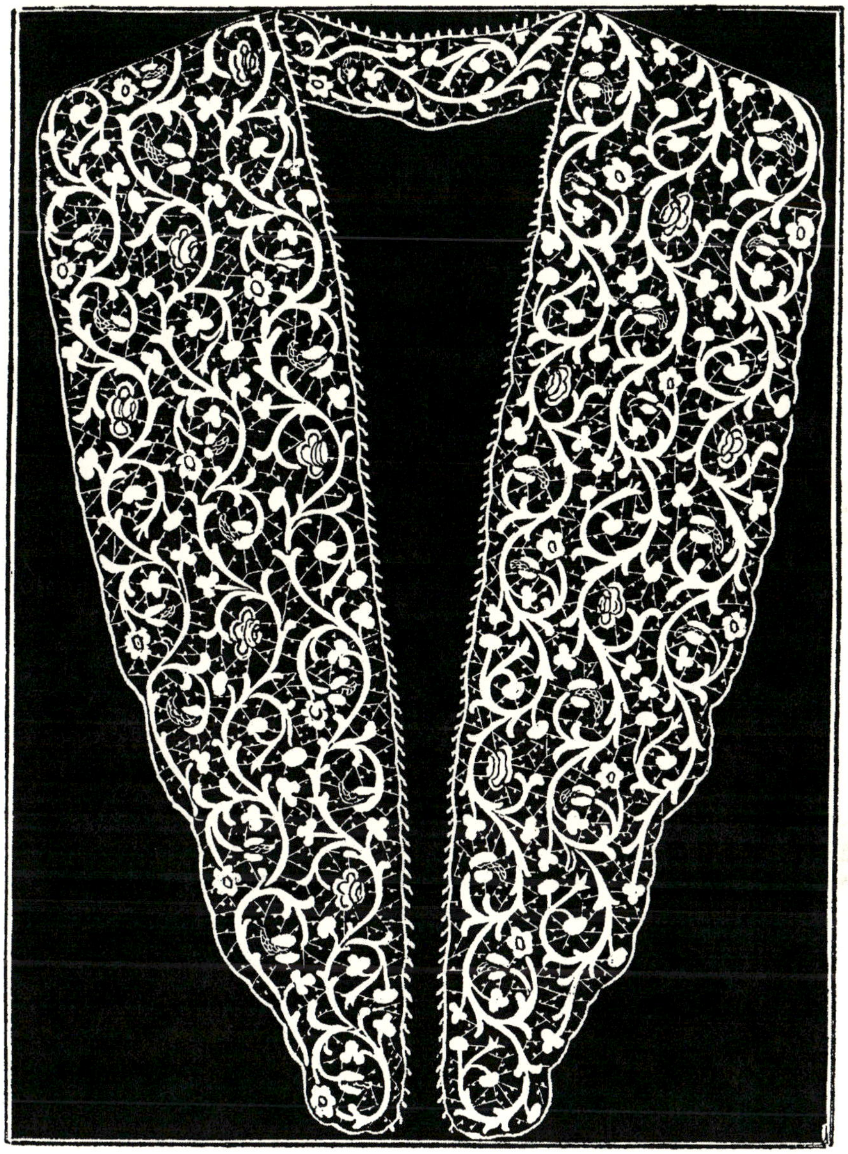

Work the centre bars as directed, page 14, to the end of the stripe.

Joining Bars—Commence in the last chain stitch of the 1st scroll of this stripe, (which must be counted as the 2nd stripe in working the bars.) Work a Bar—2 chain, join to the 22nd stitch of the centre scroll of the 2nd side of the last stripe, counting from the last oval flower; then work from the 1st bar in the 5th line of page 20, to the end of the direction, then commencing at the *, page 19, repeat the direction to the 8th line of page 22, joining to the centre of the oval flower; then work 2 chain, miss 5, 8 single on the centre scroll; 4 chain, join to the 4th stitch of the oval flower; 3 chain, join to the 4th stitch of the stem; 5 chain, miss 10, 8 single on the centre scroll of the lower stripe; 2 chain, and missing 10 stitches, join to the upper stripe, and fasten off. This finishes one side of the chemisette.

2nd Stripe of the other side—Make 29 chain instead of 47, and commencing at the * in the 1st side of the stripe, page 5, work the pattern twice, then repeat from the * to the 7 plain, 1 single worked after the 4th flower; and to form the

2nd Side of the Stripe—Work 3 single more on the stem of the flower, then 9 plain on the chain, and on the 4th scroll, 4 plain, and on the chain, 15 plain; then 6 plain on the plain stitches, and on the chain 3 plain, and on the centre scroll, 5 plain, 2 single; then work from the * *, page 10, and repeat the direction twice, then work from the * * to the end of the 2nd scroll. Work 56 plain and fasten off.

Work the centre bars as directed at page 14, ending at the 1st scroll of the 1st side.

Joining Bars—Commence in the 1st stitch of this stripe, then join to the 1st plain stitch of the 7th scroll in the 3rd pattern of the 2nd side of the long stripe. This scroll is the one which springs from the stem of the 3rd rose, and will leave half a pattern for the neck, between this stripe and the 2nd stripe of the other side, then work from the double bar in the 9th line of page 21 to the end of the direction, then commencing at *, page 19, work to the end of the direction twice, and then repeat from * to the end of the 6th line of page 20; and to finish, work 6 chain, miss 9, 1 treble on the stem of the last flower of the 2nd stripe 6 chain, join to to the 1st plain stitch of the scroll of the 1st stripe, then 1 single on the 1st 2 plain of the flower, 7 chain, join to the 12th stitch of the centre scroll of the 1st stripe; 5 chain, 1 single on the 1st treble stitch of the flower, then join to the 7th stitch of the centre scroll; 4 single on the treble stitches of the Flower, join to the next scroll of the 1st stripe, and fasten off.

3rd Stripe—Commence at the stem of the 4th flower, page 7, and work to the end of the pattern; then repeat from the * to the end of the pattern, and then work from the * to the 7 plain, 1 single worked after the 4th flower and for the

2nd Side—Work as directed for the 2nd side of the last stripe, working one repeat less; and for the

Centre Bars—Work as directed at page 14, ending with the 8 single on the 1st flower of the stripe; and for the

Joining Bars—Commence on the 1st stitch of the stripe, join to the 25th stitch of the 56 plain worked at the end of the 2nd stripe; 5 chain, miss 6, 1 single on the stem of the last stripe; 5 chain, 1 single on the 2nd 2 chain of the flower; 3 chain, turn back, and missing 5 stitches of the centre scroll of the upper stripe, work 12 single on it, turn back, 3 chain, 4 single on the 8 treble of the flower, then commence at the bar in the 16th line of page 20, work to the end of the direction; then repeat from the *, page 19, to the end of the direction; then work from the * to the end of the 6th line of page 20, and to finish, work as the end of last stripe. Fasten off, and to complete the chemisette, work a row of 8 chain, 1 treble along the 2nd side of the stripes, and for the 2nd row, miss 1, 10 plain in each 8 chain. Or make a Habit Shirt of net, and applique the outer edge to it.

THE END.

THE

CROCHET BOOK,

TEWLFTH SERIES.

BY

MLLE. RIEGO DE LA BRANCHARDIERE.

Third Edition--15,000.

LONDON:
SIMPKIN, MARSHALL, AND CO.,
ACKERMANN & CO., STRAND; OLIVER AND BOYD, EDINBURGH;
AND ALL THE BERLIN WAREHOUSES.

1853.

CONTENTS.

*** These Edgings are worked the short way.

All the Terms used are illustrated and explained in the FIRST, SECOND, and THIRD SERIES.

THE appearance of all articles in Crochet is so much spoiled by the use of cotton that becomes "heavy," loose, or fibrous *in the working*, that to prevent disappointment in the *result*, MDLLE. RIEGO particularly warns Ladies against the use of any but Messrs. I. & W. Taylor's Crochet Thread, as she cannot ensure the peculiar *lightness*, and distinctness of her patterns from any other make. This Thread is equally adapted for Point, Lacet, Knitting, Netting, and Tatting.

Post Office Orders for Eleonore Riego, to be made payable at the Post Office Old Cavendish Street.

LONDON:
Printed at the Office of E. RIEGO DE LA BRANCHARDIERE, 106, New Bond Street,

PREFACE.

IN introducing this Series, (my 17th publication on Needlework) it affords me much pleasure to inform my numerous Patronesses, that I have obtained the only PRIZE MEDAL awarded for Crochet, Point Lace, Lacet, &c., and that I intend, as soon as they can be arranged, to publish all the designs exhibited.

In this Series I have adapted the patterns to every article for which Lace is at present used; and as all these designs are worked the narrow way, they will be found very easy of execution; and to those who are unacquainted with my terms, I have only to refer them to the Rules and Instructions in my 1st and 2nd Series. I beg also to impress upon all who desire their work to look and wear well, to use the thread recommended, as from long experience, I have found no other make so suited to every purpose of needle-work as the threads manufactured by Messrs. JNO. and WM. TAYLOR. Sincerely acknowledging the extensive patronage and commendation I have received, I shall be happy in return, to give any information in my power, either personally, or by letter, to all who may experience any difficulty in the following directions.

E. R. DE LA BRANCHDARDIERE.

NEEDLEWORK ESTABLISHMENT,
106, *New Bond Street.*
Jan. 1st, 1852.

Instructions and Directions given in Point, *Lacet, Crochet, Tatting, Embroidery, Lace-work, Knitting, Netting, Tambour, &c.*

Ladies experiencing any difficulty in the following Directions, may communicate personally or by letter, enclosing a *directed stamped envelope,* and an *extra stamp* for a reply, the to Autho.ess, 106, New Bond Street.

THE CROCHET BOOK,

TWELFTH SERIES.

GIBBET PATTERN EDGING.

For Anti-Macassar, Couvre Pied, &c.—To make an Edging 4 inches deep, use Jno. and Wm. Taylor's Crochet Thread, No. 00; Penelope Needle, No. 2½, or 17 Bell Guage.

Petticoats, Drawers, &c., 3 inches deep—use Taylor's Crochet Thread, No. 2; Penelope Needle, No. 3, or 15 Bell Gauge.

Sleeves, Gilets, Childrens' Dresses, &c., 2½ inches deep—use Taylor's Crochet Thread, No. 6; Penelope Needle, No. 4, or 20 Bell Gauge.

Handkerchiefs, &c., 1¾ inches deep—use Taylor's Crochet Thread, No. 12; Penelope Needle, No. 4½, or 24 Bell Gauge.

1st STAR—Make 17 chain, turn, miss 5, 1 single in the 6th stitch to form a round loop, turn, work 1 chain to cross the chain, work 1 plain in the round loop, leaving 11 chain; and for the

1st round—9 chain, turn, and on the 9 chain, miss 4, 2 single, leaving 3 chain, work 3 chain to correspond, then 1 plain in the round loop. Repeat 6 times more, making in all 7 divisions; and to form the 8th division work 3 chain, and on the 11 chain left, miss 3, 2 single, 2 chain, miss 2, 1 single, (the last 2 chain, and the 2 chain missed will form a loop of 4 chain, the single stitch being in the centre), turn so as to cross the chain and leaving 3 chain, work 4 plain in the last loop, "that is," in the 2 chain missed, this will form half the last œillet of the next round.

E. R. de la Branchardiere, Invent., March, 1852.

2nd round, 1st œillet—1 chain, 8 plain in the 1st 4 chain of the 1st round. Work 2 œillets more the same in the 2 next 4 chains. 4th œillet—1 chain, 4 plain in the next 4 chain, and before finishing the star, work for

* The CROSS between the Stars—7 chain, turn, miss 1 and 3 single on the 7 chain, leaving 3 chain; then for the

2nd STAR—Work as the 1st star to the end of the 1st round.

2nd round, 1st œillet—1 chain, 8 plain in the 4 chain of the 1st round. Work 2 œillets more the same. 4th œillet—1 chain, 4 plain in the next 4 chain; and for the

2nd CROSS—7 chain, turn, miss 1 and 3 single on the 7 chain; and for the

3rd STAR—Work as the 1st star to the end of the 1st round.

2nd round, 1st œillet—1 chain, 8 plain as before. 2nd œillet—1 chain, 4 plain, in the next 4 chain; and before finishing the star, work the

4th STAR—Work as the 1st star to the end of the 1st round.

2nd round, 1st œillet—1 chain, 4 plain; join to the centre of the 8 plain worked for the 1st œillet in the last star, then 4 plain to finish this œillet. Work the 2nd œillet the same as last, joining it to the 1st single stitch of the 2nd cross. Work the 3rd œillet, joining it to the centre of the 3rd œillet of the 2nd star. 4th œillet—1 chain, 4 plain; and leaving this star unfinished, work the

CENTRE CROSS—7 chain, join to the 2nd œillet of the 2nd star, miss 1 and 3 single on the 7 chain, leaving 3 chain; and for the

5th STAR—Work as the 1st star to the end of the 1st round.

2nd round, 1st œillet—1 chain, 4 plain as before, join to the 1st œillet of the 2nd star, then 4 plain to finish the œillet. Work the 2nd œillet the same, joining it to the 1st single stitch of the 1st cross. Work the 3rd œillet, joining it to the 3rd œillet of the 1st star. 4th œillet—1 chain, 4 plain as before, then 4 chain, join it to the 2nd œillet of the 1st star, miss 1 and 3 single on the 4 chain, then 4 plain to finish the œillet. 5th œillet—1 chain, 8 plain. 6th œillet—1 chain, 4 plain; and before finishing the star, work the

6th STAR—Work,as the 1st star to the end of the 1st round.

2nd round, 1st œillet—1 chain, 8 plain. Work 6 œillets more the same, and to finish the 8th œillet, 1 chain, 4 plain in the same 4 chain as the 4 plain at the end of the 1st round; then 1 single on the 1st plain stitch, and 3 single on the 3 chain; then on the 5th star, 4 plain to finish the 6th œillet. Work the 7th œillet, joining it to the 7th œillet of the 6th star; and to finish the 8th œillet, 1 chain, 4 plain, then 1 single as before, 3 single on the 3 chain, and to finish the centre cross, work 4 chain, join to 6th œillet of the 6th star, miss 1 and 3 single on the 4 chain, and 3 single on the other 3 chain; then on the 4th star, 4 plain to finish the 4th œillet. Work the 5th œillet, joining it to the 5th œillet of the 6th star; and for the 6th œillet—1 chain, 4 plain, then 4 chain, join to the 4th œillet of the 6th star; miss 1 and 3 single on the 4 chain, and 4 plain to finish the œillet. 7th œillet—1 chain, 8 plain, and to finish the 8th œillet, 1 chain, 4 plain, 1 single, as before; then 3 single on the 3 chain, and on the 3rd star, 4 plain to finish the 2nd œillet. 3rd œillet—1 chain, 8 plain. 4th œillet—1 chain, 4 plain, and leaving the first 3 stars unfinished, repeat from the *, page 7, until the length required is worked.

Then to finish the last star, work 4 plain more in the 4th œillet; and for the 5th, 6th, and 7th œillets, (1 chain and 8 plain, 3 times as before), and to finish the 8th œillet, 1 chain, 4 plain, 1 single; then 3 single on the 3 chain; and for the

* * Centre Œillet between the stars, work 10 chain, turn, miss 6, 1 single in the 7th stitch to form a round loop; turn so as to cross the chain, and work 3 plain in the round loop, then for the 1st division, 4 chain, join to the 7th œillet of the last star, miss 1 and 3 single on the 4 chain, then 5 plain in the round loop; and for the 2nd division, 4 chain, turn, miss 1, 3 single on the 4 chain, and in the round loop 3 plain, then 3 single on the 3 chain, and 3 single on the remaining 3 chain of the cross; then 4 plain on the next star to finish the 4th œillet; and for the 5th œillet—1 chain, 4 plain, join to the 2nd division in the centre œillet, 4 plain as before; and for the 6th and 7th œillets, (1 chain and 8 plain, twice); then to finish the 8th œillet, 1 chain, 4 plain and 1 single as before, then 3 single on the 3 chain. Repeat from * * to the end, and fasten off; then for the

Insertion, 1st œillet—Make 11 chain, turn, miss 9, 1 single in the 10th stitch to form a round loop, turn, 1 chain to cross, and in the round loop work 4 plain, join to the centre stitch of the 7th œillet of the 1st star, then 4 plain in the round loop, and before finishing this œillet, work the

2nd Œillet—11 chain, turn, miss 9, 1 single, leaving 1 chain, turn and cross the chain, work 4 plain in the round loop, 3 chain, join to the centre stitch of the 2nd division worked in the centre œillet, miss 1, 2 single on the 3 chain, 4 plain in the round loop.

3rd Œillet—Same as the 2nd, joining to the 1st division of the centre œillet. Repeat these 3 œillets to the end, and to finish the last œillet, work 8 plain more in the round loop, then along the œillets, work 1 single on the 1 chain, and in the next œillet, 8 plain. Repeat and fasten off.

STAR EDGING.

For Anti-Macassars—To make an Edging 2 inches deep, use Jno. and Wm. Taylor's Crochet Thread, No. 00; Penelope Needle, No. 2½, or 17, Bell Gauge.

Petticoats, Childrens' Dresses.&c., 1¼ inches deep—use Taylor's Crochet Thread, No. 4; Penelope Needle, No. 3½, or 20 Bell Gauge.

Fine Trimming, 1 inch deep—use Crochet Thread, No. 8; Penelope Needle, No. 4.

1st Œillet—Make 15 chain, turn, miss 7, 1 single in the 8th stitch to form a round loop, turn, work 1 chain to cross the chain, and in the round loop, work 6 plain; then for the

E. R. de la Branchardiere, Inventor, March 1852.

2nd Œillet—7 chain, turn, miss 5, 1 single in the 6th stitch to form a round loop, turn, 1 chain to cross, leaving 1 chain, and in the round loop work 10 plain, then 1 single on the 1 chain, and to finish the 1st œillet, 6 plain in the round loop, 1 single on the chain, leaving 6 chain; and for the

* STAR—17 chain, turn, miss 5, 1 single in the 6th stitch, turn, 1 chain to cross the chain, 1 plain in the round loop ; and for the

1st *division*—5 chain, join to the 4th stitch of the 6 plain worked in the 1st œillet, then 1 chain, and on the 5 chain, miss 1, 3 treble and 1 plain, then 1 plain in the round loop.

2nd *division*—5 chain, join to the 7th plain stitch of the 2nd œillet, 1 chain, miss 1, 3 treble, 1 plain as before, 1 plain in the round loop.

3rd *division*—6 chain, turn, miss 2, 3 treble, 1 plain, then 1 plain in the round loop; work 3 divisions more the same as the last, and for the 7th division, work down the chain, 1 plain, 3 treble, 1 single, leaving 6 chain ; then for the

1st ŒILLET of the next pattern—15 chain, turn, miss 7, 1 single, turn, work 1 chain to cross, and in the round loop 2 plain, join to the point of the 6th division of the star, then 4 plain in the round loop; and for the

2nd ŒILLET—7 chain, turn, miss 5, 1 single, turn, 1 chain to cross, 3 plain in the round loop, join to the 5th division of the star, 1 plain in the round loop, and to form the edge across the star, 6 chain, join to the 4th division of the star, 6 chain, join to the 3rd division, 6 chain, join to the 6th plain stitch of the 2nd œillet in the 1st pattern, turn, and on these 6 chains, work (1 chain, 3 treble in 1 stitch, 1 plain and 1 single, 6 times,) then to finish the 2nd œillet, 6 plain in the round loop, 1 single on the 1 chain, then 6 plain to finish the 1st œillet, and 1 single on the chain, leaving 6 chain. Repeat from * until the length required is made, then work a plain row along the chain stitches.

TREFOIL EDGING.

For Anti-Macassars, Couvre Pied, &c.—To make an Edging 4 inches deep, use Jno. and Wm. Taylor's Crochet Thread, No. 00 ; Penelope Needle, No. 2.

For Curtains, D'Oyley, Petticoats, &c., 2 inches deep—use Taylor's Crochet Thread, No. 4 ; Penelope Needle, No. 3.

Pincushions, Sleeves, Gilets, Childrens' Dresses, 2 inches deep—use Taylor's Crochet Thread, No. 8 ; Penelope Needle, No. 4.

Handkerchief, Collars, Sleeves, &c., 1½ inches deep—use Taylor's Crochet Thread, No 12; Penelope Needle, No. 4.

CENTRE OVAL—Commence with 15 chain, turn, miss 12, 1 single in the 13th stitch to form a round loop, turn, 1 chain to cross, and in the round loop, work (4 plain, 10 chain, 3 plain, 6 chain, 3 plain, 8 chain, 3 plain, 6 chain, 3 plain, 10 chain, 4 plain, in all 20 plain), then 1 single on the 1 chain that crosses the chain ; and for the

* SMALL POINT—20 chain, turn, miss 1, 3 single, leaving 16 chain ; and for the

CENTRE DIAMOND—22 chain, turn, miss 9, 1 single in the 10th stitch to form a round loop, turn, and leaving 12 chain, work 1 chain to cross.

1st round—Work 15 plain in the round loop, 1 single on the 1 chain that crosses.

2nd round—5 chain, miss 1, 1 plain on the 1st round, 8 chain, miss 1, 1 plain on the 1st round. Repeat twice more, then 5 chain, miss 1, 1 plain, 4 chain, and missing 4 stitches of the 12 chain, work 1 single on it : this will form a 4th loop of 8 chain to correspond with the other three, turn ; 1 chain to cross, leaving 7 chain.

3rd round—Work 5 plain on the left side of the loop of the chain formed by last the single stitch, miss 1, 3 plain in the 1st 5 chain of the 2nd round; and for the

E. R. de la Branchardiere, Invent., March, 1852.

1st Œillet—8 chain, turn, miss 7, 1 single in the 1st stitch of these 8 chain to form a round loop, turn, 1 chain to cross, and in the round loop, 2 plain; join to the top of the small point; then 8 plain in the same round loop, 1 single on the 1 chain that crosses, then 3 plain in the same 5 chain of the 2nd round as before, miss 1, 5 plain in the 8 chain; and for the

1st Trefoil—16 chain, turn, miss 7, 1 single in the 8th stitch to form a round loop, turn so as to cross the chain, and leaving 8 chain for the stem, work 3 chain, 2 long in the round loop; join to the 5th stitch of the 8 plain of the œillet, then in the round loop, 1 long, 3 chain, 1 single, 3 chain, 2 long; join to the 9th stitch of the 16 chain left between the centre oval and the small point, then in the round loop, 1 long, 3 chain, 1 single, 3 chain, join to the centre of the last 10 chain of the centre oval; then in the round loop, 3 long, 3 chain, 1 single, making in all 3 divisions; then on the stem 4 single, which finishes the 1st trefoil.

2nd Trefoil—13 chain, turn, miss 7, 1 single, turn so as to cross, 3 chain, join to the last long stitch of the 1st trefoil, then 3 long in the round loop, join to the last 6 chain of the centre oval then 3 chain, 1 single in the round loop, 3 chain; join to the 5th stitch of the 8 chain in the centre oval, then in the round loop, 3 long, 3 chain, 1 single, 3 chain, 3 long, 3 chain, 1 single; then 4 single down the stem, leaving 1 chain; and for the

3rd Trefoil—12 chain, turn, miss 7, 1 single, turn as before, 3 chain, join to the last long stitch of the 2nd trefoil, then in the round loop 3 long, 3 chain, 1 single, 3 chain, 3 long, 3 chain, 1 single, 3 chain, 3 long, 3 chain, 1 single, then on the stem, 4 single, and down the centre stem, 5 single, then 5 plain in same 8 chain of the 2nd round as before, miss 1, 3 plain in the next 5 chain; and for the

2nd Œillet—8 chain, turn, miss 7, 1 single, turn, 1 chain to cross, 4 plain in the round loop, join to the last long stitch but one of the 3rd trefoil, then 6 plain in the same round loop, 1 single on the 1 chain that crosses, and 3 plain in the same 5 chain of the 2nd round as before, miss 1, 5 plain in the 8 chain ; and for the

4th Trefoil—16 chain, turn, miss 7, 1 single in the 8th stitch, turn, 3 chain, 2 long in the round loop, join to the 3rd stitch of the 6 plain of the œillet, then in the round loop, 1 long, 3 chain, 1 single, (3 chain, 3 long, 3 chain and 1 single, twice), 4 single on the stem ; then 13 chain for the

5th Trefoil—Turn, miss 7, 1 single, turn, 3 chain, join to the last long stitch of the last trefoil ; then in the round loop, 3 long, 3 chain, 1 single, (3 chain, 3 long, 3 chain and 1 single, twice), 4 single on the stem ; then 12 chain for the

6th Trefoil—Same as 5th, when finished, work 5 single down the centre stem, then 5 plain in the same 8 chain of the 2nd round as before, miss 1, 3 plain in the 5 chain ; and for the

3rd Œillet—8 chain, turn, miss 7, 1 single, turn, 1 chain to cross, 4 plain in the round loop, join to the last long stitch but one of the last trefoil, then 6 plain in the round loop, 1 single as before, and 3 plain in the same 5 chain as before, miss 1, 5 plain in the 8 chain.

Repeat from the 4th trefoil, once more, which will form the 7th, 8th, 9th trefoils, and the 4th œillet; when finished, work 2 single on the 7 chain left at the 2nd round, then 9 chain, join to the 5th stitch of the 6 plain of the 4th œillet, miss 1, 3 single on the 9 chain, 8 chain, join to the centre stitch of the last trefoil ; and for the

Centre Oval—21 chain, turn, miss 12, 1 single in the 13th stitch, turn, 1 chain to cross, and in the round loop, 4 plain, 5 chain, join to the 3rd long stitch of the 9th trefoil, 5 chain, 3 plain in the round loop, 3 chain, join to the 7th long stitch of the 8th trefoil, 3 chain, 3 plain as before, 3 chain, join to the 6th long stitch of the 8th trefoil, 5 chain, 3 plain as before, 6 chain, 3 plain, 10 chain, 4 plain, 1 single on the 1 chain that crosses. Repeat from *, page 12, until the required length is worked.

Edge, 1st row—Commence on the 6th long stitch of the 2nd trefoil, 2 chain, miss 7, 1 treble of the 7th long stitch of the trefoil ; 4 chain, miss 6, 1 treble on the 3rd long stitch of the 3rd trefoil ; 4 chain, miss 7, 1 treble on the 4th long stitch ; 4 chain, 1 treble on the 6th long stitch of the 4th trefoil ; 4 chain, miss 7, 1 treble on the 7th long stitch ; 4 chain, miss 6, 1 treble on the 3rd long stitch of the 5th trefoil; 5 chain, miss 8, 1 treble on the centre stitch of the 5th trefoil ; 5 chain, miss 8, 1 treble as before ; 4 chain, miss 6, 1 treble, 4 chain, miss 7, 1 treble, 4 chain, 1 treble on the 6th long stitch of the 7th trefoil ; 4 chain, miss 7, 1 treble, 4 chain, miss 6, 1 treble, 2 chain, miss 7, 1 treble, 1 chain, 1 treble on the 6th long stitch of the 2nd trefoil in the next pattern. Repeat from commencement of the row along the patterns, and fasten off.

2nd row—Commence on the 1st stitch of the last row ; and for the

* 1st *Point*—1 single, 1 plain, 2 treble, then 6 chain, turn, and on the 6 chain, miss 2, 1 plain, 3 treble, then 1 treble in the same stitch of the 1st row as the 2nd stitch of the 2 treble, then 1 treble, 1 plain. Work 10 points more the same ; then 1 single, 3 plain between the patterns, and repeat from * along the 1st row.

DIAMOND EDGING.

For Anti-Macassars, &c., 2 inches deep—use Jno. and Wm. Taylor's Crochet Thread, No. 0; Penelope Needle, No. 2, or 17, Bell Guage.

Petticoats, Childrens' Dresses, &c., 1 inch deep—use Taylor's Crochet Thread, No. 6; Penelope Needle, No. 3½, or 20, Bell Guage.

Fine Trimming—use Taylor's Crochet Thread, No. 10; Penelope Needle, No. 4.

Centre Pattern—14 chain, turn, miss 7, 1 single in the 8th stitch to form a round loop, turn, work 1 chain to cross, and in the round loop work 5 treble, then to form

the point, 4 chain, turn, miss 1, 1 plain and 2 treble on the 4 chain, then in the round loop, (5 treble, 1 chain, 1 single), and on the chain stitches, 1 single, 3 chain, miss 3, 1 treble, 1 long, 10 chain, join to the 3rd stitch of the last 5 treble; and for the

* Flower—11 chain, turn, miss 5, 1 single in the 6th stitch to form a round loop, turn, 1 chain to cross, and in the round loop, (1 plain, then 3 chain, join to the 1st treble stitch in the point of the centre pattern, 3 chain, 1 plain in the round loop, and in the same round loop work 7 chain, 1 plain, 8 chain, 1 plain, 9 chain, 1 plain, 8 chain, 1 plain, 7 chain, 1 plain, 6 chain, 1 plain, making in all 8 plain in the same round loop); then on the stem 2 single, 7 chain, miss 6, 2 single on the 7th and 6th stitches of the 10 chain, then 3 chain, miss 3, 1 treble, 1 long; and to form the

2nd Centre Pattern—14 chain, turn, miss 7, 1 single, turn, 1 chain to cross, and in the round loop work 2 treble, join to the centre stitch of the 7 chain, then 3 treble more in the round loop, and to form the point, 2 chain, join to the centre of the last 6 chain of the flower, then 2 chain, turn, miss 1 and 1 plain on the 2 chain, and on the other 2 chain work 2 treble, then in the round loop, (5 treble, 1 chain, 1 single), and on the chain, 1 single, 3 chain, miss 3, 1 treble, 1 long, then 10 chain; join to the 3rd stitch of the last 5 treble. Repeat from *, until the required length is made.

SCALLOP EDGING.

For Anti-Macassars, &c., 3½ inches deep—use Jno. and Wm. Taylor's Crochet Thread No. 00; Penelope Needle, No. 2½, or 17, Bell Guage.

Petticoats, &c., 2 inches deep—use Taylor's Crochet Thread, No. 4; Penelope Needle, No. 3, or 20, Bell Guage.

Fine Trimming, 1 inch deep—use Crochet Thread, No. 10; Penelope Needle, No. 4.

E. R. de la Branchardiere, Invent., March, 1852.

1st Scallop—Make 34 chain, and for the centre row, turn, and down the chain, miss 1, 2 plain, 2 treble, 5 long, 2 treble, 1 plain, turn, work 1 chain to cross, leaving 21 chain, and up the other side, for the

1st round—13 plain, turn, and down the other side, 13 plain, taking both edges of the stitches of the centre row, turn, 1 chain to cross; and for the

2nd round—2 single on the plain stitches of the last round, * then 9 chain, turn, miss 6, 1 single in the 7th stitch to form a round loop, leaving 2 chain, work 2 chain to correspond, then miss 1, 1 plain on the 1st round. Repeat from *, 10 times more; then 2 single, and down the chain, 9 single, turn, work 1 chain to cross; and for the

3rd round—1 chain, then in the 1st round loop of the 2nd round, 1 plain, 3 treble, 1 plain. Repeat 10 times more, that is in each round loop, turn back, 7 chain, and keeping the work on the wrong side, join to the 3rd stitch of the 9 single worked at the end of the 2nd round; miss 1, 6 single on the 7 chain; and for the

4th round—(7 chain, miss 5 and 1 plain in the 1 chain of the last round, 11 times), turn back.

5th round—Miss 1, then in the 7 chain of the last round, 1 plain, 7 treble, 1 plain. Repeat 10 times more; then 1 single on the 1st stitch of the 3rd round. This finishes the 1st scallop.

2nd Scallop—Work the same as the 1st scallop to the end of the 4th round; and for the

5th—Miss 1, then in the 7 chain, work (1 plain, 3 treble, join to the centre stitch of the last 7 treble in the 1st scallop; then 4 treble and 1 plain more in the same 7 chain). Repeat twice more, joining it to the opposite 7 treble, then (miss 1 and in the next 7 chain, 1 plain, 7 treble, and 1 plain, 8 times); then 1 single, and repeat as the 2nd scallop, until the length required is made.

POINT LACE BORDER.

For Curtains, Couvre-Pieds, Anti-Macassars, Toilet Covers, &c.—To make a Border 3½ inches deep, use Jno. & Wm. Taylor's Crochet Thread, No. 0; Penelope Needle, No. 2½, or 17, Bell Guage.

Petticoats, Night-dresses, &c., 2½ inches deep—use Taylor's Crochet Thread, No. 4; Penelope Needle, No. 3, or 19, Bell Guage.

Childrens' Dresses, Gilets, Sleeves, Pincushions, &c., 2 inches deep—use Taylor's Crochet Thread, No. 6; Penelope Needle, No. 4, or 20, Bell Guage.

Handkerchiefs, Baby's Robings, Frocks, &c., 1½ inches deep—use Taylor's Crochet Thread, No. 10 or 12, Penelope Needle, No. 4½, or 24, Bell Guage.

The following directions are written for a straight Border, and the instructions for forming the corner will be found at the end.

To work a Bar—Make 6 chain, turn, miss 3, 1 single on the 6 chain, leaving 2 chain, work thus whenever directed to work a bar.

FIRST SIDE.

1st Leaf—16 chain, turn, miss 1, 8 plain, turn, work 1 chain to cross the stem, and up the other side, work 9 plain, turn, 8 plain down the other side, 4 single on the stem; and for the

* 1st Flower—33 chain, turn, miss 8, 1 single in the 9th stitch to form a round loop, leaving 24 chain for the stem, 1 chain to cross, work 5 plain in the round loop; and for the bars between the leaf and flower, work a bar, 7 chain, join to the 17th stitch of the 24 chain, counting from the leaf, miss 1, 4 single on the 7 chain; work a bar, 2 chain, join to the 8th stitch of the chain; work a bar, 2 chain; join to the 6th plain stitch of the leaf, counting from the point of it; work a bar, 2 chain, 1 treble on the 2 chain of the bar worked after the 4 single, 6 chain; join to the point of the leaf, miss

E. R. de la Branchardiere, Invent, March, 1852.

1, 3 single on the 6 chain; work a bar, 2 chain, 1 single on the last plain stitch worked in the round loop of the flower; then in the round loop, work 1 plain, (4 chain and 1 plain in the round loop, 3 times), 5 plain more in the round loop, then down the stem, 5 plain, and 1 single; then for

The BUD—20 chain, turn, miss 7, 1 single in the 8th stitch to form a round loop, leaving 12 chain for the stem, work 1 chain to cross, and in the round loop, 4 plain, work a bar, 3 chain, join to the 7th stitch of the 12 chain, counting from the stem of the flower; work a bar, 3 chain, join to the last plain stitch of the flower; work a bar, 4 chain, 1 single on the last plain stitch of the bud, then in the round loop, 8 plain, and down the stem, 12 plain, then on the stem of the flower, 2 plain, 1 single, leaving 15 chain for the centre stem; and for the

2nd LEAF—14 chain, turn, miss 1, 8 plain, 1 chain to cross, and up the other side, 5 plain, 4 chain, join to the 8th plain stitch of the stem of the bud, miss 1, 3 single on the 4 chain, and on the leaf, 4 plain, turn, and down the other side of it 4 plain, then to form the

CENTRE DIVISION—8 chain, turn, miss 2, 2 plain, 1 treble; and for the

3rd LEAF—18 chain, turn, miss 1, 8 plain, turn, 1 chain to cross, and up the other side, 8 plain; work a bar, 7 chain, join to the 2nd stitch of the last 8 plain of the leaf; work a bar, 3 chain, join to the point of the centre division, 6 chain, join to the point of the 2nd leaf; work a bar, 2 chain, join to the 3rd plain stitch of the stem of the bud, 4 chain, 1 treble on the 3rd stitch of the 6 chain, 3 chain, 1 treble on the 3rd stitch of the
* 7 chain, then 6 chain, join to the 5th stitch of the 8 plain of the bud, miss 1, 3 single on the 6 chain; work a bar, 4 chain, 1 single on the last plain stitch of the 3rd leaf, and to finish the leaf, 9 plain, then 4 single on the stem, leaving 5 chain for the centre stem. Repeat from *, page 21, until the required length is made; then to form the

2nd SIDE—For the centre stem, work 4 chain, turn, miss 1, 3 plain on it, then 5 plain on the stem of the last leaf, and to finish the centre division, 5 chain, turn, miss 2, 2 plain, 1 treble, then on the 3 chain of the centre stem, 2 plain, 1 single, and on the 2nd leaf of the other side, work 4 plain; and for the

1st FLOWER—8 chain, join to the point of the centre division, 16 chain, turn, miss 8, 1 single in the 9th stitch to form a round loop, leaving 7 chain for the stem, work 1 chain to cross, then in the round loop, 5 plain; work a bar, 6 chain, join to the 4th stitch of the 7 chain, miss 1, 2 single on the 6 chain; work a bar, 1 chain, join to the 1st plain stitch of the centre stem of this side; work a bar, 6 chain, 1 single on the last plain stitch of the flower, 1 plain in the round loop, then (4 chain and 1 plain, in the same round loop, 3 times), 5 plain more in the round loop, 7 plain on the 7 chain of the stem, and 5 plain on the 8 chain; and for

* * The BUD—12 chain, turn, miss 7, 1 single in the 8th stitch, 1 chain to cross, and in the round loop, 4 plain, work a bar, 3 chain, join to the 6th plain stitch of the stem of the flower, work a bar, 6 chain, join to the 3rd stitch of the 5 plain of the flower, miss 1, 3 single on the 6 chain, work a bar, 3 chain, 1 single on the last plain stitch of the bud, 8 plain in the round loop, 4 plain down the stem, 3 plain on the 3 chain, and 1 single on the 2nd leaf, then for the centre stem, 5 plain on the 5 chain, and 11 plain on the 15 chain, making in all 16 plain, leaving 4 chain; then for

The LEAF—14 chain, turn, miss 1, 8 plain, turn, 1 chain to cross, and up the other side,

8 plain, work a bar, 7 chain, join to the 2nd stitch of the last 8 plain, work a bar, 2 chain, join to the 10th plain stitch of the centre stem, counting from the 2nd leaf; work a bar, 4 chain, join to the 3rd stitch of the centre stem, miss 1, 2 single on the 4 chain, 4 chain, 1 treble on the 2nd stitch of the 7 chain, work a bar, 2 chain, join to the 5th stitch of the 8 plain of the bud, work a bar, 4 chain, 1 single on the last plain stitch of the leaf, and to finish the leaf, 9 plain, 4 single on the stem, then on the centre stem, 4 plain on the 4 chain, 5 plain on the 5 chain, and to finish the *centre division*, 5 chain, turn, miss 2, 2 plain and 1 treble on the 5 chain, then 2 plain, 1 single on the 3 chain, and on the 2nd leaf, 4 plain, then 8 chain, join to the point of the centre division; and for

The FLOWER—16 chain, turn, miss 8, 1 single in the 9th stitch, 1 chain to cross, and leaving 7 chain, work 5 plain in the round loop, work a bar, 6 chain, join to the 4th stitch of the 7 chain, miss 1, 2 single on the 6 chain, work a bar, 1 chain, join to the 4th plain stitch of the centre stem, 4 chain, 1 treble on the 3 chain of the last bar but one, work a bar, 2 chain, join to the 5th stitch of the leaf, work a bar, 3 chain, 1 single on the last plain stitch of the flower, 1 plain in the round loop, (4 chain and 1 plain in the same round loop, 3 times), 5 plain more in the round loop, 7 plain down the stem and 5 plain on the 8 chain. Repeat from * * along the 1st side, and fasten off.

The EDGE, 1st row—Commence in the point of the 1st leaf in the 1st side, *, 6 chain, 1 treble on the 2 chain of the bar between the leaf and flower; 6 chain, 1 plain in the last 4 chain of the flower, 6 chain, 1 plain on the 2nd stitch of the 4 chain in the next bar, 6 chain, 1 treble on the 3 single after the bud, 6 chain 1 treble on the 2nd stitch of the 4 chain in the next bar. Repeat from * to the end, and fasten off.

2nd row—Commence in the 1st stitch of the last row, miss 1, and 9 plain in the 6 chain. Repeat to the end.

3rd row—Commence in the 5th plain stitch of last row, work 13 single on the plain stitches, 10 chain, join to the 5th stitch of these 13 single, then in the 10 chain, 6 plain, (4 chain and 3 plain in the 10 chain, 3 times), 3 plain in the 10 chain. Repeat, and fasten off.

EDGING for the 2nd SIDE, 1st row—Commence in the last 4 chain of the 1st flower of the 2nd side, 6 chain, 1 plain on the 2 chain of the next bar, 6 chain, 1 treble on the centre of the bud, 6 chain, 1 plain on the 2nd stitch of the 4 chain in the next bar, 6 chain, 1 treble on the 4th plain stitch of the leaf, 6 chain, 1 plain in the last 4 chain of the flower. Repeat.

2nd row—Miss 1, 9 plain in the 6 chain of the last row. Repeat.

3rd row—4 chain, miss 4, 2 treble. Repeat.

4th row—Miss 2, and 5 plain in the 4 chain of the last row. Repeat, and fasten off.

CORNER FOR HANDKERCHIEFS, PINCUSHIONS, &c.

Work as directed for the 1st side, (page 21) until sufficient is made for *half* one side of the Handkerchief, ending with the leaf; then to form

The CORNER LEAF—15 chain, turn, miss 1, 8 plain, work 1 chain to cross, and up the other side, 8 plain, work a bar, 7 chain, join to the 2nd stitch of the last 8 plain, work a bar, 2 chain, join to the 5th plain stitch of the last leaf of the pattern; work a bar, 1 chain, 1 treble on the 3rd stitch of the 7 chain, work a bar, 4 chain, 1 single on the last plain stitch of the leaf, and down the side of it, 9 plain, 4 single on the stem, leaving 2 chain; and for

The FLOWER—28 chain, turn; miss 8, 1 single, 1 chain to cross, 5 plain in the round loop, work a bar, 7 chain, join to the 10th stitch of the chain, miss 1, 4 single on the 7 chain; work a bar, 2 chain join to the 5th stitch of the chain; work a bar, 2 chain, join to the 4th stitch of the leaf; work a bar, 3 chain, 1 treble on the 2 chain after the 4 single; work a bar, 4 chain, 1 single on the last stitch of the flower, 1 plain in the round loop, (4 chain and 1 plain in the round loop, 3 times), 5 plain more in the round loop, 5 plain and 1 single down the stem.

Work from the bud in the 1st side (page 23), and repeat the pattern as directed between the *s the length required for one side of the handkerchief; work another corner the same, then work the 3rd side of the handkerchief and the 3rd corner; work the 4th side of the handkerchief and the 4th corner, then work half the length of one side to correspond with the half worked at the commencement; and for the

2nd SIDE of the PATTERN—work as directed (page 24), and repeat the pattern between the * *s along the half side to the corner pattern, ending at the 1 single on the 2nd leaf, in the 20th line of page 24, then work 22 plain on the centre stem, and to finish the centre division, 5 chain, turn, miss 2, 2 plain and 1 treble on the 5 chain, then 2 plain, 1 single on the chain, and on the 2nd leaf, 4 plain, then 8 chain, join to the point of the centre division; and for

The FLOWER—16 chain, turn, miss 8, 1 single in the 9th stitch, 1 chain to cross, and leaving 7 chain, work 5 plain in the round loop, then work a bar, 6 chain, join to the 4th stitch of the 7 chain, miss 1, 2 single on the 6 chain, work a bar, 1 chain, join to the 17th plain stitch of the centre stem, work a bar, 2 chain, 1 treble on the 2 chain of the bar nearest the flower, 3 chain, join to the 7th plain stitch of the centre stem, work a bar, 4 chain, join to the 6th stitch of the stem of the bud, miss 1, 3 single on the 4 chain, 2 chain, 1 single on the last stitch of the flower, 1 plain in the round loop, (4 chain and 1 plain, twice), 2 chain, join to the last plain stitch of the bud, 2 chain, 6 plain in the round loop, and down the stem, 7 plain; then on the 8 chain, work 5 plain; and for

The BUD—12 chain, turn, miss 7, 1 single, 1 chain to cross, 4 plain in the round loop, work a bar, 3 chain, join to the 6th stitch of the stem of the flower, work a bar, 6 chain, join to the 3rd stitch of the 5 plain of the flower, miss 1, 3 single on the 6 chain, 2 chain, join to the 4th stitch of the bud to the right; work a bar, 3 chain, 1 single on the last stitch of the unfinished bud, 8 plain in the round loop, then 4 plain on the stem, 3 plain on the stem of the flower, 1 single on the 3rd leaf, then 5 plain on the 5 chain and 11 plain on the 15 chain, leaving 4 chain.

Work from the leaf, page 24, and repeat the pattern as between the * *s along the side to the next corner, &c.

The EDGE, 1st row—Work as page 25 along the 1st side, then to form a corner, work thus—6 chain 1 treble on the 2nd plain stitch of the leaf, 6 chain, 1 treble on the 2 chain of the next bar, 6 chain, 1 plain on the 2nd stitch of the 4 chain of the next bar; 6 chain, 1 treble on the leaf, (6 chain, 1 treble on each of the next 2 bars); 6 chain, 1 plain in the last 4 chain of the flower, 6 chain, 1 plain on the 4 chain, 1 treble on the 3 single, 6 chain, 1 treble on the next bar. Work the remainder of edging as page 25.

FORGET-ME-NOT EDGING.

For Anti-Macassars, D'Oyleys, Couvre Pieds, &c., 2 inches deep—use Jno. and Wm. Taylor's Crochet Thread, No. 00; Penelope Needle, No. 2½, or 17, Bell Guage.

Petticoats, Childrens' Drawers, &c., 1½ inches deep—use Taylor's Crochet Thread, No. 1; Penelope Needle, No. 3, or 19, Bell Guage.

Dress Trimming, Gilets, &c., 1 inch deep—use Taylor's Crochet Thread, No. 8; Penelope Needle, No. 4, or 22, Bell Guage.

Collars, &c.—use Taylor's Crochet Thread, No. 12; Penelope Needle, No. 4½.

E. R. de la Branchardiere, Invent., March, 1852.

1st Leaf—Commence with 21 chain, turn, miss 1, 2 plain, 5 treble, 1 plain, 1 single, which forms the centre of the leaf, turn, 1 chain to cross the stem, and up the other side for the

1st Point—5 chain, turn, miss 2, 1 plain and 2 treble on the 5 chain, and up the chain stitches of the centre, miss 2, 1 plain, work 2 points more the same; and for the

* 4th Point—5 chain, turn, miss 2, 1 plain and 2 treble on the 5 chain, then 1 plain in the same stitch as the last plain on the centre; then down the other side, work 3 points more the same as the 1st, and on the stem, 4 single, then 6 chain, join to the last point of the leaf; and for the

1st Flower—14 chain, turn, miss 8, 1 single in the 9th stitch to form a round loop, and leaving 5 chain for the stem, turn so as to cross it, work 2 chain, join to the 6th point of the leaf, 2 chain, 1 plain in the round loop, then (4 chain and 1 plain in the round loop, 7 times,) 3 single on the stem, then 4 chain, join to the centre of the last 4 chain of the flower.

2nd Flower—15 chain, turn, miss 8, 1 single as before, turn so as to cross the stem, and in the round loop, (4 chain and 1 plain, 8 times;) then 3 single on the stem, leaving 3 chain, work 4 chain, join to the last 4 chain of the flower; work 2 flowers more the same as the second; and for

The Bud—11 chain, turn, miss 7, 1 single, turn, 1 chain to cross, work 10 plain in the round loop, and down the chain stitches to form the centre stem, 32 single; which will bring the thread within 4 chain of the 1st leaf; and for the

2nd Leaf—15 chain, turn, miss 1, 2 plain, 5 treble, 1 plain, 1 single, turn, work 1 chain to cross the stem; and for the

1st Point—4 chain, join to the 24th single stitch of the centre stem, and on the 4 chain, miss 1, 1 plain, 2 treble, then on the chain stitches of the centre, miss 2, 1 plain.

2nd Point—same as the 1st, joining it to the 17th stitch of the centre stem. 3rd Point —same as the 1st, joining it to the 10th stitch of the centre stem. 4th Point—4 chain, join to the 5th stitch of the centre stem, miss 1, 1 plain, 2 treble as before, then 1 plan in the same stitch as the last plain on the centre; and down the other side, for the 5th, 6th, and 7th Points—(5 chain, turn, miss 2, 1 plain, 2 treble, then miss 2, 1 plain on the centre, 3 times); when finished, 5 single on the stem, and 6 single down the centre stem, then 6 chain, join to the last point of the leaf; 5 chain, join to the 6th point; 5 chain, join to the 5th point; 7 chain, join to the 7th plain stitch of the bud; and for the

3rd Leaf—30 chain, turn, miss 1, 2 plain, 5 treble, 1 plain, 1 single, turn, and leaving 20 chain, work 1 chain to cross. 1st Point—4 chain, join to the 8th stitch of the 20 chain, and on the 4 chain, miss 1, 1 plain, 2 treble, then on the centre of the leaf, miss 2, 1 plain. 2nd Point—6 chain, join to the 4th plain stitch of the bud, and on the 6 chain, miss 1, 2 single, 1 plain, 2 treble, then on the leaf, miss 2, 1 plain. 3rd Point—same as the 1st, joining it to the 5th 4 chain of the last flower. Repeat from *, until the required length is made, then work a plain row along the chain stitches.

VANDYKE EDGING.

For Anti-Macassars, D'oyleys, &c., 1½ inches deep—use Jno. and Wm. Taylor's Crochet Thread, No. 000; Penelope Needle, No. 2, or 16, Bell Guage.

Childrens' Petticoats, Dress Trimming, &c., 1 inch deep—use Taylor's Crochet Thread, No. 2; Penelope Needle, No. 3, or 19, Bell Guage.

Baby's Dresses, Under Clothes, &c., ¾ of an inch deep—use Taylor's Crochet Thread, No. 10; Penelope Needle, No. 4, or 22, Bell Guage.

E. R. de la Branchardiere, Invent., 1852.

1st Scallop—Make 15 chain; and for the

1st, or centre row—Turn, miss 2, 2 plain, 2 treble, 2 long, turn back, leaving 7 chain.

2nd row—6 chain, miss 3, 1 plain on the centre row; 4 chain, miss 2, 1 plain in the point of the centre row; 5 chain, 1 plain in the same stitch of the point as before; 4 chain, miss 2, 1 plain on the other side of the centre row; 4 chain, turn back, join to the 5th stitch of the 7 chain left.

3rd row—Miss 1, and in the last 4 chain work (1 plain, 1 chain, 2 treble, 4 chain, 2 treble, 1 chain, and 1 plain), these plain and treble stitches are all to be worked in the same 4 chain. Repeat 4 times more, "that is," in each loop of chain.

2nd SCALLOP—Work as the 1st scallop, to the end of the 2nd row; and for the

3rd row—Miss 1, and in the last 4 chain, (1 plain, 1 chain, 2 treble, 2 chain, join to the last 4 chain of the 1st scallop, 2 chain, and in the same 4 chain as before, work 2 treble, 1 chain, 1 plain), then *, miss 1, and in the next 4 chain, (1 plain, 1 chain, 2 treble, 1 chain, 2 treble, 4 chain, 1 plain.) Repeat from *, 3 times more; then work as the 2nd scallop, until sufficient length is made.

MOSAIC EDGING.

For Anti-Macassars, Couvre Pieds, Curtains, &c.—To make a Border, 4 inches deep, use Jno. & Wm. Taylor's Crochet Thread, No. 00; Penelope Needle, No. 2.

D'oyleys, Petticoats, &c., 2½ inches deep—use Crochet Thread, No. 4; Penelope Needle, 3.

Gilets, Childrens' Dresses, Pincushions, &c., 2 inches deep—use Taylor's Crochet Thread, No. 8; Penelope Needle, No. 4, or 22, Bell Guage.

Handkerchiefs, Sleeves, Baby's Dresses, &c., 1½ inches deep—use Taylor's Crochet Thread, No. 12; Penelope Needle, No. 4½ or 24, Bell Guage.

The following directions are written for a straight Border or insertion, and the instructions for forming the corner will be found at the end.

1st SIDE.

1st SCALLOP—Make 21 chain, turn, miss 6, 3 single, turn back, leaving 12 chain for the foundation; and for the

1st row—7 chain, and missing the 3 single, work 1 long in the round loop, (2 chain and 1 long in the round loop, 6 times), making in all 7 long; then 1 chain, turn back, and join to the 7th stitch of the foundation chain; then for the

E. R. de la Branchardiere, Invent., March, 1852.

2nd row—2 plain in the 1 chain, (5 chain, miss 1 and 4 plain in the 2 chain, 6 times), 5 chain, miss 1, 2 plain in the 7 chain, turn back.

3rd row—9 chain, miss 8, 1 plain on the centre of the 4 plain, then (7 chain, miss 8, 1 plain as before, 5 times), 7 chain, turn back, join to the 4th stitch of the foundation chain.

4th row—8 plain in the 7 chain, then (miss 1 and 8 plain in the 7 chain, 6 times); making in all 7 divisions, this finishes the 1st scallop.

* 2nd SCALLOP—Work as the 1st scallop to the end of the 3rd row; and for the

4th row—(Work 4 plain in the 7 chain, join to the centre stitch of the last division of the 1st scallop, then 4 plain in the same 7 chain), miss 1, 8 plain in the next 7 chain, miss 1, 4 plain in the next 7 chain, and before finishing this scallop, work the

CENTRE STAR—13 chain, turn, miss 8, 1 single in the 9th stitch to form a round loop leaving 4 chain, turn so as to cross the chain; and for the

1st round—Work 2 plain in the round loop, then (3 chain and 2 plain in the same round loop, 7 times), and to form the 8th loop of chain, work 1 chain, and on the 4 chain left, miss 1, 3 single; turn so as to cross, and missing the 3 single, work 1 treble in the 1 chain missed, then 1 chain, 1 single on the centre of the 1st 2 plain of the round: this forms half the last point of the star.

2nd round, 1st *point*—1 chain, (2 treble in the 1st 3 chain, join to the centre of the 2nd division of the scallop, 2 treble in the same 3 chain), then 1 chain, 1 single on the 2 plain. 2nd *point*—1 chain, (2 treble in the next 3 chain, join to the centre of the 6th division of the 1st scallop; 2 treble in the same 3 chain), then 1 chain, 1 single on the 2 plain. 3rd *point*—Same as the 2nd, joining to the 5th division of the 1st scallop. 4th *point*—1 chain, 4 treble in the next 3 chain, 1 chain and 1 single on the 2 plain. Work 3 points more the same as last; and to finish the 8th or last point—1 chain, 2 treble in the 1 chain, 1 single in the last stitch of the 3 single worked at the end of the 1st round, this completes the star; and to finish the 2nd scallop, work 4 plain in the same 7 chain as before; then (miss 1 and 8 plain in the 7 chain, 4 times), which finishes the scallop. Repeat from * until sufficient is worked, fasten off, and work the 2nd side, or if a corner is required, see page 37.

2nd SIDE.

1st SCALLOP—Commence and work as the 1st scallop of the 1st side, to the end of the 3rd row; and for the

4th row, for the 1st 3 divisions—(Miss 1 and 8 plain in the 7 chain, 3 times). 4th division—miss 1, (4 plain in the next 7 chain, join to the centre division in the last scallop of the 1st side, then 4 plain in the same 7 chain). 5th division—same as the last, joining to the 7th point of the last star. 6th division—same as last, joining to the 6th point of the star. 7th division—miss 1, 8 plain in the 9 chain.

* * 2nd SCALLOP—Work as the 1st scallop to the end of the 3rd row; and for the

4th row, 1st division—(4 plain in the 7 chain, join to the last division of the 1st scallop; 4 plain in the same 7 chain). 2nd division—same as 1st, joining to the 5th point of the same star. 3rd division—same as 1st, joining to the 4th point of the star. 4th division—as 1st, joining to the centre division of the next scallop of the 1st side. 5th division—as 1st, joining to the 7th point of the next star. 6th division—as 1st, joining to the 6th point of the star. 7th division—miss 1, 8 plain in the 9 chain. Repeat from * * in the last scallop; and to form

The BEADING, 1st row—Work 4 plain more in the last division of the last scallop, †, miss 1, 6 plain in the 5 chain left at the end of the 1st row of the scallop; miss 1, 6 plain in the next 5 chain of the foundation, (miss 1 and 4 plain in the 2 chain, 3 times). Repeat from † along the scallops and fasten off.

2nd row—Commence in the 1st stitch of last row, 2 chain, miss 2, 1 treble. Repeat and fasten off. If there is a corner, two of the treble stitches must be worked in one stitch.

3rd row—Miss 1, 3 plain in the 2 chain of the last row. Repeat and fasten off.

Work these 3 rows on the foundation of the scallops of the 1st side.

CORNER FOR MOSAIC BORDER.

After making the required length of the 1st side, page 33, work thus for the

CORNER SCALLOP—18 chain, turn, miss 6, 1 single, turn back.

1st row—5 chain, 1 long in the round loop, (2 chain and 1 long in the round loop, 9 times), 1 chain, turn back, join to the 7th stitch of the foundation chain; and for the

2nd row—2 plain in the 1 chain, (5 chain, miss 1 and 4 plain in the 2 chain, 9 times), 5 chain, miss 1, 2 plain in the 5 chain, turn back.

3rd row—(7 chain, miss 8, and 1 plain on the 4 plain, 9 times), 5 chain, turn back, join to the 4th stitch of the foundation chain.

4th row—(4 plain in the 5 chain, join to the last division of the last scallop, 4 plain in the same 5 chain), miss 1, 8 plain in the 7 chain, miss 1, 4 plain in the next 7 chain, then work a STAR the same as in page 35; when finished, work on the scallop, 4 plain in the same 7 chain as before; miss 1, 8 plain in the next 7 chain, miss 1, 4 plain in the next 7 chain; and for the

CORNER STAR—13 chain, turn, miss 8, 1 single, leaving 4 chain, turn so as to cross.

1st round—2 plain in the round loop, (3 chain and 2 plain in the round loop, 7 times), 1 chain, miss 1, 3 single on the 4 chain left, turn so as to cross; miss 3, 1 treble in the 1 chain, then 1 chain, 1 single on the 2 plain.

2nd round—(1 chain, 4 treble in the 3 chain, 1 chain and 1 single on the 2 plain, 7 times), 1 chain, 2 treble in the 1 chain, 1 single on the last stitch of the 3 single, then on the scallop, 4 plain in the same 7 chain, miss 1, (4 plain in the next 7 chain, join to the 7th point of the star, 4 plain in the same 7 chain), then (miss 1 and 8 plain in the 7 chain, 4 times), which finishes the corner; then work as the 2nd scallop, page 35, until another corner is required. And if the work ends with a corner, work thus for the

2nd SIDE, CORNER SCALLOP—21 chain, turn, miss 6, 3 single, turn back.

1st row—7 chain, miss 3, 1 long in the round loop, (2 chain and 1 long in the round loop 3 times), 1 chain, turn back, join to the 7th stitch of the foundation chain.

2nd row—2 plain in the 1 chain, (5 chain, miss 1 and 4 plain in the 2 chain 3 times), 5 chain, miss 1, 2 plain in the 7 chain, turn back.

3rd row—9 chain, miss 8, 1 plain on the centre of the 4 plain, (7 chain, miss 8, and 1 plain, twice), 7 chain, turn back, join to the 4th stitch of the foundation chain.

4th row—8 plain in the 7 chain, miss 1, (4 plain in the next 7 chain, join to the 4th point of the corner star, 4 plain in the same 7 chain), miss 1, (4 plain in the next 7 chain, join to the 3rd point of the star, 4 plain in the 7 chain), miss 1, 8 plain in the 9 chain.

NEXT SCALLOP—Work as the 1st scallop of the 1st side to the end of the 3rd row; and for the

4th row, 1st Division—4 plain in the 7 chain, join to the last division of the corner scallop, 4 plain in the same 7 chain. 2nd division—same as 1st, joining to the 2nd point of the corner star. 3rd division—join to the 1st point of the star. 4th division—join to the 4th division of the corner scallop of the 1st side. 5th division—join to the 7th point of the next star. 6th division—join to the 6th point of the star. 7th division—miss 1, 8 plain, then work from * *, page 36.

ETOILE INSERTION.

For Anti-Macassars, &c.—To make an Insertion 2 inches deep, use Jno. and Wm. Taylor's Crochet Thread, No. 0; Penelope Needle, No. 2½, or 17, Bell Guage.

Childrens' Dresses, &c.—1½ inches, deep—use Taylor's Crochet Thread, No. 6; Penelope Needle, No. 3½, or 20, Bell Gauge.

Baby's Robes, Sleeves, Gilets, Handkerchiefs, &c.—Use Taylor's Crochet Thread, No. 10; Penelope Needle, No. 4, or 22, Bell Guage.

1st ŒILLET—15 chain, turn, miss 7, 1 single in the 8th stitch to form a round loop, turn, work 1 chain to cross, and leaving 7 chain work 13 plain in the round loop, then 1 single on the 1 chain that crosses; and for the

1st STAR—29 chain, turn, miss 9, 5 single, turn so as to cross the chain, leaving 15 stitches for the foundation chain; and for the

1st round—Work 23 long stitches in the round loop, then 1 single on the last stitch of the 5 single to make it round.

2nd round—(4 chain, miss 1 and 1 plain, 11 times), then to form the 12th loop of chain,

E. R. de la Branchardiere, Invent. March, 1852.

work 2 chain, and missing 2 stitches of the foundation chain, work 3 single on it, turn so as to cross the chain, and in the 2 chain missed, work 1 treble and 1 plain, this forms half the last point of the star; and for the

3rd round, 1st *Point*—Miss 1, 1 plain and 2 treble in the 1st 4 chain of the last round, 2 chain, join to the 10th plain stitch of the œillet, then 2 chain, 2 treble and 1 plain in the same 4 chain as before.

2nd *Point*—Miss 1, 1 plain and 2 treble in next 4 chain, then 4 chain, 2 treble and 1 plain in the same 4 chain; work 9 points more as the last, and to finish the 12th point, miss 1, 1 plain and 2 treble in the 2 chain at the end of the 2nd round, 2 chain, and on the foundation chain, miss 2, 1 single, leaving 7 chain; this finishes the 1st star; then 6 chain, join to the centre of the 11th point of the star; and for

* The ŒILLET between the stars—15 chain, turn, miss 7, 1 single in the 8th stitch, turn, 1 chain to cross, and in the round loop, work 3 plain, join to the 10th point of the star, then 10 plain in the round loop, and 1 single on the 1 chain that crosses.

2nd STAR—Work as the 1st star to the end of the 2nd round, and for the

3rd round, 1st *Point*—Miss 1, 1 plain and 2 treble in the 4 chain, then 2 chain, join to the 7th stitch of the 10 plain of the œillet, 2 chain, 2 treble and 1 plain in the same 4 chain, as before. 2nd *Point*—Same as 1st, joining to the 9th point of the 1st star. 3rd *Point*—Same as last, joining to the 8th point of the 1st star. 4th *Point*—Miss 1, (1 plain, 2 treble, 4 chain, 2 treble, 1 plain in the 4 chain), work 7 points more the same as the last, then miss 1, 1 plain and 2 treble in the 2 chain, work 2 chain, and on the foundation chain, miss 2, 1 single, leaving 7 chain, then 6 chain, join to the 11th point of the star. Repeat from * until the length required is made. Work a plain row along the foundation chain, fasten off; and to form the œillets for the other side.

1st ŒILLET—Commence with 9 chain, turn, miss 7, 1 single in the 8th stitch to form a round loop, turn, 1 chain to cross, and in the round loop, 10 plain, join to the 7th point of the last star, 3 plain in the round loop, 1 single on the 1 chain that crosses, 7 chain, join to the 6th point of the star, 6 chain, join to the 5th point of the star.

* * 2nd ŒILLET—15 chain, turn, miss 7, 1 single in the 8th stitch, turn, 1 chain to cross, and in the round loop, 3 plain, join to the 4th point of the star, 7 plain in the round loop, join to the 7th point of the next star, 3 plain in the round loop, 1 single on the 1 chain that crosses, 7 chain, join to the 6th point of the star, 6 chain, join to the 5th point of the star. Repeat from * *, when finished work a plain row along the foundation chain, and fasten off.

POINT LACE EDGING.

For Anti-Macassars, Couvre Pieds, Curtains, &c., 3 *inches deep*—use Jno. and Wm. Taylor's Crochet Thread, No. 00; Penelope Needle, No. 2, or 16, Bell Guage.

Petticoats, D'Oyley, &c., 2 *inches deep*—use Taylor's Crochet Thread, No. 2; Needle, No. 3, or 18, Bell Guage.

Childrens' Dresses, Dress Trimming, Gilets, Sleeves, Pinchusions, 1½ *inches deep*—use Taylor's Crochet Thread, No. 6; Needle, No 4, or 22, Bell Guage.

Handkerchiefs, Collars, and other Fine Trimming, 1¼ *inches deep*—use Taylor's Crochet Thread, No. 12; Needle, No. 4½, or 24, Bell Guage.

1st PATTERN—Commence with 29 chain, turn, miss 5, 4 single on the chain, turn, so as to cross the stem, leaving 20 chain for the foundation.

1st round—(3 chain, and 1 long in the 5 chain, 7 times); then 3 chain, 1 single, in the last stitch of the 4 single.

2nd round—1 plain, 3 treble in one stitch, 1 plain, 1 single. Repeat 7 times more, making 8 divisions in all; then 4 single on the 20 chain, turn back.

3rd—Keep the work on the wrong side, 12 chain, miss 10, 1 treble on the 1 single between the 2 last divisions of the 2nd round; *, 8 chain, turn, miss 4, 1 single in the 5th stitch of these 8 chain to form a round loop, leaving 3 chain, then 3 chain, miss 5, 1 treble on the next 1 single of the 2nd round. Repeat from *, 5 times more; then 4 chain, turn back, join to the 8th stitch of the foundation chain.

4th—5 plain in the last 4 chain, **, miss 1, 5 plain in the 3 chain, 6 treble in the round loop, then 5 plain in the next 3 chain. Repeat from ** twice more; then 9

chain, turn, miss 5, 1 single in the 6th stitch to form a round loop, turn, 1 chain to cross, (6 treble and 1 plain in the round loop), then 3 single on the 3 chain, miss 1, 5 plain in the next 3 chain of the 3rd round, 6 treble in the round loop, 5 plain in the 3 chain, miss 1, 5 plain in the next 3 chain, 2 treble in the round loop, and before finishing the round, turn back, and work the

5th—(7 chain, miss 14, 2 single in the centre of the 6 treble, 4 times,) 1 chain, turn back.

6th—Miss 1, †, 3 plain, 4 chain, 1 single on the top of the last plain stitch. Repeat from †, 11 times more, then 1 single, and on the 3rd round, 2 treble in the same round loop as the other 2 treble; and to form

The Cross—9 chain, turn, miss 5, 1 single in the 6th stitch to form a round loop, leaving 3 chain, turn, (3 plain in the round loop, 4 chain, turn, miss 1, 3 single on the 4 chain, 3 times,) then 3 plain in the same round loop, and 3 single on the 3 chain, making in all 4 divisions; then to finish the 4th *round*, 2 treble in the same round loop as the other 4 treble, 5 plain in the 3 chain, miss 1, 5 plain in the next 3 chain, 2 treble in the round loop, join to the point of the 3rd division of the cross, then 4 treble in the same round loop as before, 5 plain in the 3 chain, miss 1, 15 plain in the 12 chain, miss 1, 10 plain in the 8 chain, 1 single on the 1st plain stitch of the 4th round, turn back, miss 1, 20 single on the wrong side of the last plain stitches, turn back, and for

The Bar between the patterns, 13 chain, turn, miss 1, 5 single, leaving 7 chain, which finishes the 1st pattern; and for the

2nd Pattern—Work as the 1st pattern to the end of the 3rd round, and in the 4th round, make the following alterations.

4th round—Miss 1, 5 plain in the 4 chain, miss 1, 5 plain in the 3 chain, 2 treble in the round loop, 3 chain, join to the top of the bar between the patterns, 4 chain; join to the last treble stitch but two in the 1st pattern, turn, miss 1, 6 single on the last chain stitches, and 2 treble in the same round loop as before; join to the point of the 2nd division of the cross; 2 treble in the same round loop as before; 5 plain in the next

3 chain of the 3rd round, miss 1, 5 plain in the 3 chain, 2 treble in the round loop, join to the point of the 1st division of the cross, then 4 treble in the same round loop, 5 plain in the 3 chain, miss 1, 5 plain in the 3 chain, 6 treble in the round loop, 5 plain in the 3 chain, then 9 chain, turn, miss 5, 1 single, turn, 1 chain to cross, 6 treble and 1 plain in the round loop, 3 single down the chain, then miss 1, 5 plain in the 3 chain, 6 treble in the round loop, 5 plain in the 3 chain, miss 1, 5 plain in the 3 chain, 2 treble in the round loop, turn back.

5th—(7 chain, miss 14, 2 single on the centre of the 6 treble, 4 times,) 7 chain, turn back.

6th—Join to the last stitch of the 6th row in the 1st pattern, then on the stitches of the 5th row, miss 1, (3 plain, 4 chain, 1 single on the top of the last plain stitch, 14 times), 1 single, then 2 treble in the same round loop of the 3rd round as before; and for

The Cross—9 chain, turn, miss 5, 1 single, turn, (3 plain in the round loop, 4 chain, turn, miss 1, 3 single on the 4 chain, 3 times), then 3 plain in the same round loop, 3 single on the 3 chain, and to finish the 4th round, 2 treble in the same round loop as before; 5 plain in the 3 chain, miss 1, 5 plain in the 3 chain, 2 treble in the round loop, join to the 3rd division of the cross, 4 treble in the same round loop, 5 plain in the 3 chain, miss 1, 15 plain in the 12 chain, miss 1, 10 plain in the 8 chain, 1 single in the 1st stitch of the 4th round, turn, work 20 single on the wrong side of the last plain stitches, turn back, 13 chain, turn, miss 1, 5 single. Repeat as the 2nd pattern, until the length required is worked.

Narrow Scallop Edging.

Material—Same as Vandyke Edging, page 32.

1st Scallop—Make 17 chain, turn, miss 9, 3 single on the chain, leaving 5 chain.

1st row—Turn so as to cross the chain, and in the 9 chain work 1 treble, (3 chain and 2 treble 4 times in the same 9 chain), turn back.

2nd row—(6 chain, miss 4 and 1 plain in the 3 chain of the last row, 4 times), 4 chain, turn back.

E. R. de la Branchardiere, Invent., March, 1852.

3rd row—Join to the 3rd stitch of the 5 chain left at the commencement, then work 7 plain in the last 4 chain, * miss 1, 3 plain in the 6 chain, (5 chain and 1 plain, 3 times in the same 6 chain), then 2 plain more in the same 6 chain, making in all 8 plain. Repeat from * twice more, then miss 1, 7 plain in the last 6 chain.

2nd Scallop—Work the same as the 1st to the end of the 2nd row; and for the

3rd row—Join to the 3rd stitch of the 5 chain, then 3 plain in the 4 chain, join to the centre stitch of the 7 plain in the 1st scallop, then 4 plain in the same 4 chain, and repeat from the 1st * in the 1st scallop.